TABLE AND TEMPLE

Table and Temple

The Christian Eucharist and Its Jewish Roots

David L. Stubbs

WILLIAM B. EERDMANS PUBLISHING COMPANY
GRAND RAPIDS, MICHIGAN

Wm. B. Eerdmans Publishing Co.
4035 Park East Court SE, Grand Rapids, Michigan 49546
www.eerdmans.com

26 25 24 23 22 21 20   1 2 3 4 5 6 7

ISBN 978-0-8028-7480-1

Library of Congress Cataloging-in-Publication Data

Names: Stubbs, David L. (David Leon), 1964– author.
Title: Table and temple : the Christian eucharist and its Jewish roots / David L.
    Stubbs.
Description: Grand Rapids, Michigan : William B. Eerdmans Publishing Com-
    pany, 2020. | Includes bibliographical references and index. | Summary:
    "A biblical and theological study of the Christian Eucharist in relation to its
    roots in Israelite theology, especially with regard to the temple"—Provided by
    publisher.
Identifiers: LCCN 2020010604 | ISBN 9780802874801 (hardcover)
Subjects: LCSH: Lord's Supper. | Lord's Supper—History of doctrines. | Fasts
    and feasts in the Bible. | Fasts and feasts—Judaism. | Christianity and other
    religions—Judaism. | Judaism—Relations—Christianity.
Classification: LCC BV825.3 .S8 2020 | DDC 234/.163—dc23
LC record available at https://lccn.loc.gov/2020010604

To the students of Western Theological Seminary

CONTENTS

Foreword

The book you are holding is not just a book about cognitive, propositional, doctrinal claims. It is therefore not only a book to think about.

For while this book will cause you to think, its aim is ultimately to engage us at a much deeper level—at that place deep in our hearts where our thinking, our emotions, our sense of identity, our cultural context, our fundamental attachment to the world and to others, and our awareness of God all intermingle, shaping our way of being in the world.

Ultimately, God's temple is not only an ancient building or a metaphor to describe, analyze, and unpack. It's a potent way of eliciting and evoking a stunning, countercultural way of construing the world and our place in it, a world in which, through Christ, we discover what it is like to love a God "in whom we live and move and have our being."

In my own teaching, I work as persistently as I can to help my students to see doctrine as an indispensable resource for moving into this deep dimension, this site of some of the Holy Spirit's most remarkable work. This makes me profoundly grateful to David Stubbs for writing a book that patiently engages one of the most pervasive and central biblical images with a keen eye for how it can transform our worship of God by reshaping our own theological imagination at this very deep level.

This is challenging work, in part because temple imagery is so pervasive, and because it often is used in any number of contemporary contexts without careful thought. In recent years, highly influential worship movements have been based on a vision of what it means for worship leaders to help us "enter God's courts with praise" and to "approach the holy of holies with awe." How important it is, then, for us to pay attention to the full meaning of the temple in the Old and New Testaments, drawing on insights from thirty centuries rather than just twenty years of Christian reflection.

One of the gifts of this book is that David Stubbs does this careful work in such a generously orthodox and symphonic way, weaving together insights from biblical, historical, systematic, and practical theology, defying the tight boundaries that too often keep these disciplines apart. He does so in ways that invite all of us to pay attention to some of the most dearly loved and also some of the most rarely read passages of the Bible.

The fruit of this work comes together in a highly focused way as we consider how we approach the lavishly generous table of grace God provides in the Lord's Supper or Eucharist. As I worked through this volume, I was struck again by how the Eucharist, though a single sacrament, can simultaneously be celebrated in ways that resist so many distinct spiritual temptations or heresies, including the classic Christian heresies of Marcionism, moralism, and deism. I was struck by the expansive vision of the Eucharist that, even though it ultimately focuses on consuming but a bit of bread and wine, turns our attention outward to the breadth and length and height and depth of God's love for the entire creation. I was struck by the complementary dimensions of this single practice—how participation at the table is at once about thanksgiving, remembrance, and hope.

To experiment with a metaphor, I was led by this book to wonder about how we could better learn to see the Eucharist is a "fractal" of the gospel. A fractal describes a shape that, remarkably, is profoundly similar at both macro- and micro-levels. For example, a snowflake consists of microscopic crystals that have a shape similar to the flake itself. Mathematicians and scientists offer dozens of other mind-boggling examples of this kind of "self-similarity" in nature. What would it mean for us to approach the Eucharist as a fractal of the lovingkindness of God made manifest in the First Temple and especially in the person of Jesus Christ, the ultimate temple of God in human flesh? How might we then more compellingly taste and see the goodness and graciousness of God as we gather together at the table?

As readers engage this book, much will depend on context.

Some Christian worshippers will read this from within robust communities of Eucharistic practice, where temple imagery is already abundant. For them, may this book help them cherish this legacy and embrace and promote it with greater love and care.

Some Christian worshippers will read this from within communities that have long separated temple imagery and Eucharistic practice, where temple insights inform the praise of God but not the act of praying doxologically at the Lord's Table. For them, may this book inspire liturgical reform and change, leading to a profound recovery of what has been lost or missing.

Some Christian worshippers will read this but realize they have little or no authority to propose any changes in how their communities celebrate the Lord's Supper. For them, may this book transform how they participate at the table and how they perceive connections between the table and every other aspect of their Christian life.

Some Christian worshippers will read this and realize the profound responsibility they have for giving shape to Eucharistic practice. For them, may this book offer a generous and encouraging vision for liturgical reform, inspiring change for the joy that awaits us when we grow up into full maturity in Christ.

Some readers may engage this book, whether in formal religion or divinity school classes or in informal reading, and bring to it little, if any, Christian faith and perhaps even opposition to any Christian message. For them, may this book be used by God's Spirit to correct the many distorted visions of the Christian faith that are prominent in the public square and elicit a sense of wonder about what God truly offers us in Christ.

For all of us, may God's Spirit continue to be at work, using the words and sentences and paragraphs found in books like this to accomplish within us and our communities something that far surpasses the capacity of any words, drawing us into unspeakably robust communion with each other and the God who creates and redeem us. To use the words with which Prof. Stubbs concludes the book, may God's Spirit help us to be "watchful in prayer, strong in truth and love, and faithful in the breaking of bread," confident that, in the end "all peoples will be free, all divisions healed, and with your whole creation we will sing God's praise through Jesus Christ."

JOHN D. WITVLIET
Calvin Institute of Christian Worship
Calvin College and Calvin Theological Seminary
Grand Rapids, Michigan

PREFACE

We live in an age of lost and missing connections.

The church has for a long time been disconnected from its Jewish roots. In response to this loss, the first task of this book is to draw bold lines of connection from the Eucharist back to the Jewish temple and its main worship services. Such lines are evident in the writings of the early church. By highlighting these connections to our common Jewish roots, I hope that this book will be helpful for the Christian church today on its long journey toward unity. Much of the eucharistic theology and practice of at least the Western church, both Protestants and Roman Catholics, is based in large part on a small range of New Testament texts, texts whose diverse interpretations have led to diverse eucharistic understandings and practices. These differences have led to painful divisions and schisms in the West. By regrounding the central meanings of the Eucharist on the Old Testament and central Old Testament temple practices, in addition to the usual New Testament texts, which I argue is precisely what the early leaders of the church did, I hope that Christians from various denominations and traditions might find their imaginations enriched, that they might rediscover a solid, biblical foundation upon which a fuller ecumenical understanding and common practice might be renewed. By reconnecting with our past we will become better connected to one another in the present.

Another hope is that readers of this book will be encouraged to see how the Eucharist prompts other reconnections—reconnections between God and humanity, between humanity and the rest of creation, and between us and our identity, purpose, and future as individuals and as a community. I believe the

Eucharist was intended to be precisely this expansive in meaning. I hope that the central meanings of the Eucharist highlighted in this book, as well as the many suggestions about practice scattered throughout it, might help people to see more fully the beauty and multifaceted fullness of this gem we have been given by God through Christ.

We live in an age of lost connections to God and each other, both inside and outside the church. Doubts about faith, declining attendance, schisms, and political divisions characterize the church in our time. And yet we are not without hope. Beginning a few decades ago, we have also been living in an age of great and significant transition—some people in their more positive moments even talk about a "new Reformation." Renewed interest in the theological interpretation of Scripture, renewed connections with the early church, shifts in epistemology that question many modern assumptions, liturgical renewal movements, renewed emphasis on the visibility and mission of the church, and some quite remarkable ecumenical convergences—these and other movements are hopeful signs of life and renewal. A renewed hunger for the Eucharist and renewed Eucharist practice have been part of a great number of these movements. While the Eucharist as practiced in many contemporary churches is certainly not the same as the Eucharist in its fullness, the Eucharist has the potential to be—and I argue was intended to be—a practice that expansively reconnects us to God, each other, the creation, and our identity and mission. It has the potential to play a role in the renewal of our individual and corporate lives.

I have personally seen such signs of renewal, and would like to acknowledge those Christian communities where I have personally experienced real foretastes of what the Eucharist itself points to and participates in. I first experienced a rich Eucharist-centered community in college, as part of the university group of Menlo Park Presbyterian Church, where we had Thursday night communion services on the college campus led by Rev. Jerry Lambert. Other communities fed me and welcomed me into a rich communal life gathered in part around the Lord's table. Golden Gate Community Church, a quirky and wonderful Nazarene and evangelical church in San Francisco, led by Rev. Barry Brown, and St. Joseph's Episcopal Church in North Carolina, led by Father Steven, were wonderful communities during my sojournings in those places. The Sacramental Study Group of the Presbyterian Church (USA), hereafter PC(USA), and other groups and committees formed by the then-titled Office of Theology and Worship were homes away from home, in which a quite diverse group of pastors and theologians gathered for study, work, and eucharistic connection to God and each other. Such times of work and eucharistic fellowship were often led by Rev. Marney Wasserman, Rev. Dr. Neal Presa, Rev. Dr. Martha Moore-Keish, and Rev. Chip Andrus. Grace Episcopal Church, led by Rev. Jen Adams, is a beautiful table-centered community, and finally, my beloved Western Theological Seminary, with its daily chapel and weekly communion services organized by Rev. Dr. Ron Rienstra has been a place where I and others are invited to move rather seamlessly between office, classroom, library, community atrium, community kitchen, font, pulpit, and eucharistic table. This book is indebted to the inspiration those Christian communities lent me in my work.

This project has been a long one, and during my time working on it many people and institutions have come alongside me and offered me hospitality, support, wisdom, and encouragement. Work on this project started during a sabbatical leave in which I was able to work as a visiting scholar at the University of Otago in Dunedin, New Zealand, thanks to the gracious hospitality of Dr. Murray Rae and others on the faculty and staff of that wonderful center of Reformed thought and life. The time and conversations there helped to get the project off to a good start. Several years later, I was able to substantially complete the project during another sabbatical leave in Rome, this time aided by the generous hospitality, sponsorship, and resources of Dr. Fulvio Ferrario and the Waldensian seminary, *Facoltá Valese di Teologia*, as well as the resources available at the Gregorian Institute. Many thanks to Rev. Dana English, who was an ever-able guide to many of the earliest still-existing worship sites, churches, and artwork of the ancient Christian community there in Rome. Being included in the *Churches Together in Rome* ecumenical group during the five-hundred-year commemoration of the Reformation, hosted by the Waldensian seminary, at the center of Roman Catholicism, surrounded by the sites and relics of the early Roman church, all while working on a book on the Eucharist was a rich and productive time that I will always be grateful for. None of this would have been possible without the support and leave of my own home institution, Western Theological Seminary. Its board, faculty, staff, and students all make it an academic community that is a true pleasure to work in and an inspiring place to pursue my calling. My wife Lynn has continued her lifelong support of me and is an ever-present and wise sounding board for theological ideas. Let me also express my deepest thanks to Dr. Suzanne MacDonald, Rev. Jen Rozema, and Dr. Sue Rozeboom, who all tirelessly read through a draft of the entire manuscript, commented extensively, offered wonderful suggestions for improvement, and gave great encouragement. Finally, many thanks to the good and wise people of Eerdmans, especially Michael Thompson, who helpfully began the editing process with me, Cody Hinkle, for his wise comments and edits, and James Ernest, whose comments, work, and supervision brought the book to a successful completion.

PART ONE

Bridging the Gap between Table and Temple

1

Ancient Connections, Modern Gaps

Table and Temple in Church and Academy

Happy are those whom you choose
  and bring near to live in your courts.
We shall be satisfied with the goodness of your house,
  your holy temple.
                                              —Psalm 65:4

The Eucharist. It is a celebration in which God is specially present. It is a re-membrance of the death and resurrection of Christ, a communion celebra-tion in which the new covenant relationship between God and God's people is renewed, and a foretaste of the feast to come. Remembrance; commu-nion and covenant renewal; hope—such phrases and images point to cen-tral meanings of the eucharistic rite which Christians celebrate around the communion table.

And yet there are still more ways to describe it: it is a thanksgiving to the Father, a calling on the Spirit, a meal of the kingdom, a communion of the faithful, a rite in which Christ is truly present, a means of grace and blessing. Many meanings and images are used to understand and explain this central Christian sacrament. This plurality of images and meanings is quite rich and evocative, but it can also cause confusion. It raises questions: Which mean-ings are central? How are such meanings grounded in Scripture and tradition? These questions have received a variety of answers over the centuries. I think the Jewish temple provides the key to answering them well.

The temple. It was a place where God was specially present to God's people. It was a place where Israel regularly gathered and at the three principal yearly celebrations, the three pilgrim feasts, remembered God's deliverance of God's people, celebrated and renewed the giving of the covenant on Mount Sinai, and looked forward to the great feast to come. Remembrance; communion and covenant renewal; hope—such were some of the central meanings of the most important worship celebrations at the temple.

It is not difficult to see that the core meanings of these central celebrations of the people of God in the Old and New Testaments have strong parallels. The core meanings of the most important Old Testament celebrations are similar to those of the most important celebration of the New—it is as if those Old Testament motifs have been combined and transposed into a different key. I will argue that examining these transposed motifs is the best way to determine the Eucharist's central meanings. Highlighting these relationships and drawing bold lines of connection from the table back to the temple is the main task of this book.

But what precisely is the nature of those connections between table and temple?

One way in which the gap between New Testament eucharistic worship and Old Testament temple practices can be bridged and connected is by *typology*. Typology involves understanding certain Old Testament people, places, events, or practices as "types," "figures," or "shadows" of New Testament ones. The Eucharist is a prime example of a New Testament practice that can be understood to be "prefigured" in the Old Testament. Indeed, many early church writers allude to or draw out such typological relationships.

But if this is the case, and the central celebrations of the Old and New Covenants are as intimately related as I am arguing they are, why do these connections not figure more prominently in discussions of the Eucharist? In most modern discussions of the Eucharist and its origins such typological relationships have not played a large role. Often mentioned in passing, such relationships do little work in grounding, organizing, or explicating what is happening in the eucharistic celebration. Many, if not most, modern theologians have found such typological relationships unhelpful, almost quaint, and not up to the standards of modern readings of Scripture. Moreover, there have been several Protestant and modern prejudices against the religion of Israel centered at the temple that have obscured such connections and created a large gap between temple and Eucharist in discussions of the origins and meanings of the Eucharist.

But consider Eusebius of Caesarea. This important Palestinian bishop and teacher of the early church writes in his treatise *The Proof of the Gospel* that "we . . . have received both the truth and the archetypes of the early images."[1] In saying this, he is claiming that Jesus Christ and the practices which Christ handed on to his disciples—he refers to practices such as the Eucharist and baptism—are "the archetypes" of the images found in Israelite religion. That which went before—prophecies, the temple, the law, the worship rituals of Israel—are images, sketches, or shadows of the things that came after them. And for Eusebius, these typological relationships demonstrated the truth of the gospel.

But how can this be? What does it mean to call something that came a thousand years before the gospel a "sketch" or "shadow" of the gospel? And what kind of "proof" is this?

For Eusebius, the answer to these questions rests on several deep theological assumptions. The New Testament, or New Covenant—meaning both the biblical *writings* that witness to Christ and also the *way of life* inaugurated by Jesus Christ as he was empowered by the Holy Spirit to the glory of the Father—is for Eusebius a new revelation. In fact it is the greatest revelation of the relationship that God desires with humanity. This relationship between God and humanity is incarnated in the person or "body" of Jesus Christ; his divine-human person is the prototype of the new humanity in proper relationship to God. He is the true archetype for the many biblical types in which the relationship between God and humanity is imaged.

Another assumption he makes is that Christ called others to participate in his renewed humanity in proper covenantal relationship with God. This renewed relationship, this renewed way of life, is imaged in and enabled through Christ's teachings and through the practices that Christ handed on to his disciples, the most central practices being baptism and the Eucharist. Furthermore, this new relationship between God and the people of God, this new covenant, was imaged or sketched out in the institutions, laws, prophecies, and ceremonies of Israel, as recorded and witnessed to in the Old Testament. Such theological assumptions would have informed Eusebius as he read the saying

---

1. Eusebius of Caesarea, *Demonstration of the Gospel* (PG 22:89a), lib. 1, c. 10. Eusebius lived from 260/265 AD to 339/340 AD.

of Jesus Christ, "Do not think I have come to abolish the law or the prophets; I have come not to abolish but to fulfill" (Matt. 5:17).

In this book I will travel down paths like those that Eusebius trod. He and many other Christians throughout the ages have understood there to be a "typological" or "figural" relationship between the Old and the New Testaments, a relationship in which Christ is the linchpin. They have understood this to be in fact a central Christian way to read Scripture and to understand the history of God's interactions with God's people, and an important way to understand, in particular, the Eucharist.

The main task of this project is thus to draw bold lines connecting Christian worship centered on the reading of the Word and celebration of the Eucharist with Old Testament tabernacle and temple worship.[2] In this way our understanding of the Eucharist and our practice of the Eucharist can be more solidly grounded and deeply enriched.

In the following chapters, I begin with the temple, exploring the central meanings and practices of Israelite worship at the wilderness tabernacle and Jerusalem temple. We find in these practices, commanded by God at Mount Sinai, foundational patterns of worship that are appropriate responses to the creating and saving works of God. Moving then to New Testament and early church authors, we find that these foundational patterns were not abandoned by the earliest Christians, but rather transformed in light of the incarnation and work of Jesus Christ. The fact that such connections between table and temple are consistently being drawn by the leaders of the early church is an important data point for those who seek to follow in the apostolic tradition. Such early traditions and ways of thinking have great authority for most Christians (including me). But the ultimate payoff of seeing such connections is that they help to ground, structure, renew, and enrich contemporary eucharistic theology and practice, especially contemporary Protestant practice. Such typological connections can pressure and guide our thinking, sparking the imaginations of Christians in church and academy who discuss and decide upon best eucharistic practices. They can also deepen the faith, imagination, and practice of all those who celebrate the Eucharist together.

2. While certain distinctions between the earlier tabernacle in the wilderness and the later temple in Jerusalem are important to make, throughout this book I assume in general that the theologies surrounding the tabernacle and temple and their main acts of worship are similar enough to be interchangeable unless otherwise noted.

How This Book Is Organized

The book as a whole is structured around what I consider the most central, encompassing, and enduring figures, images, and types related to the temple and its worship.

After explaining the context and method of the project in Chapters 1 and 2, in Chapter 3 I turn to the image or figure of the temple itself, the "house" where the Name of God dwelt. Israel's understanding of the purpose of that building and place, how God and God's kingdom were present there, and humanity's role there helps to guide our thinking about what Christian worship is and how God might be present in worship. The temple's role in Israel provides a foundation for understanding what is happening in worship centered on Word and Table. Chapter 4 examines the connections drawn in the New Testament and the early church between the temple and Christian worship. Chapter 5 asks how such connections might guide or pressure contempory reflection upon and practice of Christian worship, especially with respect to our sacramental practices. This movement from Old Testament foundations, to New Testament connections, to the pressure these connections put on contemporary thought and practice is repeated for each of the main worship rites at the temple in each of the following chapters.

I use the word "pressure" throughout the book to indicate the kind of multifaceted force that these images and types exert on our thinking, a force that molds and shapes our thinking in certain ways, somewhat like the pressure the hands of a potter exert on wet clay. I take that word-image from an article by C. Kavin Rowe who in turn takes it from the work of Brevard Childs. Rowe argues that not only the text, but ultimately God speaking through the text is at work to mold and shape Christian thinking and practice. Rowe writes that "the two-testament canon read as one book pressures its interpreters" to make certain kinds of theological judgments about trinitarian theology.[3] I think the two-testament canon read as one book also does so concerning eucharistic theology and practice.

Chapters 6 through 10 address connections between the main, prototypical practices of worship at the temple and the Eucharist. These are outlined in

---

3. C. Kavin Rowe, "Biblical Pressure and Trinitarian Hermeneutics," *Pro Ecclesia* 11, no. 3 (2002): 308.

the Old Testament liturgical calendars in Numbers 28–29 and Leviticus 23, which themselves follow the enduring structure of Israel's corporate worship first seen in Exodus 23 (introduced in chapter 6). These passages specify the daily, weekly (Sabbath), and monthly services (chapter 7), and the three yearly pilgrim feasts which every Israelite male was required to attend (chapters 8, 9, and 10). The three feasts or festival seasons are *Pesach* (Passover), *Shavuot* (the Feast of Weeks), and *Sukkot* (the Feast of Booths).[4]

The daily, Sabbath, and monthly services feature Israel's thanksgiving for and commitment to God's regular creational order. God is celebrated as creator, and Israel as a representative of all humanity takes its rightful place as a "priest" of all creation in these regular services. In contrast, each of the three pilgrim feasts commemorates God's saving work with Israel: the deliverance from Egypt, the gift of the Law covenant at Mount Sinai, and the future fulfillment of all those covenant promises and hopes. Together, these feasts provide a sweeping portrait of this saving history.

I draw the book to a close in Chapter 11 by drawing out several important practical implications for contemporary practice of the Eucharist.

This multifaceted view of the temple and its central practices provides a helpful and trustworthy framework for understanding the Eucharist. Understood in this way, the Eucharist is like a fractal. It is a beautiful jewel. It is a microcosm. It is a complex and multifaceted celebration in which the full pattern of God's creating, reconciling, and redeeming work, centered on the work of Christ and the gift of the Spirit, can be seen and comes into ritual focus.

Such a project is quite timely, given recent developments in both the church and the academy. In the church—at least in mainline and evangelical Protestant churches in English-speaking countries—there has been a renewed hunger for the sacraments in general and a renewal of eucharistic liturgy. At the same time there are continued confusion about and contradictory understandings of its central meanings. In the academic context, for the last several hundred years, common prejudices which are discussed below have made a project such as this unattractive and implausible for most modern Protestant theologians, biblical scholars, and historians. But those prejudices have been

---

4. Details about terminology, such as the distinctions between the names for festival seasons as a whole and the individual gatherings or services (which often were feasts) that were parts of the larger seasons, will be discussed in those chapters.

decisively challenged in recent decades. Growing bodies of literature highlight the Jewish background of New Testament beliefs and practices; they specifically highlight the importance of the temple and its worship for understanding both the Old Testament and the New. All this creates a new openness to figural readings of both Scripture and the practices of the church.

In the remainder of this introductory chapter, I will examine those two contexts more carefully. I will both highlight reasons for the modern gaps between table and temple, and also describe new possibilities in both church and academy for bridging that gap. In the following chapter, I will explain in more detail my methodological assumptions concerning figural reading, the bridge that can reconnect table and temple in our understandings. Then, in the following chapters, the real work begins.

The Church Context: Gaps between Eucharistic Theology and Practice

Hungry, but confused. These two adjectives, paired in this contrasting relationship, go far in describing current Protestant eucharistic practice and doctrine.

The Eucharist has not typically been at the center of Protestant worship, spirituality, or theology. As recently as 1989, James F. White wrote: "The eucharist is usually not the most important service for Protestants, at least not in terms of frequency. Most Protestant worship, historically and at present, has not made the eucharist its central service. . . . For major segments of their history, churches that now have weekly celebrations were quite content with only occasional ones."[5] Chuck Fromm, the editor of *Worship Leader* magazine, made a similar point in a 2008 conversation he had with Robert Webber. Fromm said to Webber, "Bob, face it, the Eucharist was the focal point of God's presence in the ancient church, the Reformation made the Word the center of God's presence, and today the presence of God is found in music."[6]

However, as White also notes, there is a growing hunger for the Eucharist within many Protestant churches and traditions today. The great increase in

5. James F. White, *Protestant Worship: Traditions in Transition* (Louisville: Westminster John Knox, 1989), 14.

6. Robert Webber, *Ancient-Future Worship: Proclaiming and Enacting God's Narrative* (Grand Rapids: Baker Books, 2008), 133.

the frequency of eucharistic celebration in many churches is one indication of this. Using my own denomination, the PC(USA), as an example, around 80 percent of those surveyed in 2009 were part of congregations that celebrate communion either monthly or weekly. That is almost double the 41 percent of churches celebrating monthly or more in 1989.[7] In addition, one third of PC(USA) ministers in 2009 said they would like to have their congregation celebrate weekly.[8] Those numbers represent a historic shift.

As part of this change, the current Book of Common Worship of the PC(USA), the book that officially guides the worship of most Presbyterian churches in the United States, states that the Eucharist should be a standard part of a typical Lord's Day service. Not quarterly, not monthly, but rather weekly eucharistic celebration is considered the norm.[9] While the facts on the ground do not match this norm, the mere existence of this norm is further evidence of the growing appreciation for the Eucharist within large segments of Protestant churches.[10]

The fact that this hunger for and increased frequency of eucharistic celebration are relatively recent phenomena leads to a second observation: our written liturgies and our genuine receptivity to eucharistic practice have progressed at a greater pace than our eucharistic theology. This leads to some confusion. Many of the *liturgical resources* available today are fruits of the modern liturgical renewal movement which blossomed among mainline Protestants starting in the 1960s,

7. In 2009, "Three-quarters of panelists (members, 72%; elders, 78%; pastors, 75%; specialized clergy, 72%) are part of congregations that celebrate the Lord's Supper every month. . . . Fewer than one in five panelists in each group (members, 6%; elders, 5%; pastors, 9%; specialized clergy, 16%) are part of a congregation that celebrates the Lord's Supper every week." PC(USA), Office of Research Services, "The Presbyterian Panel: The Sacraments: The February 2009 Survey" (Louisville: PC[USA], 2009), 1. In 1989, 40% of congregations celebrated monthly and 1% weekly, in PC(USA), "How Frequently Do PCUSA Congregations Celebrate the Lord's Supper?" (Louisville: PC[USA], 2007).

8. PC(USA), "The Presbyterian Panel," 1.

9. PC(USA), Theology and Worship Ministry Unit, *Book of Common Worship* (Louisville: Westminster John Knox, 1993), 8–9.

10. On a more anecdotal level, I have seen this increased hunger and appreciation for the sacraments at the Reformed Church in America seminary where I now teach, Western Theological Seminary, in Holland, MI. Every year, each graduating student participates in an exit interview. In the last decade, the aspect of our seminary community that students mention more than any other is our weekly celebration of the Eucharist as a community. They find it deeply formative and say they will greatly miss it when they leave seminary.

and which itself draws heavily from the texts and practices of the early church. However, the eucharistic *theology* that still shapes Protestant churches and finds its way into basic theological textbooks often centers on Reformation-era points of division about the Eucharist—and perhaps not even the best understanding of them.[11] This is a situation of instability. Our eucharistic imagination—the thought forms, metaphors, and theological substructure through which we view our performance of the Eucharist—is insufficient for comprehending the written liturgies and communion prayers that are commonly used.

For one significant example of the lack of fit between our theological imagination and our practice, consider the *Sanctus*. In many celebrations of the Eucharist in mainline Protestant churches, the congregation sings or says these words: "Holy, holy, holy is the Lord of hosts; the whole earth is full of his glory." Using these words as part of the eucharistic prayer goes back to very early Christian celebrations. Why these words? They first occur in Isaiah 6 where Isaiah has a vision of angelic beings calling these words to one another as they encircle the throne of God at the temple.[12] If the Eucharist is understood primarily as a memorial meal in which Christ's substitutionary death on the cross is remembered—a common view of many mainline Protestants and evangelicals—why would we join in this angelic song set in the holy of holies of the temple, implicitly imagining that we too are coming into the presence of God seated on his throne?[13]

---

11. For example, Alister McGrath's *Christian Theology: An Introduction*, 3rd ed. (Malden, MA: Blackwell Publishing, 2001), 508–33. However, Protestant authors such as Martha Moore-Keish, *Do This in Remembrance of Me: A Ritual Approach to Reformed Eucharistic Theology* (Grand Rapids: Eerdmans, 2008), Michael Welker, *What Happens in Holy Communion?* (Grand Rapids: Eerdmans, 2000), and Peter Leithart, "Embracing Ritual: Sacraments as Rites," *Calvin Theological Journal* 40 (2005): 6–20, are exploring what is taking place in the sacramental encounter of the Eucharist in fuller dialogue with contemporary liturgical and ritual studies, and going beyond traditional questions of real presence. See Leithart's quick review of recent Protestant and evangelical books on the Lord's Supper in his article.

12. Cf. Ezek. 1:1–28; 10:1–22; Rev. 4:1–11. For a history of these words, see Bryan Spinks, *The Sanctus in the Eucharistic Prayer* (New York: Cambridge University Press, 1991). Cf. Rachel Elior, *The Three Temples: On the Emergence of Jewish Mysticism*, trans. David Louvish (Oxford: The Littman Library of Jewish Civilization, 2004), who points out the prominent place this scene and these words have in Qumran worship and Jewish mysticism (e.g., pp. 16, 33).

13. Because such words, which were part of the Christian Eucharistic liturgies through most of Christian history, do not in fact fit very well with common Protestant ways of

Other churches that structure their eucharistic celebrations more spontaneously, so-called "non-liturgical" churches, often pull the participant in a variety of directions. The music, the way the bread and wine are handled, and the words that are used by the presider often present a mosaic of possible meanings that often do not create a coherent whole.

So, we find ourselves amidst a "cacophony of evangelical and Reformed sacramental theologies," using liturgical resources that those theologies cannot comprehend.[14] We are hungry for the Eucharist once again, but we lack a coherent Protestant eucharistic imagination. This project of understanding the Eucharist in light of the worship of the temple can help ground, organize, and enrich our doctrine of and imagination concerning the Eucharist. It does so in a way that is biblically grounded and that resonates well with early church liturgies and practices.

The Academic Context: Prejudice against and Recovery of the Jewish Roots of Christianity and Christian Worship

Alongside this growing hunger for the Eucharist in the church are a new openness to and recovery of the Jewish background of Christianity in the academy. More specifically, there has been an increasing recognition of the importance of Israelite worship at the temple within the context of Old Testament theology. This has only recently been the case. In fact, we find in our history as Protestant Christians several factors that have resisted such Jewish roots—meaning both the explicit words and structures of Israelite worship,

---

imagining what we are doing, many Protestant celebrations of the Eucharist leave them out. Yet even Luther, who took out almost every other biblical reference that appeared sacrificial other than the words of institution from the 1526 *Deutsche Messe*, still retained the Sanctus. William Cavanaugh explains the logic of Luther's reforms in "Eucharistic Sacrifice in the Social Imagination in Early Modern Europe," *Journal of Medieval and Early Modern Studies* 31 (2001): 585–605. Cavanaugh's main critique of Luther is that his "reaction against late medieval practices often shares in some of the problems associated with those practices" (595), namely an understanding of sacrifice which "precludes mutual participation" (597). As will be argued below, it is important that the recovery of a temple imagination should not simply recover the notion of sacrifice for the Eucharist, but should recover a *better* notion of sacrifice.

14. The phrase is Peter Leithart's, "Embracing Ritual," 20.

as well as the underlying theology and spirit that undergird Jewish forms of public worship centered in temple and synagogue. The past few centuries in particular have witnessed great resistance within academia to acknowledging those Jewish roots. Retelling this history is important for understanding forces which have obscured our ability to see the connections between the temple and the Eucharist.

Walter Brueggemann, in his *Theology of the Old Testament,* names several of these forms of resistance.[15] The first is that Christian interpreters of the Old Testament, who have dominated Old Testament scholarship, have often operated with a "largely hidden and unacknowledged" propensity toward supersessionism, here meaning that the work of Christ has *superseded* Old Testament worship traditions, making them obsolete and thus unimportant.[16] Furthermore, the anti-Judaism that often accompanied certain forms of supersessionism created even more pressure to devalue the Jewish roots of Christianity.[17] Even when acknowledged as types, the reigning understandings of typology itself devalued the Old Testament practices which foreshadowed those of the New.[18]

A second largely unacknowledged prejudice against Old Testament temple worship comes from the fact that many of the most important Old Testament scholars were, and are, Protestants. Many of the historic and modern

---

15. While I greatly appreciate what Brueggemann writes about the temple in his magnum opus, *Theology of the Old Testament* (Minneapolis: Fortress, 2012), it is telling that he begins his work on the temple and "The Cult as Mediator" on p. 650. In other words, Brueggemann, who is well-known for his work on the prophets, still decenters priests and the cult, the worship life of the temple, in his exposition of the theology of the Old Testament as a whole. He certainly is aware of this propensity to "sideline the worship materials of the Old Testament" and sees it as a problem (p. 653), but he has not yet fully incorporated that material into the center of his own project of giving an overarching theology of the Old Testament.

16. Brueggemann, *Theology,* 651. There are several ways "supersession" has been defined and understood. Such definitions are undergoing lively contemporary debate.

17. For example, F. F. Bruce, explaining the countercultural significance of Leonhard Goppelt's well-known book on typology, writes, "It was first published in 1939, at a time when it was politically expedient in Germany to play down the importance of the OT for Christianity. The author was concerned to show how essential the Old Testament was for the life and faith of the church, and how Christians could read it with understanding and profit." Back cover of Leonhard Goppelt, *Typos: The Typological Interpretation of the Old Testament in the New,* trans. Donald H. Madvig (Grand Rapids: Eerdmans, 1982).

18. See pp. 21–46 below for a discussion of various understandings of types and figures.

prejudices, stereotypes, and theological pairings by which Protestants have understood their differences with Roman Catholicism—dualities such as grace versus works righteousness, "democratic" congregationalism versus "monarchical" priestly hierarchy, modern versus primitive, life-giving charismatic leadership versus death-dealing institutionalized authority, scientific versus magical, heartfelt spontaneity versus unfeeling "dead" ritualism—were translated into prejudices against and dismissals of the Old Testament priesthood and temple worship. As Brueggemann admits, "This general Christian attitude toward the Old Testament is intensified by classical Protestantism, which has had a profound aversion to cult, regarding cultic activity as primitive, magical, and manipulative, thus valuing from the Old Testament only the prophetic-ethical traditions."[19]

For example, Ludwig Koehler, an influential twentieth-century Protestant Old Testament scholar, writes in his *Old Testament Theology*: "There is no suggestion anywhere in the Old Testament that sacrifice or any other part of the cult was instituted by God. It is begun and continued and accomplished by man; it is works, not grace; an act of self-help, not a piece of God's salvation. Indeed, the cult is a bit of ethnic life. Israel took it from the heathen."[20] Given such presuppositions of leading Protestant scholars, it is little wonder that they paid little appreciative attention to temple worship. They have instead laid emphasis on the prophetic literature and the importance of historical events, even though temple life was equally formative for Israel.[21]

Finally, modern academic methods for reading and understanding the Old Testament itself—approaches that have been standard for over a century, but which have been under increasing critique, such as the history of religions approach and Julius Wellhausen's Documentary Hypothesis—have created dismissive attitudes toward the temple and its worship.

For example, the history of religions approach seeks to understand the practices and beliefs of Israelite worship through comparison with beliefs and

19. Brueggemann, *Theology*, 651.

20. Ludwig Koehler, *Old Testament Theology* (London: Lutterworth, 1957), 181. Cited in Brueggemann, *Theology*, 152n5. Other examples of such understandings by Protestant scholars are given in Richard D. Nelson, *Raising Up a Faithful Priest: Community and Priesthood in Biblical Theology* (Louisville: Westminster John Knox, 1993), 101–5.

21. A good example can be found in the mid-twentieth-century biblical theology movement, started in part by G. E. Wright, *God Who Acts: Biblical Theology as Recital* (London: SCM, 1952).

practices of other ancient Near Eastern peoples. Such a comparative approach certainly has its merits, but, as Brueggemann notes, given this approach, "It is not difficult to conclude that practices which strike an interpreter as primitive are in fact borrowed, and therefore 'not really Israelite.'"[22] In this way, sacrifices and other practices were often written off as contaminating true Israelite religion, as in the quote above from Koehler.

The Documentary Hypothesis, a way of reconstructing the compositional history of the Pentateuch associated with the work of Wellhausen, has also contributed to prejudices against the importance of the temple and its worship. The Priestly (P) material of the Pentateuch, the hypothetical source material in which the tabernacle, and by extension, the temple and its worship practices are described and valued, was typically dated as the latest stratum of material that went into the composition of the Old Testament. "Latest" in this context was not a compliment. It suggested an author or authors far removed from God's revelatory events. Most scholars also described P as "legalistic, punctilious, and religiously inferior," descriptions informed by the kinds of modern, Protestant, and supersessionist tendencies mentioned above.[23]

In addition to the factors Brueggemann mentions, another technical yet quite important factor, in my opinion, has also led to the devaluing of Old Testament worship and its typological relationship to the worship of the New Testament—that of the modern scientific understandings of causation. This additional prejudice against sacramental rites stems more from the worldview associated with Isaac Newton than the theologies of Luther or Calvin. Given a Newtonian scientific imagination, we have lacked categories for, and are consequently suspicious of, special divine action in the sacraments and in worship. Modern people have, of course, tended to be suspicious of any special divine action whatsoever. But even allowing that God is involved with the creation in ways other than upholding the general laws of nature, our understanding of causality has crippled our sacramental imaginations. Modern people tend to think of all causality in terms of "efficient causality"—i.e., we think things "happen" because masses are striking or bumping up against one another.[24]

22. Brueggemann, *Theology*, 652.

23. See similar evaluations of the tendency to denigrate priestly traditions in Nelson, *Raising Up a Faithful Priest*, ix–x, and Rodney Hutton, *Charisma and Authority in Israelite Society* (Minneapolis: Fortress, 1994), 1–5, 138.

24. See Alasdair MacIntyre, *First Principles, Final Ends and Contemporary Philosophical Issues* (Marquette: Marquette University Press, 1990).

Such a limited modern toolbox for thinking about causality has a difficult time comprehending both typology and the formative action of God through sacramental rites. Yet it is precisely such a typological hermeneutic that allows us to take a middle road between supersessionism and requiring "literal" obedience to the Old Testament law.

Summing up these various factors leading to the devaluing of the temple and its worship throughout much of the past two to three hundred years in modern academic work, Christian supersessionism (of a certain kind), modern Protestant allergies to anything smelling "Catholic," the reigning paradigms of Old Testament scholarship, and the typical modern scientific worldview have created a toxic climate for serious consideration of the temple and its worship. Brueggemann writes:

> I must confess, at the outset, that I have been nurtured, as a Protestant Christian, with the limiting, dismissive perspective noted above. I am, moreover, nurtured in that way as an Old Testament scholar, for critical scholarship has been little interested in the theological intention of Israel's worship. Therefore, I propose a model for considering this material theologically, but I do so with considerable diffidence, recognizing that we are only at the beginning of a reappropriation of the serious worship of Israel as an important theological datum.[25]

"Only at the beginning," yes, but such a reappropriation has gained momentum in the past decades. While much could be said about the ways that all the prejudices Brueggemann mentions are being challenged, let me highlight one: the wide-scale reconsideration of Judaism's relationship to Christianity.

After the Second World War, Christians reassessed their attitude toward Jews and Judaism. Certainly a great impulse for this was the realization that at least part of the blame of the Holocaust lay at the feet of Christians who, because of their overly negative view of Judaism, helped to create an atmosphere in which such a tragedy was possible.

A shining example of this major shift of Christian attitudes toward Judaism is the Roman Catholic document *Nostra Aetate: Declaration on the Relationship of the Church to Non-Christian Religions*. This declaration came out of Vatican II

25. Brueggemann, *Theology*, 653.

and was promulgated in 1965 by Pope Paul VI. It was a watershed document. In the United States alone it spurred the creation of over two dozen centers for Catholic-Jewish studies on Roman Catholic educational campuses. It sparked similar documents and discussions in many Protestant denominations.[26] It and the ensuing discussions did much to change many Christians' views on Judaism. In it, the pope pointed to the way Christ's work of salvation is "foreshadowed" in the Exodus, affirming that Gentiles draw sustenance from the "root of that well-cultivated olive tree," Israel, that God does not repent of God's call to Israel, that Jews and Christians share the same "patrimony," and that all forms of anti-Semitism are to be rejected.[27]

As a result of this wide-scale reassessment, many have called into question older views of supersessionism. This has in turn led to backlash, but also created ongoing contemporary discussions about different kinds of supersession

---

26. See the website of the International Council of Christians and Jews for the latest statements and news in ongoing Jewish-Christian relations: http://www.jcrelations.net/. From my own denomination, see the recent compilation of resources from the Presbyterian tradition in the PC(USA) document *Christians and Jews: People of God* (Louisville: PC[USA], 2010). Noteworthy in that collection is the statement, *Dabru Emet: A Jewish Statement on Christians and Christianity*, written in 2000 by prominent Jewish scholars who were responding to the many statements by Christian traditions in the wake of *Nostra Aetate*.

This paragraph in *Dabru Emet* is especially apropos, in that it mentions favorably the efforts of many Christian theologians:

> *Nazism was not a Christian phenomenon.* Without the long history of Christian anti-Judaism and Christian violence against Jews, Nazi ideology could not have taken hold nor could it have been carried out. Too many Christians participated in, or were sympathetic to, Nazi atrocities against Jews. Other Christians did not protest sufficiently against these atrocities. But Nazism itself was not an inevitable outcome of Christianity. If the Nazi extermination of the Jews had been fully successful, it would have turned its murderous rage more directly to Christians. We recognize with gratitude those Christians who risked or sacrificed their lives to save Jews during the Nazi regime. With that in mind, we encourage the continuation of recent efforts in Christian theology to repudiate unequivocally contempt of Judaism and the Jewish people. We applaud those Christians who reject this teaching of contempt, and we do not blame them for the sins committed by their ancestors.

27. Second Vatican Council, "Declaration on the Relation of the Church to Non-Christian Religions, Nostra aetate, 28 October, 1965," in Austin Flannery, O. P., ed., *Vatican Council II: Constitutions, Decrees, Declarations: A Completely Revised Translation in Inclusive Language* (Northport, NY: Costello, 1996), §4.

and the precise relationship between Christianity and Judaism—discussions which often feature an examination of typology.[28]

Two of the Roman Catholic cardinals who most worked against anti-Semitism both during World War II and in the movements that led to Vatican II, Jean Daniélou and Henri de Lubac, also produced seminal scholarly works that showed the importance of the Jewish background to much of the New Testament and early Christian thought and worship. Daniélou, in his 1956 work *The Bible and the Liturgy,* argued that the worship of both synagogue and temple definitively shaped the early worship of the church. His later book *The Theology of Jewish Christianity* argued that early Christian life and thought drew much more from Jewish thought forms and Jewish patterns of worship than was previously recognized. This was in marked contrast to typical modern Protestant histories of the early church that emphasized the distinctions between Old and New Covenants and the Greek influences on early Christian thought.[29] Daniélou and his teacher, de Lubac, also highlighted typology as the central means by which early Christian interpreters understood continuity and discontinuity between Judaism and Christianity.

So, in a variety of ways, Protestants and Catholics since especially the 1960s have been retrieving a deeper sense of Christianity's basis in and ties to Judaism in general, and more specifically the Jewish background of Christian worship practices. While the details of the relationship between Christians and Jews are still being negotiated, stark contrasts between the Old Testament and New Testament implied by frameworks such as law and gospel have in general been called into question. Christians are seeing the continuities between Israelite religion and Christianity much more clearly.

28. For example, see Matthew Boulton, "Supersession or Subsession? Exodus Typology, the Christian Eucharist and the Jewish Passover Meal," *Scottish Journal of Theology* 66, no. 1 (Feb 2013): 18–29. From the perspective of an important Jewish scholar, see Peter Ochs, *Another Reformation: Postliberal Christianity and the Jews* (Grand Rapids: Baker Academic, 2011), in which Ochs examines the positive correlation between what he calls "non-supersession" and postliberalism.

29. Daniélou, *The Bible and the Liturgy* (Notre Dame: University of Notre Dame Press, 1956); *The Theology of Jewish Christianity* (London: Darton, Longman & Todd, 1964). While many have critiqued the overly rigid categories of Daniélou's *Jewish Christianity* and even the term "Jewish Christianity," his work has helped redirect the understanding of Christian origins. For such an appreciative critique, see R. A. Kraft, "In Search of 'Jewish Christianity' and Its 'Theology,'" in *Early Christianity and Judaism,* ed. Everett Ferguson (New York: Garland, 1993), 1–13.

Reconnecting the Eucharist to the Temple

This revolutionary renewed appreciation of the continuities of Christianity with its Jewish roots in the past decades, in addition to the many significant mid-twentieth-century archaeological discoveries that have shed light on first-century Judaism, has substantially affected discussions about the origins and meanings of the Eucharist.[30]

In the past, within the field of liturgical studies and the history of Christian worship, discussions about the origins of the Eucharist have largely focused on the development of eucharistic rites *after* Christ's Last Supper up until the full and detailed eucharistic liturgies of the fourth and fifth centuries, not primarily on what came *before* the Last Supper. Even so, cultural influences behind and before the Last Supper have played a minor role in the origins discussion. Such influences provided the frameworks of ritual and meaning for the earliest Eucharist celebrations and continued to pressure their development.

Potential influences often considered include Jewish rites, rituals, and prayers from which the Eucharist might have developed. Meanwhile, temple and typology are rarely mentioned. Scholars typically examine Jewish meal rites and rituals set in homes (as opposed to the temple), and the textual traditions of eucharistic prayers (as opposed to types and images). They attempt to trace early Christian liturgies back to those home rituals through exact words and phrases carried over from Jewish prayers.

In such work throughout the twentieth century several Jewish influences have been routinely cited; however, no one source has been convincingly received as *the* Jewish precursor to the Eucharist. In the early decades of the twentieth century, many scholars argued that the Last Supper took over the forms of the Passover Kiddush meal or Kiddush blessing.[31] Another common opinion was that it was an adaption of a *chaburah* meal, a meal shared by cer-

---

30. The most important of these discoveries are the Dead Sea Scrolls, found in 1947, and the Nag Hammadi library, discovered in 1945. See McGowan's summary of "Jewish Evidence" in Andrew McGowan, *Ancient Christian Worship: Early Church Practices in Social, Historical, and Theological Perspective* (Grand Rapids: Baker Academic, 2014), 10–12.

31. The Kiddush rite was a ritual blessing of the Sabbath in homes which involved blessing the wine and breaking bread.

tain fellowships or societies of Jews.[32] Such opinions began to fall out of favor in the mid-twentieth-century due in part to the arguments of Joachim Jeremias who, in his influential *The Eucharistic Words of Jesus*, argued that the Passover Seder meal was the most likely and most obvious background to the Last Supper.[33] However, in the last few decades theories that either simply identify the Last Supper as a transformed Passover Seder meal or create a simple narrative of development from Passover Seder meal to eucharistic rite have also been called into question.

Andrew McGowan's book *Ancient Christian Worship* is a good representative of such recent work on the origins of the Christian Eucharist. Besides examining claims that eucharistic practices developed from Jewish prayers and meals, he also takes into consideration arguments that place the Eucharist in the tradition of Greco-Roman symposiums or banquets. While he thinks both Jewish and Greco-Roman traditions add to our understanding of the context out of which the Christian celebration arose, he also argues that none of these traditions—whether Greek symposium meal or Jewish Passover meal or some other Jewish ritual—can explain the shape or meaning of the Last Supper, much less the Eucharist. He writes:

> The Christian meal began as a form of ancient Mediterranean banquet, a varied but recognizable tradition fundamental to social and cultural, as well as religious, life. Banquets did not have a single or simple meaning inherent in their celebration, but might be venues for contest as well as celebration, for struggle as well as solidarity, for experimentation as well as consolidation. The Eucharist appears as a tradition within this tradition, with meanings and values attached, yet not simply one single or simple "word" spoken within that "language" of communal and convivial signification.[34]

32. Dom Gregory Dix, a leading liturgical scholar, in *The Shape of the Liturgy* (New York: Seabury, 1982), originally published in 1945, argues the background to the Eucharist was not the Passover, but rather *chaburah* meals.

33. Joachim Jeremias, *The Eucharistic Words of Jesus*, trans. Norman Perrin from the 3rd German ed. (London: SCM, 1966). See pp. 15–89 for a review of his arguments against other options and his own argument that the Last Supper was a Passover Seder meal. The Passover Seder meal was eaten in homes after the Passover celebration at the temple.

34. McGowan, *Ancient Christian Worship*, 63.

Not only is its meaning not determined by its background, but McGowan notes too that the Eucharist has more than one meaning: "The Eucharist is a field of Christian practice characterized (like early Christian doctrine) by diversity and not just a single idea represented in bread and wine."[35] While trying to find a single meaning is tempting, the evidence suggests there is a "real feast of meanings" included in it.[36]

McGowan makes little mention of the worship rites of the temple as possible background practices. Instead he understands allusions to the temple made by writers such as Cyprian as a later change to the earlier practice. McGowan notes allusions to the temple were widespread by the year 300 but suggests those widespread allusions developed as a counter-practice to non-Christian Roman sacrifice.[37]

Bryan Spinks, in his book *Do This in Remembrance of Me,* also sums up many of the latest discussions about the possible background contexts of the Christian Eucharist. Similar to McGowan, Spinks centers his discussion on meal practices in homes and written prayers. He is cautious about claiming direct connections to such precursors. He cautions first about prayers, such as the *berakot* prayers of the Jewish Seder, arguing we know very little for certain about the exact form or wording of Jewish prayers in the first century: "We have scant information as regards the actual forms of Jewish meal prayer in the first century CE and therefore precious little on which to speculate about some evolution of Christian Eucharistic Prayers."[38]

Regarding the various forms of meals in both Greco-Roman and Jewish cultures of the time, he examines the forms and meanings of those meals and the ways they might have influenced the forms of the Christian Eucharist. Aspects of the Greco-Roman symposium or banquet, for example, seem to have influenced the ways the Passover Seder meal was celebrated. However, he writes that it is not the similarities that are especially significant, but rather "their *differences* and their *theological significance*" that one should pay attention to.[39]

Along with these more typically examined antecedents, Spinks examines recent claims connecting the Eucharist to the temple and temple-inspired

---

35. McGowan, *Ancient Christian Worship,* 62.
36. McGowan, *Ancient Christian Worship,* 62.
37. McGowan, *Ancient Christian Worship,* 53–55.
38. Spinks, *Do This in Remembrance of Me,* 2.
39. Spinks, *Do This in Remembrance of Me,* 5.

practices. Some scholars have argued the Eucharist was influenced by a certain hypothetically reconstructed temple sacrifice, or alternatively, the *todah* sacrifice, or meals of the Essene community led by a priest which prefigured the awaited messianic banquet led by the Messiah who is also Priest.[40] While Spinks give little weight to these claims, he notes that these claims of possible backgrounds gives "a broad context in which the meals of the Gospels and the distinct Last Supper narratives of Jesus can be evaluated."[41]

Paul Bradshaw is a final example of an important liturgical scholar who argues that the search for the words of the earliest eucharistic prayers in order to arrive at some pristine original understanding and model of those prayers is misguided. He argues the earliest Christian eucharistic prayers show great diversity in theology, imagery, and wording.[42] In fact, he claims that those earliest prayers "were much less developed and explicit as to their eucharistic theology than were the beliefs of those who used them and preached about them. Thus they provide less than satisfactory models for modern liturgical compilers to imitate than do the more fully formed examples from later centuries."[43]

McGowan, Spinks, and Bradshaw all agree that the search for a single Jewish prayer precedent for early Christian eucharistic prayers should be abandoned. It does not seem that there were, in fact, fixed prayers that all Jews used for any celebration. The exact forms of prayers that are recorded in later rabbinic literature were, at least in some opinions, creations of the rabbis to systematize and standardize practices which were diverse at the time of Christ. As Joseph Heinemann writes: "Only after the numerous prayers had come into being and were familiar to the masses did the Sages decide that the time had come to establish some measure of uniformity and standardization."[44] As a result, "The widely accepted goal of the philological method—viz., to discover or to reconstruct the one 'original' text of a particular composition . . . is out of place in the field of [early] liturgical studies."[45]

---

40. Spinks, *Do This in Remembrance of Me*, 7–11.

41. Spinks, *Do This in Remembrance of Me*, 11.

42. Paul F. Bradshaw, *Eucharistic Origins* (London: SPCK, 2004), and Bradshaw, *Reconstructing Early Christian Worship* (London: SPCK, 2009).

43. Bradshaw, *Reconstructing Early Christian Worship*, 52.

44. Joseph Heinemann, *Prayer in the Talmud: Forms and Patterns*, Studia Judaica 9 (New York: De Gruyter, 1977), 37. Quoted in Spinks, *Do This in Remembrance of Me*, 24.

45. Heinemann, *Prayer in the Talmud*, 43. Quoted in Spinks, *Do This in Remembrance of Me*, 24.

In contrast to the philological method, i.e., starting with the exact words of early Christian eucharistic prayers and then attempting to trace those words back to the exact language of Jewish models, this book will focus on types and images. It will connect Christian eucharistic theology and practice, organized around central images and types, back to the central images and types of Jewish temple theology and practice. Indeed, Spinks thinks that highlighting "theological motifs" and tracing these motifs back to Jewish precedents is a more interesting and fruitful project, which is precisely what I am doing by focusing on the "central meanings" of the temple and its rites.[46]

So, as we have seen, the temple has not played a large role in the work of most liturgical historians. But in contrast, there has been a much larger and increasing interest in the temple among Old Testament scholars and biblical theologians. The temple is increasingly understood to have held an important place in the imaginations and writings of first-century Jews, a phenomenon mentioned by Walter Brueggemann above.

One reason for this is the overturning of the many prejudices named above. Another impetus has been the significant archaeological discoveries of writings this past century, most prominently the Dead Sea Scrolls. These have thrown greater light on the thought and practice of first-century Jewish groups. In these writings we find that the temple, worship at the temple, and the priesthood of Israel played a much more important role in Jewish imagination and piety than previously understood.[47] The result is that temple themes in Old Testament theology and in reconstructions of first-century Judaism are becoming more and more prominent.[48]

Going hand in hand with this, a growing number of Christian theologians and biblical scholars argue that the temple and its imagery are hermeneutical keys for narrating the larger story of God and God's people in ever more satisfying ways. More scholars are recognizing the importance of temple imagery

46. Spinks, *Do This in Remembrance of Me*, 27.

47. Elior, *Three Temples*. See also C. T. R. Hayward, *The Jewish Temple: A Non-Biblical Sourcebook* (New York: Routledge, 1996).

48. E.g., Jon D. Levenson, *Sinai and Zion: An Entry into the Jewish Bible* (San Francisco: HarperSanFrancisco, 1985); Samuel Balentine, *The Torah's Vision of Worship* (Minneapolis: Fortress, 1999); Peter Leithart, *A House for My Name: A Survey of the Old Testament* (Moscow, ID: Canon, 2000); Craig Koester, *The Dwelling of God: The Tabernacle in the Old Testament, Intertestamental Jewish Literature, and the New Testament* (Washington, DC: Catholic Biblical Association of America, 1989).

in both christology and ecclesiology.[49] And in this literature, more and more connections are being made between temple worship and the Eucharist.[50]

Among scholars who explicitly highlight the importance of temple motifs and themes for early Christian worship and for the Eucharist in particular, both Margaret Barker and Brant Pitre stand out as persistent and important voices who have written extensively on the topic.

Margaret Barker in many of her books and writings argues that many early Christian theologians and leaders of the church from the very beginning drew deeply from temple traditions in their understanding of the gospel and the practices of Eucharist and baptism.[51] Such traditions of imagination, practice, and understanding are the "unwritten traditions" written about by several early church Fathers that were handed down by Jesus to his disciples and from them to the succeeding generations.

In this regard, Barker often draws on Basil of Caesarea (d. AD 379) who in his treatise *On the Holy Spirit* writes: "Concerning the teachings of the Church, whether publicly proclaimed (*kērygma*) or reserved to members of the household of faith (*dogmata*), we have received some from written sources, while others have been given to us secretly, through apostolic tradition. Both sources have equal force in true religion."[52] Some of these teachings that Basil gives

---

49. E.g., G. K. Beale, *The Temple and the Church's Mission: A Biblical Theology of the Dwelling Place of God* (Downers Grove, IL: InterVarsity Press, 2004); Oskar Skarsaune, *In the Shadow of the Temple: Jewish Influences on Early Christianity* (Downers Grove, IL: InterVarsity Press, 2002); Matthew Levering, *Christ's Fulfillment of Torah and Temple* (Notre Dame: University of Notre Dame Press, 2002); Kurt Paesler, *Das Tempelwort Jesu: Die Traditionen von Tempelzerstörung und Tempelerneuerung im Neuen Testament* (Göttingen: Vandenhoeck & Ruprecht, 1999); Alan Kerr, *The Temple of Jesus' Body: The Temple Theme in the Gospel of John* (Sheffield, UK: Sheffield Academic, 2002); Paul Hoskins, *Jesus as the Fulfillment of the Temple in the Gospel of John* (Bletchley, UK: Paternoster, 2006).

50. E.g., Levering, *Christ's Fulfillment*, 120–25; Matthew Levering, *Sacrifice and Community: Jewish Offering and Christian Eucharist* (Malden, MA: Blackwell, 2005); Marvin Wilson, *Our Father Abraham: Jewish Roots of the Christian Faith* (Grand Rapids: Eerdmans, 1989), 237–50; Skarsaune, *In the Shadow of the Temple*, 399–420; Margaret Barker, *Temple Themes in Christian Worship* (London: T&T Clark, 2007); Brant Pitre, *Jesus and the Jewish Roots of the Eucharist* (New York: Doubleday, 2011); Pitre, *Jesus and the Last Supper* (Grand Rapids: Eerdmans, 2015).

51. Barker, *Temple Themes*; Barker, *On Earth as It Is in Heaven: Temple Symbolism in the New Testament* (Edinburgh: T&T Clark, 1995); Barker, *The Great High Priest: Temple Roots of Christian Liturgy* (London: T&T Clark, 2003); Barker, *Temple Theology: An Introduction* (London: SPCK, 2004).

52. St. Basil the Great, *On the Holy Spirit* (New York: St. Vladimir's, 1980), 27, §66.

as examples of unwritten traditions are signing catechumens with the sign of the cross, praying facing East, "the words to be used in the invocation over the Eucharistic bread and the cup of blessing," the way to bless the baptismal water and the oil for chrismation, and baptizing with three immersions—all parts of sacramental worship.[53] Basil also thinks that if these "unwritten customs" were forgotten, "we would fatally mutilate the Gospel."[54] He likens these customs, and the way they are passed on only to the initiated, to the way that Moses and the Levites did not pass on all the knowledge about the practices of the temple to all the Israelites in public writings, but rather passed that knowledge down through unwritten priestly traditions.[55]

But rather than simply pointing to general ways that temple traditions influenced Christian worship, Barker makes the case that the early Christians understood themselves to be carrying on the traditions of the *first* temple, the Temple of Solomon, traditions which had been neglected, abused, and purposely changed during the time of the *second* temple. For Barker, these early Christians understood that in their worship, they, the new spiritual temple, were renewing the true worship of the first temple. Barker even suggests that the Old Testament texts that are the basis of Christian scripture were altered during that time and that Jesus and his disciples used earlier versions, which are now lost.

Many of her more speculative claims about historical reconstructions and textual alterations I find under-supported and difficult to evaluate.[56] That being said, the connections she draws between early Christian worship, the explanations of such worship in early Christian authors, and the worship of the temple are quite compelling. Barker has certainly done a great service in bringing to light the importance of the temple for both the religion of Israel and the imagination of the leaders of the early church.

---

53. Basil, *On the Holy Spirit*, §66.

54. Basil, *On the Holy Spirit*, §66.

55. Origen makes the same connections in his fifth homily on the book of Numbers. See Barker, "The Temple Roots of the Liturgy" (unpublished, 2000), 3. www.marquette .edu/maqom/Roots.pdf, accessed December 29, 2019.

56. I am predisposed to not follow Barker toward her conclusions in part because of my commitments to the canonical status of the Old Testament. Specifically, she argues that later Deuteronomistic redactors distorted the older religion of Israel, but that certain Jewish sects and the early Christians carried on and/or recovered those earlier traditions. A quasi-Marcionism of a higher critical kind seems to follow.

Brant Pitre similarly highlights connections between Jewish temple worship and the Eucharist, but with different results. Instead of highlighting those connections in service of a historical project with many revisionist aspects, Pitre finds the connections he researches fill out understandings of both the Eucharist and Jesus Christ that resonate well with traditional Roman Catholic theology and practice. In *Jesus and the Jewish Roots of the Eucharist*, Pitre focuses primarily on three such connections: the Passover celebration, the bread of the Presence, and the manna that was preserved in the ark of the covenant. It is these aspects of "the faith and hope of the Jewish people" that help one best interpret "Jesus' words at the Last Supper."[57] In *Jesus and the Last Supper*, Pitre amplifies his work on the Jewish background of the Last Supper. He argues that background undergirds the historical plausibility of the Last Supper and provides a central key to historical portraits of Jesus of Nazareth. In doing so, Pitre paints a historical portrait of Jesus that is deeply orthodox, historically rigorous, and yet fresh and full, given the way it emerges from the milieu of Jewish beliefs and worship.

I have great appreciation and gratitude for all the work of Barker and Pitre and understand my investigation corroborates and builds on their work in many ways. In one major way I hope to extend their work. Given my understanding of God's providential activity in inspiring the final canonical form of the Old Testament, a point at which I differ from Barker, I expect the broadest and most comprehensive images or types of the ideal canonical forms of Israelite worship at the temple and tabernacle to provide the most important background to the Eucharist. It would make sense that the central ritual celebration of the New Testament people of God would be foreshadowed by the central ritual celebrations of the Old Testament people of God. By attending to the structure and patterns of Israelite worship at the temple more fully than Barker and Pitre do, I argue that these central ritual structures found in plain sight and bold print in the canonical texts provide the most satisfying framework of symbols and meanings for illuminating both the Last Supper and the Christian Eucharist.

The theological center of the Old Testament is the Torah, the five books of Moses. At the center of the Torah is the covenant given to Moses on

57. Pitre, *Jesus and the Jewish Roots*, 9.

Mount Sinai as recorded in Exodus 19 to Numbers 10. At the center of the covenant are the detailed instructions for the building of the tabernacle and detailed instructions for the overall liturgical life of the people of God. The five most prominent symbolic and ritual components of that worship described in those texts are (1) the temple itself, (2) the regularized daily, Sabbath, and monthly services, and the three annual pilgrim feasts of (3) Pesach or Passover, (4) Shavuot or Pentecost, and (5) Sukkoth or the Feast of Booths.[58] These symbols and practices and their main meanings form the structure of my investigation, my book, and my understanding of the Eucharist itself. I believe this structure can go far in bringing a stable, biblical, and providentially given structure to a Christian understanding and practice of the Eucharist.

In my own research I sought in vain for an early church theologian who spotted and structured their own understanding of the Eucharist around these five components of the temple and its worship, or even around just the three pilgrim feasts. I was excited to find that Hippolytus, an important leader of the church in Rome, in a work of his quoted by Theodoret, did see Christ as the typological fulfillment of the three pilgrim feasts: "Wherefore three seasons of the year typified the Saviour Himself that He might fulfil the mysteries predicted about Him. In the Passover, . . . At Pentecost. . . ."[59] And yet, even though I did not find a conscious use of the overall structure I am presenting here in early Christian theologians, many, if not most, early church leaders and theologians consistently spotted typological relationships between the Eucharist and one or more of the feasts or celebrations at the temple. So, while my fivefold structure for organizing eucharistic theology cannot claim the historical gravitas of patristic precedent, it is a clear structure found in the Torah, and it is a clear way to organize the many meanings of the Eucharist. The words of Christ at the Last Supper as recorded in the

---

58. As mentioned above, daily, Sabbath, and monthly celebrations and the three pilgrim feasts are laid out clearly and in this order in Numbers 28–29. Instructions for the Sabbath and the three pilgrim feasts are given in Leviticus 23:1–44 and Exodus 23:12–17. The three pilgrim feasts are commanded in Exodus 23:14–17, 34:18–23 and Deuteronomy 16:1–17.

59. Quoted by Theodoret in Dialogue 2, "The Unconfounded" (*NPNF2* 3:202).

Gospels also resonate with the central meanings of all three pilgrim feasts at the temple (see Chapter 6).

But before drawing out these figurative relationships and showing their implications for doctrine and worship in the following chapters, it will be beneficial first to take a close look at typology and the assumptions that undergird it, this bridge between table and temple.

2

RECONNECTING TABLE AND TEMPLE

Roots, Echoes, Images, and Figural Performances

God is a typological poet.

—Matthew Boulton,
"Supersession or Subsession?"

We . . . have received both the truth and the archetypes of the
early images through the mysterious dispensation of Christ. . . .

—Eusebius of Caesarea,
Demonstration of the Gospel

The importance of the temple and its rites in the imaginations of the writers of
the New Testament writers and the leaders of the early church is being recovered in the academy, as discussed in the previous chapter. But *how* did it make
a difference in their understanding of Christ and of the Eucharist? How does it
matter for contemporary eucharistic theology and worship? More specifically,
what does it mean to speak of the temple and its rites as *images* or *types* of the
practices surrounding the Eucharist?

The historic reassessment of Christianity's relationship to Judaism that has
taken place in the last quarter century has gone hand in hand with important
reassessments of how to read Scripture, and in particular how to read the New
Testament in relation to the Old Testament.[1] The history of these intertwined

1. Many of these developments have been brought together under the phrase "the
theological interpretation of Scripture," a broad movement that is helpfully marked by

reassessments could be narrated in a variety of ways,[2] but for the purposes of this study, rather than trying to summarize the vast literature that has been written on these topics in the last twenty-five years, I will merely emphasize a few ways of thinking about the relationship of the Old Testament to the New Testament, and more specifically of the temple to the Eucharist, that I have found to be most illuminating.[3]

Brant Pitre: Jewish Roots

Considered most broadly, this project involves the recovery of the Jewish roots of Christianity. The image of Jewish roots is related to Romans 11:16–18, where Paul is reflecting on the relationship of the new followers of Christ to Israel: "If the root is holy, then the branches also are holy. But if some of the branches

the *Dictionary for Theological Interpretation of the Bible*, ed. Kevin J. Vanhoozer (Grand Rapids: Baker Academic, 2005). From the preface: "*DTIB* responds to two crises precipitated by Enlightenment and post-Enlightenment developments in biblical interpretation respectively: to the modern schism between biblical studies and theology, and to the postmodern proliferation of 'advocacy' approaches to reading Scripture where each interpretive community does what is right in their own eyes" (20). A positive recovery of Jewish roots is often involved in those interested in the theological interpretation of Scripture, a movement with many crossovers with "postliberalism," which is itself often seen as a third-way between modern and post-modern hermeneutical strategies. The title of Peter Ochs's book, *Postliberal Christianity and the Jews: A New Reformation* (Grand Rapids: Baker Academic, 2011), suggests that such developments are of the same magnitude of historical importance as the sixteenth-century Reformation. Phyllis Tickle, in *The Great Emergence: How Christianity Is Changing and Why* (Grand Rapids: Baker Books, 2008) argues the paradigms for reading Scripture are undergoing great transformation in our time comparable to the Reformation. Finally, the Vatican II document *Dei Verbum* in 1965 signaled a rethinking of the relationship of tradition and Scripture within the Roman Catholic Church in a way that finds much convergence with the Protestant approaches mentioned above.

2. Given the great influence of Richard Hays on my own thinking, I find his own listing of "important influences" on his thought about "the interpretation of the OT in the NT" to be illuminating. See Richard Hays, *Reading Backwards: Figural Christology and the Fourfold Gospel Witness* (Waco, TX: Baylor University Press, 2014), xv-xviii.

3. See also Beale's discussion of "extended meaning" in his book, *Temple and the Church's Mission*, in his section "Hermeneutical reflections on the theological relationship of the Old Testament temple to the temple in the New Testament," 373–85. There Beale frames part of the question of the relationship between OT and NT in terms of "literal" fulfillments.

were broken off, and you, a wild olive shoot, were grafted in their place to share the rich root of the olive tree, do not boast over the branches. If you do boast, remember that it is not you that support the root, but the root that supports you." In this analogy, gentile followers of Christ are made holy through their being "grafted" onto the tree and the root of Israel. Gentile followers of Christ as well as the faith-filled "branches" of Israel who were following Christ drew life from the same roots. Although not a fully nuanced account of the New Testament's relation to the Old, Paul's image here at the very least indicates that understanding the new covenant as having totally overcome or replaced the old covenant is problematic.

This image of Jewish roots which support and nourish the engrafted Gentile church has become increasingly popular in many settings, from recent academic discussions of "the new black theology" of Willie Jennings and J. Kameron Carter to more popular writings in the emerging church movement.[4] Despite being a powerful and suggestive metaphor and a good place to begin methodologically, the roots image does not precisely identify the kinds of relationships that are involved between, for example, the temple and the Eucharist.

Consider again Brant Pitre's book *Jesus and the Jewish Roots of the Eucharist*. Pitre reads Jesus's eucharistic sayings in light of Jewish beliefs found in both the Old Testament and rabbinic literature, especially the Mishnah and the Talmud.[5] Pitre writes: "If you really want to know who Jesus was and what he was saying and doing, then you need to interpret his words and deeds in their historical context. And that means becoming familiar with not just ancient Christianity but also with ancient Judaism."[6]

Pitre connects the Eucharist to the Passover, to expectations about the new manna of the Messiah, and to the bread of the Presence at the temple. Using

---

4. Jennings argues for connections between the history of Christian supersessionism and modern racism, and argues the Christian church must recover our rootedness in Israel. The image of the wild olive branch being grafted onto the olive tree and roots of Israel plays an important role in the positive trajectory he argues for. William Jennings, *The Christian Imagination: Theology and the Origins of Race* (New Haven: Yale University Press, 2010). As one example among many of the recovery of Jewish roots in emerging church movements, Dan Kimball writes, "In the emerging church we need to bring back the ancient symbols and talk about the Jewish roots of our faith." Kimball, *The Emerging Church: Vintage Christianity for New Generations* (Grand Rapids: Zondervan, 2003), 149.

5. See Pitre, *Jesus and the Jewish Roots*, 18–21 for his discussion of sources.

6. Pitre, *Jesus and the Jewish Roots*, 8.

these connections, Pitre shows how an understanding of the Eucharist that is in line with the Catechism of the Catholic Church is not only supported but comes alive in a fresh way.

Pitre points out many important connections and his work does a great service, especially for Roman Catholics by alerting them to the importance of the Eucharist's Jewish roots. However, given the limitations of scope and audience of this book, Pitre does not provide an in-depth discussion about how such roots and contexts matter. For example, as he argues against a Zwinglian "symbolic" understanding of the bread and wine he simply refers to the idea of typology without further elaboration:

> Now let's ask a pivotal question: If a first-century Jew believed that the old manna was supernatural bread from heaven, then could the new manna be just a symbol? . . . If so, that would make the old manna *greater* than the new! But that is not how salvation history works in the Bible. Old Testament prefigurations (known as types) are never greater than their New Testament fulfillments (known as antitypes). . . . In short, *if the old manna of the first exodus was supernatural bread from heaven, then the new manna of the Messiah must also be supernatural bread from heaven.*[7]

While I appreciate the point, in order to convince a Zwinglian, a longer discussion about types, figures, and the theological relationship between the Old and New Testaments is needed.

In his *Jesus and the Last Supper*, however, Pitre does provide a rigorous methodological discussion about how such roots and contexts matter.[8] In fact, this book represents perhaps the most in-depth discussion of the Last Supper in print. By drawing on Old Testament images and types, most centrally Moses, manna, Passover, and the Messianic banquet, Pitre convincingly shows how Jesus's actions and words at the Last Supper are embedded in their Jewish context. But in this work Pitre is most centrally engaged in debates about the historicity of the Last Supper. As such, his emphasis on how such roots and background images contribute to the historical plausibility of the Last Supper accounts and its coherence with an overall picture of Jesus's aims and purposes,

7. Pitre, *Jesus and the Jewish Roots*, 103.
8. Brant Pitre, *Jesus and the Last Supper* (Grand Rapids: Eerdmans, 2015), 28–52.

aims and purposes that include establishing a new covenant community centered on "the new sacrifice of a new cult."[9]

But for the purposes of my project, I am interested not so much in the ways such roots and connections matter for the historical plausibility of the Last Supper but in the ways those roots influence and shape our understanding of the central meanings of the Eucharist. So, what tools are available for bringing more control to the ways such roots influence our understanding of the meanings of Eucharist? One such tool is intertextual linkages, which Pitre himself speaks of: "'intertextual linkage' is often one of the most helpful ways of deepening our understanding of the meaning Jesus' words and deeds might have had in the overall context of his public ministry."[10] For a thorough discussion of such intertextual linkages or echoes, the work of Richard Hays has been groundbreaking.

Richard Hays and Christopher Seitz: Intertextual Echoes and Figures

Richard Hays has had a profound impact on the field of New Testament studies and my own theological vision by highlighting how New Testament writers' imaginations were formed by the Old Testament. Hays argues New Testament texts are best understood when one considers the "vast intertextual network of scriptural citations, allusions, and echoes" that form the substructure of their writings.[11]

Of particular interest is his analysis of the use of a literary device called "metalepsis" in the New Testament. For example, he argues that Paul's allusions to and quotations of OT Scripture "frequently exemplify the literary trope of metalepsis."[12] Hays defines metalepsis as "a rhetorical and poetic device in which one text alludes to an earlier text in a way that evokes resonance of the earlier text *beyond those explicitly cited.* The result is that the interpretation of a metalepsis requires the reader to recover unstated or suppressed correspondences between the two texts."[13] When one encounters an instance

9. Pitre, *Jesus and the Last Supper,* 517.
10. Pitre, *Jesus and the Last Supper,* 39.
11. Hays, *Reading Backwards,* ix. See also Hays, *Echoes of Scripture in the Letters of Paul* (New Haven: Yale University Press, 1989), *The Conversion of the Imagination: Paul as Interpreter of Israel's Scripture* (Grand Rapids: Eerdmans, 2005), and Richard B. Hays and Ellen Davis, eds., *The Art of Reading Scripture* (Grand Rapids: Eerdmans, 2003).
12. Hays, *Conversion of the Imagination,* 2.
13. Hays, *Conversion of the Imagination,* 2.

of metalepsis, one should go back and examine the wider scriptural context of the precursor text in order to fully appreciate the "figurative effects" that are created through the interplay between these two, or perhaps more, texts.[14]

For example, Jesus at the Last Supper said, "This is my blood of the covenant, which is poured out for many" (Mark 14:24; cf. Matt. 26:28, Luke 22:20, 1 Cor. 11:25). The phrase "blood of the covenant" echoes Exodus 24:8: "Moses took the blood and dashed it on the people and said, 'See the blood of the covenant that the Lord has made with you in accordance with all these words.'"[15] If this is an instance of metalepsis, what "figurative effects" are created through the interplay of these texts?

The larger context of the Exodus text is quite familiar—it is the original covenant ratification ceremony performed on Mount Sinai between Israel and the Lord. In Exodus 24, Moses speaks to the people the words of the Lord which form the center of the covenant (24:3), writes down all the words of the Lord (24:4), builds an altar (24:4), has men offer burnt offerings and sacrifices of well-being (24:5), and dashes half the blood from those offerings on the altar (24:6). The people voice their vow of obedience (24:7), and then Moses dashes the other half of the "blood of the covenant" on the people (24:8). After this sealing of the covenant, the leaders "went up" (24:9) and "they beheld God, and they ate and drank" (24:11).

A more detailed treatment of this example will be provided in chapter 9 where I will examine the feast of *Shavuot*, the pilgrim feast where the giving of the Law is celebrated and the covenant renewed. For now let me simply point out a few ways both the immediate and larger scriptural contexts of Exodus 24:8 might put pressure on our interpretation of the New Testament "words of institution" passages.

First, it suggests that the Eucharist was intended to be, among other things, a covenant renewal ceremony. By drinking the wine, those who participate are, like the people of Israel in Exodus 24:7, both receiving a gift from God and pledging their vow of obedience to follow the new law of Christ. Second, it corrects the false distinctions people often draw between table and altar, and sacrifice and meal. In Exodus 24, sacrifices and meals went together. Third, the

---

14. Hays, *Conversion of the Imagination*, 3.

15. The only Old Testament instances of the phrase "the blood of the covenant" are Exod. 24:8 and Zech. 9:11.

phrase "the blood of the covenant" suggests that the New Testament authors understood Jesus's action as a figurative extension of the Mount Sinai episode rather than as a more typical Jewish or Greco-Roman meal. Fourth, since the Passover is not in view in Exodus 24, this background suggests that the Eucharist is not merely a transformation of a Passover Seder meal. Fifth, it suggests that as the church celebrates the Eucharist, God is present in a powerful way similar to how God was present in the events written about in Exodus 24 (as some who see the Eucharist as an "ordinance" and not a "sacrament" often deny). Of course all these points must be argued more carefully, but simply by putting this phrase against the background of Exodus 24 and tracing possible unstated correspondences, these theological pressures can be felt.

So, given this understanding of intertextual echoes and figures, this study considers how one might better understand New Testament and early church texts about the Eucharist by examining the larger Old Testament contexts that they allude to or are drawn from.

While this is a crucial place to start, methods of figural interpretation raise questions that go deeper than texts and their historical contexts. They raise questions that concern God's relationship to them both, namely, how are God's providence and activity involved in the production of these textual and figural relationships? Christopher Seitz, in writing about both the loss of figural interpretation in the past few centuries and its recent recovery, claims: "The loss of figural reading is not the loss of an exegetical technique. It is the loss of location in time under God."[16] By reading Scripture with eyes and ears that are attuned only to their immediate literary or historical context, we may fail to notice the relationship of texts, people, and events to the unified providential molding of God. Figural readings of Scripture suggest that God has shaped not only texts, but also the imaginations of the many scriptural authors and the many events and people to which Scripture points, forming them into recognizable and analogous patterns, figures, and types. Those figures are "figured" *by God*, who has desired to reflect both who God is and God's overarching intentions for God's creation in a variety of creaturely materials: texts, imaginations, and events.

This theologically freighted understanding of figuration is important because some of the most important figures for our understanding of the Eu-

---

16. Christopher Seitz, *Figured Out: Typology and Providence in Christian Scripture* (Louisville: Westminster John Knox, 2001), viii.

charist are not textual. They are instead the figure of the temple itself and its ceremonies that anchored the worship of the Jewish people at the temple. Furthermore, the goal of this study is not a better text about the Eucharist, but Christian celebrations of the Eucharist that figure God's intended transactions with God's people in the Eucharist more fully and richly.

In understanding these figurative readings of Scripture and of certain people, places, and events and their ramifications, the writings of Austin Farrer and John David Dawson have been particularly formative for me.

Austin Farrer: Master Images

Austin Farrer (1904–1968) was an Oxford theologian and philosopher who kept good company, having notable friends such as C. S. Lewis, J. R. R. Tolkien, and Dorothy Sayers. Archbishop Rowan Williams once said he is "possibly the greatest Anglican mind of the twentieth century."[17] In his 1948 Bampton Lectures, *The Glass of Vision*, he sought to better understand the process of inspiration and divine revelation. In Farrer's words, he was interested in "the form of divine truth in the human mind."[18] Working through Farrer's lectures, one finds that revealed divine truth is formed in the human mind through a process of inspiration and revelation that involves the interplay of both "images" and "events."[19] While not a theory of typology per se, his understanding of this interplay sheds much light on it.

His combined emphasis on image and event creates a path between two extremes. He seeks to avoid, on the one hand, a theory of inspiration in which God directly inspired the writers of Scripture to write each particular word on the page, and on the other hand, the theory that only the events behind the scriptural texts were inspired and that the scriptural writers were simply in a unique position to record such events. Farrer is unsatisfied with both of these

---

17. "Debate on The Gift of Authority: Archbishop of Canterbury's Remarks," 13 February 2004 (http://www.archbishopofcanterbury.org/sermons_speeches/040213a .html).

18. Austin Farrer, *The Glass of Vision*, in *Scripture, Metaphysics, and Poetry: Austin Farrer's* The Glass of Vision *with Critical Commentary*, ed. Robert MacSwain (Surrey, England: Ashgate Publishing Limited, 2013), 15.

19. Farrer, *Glass of Vision*, 42.

common ways of understanding inspiration and revelation and the resulting ways of reading and interpreting Scripture associated with them. As he puts it, "the prevalent doctrine about Scriptural inspiration largely determines the use men make of the Scriptures," and his ideas about inspiration avoid conservative and liberal extremes, opening up a middle way to more figural readings and uses of Scripture.[20]

For his model of inspiration, Farrer points to the divine-human mind of Jesus Christ as the quintessentially inspired mind. He further reasons that "the interpretive work of the Apostles [as they composed scriptural texts] must be understood as participation in the mind of Christ, through the Holy Spirit: they are the members, upon whom inflows the life of the Head."[21]

So how did Jesus express his thinking? Through images that interpreted the events of his life. Farrer writes: "Now the mind of Christ himself was expressed in certain dominant images."[22] That is, Christ took certain dominant or master images from the life and traditions of Israel and applied them to himself in order to explain and interpret his own self and activity.

Farrer names five dominant or master images. The first two are Kingdom of God and the Son of Man. Third, "He set forth the image of Israel, the human family of God, somehow mystically contained in the person of Jacob, its patriarch. He was himself Israel, and appointed 12 men to be his typical 'sons.'" The fourth are the images that are part of his prophecies of redemptive suffering. His final image is the Eucharist, or as he put it, "the action of the supper, the infinitely complex and fertile image of sacrifice and communion, of expiation and covenant."[23]

While such images were not the sum of what Christ taught, "They set forth the supernatural mystery which is the heart of the teaching."[24] These images were not free-floating concepts, but rather ways of seeing and interpreting specific events or activities in which God was involved with God's people, a history centered on the incarnation of Christ. "The great images interpreted the events of Christ's ministry, death and resurrection, and the events interpreted

---

20. Farrer, *Glass of Vision*, 37.
21. Farrer, *Glass of Vision*, 42.
22. Farrer, *Glass of Vision*, 42.
23. Farrer, *Glass of Vision*, 42.
24. Farrer, *Glass of Vision*, 42.

the images; the interplay of the two is revelation."[25] Without the image of the kingdom of God, events in Christ's healing ministry would not be properly seen as the in-breaking of the reign of God; without the image of the supper, the events of Christ's life, death, and resurrection would not be seen and understood in their fullness. The images are the key to a revelatory interpretation of the events—they are a central and crucial part of the "word" that interplays with "deed" in the revelatory life of Christ.

While much of Farrer's thought remains undeveloped, at least two aspects of it are especially fruitful and important. First, Farrer's emphasis on inspired images resonates well with premodern figural interpretations of Scripture and so can help us understand how New Testament, early church, and rabbinic writers thought. As Farrer writes, "In taking up the topic of Scriptural inspiration, we should like to attach ourselves to the thought of the ancient Church: but this we are told, is just what we have not to do." In putting it this way, Farrer is noting that, at least in 1948, any form of premodern exegesis was seen as quite questionable and unscientific. In the first chapter above, we saw many reasons for this prejudice. But this is how the scriptural writers of both Testaments thought. In the Old Testament, revelation can well be understood as the coincidence of divinely inspired events—such as the exodus from Egypt, the giving of the Law, the building of the temple—and the inspired interpretation of those events by the prophets and writers of Scripture, who often employed images in their interpretations. And to take just one example from the New Testament, the apostle Paul understood the worship and life of the disciples of Christ as a new temple.[26] In such premodern interpretations, divinely inspired events were understood in light of their attendant images.

Second, his trinitarian and incarnational account of revelation and inspiration helps chart a third way beyond the common modern options of "dictated propositions" on the one hand, and "events only" on the other. As Ingolf Dalferth approvingly writes, for Farrer, "Revelation is the *coincidence of divine incarnation and apostolic inspiration*, that is God's inspiration of the apostles to explicate the truth implicit in the incarnation."[27]

In both these ways, Farrer's work shows us that this typological way of

25. Farrer, *Glass of Vision*, 42.

26. See 1 Cor. 3:16–17; 2 Cor. 6:16; Eph. 2:21–22.

27. Ingolf Dalferth, "The Stuff of Revelation: Austin Farrer's Doctrine of Inspired Images," in MacSwain, *Scripture, Metaphysics, and Poetry*, 155.

thinking not only helps us understand premodern writers better but can also help us move forward past conservative versus liberal polarities that characterize modern biblical interpretation and still divide the church.

Farrer's thought shapes our understanding of the interplay of the Lord's Supper and the temple worship of Israel in two main ways. It first of all emphasizes that the Eucharist is one of the five most important images that reveal the saving work of God in its fulness and that link the Old Covenant with the New. It also suggests that as we try to understand the Eucharist, we should be on the alert for how the master image of the Eucharist is rooted in and a development or fulfillment of images in the Old Testament and life of Israel. In the following I argue the Eucharist grows out of and is a refinement of the image of the temple itself, as well as a refinement of the images of the most typical and central services of the temple: the daily thanksgiving to God at the temple, and the pilgrim feasts of the Passover, *Shavuot*, and *Sukkoth*—each of which is linked to particular events in the history of God's interaction with Israel: creation and providence, deliverance from the bondage of Egypt, covenant ratification and renewal, and the coming day of the Lord, a day that includes judgment, atonement, and the final great feast with God.

John David Dawson: Figural Performances

What Farrer suggests, Dawson clarifies and extends. In his careful study *Christian Figural Reading and the Fashioning of Identity*, Dawson looks in detail at the work of three important contemporary thinkers who engage with allegorical and figurative readings of Scripture: Daniel Boyarin, Erich Auerbach, and Hans Frei.[28] He compares them to one of the best-known early church exegetes of Scripture, Origen. In his analysis of these scholars, Dawson clarifies many of the theological issues surrounding figural interpretation. For our purposes, two aspects of Dawson's approach to figural interpretation are quite helpful for understanding the relationship between the temple and its worship and the Eucharist.

The first is his emphasis on embodied performances. Figural interpreta-

28. John David Dawson, *Christian Figural Reading and the Fashioning of Identity* (Berkeley: University of California Press, 2001).

tion—a phrase that Dawson borrows from Auerbach—is a description of the relationships between two realities, which could be people, texts, or events. In Hays's work, the two realities put into relationship are primarily textual images or figures and their meanings. Farrer goes further to suggest that such textual images are the keys for interpreting events that are in some ways outside of the images, yet intertwined with them. But Dawson suggests that underlying most texts and images are embodied performances. These events, occurrences, people, and practices outside of the text are the figures which are being put into relationship with one another in the biblical texts. And for Dawson, such embodied figures should ultimately be understood as "God's historical performances."[29]

Dawson stresses these points quite strongly. Using the text of the Ethiopian eunuch (Acts 8:26–40) as an example, he points out that the question posed by the eunuch about the Isaiah text was not fundamentally about a literary figure or image. As the eunuch learned, the text ultimately referenced the life and activity of Jesus Christ, even though it originally referenced another embodied historical figure. The questions the eunuch raised were not most fundamentally about a text and its meaning, but about persons and activities. Ultimately his questions centered on the person of Jesus Christ and the activity of God through him. Dawson writes, "Any effort to understand Christian figural reading as fundamentally a matter of texts and the presence or absence of meaning, rather than a matter of rendering God's historical performances intelligible, is doomed to theological irrelevance, however much contemporary theoretical sense it might make."[30] When one contemplates a figure in the text, one should understand that "the biblical figure is regarded as simultaneously bodily reality *and* textual signifier precisely because the text reflects the intervention of God in historical life, among embodied persons, in order to enact a divine plan for transformation."[31]

29. Dawson, *Christian Figural Reading*, 6.

30. Dawson, *Christian Figural Reading*, 6. Dawson's analysis of Boyarin's interpretation of Paul stresses this point. Dawson agrees with Boyarin that Christian figural reading must avoid a kind of allegorizing which erases or spiritualizes the embodied life of Israel, making the point of Old Testament texts an abstract moral or spiritualized point. This kind of allegorical reading has been part of a kind of supersessionism which both Dawson and Boyarin seek to avoid. However, Dawson argues, against Boyarin, that neither Paul nor Origen ultimately falls prey to this critique.

31. Dawson, *Christian Figural Reading*, 210.

Related to this first point is a second: Dawson's distinction between *figural* reading, and *figurative* or allegorical reading. The primary difference is that for figurative and allegorical readings and relationships, the original figure is in some way replaced or subverted by the second, while for figural readings and relations, the historicity of the first figure is preserved.[32]

An example here is helpful. Consider the relationship between the exodus and Christian baptism. Some texts refer to baptism as a kind of new exodus. In a purely *figurative* or allegorical reading of the two and their relation, the meanings of baptism can be stated "apart from the representation without loss; the representation is, at best, a useful but dispensable illustration."[33] For example, the death of the Egyptian soldiers in the Exodus story can be interpreted as a representation of the death of a person's sins in baptism. In this case, baptism means what it means with or without the exodus event—even though the exodus text is a useful figurative illustration.

In contrast, given a *figural* understanding of the relation between the two, the exodus is seen as a figure which "announces something else that is also real and historical."[34] Baptism is in this way understood as a practice that is part of a larger historical trajectory foreshadowed in Israel's exodus but continued in a new way post-Christ in which God continues to free and transform a people group for a special vocation. As Dawson writes, such figures "are persons or events that exist *in order to* signify something, and they do so because they are the means by which God is executing a divine plan for human life."[35] So, rather than being merely an interesting analogy to something else—like parables and sermon illustrations—it is through the activity and intentionality of God that the relationship is established. Figural reading in this way is not a literary

32. He draws this point especially from Auerbach. A similar point is made by E. Earle Ellis in his new foreword to Goppelt's *Typos*. Typology provides a third way between two early church tendencies: Marcionism and what has been called "Judaizing," or requiring "literal" obedience by all Christians to the Old Testament law. "Unlike a Judaizing hermeneutic, typology views the relationship of OT events to those in the new dispensation not as a 'one-to-one' equation or correspondence, in which the old is repeated or continued, but rather in terms of two principles, historical correspondence and escalation" (x).

33. Dawson, *Christian Figural Reading*, 86. The illustration from the exodus I take from Dawson.

34. Dawson, *Christian Figural Reading*, 87. Here Dawson is quoting Auerbach.

35. Dawson, *Christian Figural Reading*, 87.

creation by either the human authors or the human readers; it is instead the discernment of God's providential activity in history.

The relation between the two figures in this way is not a matter of abstracting transhistorical meanings from a previous historical event. Rather, one discerns a transformation from one embodied reality to a later embodied reality, a transformation brought about by God. Origen and other early church interpreters of Scripture are often accused of such abstraction or "allegorization," but Dawson defends them. He examines the distinction between body and spirit that Origen uses to speak of the difference between Old and New Testaments. Some understand Origen to be contrasting "embodied" historical events (such as the death of the Egyptians) with abstract and universal "spiritual" *meanings* (God removes our sins from us).[36] But Dawson claims that for Origen, this is a contrast between an earlier "body" event and a later "spirit" *event*. It is a matter of "transformation" rather than abstraction, the transformation from a materiality lacking in or devoid of spirit, to a "spiritualized materiality." While Dawson does not defend every scriptural interpretation of Origen, he convincingly shows that in general Origen is not making the kinds of modern supersessionist contrasts which combine modern body-spirit dualism with anti-Judaism. The "embodied practices and identities of Jews" are not undermined by Origen; instead, they are understood to be transformed by a further work of God.[37]

Dawson's concerns can guide our own thinking about the relationships between the temple and its practices and the Christian practice of the Eucharist. Following Dawson's thinking, both realities should be understood as parts of a larger historical performance by God. The practices of the temple should be understood as figured by God in order to announce the practice of the Eucharist.

The "meanings" of the temple and its worship are in this way not simply useful illustrations of the meanings of the Eucharist, nor are the Eucharist and New Testament texts associated with it simply making allusions to or allegories of past practices. Nor is the Eucharist seen as a "spiritual" practice (understood

36. Dawson claims such an understanding reflects modern contrasts between body and spirit that modern interpreters impose upon Origen and premodern interpreters. See for example his treatment of Boyarin's reading of Origen, *Christian Figural Reading*, 47–50.

37. Dawson, *Christian Figural Reading*, 50.

as abstract, universal, and free from the constraints of the body) that overturns a faulty, primitive, and corrupt practice. Nor is the contrast between literal (applied to the Eucharist) and nonliteral (applied to the temple) apt or helpful.

Instead, following Dawson's lead, I consider the basic patterns of God's providential activity in the temple and its practices, and then consider ways the practices of the temple are being "spiritualized," or better, transformed in the feast of the Eucharist because of the further work of God in the life, death, resurrection, and ascension of Jesus Christ through the power of the Holy Spirit. It is in these ways that I will attempt to understand the temple and its practices as "figures" of the Eucharist.

To conclude, as I "read" the Eucharist against the background of the temple and its worship, I will be looking especially for three things: intertextual echoes, an interplay of images, and historical performances which providentially function as figures or types. These are the primary tools and associated assumptions I bring to the task of drawing connections between the Eucharist and its Jewish roots, between table and temple.

This discussion of roots, echoes, images, and figural performances helps to pinpoint what I mean when I talk about the meanings or central meanings of the Eucharist. "Meaning" is, to put it lightly, a complicated word. Generally, I take the meaning of a communication, text, or activity to be its impact on someone (i.e., its import), which is often but not always related to the intended impact by its author (i.e., its purport). In speaking of the central meanings of the Eucharist my intention is to bring into focus the latter (i.e., its divinely intended meanings), which again may or may not align with its imported meanings (i.e., those received by its participants). Thus, discerning the central meanings of the Eucharist means discerning how God intends the practice to affect people's hearts, minds, and being. Discerning the central meanings of it involves trying to understand what God is up to and what God intends for those who participate in it.

The word "central" is important because it recognizes that the actual meaning or impact a particular Eucharist has on a particular person at a particular time might vary greatly, perhaps because God is doing something unusual on that particular occasion, perhaps because the practice of the Eucharist in that occasion distorts or occludes what God intends, or perhaps because of some problem in the reception of the practice by the people involved. So the Eucharist's central meanings refer to God's general intentions with respect to the practice. We must discern how God intends to transform people and discern people's proper responses to God's action. Such discernment of these central meanings is helped by making these connections between table and temple.

The Goal: Grounding and Enriching Eucharistic Theology and Practice

Drawing bold lines of connection from the Lord's Supper back to the temple and its worship is helpful both for the theology of the Eucharist and for its practice.

With regard to eucharistic theology, drawing typological connections from temple to table can impart a biblical framework, balance, and richness to our eucharistic theology. As mentioned above, I will structure my own thinking and the following chapters around five embodied symbols and practices: the temple itself; the daily, Sabbath, and monthly sacrifices; and the three yearly pilgrim feasts. This will result in five central meanings that can structure eucharistic theology and practice.

One way to summarize the key theological implications resulting from this project is in terms of the intentions or main thoughts that someone would bring to their practice of the Eucharist. Given these main typological relationships, members of the church could confidently think these things as they approach the table:

- "God is really and personally present; the kingdom of God is breaking in."
- "We give thanks for God's creation and providence; we commit ourselves to wisely and creatively participate in God's creational order."
- "We remember God's deliverance of us through Christ's sacrificial life and death; in faith, we reject the old way of life and follow in the steps of Christ."
- "We give thanks for and recommit ourselves to the new covenant way of Christ; we call on the Holy Spirit to unite us with Christ and one another, empowering us to live as Christ's body for the world."
- "We celebrate with hope the feast to come in God's kingdom; we will be judged, yet forgiven, and so we rejoice that we can experience a foretaste of that feast even now."

Or, more briefly:

- God and God's kingdom are here.
- We give thanks for God's creation and providence.
- We remember Christ's sacrificial life and death.
- We recommit ourselves to the New Covenant.
- We celebrate with hope the feast to come.

Each of these intentions stem from the central figures we find in the worship of the temple but are transformed and find their fulfillment in the New Covenant brought about by Jesus Christ through the power of the Holy Spirit to the glory of the Father.

This way of organizing the primary meanings of the Eucharist is a robust, biblical structure based on the primary liturgical patterns or figural performances given to Israel by God on Sinai. At Sinai, God commanded that the tabernacle should be constructed, that daily, weekly, and monthly sacrifices be made, and that all the males of Israel should three times a year "appear before the LORD your God at the place that he will choose" (Deut. 16:16). Why? It would make sense that God was setting up a central symbol and regular practices in which the main transactions or relational moves God desired between God and his chosen people would be highlighted, namely, that God would be present to God's people and "dwell" with them (Deut. 16:6), that the people would give thanks for the "blessing" that God had given them through God's providence (Deut. 16:17), and more specifically, they would "remember" God's acts of deliverance (Deut. 16:3), "rejoice" in and recommit themselves to "observe" the covenant life God outlined for them (Deut. 16:10–11), and "rejoice" in the hope of a good future God has planned for them and all of creation (Deut. 16:14). Such a structure transformed through the work of Christ is discernable in the Eucharist as well.

These meanings can provide balance and a specific structure for our theology of the Eucharist. I find that often one or more of these main themes are emphasized to the exclusion of the others (for example, remembrance of Christ's sacrifice) or that words or phrases are used to organize one's eucharistic theology that are too general to be used without further explanation (for example, "grace and gratitude": What is the content of that grace? Gratitude for what?). My hope is that such a biblical structure would help bring coherence and some convergence to the various eucharistic theologies in the church and academy.

These typological relationships can also help us better discern, think through, and articulate the details of eucharistic theology. For example, questions concerning eucharistic presence, questions about open tables, and questions of best practice will receive helpful pressure and enrichment not only by reading through New Testament texts and being guided by the apostolic tradition, but also by drawing connections to the mode of God's presence in the temple, thinking through who was allowed to celebrate in the temple feasts of Israel, and considering analogies to and transformations brought about by Christ's work to temple practices. Such issues will be considered throughout the following chapters.

Basing and organizing one's eucharistic understanding on this typological structure also has many implications for the contemporary practice of the Eucharist. These primary meanings and the kind of typological imagination involved provide a useful and flexible center for evaluating various eucharistic prayers and practices. Rather than being a limiting factor, such an understanding leads to an enrichment of prayers and practices in order to shine more light on the complex and beautiful transactions between God and God's people in this central rite. I will examine some of the implications of these typological relationships for the practice of the Eucharist in the final chapter. These relationships between temple and table will greatly enrich our understanding of what "this" is and might be as we "do this" in remembrance of the work of Jesus Christ, empowered by the Spirit, to the glory of the Father.

PART TWO

The Table in Light of the Temple

3

The Jewish Temple

God with Us and a Conduit of the Kingdom

[In the Eucharist] . . . the time of the Kingdom of God . . . now
enters into the fallen time of "this world" in order that we, the
Church, might be . . . transfigured into "that which she is"—the
body of Christ and the temple of the Holy Spirit.

—Alexander Schmemann,
The Eucharist: Sacrament of the Kingdom

Place to person to practice.

As we begin to draw bold lines of connection from the place and practices
of the Israelite temple, through the person of Christ, to the practice of the
Christian Eucharist, we begin with the temple itself—as a place. The temple
was in one sense simply a building, or better put, a series of buildings. It was
apparently modeled in its main features on the wilderness tabernacle used
by Moses, and built in Jerusalem on Mount Moriah by Solomon in the tenth
century BC.[1] It was destroyed by the Babylonians in the sixth century BC and

1. This relationship of temple and tabernacle is the most common sense way to read
their relationship as presented in Scripture. However, given debates about the composition history of the Pentateuch, the relationship between temple and tabernacle, and
even the garden in Eden, could be more complicated. While taking a stance on the documentary history of the Pentateuch is not important for my purposes, if one assumes
a composition history of the Pentateuch in which it was finally redacted in the fifth
century BC, the temple was built before the stories of the garden and laws concerning
the tabernacle reached their final form. The form and worship of the temple would have

rebuilt after the exile by Zerubbabel. It was later expanded in the pre-Herodian era and then expanded again to its greatest extent by Herod the Great starting about twenty years before Christ was born. It was finally destroyed in AD 70 by the Romans.[2]

For first-century Jews, however, it was much more than a building. In many ways, it was the center of their lives. It was a highly important and symbolic place. It was a figure or image with many meanings associated with it.

One can sum up many of the central meanings of the temple—God's generally intended purposes for it and also what it symbolized and how it functioned in the lives and imaginations of the people of ancient Israel—by examining some of the central images, symbols, and ideas associated with it: the name of God, the house of God, clouds, glory, ladders, the throne, tablets of the covenant, Adam, the garden of Eden, altars and tables, priests, sacrifices, prayers, bread, blood, wine, light. As discussed in the previous chapter, it is these images and types that get picked up by Christ, transformed, and then associated with the practice of the Eucharist.

While it may seem odd at first to seek connections between the meanings of a place (the temple) and a practice (the Eucharist), many of the core meanings of the temple are indeed mapped onto the Eucharist in the New Testament and in the writings of the early church. The reasons for this connection become clearer when one sees that Jesus Christ is the hinge in this relationship.

---

influenced the inspired imaginations of those who wrote or redacted the creation stories in Genesis and descriptions of the tabernacle. On the other hand, if one assumes that the creation accounts in Genesis, whether in oral or written form, go back to very early traditions, the interplay between the garden of Eden and the layout of the tabernacle would still have been apparent to the authors of those traditions. Whatever the case may be, if one traces the inspiration of those stories and directions back to the mind and plans of God and the work of the Holy Spirit, such deep typological resonances between the garden, tabernacle, and temple, which find further expression in the person of Jesus Christ and the celebration of the Eucharist, need not be seen as some kind of literary sleight of hand (on the part of a late priestly writer), but rather a cause for wonder and praise for the providence of God. See S. Dean McBride, Jr., "Divine Protocol: Genesis 1:1–2:3 as Prologue to the Pentateuch," in *God Who Creates: Essays in Honor of W. Sibley Towner,* William Brown and S. Dean McBride Jr., eds. (Grand Rapids: Eerdmans, 2000), 3–41; and Beale, *Temple and the Church's Mission.*

2. For a brief history, see Dan Bahat, "The Second Temple in Jerusalem," in *Jesus and Temple: Textual and Archaeological Explorations,* ed. James H. Charlesworth (Minneapolis: Fortress, 2014), 59–74.

Many of the meanings of the place (the temple) are first fulfilled in a person (Jesus Christ). These are then extended to the people who are and are called to become "the body of Christ" and "the temple of God" (1 Cor. 3:16) and become so most centrally through a practice (the Eucharist).

This chapter unpacks the central meanings of the temple, the house for God's name (1 Kings 8:29). The following chapters trace the ways in which those meanings are mapped onto the Christian church especially through the practice of the Eucharist. But before discussing the central meanings of the temple, a few words are necessary regarding the sources used for understanding the temple and its meanings.

Sources for Understanding the Meanings of the Temple and Its Worship

As we begin, an important question arises: how do we know what the temple signified to ancient Israelites? And especially important for our purposes: how do we know what the temple and its worship signified to Jesus and his early Jewish followers? For it is the imagination and understandings of first-century Jewish people concerning the temple that are transformed into and shape early Christian understandings of Jesus and the Eucharist.

A great variety of sources give us insight into these questions. The most important of these are the Old and New Testament Scriptures, archaeological evidence, rabbinic literature, and other Jewish and non-Jewish writings of the Second Temple period, including many of the Dead Sea Scrolls.

Regarding the Old and New Testament Scriptures, there is a great amount of information about the temple in them. The layout, measurements, and materials of the tabernacle as well as many aspects of the regular worship services held at the tabernacle and later the temple are described in detail in Exodus, Leviticus, and Numbers, and are reiterated in Deuteronomy. The layout and measurements of the tabernacle are clearly given in Scripture (see figs. 1 and 2, page 52). Indeed, guidelines for the tabernacle and its worship are a central part of the Law given to Israel through Moses on Mount Sinai. First Kings and 1–2 Chronicles tell of the building of the First Temple in Jerusalem. These books indicate that the temple was modeled on the plan of the tabernacle and intended to be a permanent replacement of it. They also provide many details about the layout of the temple and its worship practices. The book of

Psalms provides insight into the music, worship, and theological speech that resounded through the temple. Genesis offers typological resonances between the temple and creation as a whole, as well as foreshadowings of the temple in Jacob's dream of the ladder at Bethel. In Ezekiel's eschatological vision, there is an idealized vision of the temple that is part of God's good future, providing further theological data for all that the temple symbolized. The prophets'

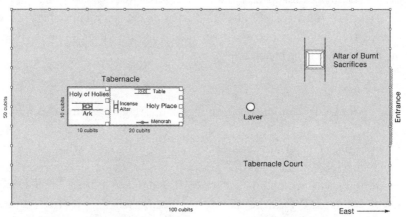

Figure 1. Plan View of the Tabernacle. © Ritmeyer Archaeological Design

Figure 2. The Tabernacle. © Ritmeyer Archaeological Design

critiques of deficient practices at the temple reveal how Israel fell short of the true intentions of the temple and its worship. The New Testament offers further descriptions of and theological reflections on the practices of the temple at the time of Christ. We also see ways in which early Christians critiqued and transformed temple practices.

As a whole, Scripture provides authoritative boundaries for proper worship at the temple, a framework upon which the actual practice of the Jewish people was consciously based. It also provides the most important threads out of which the rich tapestry of meaning that covered that framework was woven. That being said, in Scripture we more often find laws concerning details of buildings, furniture, and practices than a thorough discussion of the theology, symbolism, and intentions undergirding those items and practices. In Scripture, the framework is clearer than the tapestry of meaning that covers it.

Regarding archaeological evidence, the many archaeological discoveries of the nineteenth and twentieth centuries both on the Temple Mount itself and in its vicinity, as well as depictions of the temple on coins and in ancient drawings—all used in combination with texts such as the rabbinic tractate *Middot* and the writings of Josephus—give us a fairly accurate picture of what the first-century temple looked like (see Figs. 3 and 4, page 54).[3] For the purposes of this work, the many details of the temple building in such reconstructions give assurance that there was a general continuity between the tabernacle, the First Temple, and the Second Temple in their most important symbolic features, even though the expanded Second Temple was a much more massive and complex structure. They also give insight into the details of its main symbolic features that shaped the meanings of the temple and its worship.

Regarding rabbinic literature, of the vast amount of extant early rabbinic material that deals with the temple and its worship, the earliest strands are most relevant for this project. Of these the Mishnah is central. It is the first major compilation of Jewish oral tradition and generally considered the most authoritative. It is divided into six major sections. The second section, *Moʿed* ("Festivals"), has twelve tractates which cover religious laws concerning the Sabbath and annual festivals, and the sixth section, *Qodashim* ("Sacred

3. See Leen Ritmeyer, "Imagining the Temple Known to Jesus and to Early Jews," in Charlesworth, *Jesus and Temple*, 19–57, for a contemporary discussion of such reconstructions.

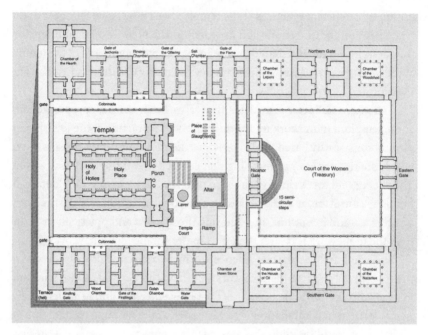

Figure 3. Plan View of the First-Century Temple. © Ritmeyer Archaeological Design

Figure 4. The Temple as Seen from the Women's Court. © Ritmeyer Archaeological Design

Things"), includes eleven tractates discussing religious laws concerning the temple and offerings at the temple. The Mishnah received its final form before AD 217 (when Rabbi Judah, the compiler and redactor of the Mishnah, died) but drew upon earlier traditions, the majority of which date from the middle of the first century. David Instone-Brewer, in his recent multi-volume work *Traditions of the Rabbis from the Era of the New Testament*, has done a great service by untangling the strands of traditions in the Mishnah, and attempting to identify the strands that reflect traditions dated AD 70 or earlier. In this way Instone-Brewer gives us greater confidence in our knowledge of practice at the temple before it was destroyed.[4] While the Mishnah is of central importance, the Jerusalem Talmud and the Babylonian Talmud (early commentaries on the Mishnah), the Tosefta (oral traditions from the time of the Mishnah that are not included in it), and various midrashim (works of biblical exegesis) also help to shed light on temple practices and their meanings.

Non-rabbinic Jewish writings and non-Jewish writings of the Second Temple period shed further light on the meanings of the temple and its services. These include the writings of Josephus and Philo, the work *Liber Antiquitatum Biblicarum* by Pseudo-Philo, and many of the writings that are part of the findings in the Dead Sea caves, such as Jubilees, the Community Rule, and the Temple Scroll.[5] The Dead Sea Scrolls include copies of every book in the Old Testament (with the exception of Esther) as well as many writings collected or written by, what is most likely, the Essene sect who lived in that location up until about AD 68 when the settlement was overrun and destroyed by Roman soldiers.[6] Many of these were originally written in the century before Christ. They give us great insight into the theologies and understandings of the Qumran community as well as Jewish practices at the temple. They have also shed much light on the importance of apocalyptic and mystical traditions. The Qumran community understood themselves to be in some opposition to and a replacement of what they considered the corrupted worship at the temple

---

4. Most important for this book is David Instone-Brewer, *Feasts and Sabbaths: Passover and Atonement*, vol. 2a of *Traditions of the Rabbis from the Era of the New Testament* (Grand Rapids: Eerdmans, 2011).

5. Many of these are included in Hayward, *The Jewish Temple*, and Geza Vermes, *The Complete Dead Sea Scrolls in English, Revised Edition* (London: Penguin Books, 2004).

6. While still debated, the majority of scholars agree with this understanding of the provenance and dating of the scrolls. See the "Introduction" in Vermes, *Complete Dead Sea Scrolls*, for an overview of the history of the discussion.

in Jerusalem. They were what some scholars call a "counter-temple" sect, not because they were against the temple, but rather because they were against the contemporary leadership of the temple. Their writings often detail ideal temple and worship practices and include hymns, prayers, ritual instructions, and liturgical calendars. These writings highlight the importance of the temple for Jesus and the New Testament writers.

These sources result in a fairly accurate understanding of both the layout of the temple and its ritual practices. We can also sum up with some confidence the central meanings of that great building and many of the worship services and rituals that were conducted there.

It is worth anticipating at least two areas of questioning related to these sources and claims to knowledge about the worship practices at the temple in the first century. The first pertains to the reliability of rabbinic sources for understanding worship practices at the temple before its destruction in AD 70. As briefly mentioned above, scholars in recent years have raised questions about whether or not later rabbinic traditions, which came to their final form in AD 217, were simply idealized projections back onto the time of the temple, whether or not statements attributed to early rabbis were highly edited in their oral and written transmission, and which parts of the Mishnah were discussions of actual practice before AD 70. Instone-Brewer writes that he began his own work with some of this skepticism: "When I started this project, I was skeptical about finding any actual words which have survived unedited from before 70 CE. I was hopeful of finding laws and concepts which formed the foundation of later Judaism, but I assumed that later editors had rewritten their past so completely that all the original wording would be lost." But he continues, "In the first volume I started to realize that the editors were often reluctant to edit traditions which they had received, even if this resulted in a clumsy or untidy final text. During my work on this volume [2a] . . . I have changed my mind further. I now acknowledge it is possible that some texts from the early first century [AD] or even earlier may have survived within Mishnah."[7] At the very least Instone-Brewer and others are arguing that rabbinic traditions have not grossly distorted what happened at the temple; instead, they arguably were careful to preserve earlier traditions even as they added onto them. Taken together with and checked

7. Instone-Brewer, *Feasts and Sabbaths*, xi.

against biblical and other extrabiblical sources, rabbinic sources can help us achieve confidence in our reconstructions. Skepticism about the use of these sources has tempered over time.

The second related area where questions emerge, especially among non-scholars, has to do with the extent to which the purported "secrets" of the Dead Sea Scrolls have changed our understanding of the landscape of Judaism and early Christianity. Given the way they have been discussed at a popular level, people may wonder whether they have fundamentally altered or overturned older perceptions of the meanings surrounding the temple. In general the answer is no. Certainly these textual discoveries have greatly sharpened and deepened our knowledge of the details of, and challenged some older assumptions about first-century Judaism and different groups within Judaism. But, as argued in the previous chapters, the main obstacles to seeing the relationships between worship at the temple and Christian worship have not been our lack of data or grossly misguided perceptions of what the temple and its worship services were like, but rather lack of trust in that understanding combined with the theological, religious, and cultural prejudices against seeing a positive relationship between Christianity and its Jewish roots.

The Central Meanings of the Jewish Temple

When a first-century Jewish person viewed the temple, there were a host of possible meanings, stories, and images that they might have associated with it. Like any symbol, the range of possible meanings for different viewers is infinite. And yet, like most symbols, the temple possesses certain central connotations within traditions of thought and practice.

For the sake of simplicity, one can organize the many images, stories, and meanings first-century Jews associated with the temple into four central meanings. (1) The temple was the dwelling place of the *real, yet elusive* presence of God. It was a place where God promised to be *personally* present. (2) Not only did God dwell there, but it was a place where *heaven and earth met,* a place where the ways of heaven were mediated to earth and where earth was connected to or aligned with the ways of heaven. (3) Since heaven and earth met there, the temple was a place where the ways of humanity and creation were set right. The reign of God, which was perfectly accomplished in heaven, was extended into the earth. Wrong was dealt with and typical righteous practices of humanity in relationship to God were seen, practiced, and extended outwards. It was *a conduit of the kingdom of God*. (4) Given these connections to the kingdom of God, the temple also had deep *connections to the past and the future*. It was a reminder of the past, the garden of Eden. It also pointed to a future day when God's reign would be fully realized on earth.

The following image binds these four central meanings together. Imagine, if you will, God's presence and reign coming down from heaven to the temple—like a pillar of fire or a ladder that connects earth and heaven—and then God's presence and kingdom flowing out from the temple into the earth—like streams of life-giving water. That is what first-century Jews most centrally "saw" when they viewed the temple.

In the following chapter, we will see that these meanings also illuminate the person and work of Jesus Christ and the practice of the Eucharist.

1. The Dwelling Place of the Real and Personal Presence of God

The temple was principally understood to be the dwelling place of God. In Exodus 25:8, God tells Moses, "Have them make me a sanctuary (*miqdash*), so that I may dwell among them." This original holy place or sanctuary was also called the tabernacle (*mishkan*), a term meaning dwelling place. It was understood to be a place where God would dwell (*shakan*) among the people of Israel. When the tabernacle was completed by Moses, God did in fact inhabit it: "So Moses finished the work. Then the cloud covered the tent of meeting, and the glory of the LORD filled the tabernacle" (Exod. 40:33–34).

Later, when the tabernacle was replaced by the temple planned by David and built by Solomon, one of the most typical ways that the temple was referred to was simply as "the house" (*habbayit*), the house of God. It was understood by all of Israel that God dwelt there. The presence of God was specifically seen to dwell in the holy of holies between the cherubim as the psalmist says: "You who are enthroned upon the cherubim" (Ps. 80:1).

For Israel, the temple was not simply a symbol of God's presence among Israel, but in some way God was really present, dwelling with his people in "the house."

While God was in some way specially present there, it was also understood that God does not dwell in the tabernacle or temple in a crassly physical way—God's transcendence was always held in tension.[8] As Solomon says at the dedication of the temple, "But will God indeed dwell on the earth? Even heaven and the highest heaven cannot contain you, how much less this house that I have built!" (1 Kings 8:27). Similarly, both Isaiah's and Ezekiel's visions of God in the temple suggest, on the one hand, that God is specially present there, but also that God's glory fills the whole earth. The ancient Kedushah prayer, part of the temple and later synagogue rites, combines these emphases together. In the prayer, one echoes the seraphim's cry, "Holy, holy, holy is the LORD of hosts; the whole earth is full of his glory" (Isa. 6:3), emphasizing the transcendence of God, the fact that God is not contained by the temple. This is followed by the phrase "Blessed is the glory of the Lord in its place" (Ezek. 3:12), which points to the particularity and immanence of God's presence.[9] God was in some special way really present and available to humans at the temple—and yet God was not contained by it.

Nor was God's presence tied to the temple by necessity. Jeremiah's famous temple sermon (Jer. 7:1–15) is instructive. In it Jeremiah mocks those who think that God's protective presence is "automatic" and forever tied to the temple. His jeremiad reveals both common conceptions about God's presence at the temple and their limits.

God's free, elusive, and yet real and local presence is talked about in several ways.[10] In biblical traditions, the *kabod* ("glory") or *shem* ("name") of God is said to dwell in the temple, while in rabbinic traditions, it is spoken of as the *shekinah*.

God's Name being in a chosen place is the preferred description of God's presence in Deuteronomy and in other writings (Deut. 12:5, 11, 21; 16:6; 26:2; 1 Kings 8; Jer. 7:10–14). In Deut. 12:5-7, "name" and "presence" are explicitly connected: "You shall seek the place that the Lord your God will choose out of all your tribes as his habitation to *put his name there*. You shall go there, . . . and you shall eat there *in the presence of the Lord* your God."

For us modern nominalists, the idea of a name being something more than

8. Here I am using transcendence in its broader, less technical meaning.
9. L. H. Schiffman, *Reclaiming the Dead Sea Scrolls: The History of Judaism, the Background of Christianity, the Lost Library of Qumran* (Philadelphia: Jewish Publication Society, 1994), 76.
10. See Samuel Terrien, *The Elusive Presence: Toward a New Biblical Theology* (San Francisco: Harper & Row, 1978).

a linguistic signpost is difficult to comprehend. But names, for the Israelites and other non-modern people, are intimately tied to those who bear them. Tryggve Mettinger describes the Israelite view in this way: "A person's name tends to be her or his alter ego and reflects her or his nature, power, and reality."[11] God reveals Godself to Moses not by showing Moses his face (Exod. 33:20), but instead by speaking God's name to him (34:5).

God's presence in the temple was not only real, yet elusive; it was also *personal*. God sharing his name with Israel at the temple, as he shared it earlier with Moses (Exod. 3:13–15), suggests that God was accessible for the kinds of interactions and relationships that are appropriate to human persons. In the rites of the tabernacle and temple, personal interactions with God's people were being conducted and realized. Covenantal relationships were formed, remembered, renewed, and strengthened; the breakdown of those relationships was lamented; forgiveness was asked for and received; and the relationships that constituted the coming kingdom of God were being longed for and hopefully celebrated.

The understanding that God is really and personally present in and to the Israelites in the temple is also reflected in the Jewish practice of turning toward the temple when praying. Praying toward the temple is like turning to address someone as you are speaking to them. In Solomon's prayer of dedication, in several places he speaks of people praying "toward this place" (1 Kings 8:30, 35, 38, 42, 44, 48). It is promised that God will hear them, even though he dwells in heaven (1 Kings 8:30). In rabbinic tradition, people are taught to "turn [their] face" toward the temple, especially the holy of holies, or if they cannot, to at least "concentrate [their] thoughts toward the Chamber of the Holy of Holies" (*y. Berakhot* 4:5–6).

Furthermore, names created intimate ties to others who took them on. The ancient Israelites had a practice in which one called out his/her name over a person or piece of property. As a result, the relationship of that person or piece of property to the one named would change. The practice might be understood as merely making a public claim to legal possession, but more likely, it seems analogous to the creation of a kinship bond (Ps. 49:11; 1 Kings

11. Tryggve N. D. Mettinger, *In Search of God: The Meaning and Message of the Everlasting Names* (Philadelphia: Fortress, 1988), 11. For a contemporary expression of the power of names in story form, see the epic fantasy novel by Patrick Rothfuss, *The Name of the Wind* (New York: Daw Books, 2009).

8:43; Isa. 4:1; Jer. 14:9; 15:16).[12] Conversely, the idea of a name "dwelling" in someone might also partially reflect how Israelites perceived kinship bonds. Related to the idea of taking on a name is the locution "son of." This expression is sometimes used to name biological ties, such as one might see in a genealogy, but it can also point to a sharing of personal characteristics, roles, or ways of being (cf. John 8:39).

All this illuminates an important practice at the temple. At the end of most worship services at the temple or tabernacle, God's Name is "put on" the Israelites in the act of blessing. The priest lifts his hands and pronounces the familiar Aaronic blessing upon those gathered. In so doing, "They shall put my name on the Israelites, and I will bless them" (Num. 6:27). In this act, God's presence is extended toward and upon the Israelites, creating a kind of intimate kinship bond, one in which some of the characteristics or ways of God are being shared with or put on the people who are called by God's Name.

Such ties between name, glory, personal presence, and intimate relationship are reflected in certain non-sectarian writings of the Dead Sea Scrolls, such as in this non-canonical psalm:

> [Jeru]salem [the city which the Lo]rd [chose] from eternity,
> [as a place of residence for] the holy ones.
> [For the na]me of the Lord has been invoked upon it,
> [and His glory] has appeared over Jerusalem [and] Zion.[13]

All these images, practices, and ways of speaking and writing reflect the understanding that God is really and personally present to God's people in and through the temple. Put differently, God's Name dwells there and God hears from there. Even though God's presence is not limited to it, the temple is the place where God specially dwells. The psalmist sees no tension as he proclaims:

> The LORD is in his holy temple;
> the LORD's throne is in heaven. (Ps. 11:4)

---

12. Mettinger, *In Search of God*, 10.
13. Non-Canonical Psalms A Scroll (4Q380) 1.I.1–8, in Schiffman, *Reclaiming the Dead Sea Scrolls*, 388.

2. The Meeting Place of Heaven and Earth

Not only was *God* really and personally present there. The temple was further understood to be a place where the *heavenly realms* intersected with the earth, with the entire cosmos, and with the special priestly people of Israel.

It is helpful to "read" the layout of the temple as you would read a figure or type, like an icon,[14] in order to clearly see its meanings. In both the tabernacle and temple, a significant feature was their division into three parts: the holy of holies, the holy place, and the outer courts. Inside these spaces were important symbols. In the holy of holies was the ark of the covenant. In the holy place, the veil, the altar of incense, the menorah, and the table of the bread of the Presence were placed. In the courts were the altar of sacrifice and the bronze sea. Moving throughout these areas was the high priest, who wore highly symbolic vestments. These places and items are meticulously described in the Law given to Moses on Mount Sinai.

So what do they represent? In broad strokes, the holy of holies represents God's presence and the heavenly realms where God dwells with the angelic hosts. Moving outward, the holy place represents, on one level, the entire cosmos, and on another level, the priestly people of Israel.

While the language of representation is accurate, the relationship is much more than that. The ark of the covenant is situated in the holy of holies as a symbol of God's presence, yet God's presence is not merely represented: first-century Jews understood God was specially present there in the elusive sense described above. Similarly, the relationships symbolized by the architecture and furniture of the temple represent the relationship of God and God's heavenly kingdom first to the entire cosmos, and second to the people of Israel. But the temple is not only understood to represent those relationships; it is where those relationships were really maintained and transacted.

Let us examine those relationships more closely.

The veil between the holy of holies and the holy place was understood to represent the created heavens. Josephus explicitly makes this connection: "Now in front of these was a veil . . . of Babylonian woven cloth embroidered in

---

14. Here I refer to the way that icons are understood to be "windows of the kingdom" by Eastern Orthodox Christians. See Vladimir Lossky and Léonide Ouspensky, *The Meaning of Icons* (Crestwood, NY: St. Vladimir's Seminary Press, 1982).

blue and linen as well as scarlet and purple, worked in marvelous fashion. The combination of material it possessed did not lack theoretical significance, but was like an image of the universe. . . . And the woven cloth was embroidered with the spectacle of the whole heaven, except for the signs of the Zodiac."[15] For Philo and Josephus, the vestments of the high priest also represented various parts of the creation, and the seven lamps of the menorah represented the seven known planets. Josephus writes that the twelve loaves of the bread of the Presence represented the twelve months of the year with their corresponding signs of the Zodiac.[16] And, of great significance, the sacrifices of the high priest in many writings are linked with the sacrifice of Noah, who is himself a kind of second Adam. Adam and Noah are priestly representatives of all of humanity, not just Israel. While more will be said of this "cosmic worship"[17] in the chapter below detailing the daily, Sabbath, and monthly sacrifices, it is already clear that the temple was a place where heaven and earth met and where worship and sacrifice took place that was fitting of all humanity and the cosmos.

In several writings it is clear that this worship—especially the daily, Sabbath, and monthly celebrations—was patterned on and reflective of the worship of God by the angels in heaven. For example, where Jacob blesses Levi in the book of Jubilees, he says, "And may the Lord give to thee and to thy seed greatness and great glory, and cause thee and thy seed, from among all flesh, to approach Him and to serve in His sanctuary as the angels of the Presence and as the holy ones."[18] This worship of God by humanity was fitting of them. It was their rightful duty, and even helped contribute to the stability of the order of the cosmos.[19]

Not only were aspects of the temple a figure of the entire cosmos; they also figured the people of Israel. One can make sense of this dual signification by considering Israel's fundamental vocation: "Now therefore, if you obey my voice and keep my covenant, you shall be my treasured possession out of all the peoples. Indeed, the whole earth is mine, but you shall be for me a priestly kingdom and a holy nation" (Exod. 19:5-6). Israel is called to a special func-

---

15. Josephus, *J. W.* 5.212–214.
16. See larger discussion of the cosmic significance of the temple in Hayward, *Jewish Temple*, 8–10.
17. A phrase Josephus uses in *J. W.* 4.324.
18. Jubilees 31:14. Quoted in Hayward, *Jewish Temple*, 87.
19. See Hayward, *Jewish Temple*, 6–13.

tion, to be a priestly kingdom. A priest represents and mediates; they represent and mediate God and God's words and ways to the nations, and they also represent and mediate all the peoples, all humanity to God. So as Israel worships as Israel, they also worship on behalf of, as representatives of, the nations and the entire created cosmos. As such, the menorah's seven lights not only represent the planets and their reflected light, but the menorah also symbolizes Israel, the people of God.[20] The menorah is a lampstand with seven lamps, shaped like a plant, bush, or tree. Lit by the sevenfold spirit of God, Israel, like the menorah, burns with the presence and light of God but is not consumed. Israel, as it obeys the covenant, shines like a lamp before the nations with the knowledge and wisdom of God. As rabbinic tradition says, "The Menorah is testimony to the world that the Shekinah dwells amidst Yisrael."[21]

Similarly, the twelve loaves of showbread on the table of the Presence are often understood as representing the twelve tribes of Israel. Just as the high priest had the names of the tribes of Israel carved into the onyx stones on his shoulders, six on one stone and six on the other (Exod. 28: 6–14), so too there were twelve loaves in two rows set onto the table of the bread of the Presence (Lev. 24:5–9). The light of the menorah and the bread of the Presence were not primarily food and light for God, but rather showed that God provided light and blessing to his people.

While much more will be said about temple worship and its symbolism, one can see that the temple represented not only the presence of God, but was further understood to be a place where God and God's kingdom came into contact with all of creation. The temple was a microcosm of all of creation; Israel, in turn, was a further microcosm. Put differently, Israel in its worship at the temple was the priestly representative of all of humanity and creation.

But for the Jewish people, heaven and earth meeting in the temple was not simply like the meeting of two negotiators on opposite sides of a table. Rather, the temple was a kind of "thin" place, a liminal space, a place in which the realms of heaven and earth overlapped.[22] Perhaps the central biblical image for this aspect of the temple is the ladder of Jacob:

20. Samuel R. Hirsch, "The Menorah: Components and Workmanship," in *Collected Writings* (New York: Philipp Feldheim, 1996), 1:209–35.

21. *b. Menah.* 86b.

22. An analogous contemporary literary image could be the wardrobe in C. S. Lewis's

Taking one of the stones of the place, he put it under his head and lay down in that place. And he dreamed that there was a ladder set up on the earth, the top of it reaching to heaven; and the angels of God were ascending and descending on it. . . . And he was afraid, and said, "How awesome is this place! This is none other than the house of God, and this is the gate of heaven." So Jacob rose early in the morning, and he took the stone that he had put under his head and set it up for a pillar and poured oil on the top of it. He called that place Bethel . . . saying, . . . "this stone, which I have set up for a pillar, shall be God's house . . ." (Gen. 28:11–12, 17–22)

Jewish tradition understands that the very stone Jacob had put under his head became the foundation stone for the temple in Jerusalem.[23] The temple was like a ladder, allowing heavenly things access to earth and earthly things access to heaven.

But what kinds of heavenly things are being extended into, or mirrored upon earth? A primary emphasis in Scripture is that certain patterns of activity, ways of being, acting and doing that are pleasing to God, are being communicated. As the Psalmist writes in Psalm 103, the angels are obedient to the ways and rule of God. These patterns of obedient heavenly activity are then extended into, or reflected on the earth.

> The LORD has established his throne in the heavens,
> and his kingdom rules over all.
> Bless the LORD, O you his angels,
> you mighty ones who do his bidding,
> obedient to his spoken word.
> Bless the LORD, all his hosts,
> his ministers that do his will.
> Bless the LORD, all his works,
> in all places of his dominion. (Ps. 103:19–22)

The Lion, the Witch and the Wardrobe (New York: HarperCollins, 2008), in that it connects the realm of Narnia with the realm of England.

23. *Pirqe R. El.* 35; *Midr. Ps.* 91:7. See Emmanouela Grypeon and Helen Spurling, *The Book of Genesis in Late Antiquity: Encounters Between Jewish and Christian Exegesis* (Leiden: Brill, 2013), 291–92.

Given this, it makes sense that the temple in Jewish traditions was understood to be a symbol of the real temple in heaven. As a symbol, it participated in that which it points to, or was a manifestation of an essential reality, somewhat like a physical manifestation of a Platonic "form" (Gr. *eidos*). And, just as in Plato's conceptuality, a "form," such as "justice," was more like a ratio or a way of acting than a "thing" or "substance." The temple was like an incarnation of certain patterns of activity found in its heavenly prototype. As quoted above, the human worship practices mirrored heavenly ones: "And may the Lord . . . cause thee and thy seed, from among all flesh, to approach Him to serve in His sanctuary as the angels of the presence and as the holy ones" (Jub. 31:14).

Jon Levenson, in his masterful book *Sinai and Zion*, documents these connections between heaven and earth at length.[24] The temple's decorations suggested that it was "'the meeting place of heaven and earth,' the tangent of celestial and mundane reality."[25] Commenting on Isaiah's vision at the temple (Isaiah 6) he writes, "The earthly Temple is thus the vehicle that conveys the prophet into the supernal Temple, the real Temple, the Temple of YHWH and his retinue, and not merely the artifacts that suggest them. This Temple is an institution common to the heavenly and the terrestrial realms; they share it."[26]

These connections between the earthly and heavenly temples were also at the root of the Jewish mystical *Merkavah* tradition which developed in the second and first centuries BC. Rachel Elior, in *The Three Temples: On the Emergence of Jewish Mysticism*, documents how Jewish priestly writers understood the ark/throne in the temple to be connected to the heavenly chariot-throne (Heb. *merkavah*) of God in heaven, and later, that the worship of the people on earth was a mirror of the worship of the angels in heavenly sanctuaries (Heb. *hekalot*).[27]

Thus, in this Jewish theology of ascent and descent, as the Jewish people gathered at the temple, they understood that they were coming into contact

24. Levenson, *Sinai and Zion*, especially the chapters "Zion as the Cosmic Mountain" and "The Temple as Sacred Space," 125–55.

25. Levenson, *Sinai and Zion*, 111. Here Levenson is working with and quoting the work of Richard J. Clifford, *The Cosmic Mountain in Canaan and the Old Testament*, HSM 4 (Cambridge: Harvard University Press, 1972). It was a "microcosm of the entire heaven and earth," according to Beale, *Temple and the Church's Mission*, 31.

26. Levenson, *Sinai and Zion*, 137.

27. Elior, *Three Temples*.

with heavenly realms, and the heavenly realms were breaking into or overlapping with the earth. The temple was the meeting place of heaven and earth; it was the ladder of Jacob.

3. *The Conduit of the Kingdom of God*

Not only did the temple symbolically represent and exist as a place where God and the heavenly realms intersected with the earth; it embodied a dynamic relationship. As they met the kingdom of heaven flowed into the earth through the temple, and as it did so all creation was set right. Outside the temple precincts, the wicked "take the path that sinners tread" (Ps. 1:1) and "the nations conspire" (Ps. 2:1), but at the temple, God's will for all creation and humanity was done on earth as it is in heaven. All creatures were in full health, life was abundant, and proper relationships between God, God's creation, and God's people were maintained, symbolized, and set right. The reign of God was realized there in the temple. It was hoped that such holiness, righteousness, and justice would "roll down like waters" (Amos 5:24) from the temple to Jerusalem, Samaria, and the ends of the earth. The temple was a conduit of the kingdom of God.

One sees this central meaning of the temple symbolized in several overlapping ways. First, the overall layout of the temple and the symbolism of its major furnishings, especially the ark of the covenant, suggested that God's rule and kingdom emanated from the holy of holies outward. In addition, the temple reflected the garden of Eden, a place where creation functioned as it was intended to. Finally, the requirements for purity and holiness at the temple also suggest that God's rule and reign is being extended from heaven to earth through the temple.[28]

Let us examine those symbols more carefully, starting with the temple's overall layout and furnishings. The epicenter of the temple was the holy of holies, the place of God's special presence. In that most holy precinct the ark of the covenant was placed—at least until it disappeared, probably during the Babylonian captivity. Described in Exodus 25:10–22 (cf. Exod. 37:1–9), it functioned first of all as a throne for YHWH from which God would give

---

28. While much has been written on all these topics, this threefold division follows Balentine, *Torah's Vision of Worship*, chaps. 4–6.

commands: "You shall put the mercy seat on the top of the ark; and in the ark you shall put the covenant that I shall give you. There I will meet with you, and from above the mercy seat, from between the two cherubim that are on the ark of the covenant, I will deliver to you all my commands for the Israelites" (Exod. 25:21–22). The ark was a clear symbol that God actively and personally ruled over Israel from the holy of holies.

But what was the form or shape of that rule? God's will for God's people was not arbitrary, but rather had a specific shape to it, a specific way of life. As the quote above says, the ark was also a depository for the covenant. The covenant, with its laws and prescriptions, drew a picture of the *torah*, the way of life that God desired for Israel and commanded Israel to follow. The goal of the covenant way was blessing and abundant life. If Israel followed the commands and reign of God, God promised that blessings would fall upon Israel (Deut. 7:12–26; 28:1–14). If they heeded God's commands and followed God's way, they would be like "trees planted by streams of water" (Ps. 1:3). The word and statutes of God would be like "a lamp to [their] feet and a light to [their] path" (Ps. 119:105), showing them the paths of life. As such, the covenant and reign of God were often compared to a light in the darkness or a life-giving stream pouring forth water.[29] And like a stream in the desert, as the heavenly realm and rule of God intersected with the earth, the life-giving, creative energy and rule of God would make earthly realities whole, holy, and fruitful—like a garden.

But the throne of God in the holy of holies also brought to mind the judgment of God. While one path led to life, others led to death. In the covenant stored in the ark, blessings were promised for obedience, but curses were also pronounced if one turned away from God's ways. Similarly, God's very being, God's holy presence, was like a plumb line, creating a standard by which human lives and ways were judged. God's presence brought life for created beings who were in harmony with it, but sin and impurity were judged and rejected. Given this, Isaiah's reaction to his vision of God in the temple is understandable: "Woe is me! I am lost, for I am a man of unclean lips, and I live among a people of unclean lips; yet my eyes have seen the King, the LORD of hosts!" (Isa. 6:5).

Moving outward from the holy of holies, one comes into the holy place.

29. See Levenson, *Sinai and Zion*, 112.

There, the menorah and the table of the bread of the Presence were the central symbols. As mentioned above, the light of the menorah and the bread on the table are symbolic of, on the one hand, the wisdom and enlightenment, and, on the other hand, the prosperous life Israel would experience as they lived in harmony and peace with the ways and presence of God.[30]

In a related set of images, the temple was seen to be like the garden in Eden, a place of creation as it was intended to be.[31] Or, reversing this relationship, one could say that the garden in Eden was likened to the temple.[32] In the Genesis accounts of the garden of Eden (Gen. 2:5–3:24; cf. Ezek. 28:11–19, 31:1–18, esp. 36:16–38; Isa. 51:1–3), we see first of all that the garden was a place where God dwelt with humanity, with Adam and Eve. Right before the sin of Adam and Eve was discovered, God was "walking in the garden at the time of the evening breeze" (Gen. 3:8). God is similarly described as "walking among Israel" as he dwells in the tabernacle (Lev. 26:12; cf. Deut. 23:14 and 2 Sam. 7:6–7).[33] The garden was a beautiful and healthy place: "Out of the ground the LORD God made to grow every tree that is pleasant to the sight and good for food" (Gen. 2:9). Similarly, the furnishings and decorations of the temple—palm trees, fruit, and cherubim—and its purity—there are no blemished people or animals present in the temple precincts—further suggested it was like a new garden. As Levenson writes, "Words like 'ideal,' 'perfection,' and 'unblemished,' suggest that the Temple was, in fact, a paradise."[34]

30. David Stubbs, *Numbers*, Brazos Theological Commentary on the Bible (Grand Rapids: Brazos, 2009), 96–97. See also Qumran's *Hymn Scroll*, in which the righteous person is compared to the menorah: "I will shine with a seven-fold li[ght] in the E[den which] Thou hast [m]ade for Thy glory" (1QH 7.24). See discussion of the translation by Dupont-Sommer in Beale, *Temple and the Church's Mission*, 79.

31. See, for example, Beale, *Temple and the Church's Mission*, 66–80. Beale shows the numerous links between the temple and Eden, and shows in biblical and other literature where such links are made. See p. 66n87 for a list of other authors and literature that also make these connections. See Leithart, *House for My Name*, for a very accessible linking of the temple to the creation accounts. See Elior, *Three Temples*, e.g. 78, 128–29, 245–49, for ways that writings found at Qumran and later mystical literature linked especially the holy of holies with the garden of Eden and paradise.

32. Here I am again alluding to scholarly discussions about the composition history of the Pentateuch. See n. 1 above.

33. It is the same Hebrew verbal form, *mithallek* (hithpael). See Beale, *Temple and the Church's Mission*, 66 for discussion.

34. Levenson, *Sinai and Zion*, 128. For connections to the garden of Eden, see Levenson, *Sinai and Zion*, 128–33. That the temple was also considered the epicenter of God's

The layout of the temple also has analogies to the geography of Eden and its garden. The source of life in Eden is in the west, the garden is just to the east of this source, and east of the garden is the rest of the world.[35] "A river flows out of Eden to water the garden, and from there it divides and becomes four branches" (Gen. 2:10). Similarly, the holy of holies is in the west. Going east one moves to the holy place, and from there to the temple courts, Jerusalem, and the nations. In several prophets' visions of the future, a stream of water similarly flows out from the temple eastward; it is a river of life that will bless the nations (Ezek. 47:1–12; Zech. 14:8; Joel 3:18).

This might at first seem odd, for such a stream of water is not mentioned in the directions concerning the tabernacle or temple given in the Pentateuch. But historical descriptions of the temple do in fact show that water features prominently in the Second Temple. In the Letter of Aristeas to Philocrates, written in the second century BC, we find mention of an elaborate water system that utilizes a "natural spring" that "gushes up from within the temple area." His description of the temple is fascinating, and so I quote it at length:

> The Temple faces the east and its back is toward the west. The whole of the floor is paved with stones and slopes down to the appointed places, that water may be conveyed to wash away the blood from the sacrifices, for many thousand beasts are sacrificed there on the feast days. And there is an inexhaustible supply of water, because an abundant natural spring gushes up from within the temple area. There are moreover wonderful and indescribable cisterns underground, as they pointed out to me, at a distance of five furlongs all round the site of the temple, and each of them has countless pipes so that the different streams converge together. And all these were fastened with lead at the bottom and at the sidewalls, and over them a great quantity of plaster had been spread, and every part of the work had been most carefully carried out. There are many openings for water at the base of the altar which

---

creation of the world is also attested in rabbinic literature. Rabbi Eliezer the Great linked the creation of the world to Mount Zion: "The offspring of heaven were created from heaven, and the offspring of the earth were created from earth. But the sages say, Both were created from Zion . . . as the Bible says, 'From Zion, perfect in beauty, God shone forth' (Ps. 50:2)." Quoted in Levenson, *Sinai and Zion*, 118.

35. Beale, *Temple and the Church's Mission*, 74. J. H. Walton, *Genesis*, NIV Application Commentary (Grand Rapids: Zondervan, 2001), 167.

are invisible to all except to those who are engaged in the ministration, so that all the blood of the sacrifices which is collected in great quantities is washed away in the twinkling of an eye. Such is my opinion with regard to the character of the reservoirs and I will now show you how it was confirmed. They led me more than four furlongs outside the city and bade me peer down towards a certain spot and listen to the noise that was made by the meeting of the waters, so that the great size of the reservoirs became manifest to me, as has already been pointed out. (*Aristeas*, 88–91)

Other testimonies likewise speak of the relationship of the temple to water that flowed through it (Tacitus, *Hist.* 11–12; 1 Enoch 26:2–3; cf. Josephus, *J. W.* 7.28–30).

So, at the temple, a great stream of water, often mixed with the blood of the sacrifices made there, flowed eastward from the south side of the central temple building, from the altar of sacrifice, and then down away from the Temple Mount into the Kidron valley. This mixture of water and blood is, in the visions of the prophets, transformed into a river of life, a river that flows outward from the temple, watering and providing life first for Israel and then for the nations. The psalmist mentions this stream as well:

> How precious is your steadfast love, O God!
> All people may take refuge in the shadow of your wings.
> They feast on the abundance of your house,
>   and you give them drink from the river of your delights.
> (Ps. 36:7–8)

Analogies to Christ's side (John 19:34) and further to the cup of the Eucharist are not difficult to spot and were often made in the Christian tradition (one result is the tradition of adding water to the Communion wine).

The traditions and biblical passages in which Adam functions in the garden similarly to how the priests functioned in the Jerusalem temple form a final connection to the garden. For example, the book of Jubilees recounts an unbroken line of priestly leaders of Israel from Adam forward, all of whom play the role of a kind of priest-king, a priest-king who is to bear God's image.[36]

---

36. See the longer discussion in Beale, *Temple and the Church's Mission*, 81–121.

In all these ways the temple was like a new garden of Eden, a conduit of heavenly life directed toward the earth.

Finally, one can spot this dynamism of the kingdom breaking into the earth through the temple in the holiness and purity laws of the temple. These laws described and created a space at the center of the temple, the holy of holies, in which the holiness and purity of God's heavenly kingdom was preserved and then radiated outward.[37]

At the center of Israel's vision of holiness and purity is God. "Holy, holy, holy," cry the angels in Isaiah's vision of God in the temple (Isa. 6:3). God's holiness means that God is totally separate—but separate from what? While God as Creator is totally other than creatures, the laws of Sinai focus on God's separation from all corruption and chaos, from all moral impurity and sin. Persons, places, times, and objects that are marked as "holy" (*qodesh*) to God are separated from the "common" (*hol*). God tells Aaron and the priests of Israel: "You are to distinguish between the holy and the common, and between the unclean and the clean" (Lev. 10:10). This is done not to separate creatures from God, but rather to create and preserve a holy sphere in the world where physical corruption and sin are excluded so that God and creatures may draw near to one another and dwell with each other.

To explain why holiness is required for proximity to God, analogies are helpful. Consider the image of vibrating musical strings and the attunement or dissonance between them. Musical strings are sympathetic to or harmonize with certain frequencies and are dissonant with others. The being of God might be thought of as having a certain frequency, harmony, or even rhythm to it.[38] This harmony or pattern is reflected throughout the creation to the extent that creatures are capable of such harmony, but it occupies the tabernacle and temple in a powerful way.

Only creatures that resonate with such tuning in both physical and moral ways can bear and come into God's presence. If they do not, the wrath of God

37. See Stubbs, *Numbers*, 52–57, for a more thorough discussion of holiness and purity and the pertinent literature. In the following paragraphs, I draw substantially from those pages.

38. This idea is a familiar concept in Hasidic Judaism. Madeleine L'Engle's 1973 novel *A Wrinkle in Time* and C. S. Lewis's 1965 novel *That Hideous Strength* both illustrate evil having a physical and moral rhythm to it. Karl Rahner's *Hearers of the Word*, trans. M. Richards (New York: Herder & Herder, 1969) makes much of the idea of attunement with God.

might break out, as it did in the story of Nadab and Abihu (Lev. 10:1–7). God's "fire" (v. 2) and "wrath" (v. 6) consumed them when they offered "unholy fire before the LORD" (v. 1). God's wrath in that passage is like the anger of a person, breaking out as the result of an intentional choice. But elsewhere, such as with an inappropriate entry into the tabernacle, God's wrath acts also like a physical field of power, like the unintentional dissonance and "beating" created when two out-of-tune strings vibrate near each other.[39]

This creaturely holiness is on a graduated scale. Things can be more or less holy. Gradations of holiness are reflected throughout the architecture and laws concerning the tabernacle and the priests.[40] Creatures selected to be closer to God—for example, in the holy of holies as opposed to simply in the camp (for the tabernacle) or the outer courts (for the temple)—must exhibit better attunement or holiness.

Attunement or dissonance can occur both at a physical/biological level and at the level of human thoughts, actions, and intentions.[41] At the physical/biological level, creatures that are blemished, temporarily impure, or that in some way do not reflect well the orders or harmonies of God's creation are to some extent excluded from either the precincts of the temple or "the camp." At the moral level, humans who have sinned—acted out of harmony with God's desires for human life and community—are also required to make amends in some way, often by sacrifice to God and/or some form of restitution to those harmed, in order to approach God.

Interpreters often distinguish between physical and moral laws. In the Christian tradition, many have made a distinction between "ritual" and "moral" impurity, or a distinction between "ceremonial" and "moral" law. However, the Israelites did not make this kind of distinction.[42] Instead of strong distinctions,

39. For an analogy using disease or contagion, see Jacob Milgrom, "Encroaching on the Sacred: Purity and Polity in Num. 1–10," *Interpretation* 51 (1997): 243–44.

40. In the Mishnah, ten levels of holiness are differentiated, starting from the nations to the land of Israel itself, through the city of Jerusalem, through the various courts of the temple, up to the highest level of holiness in the holy of holies (*m. Kelim* 1:6–9; cited in Schiffman, *Reclaiming the Dead Sea Scrolls*, 81).

41. Jonathan Klawans, *Impurity and Sin in Ancient Judaism* (New York: Oxford University Press, 2000), 3–20. See also Balentine, "Covenant Holiness," *Torah's Vision of Worship*, 148–76.

42. Klawans draws a sharp distinction between ritual and moral impurity. He then shows how the relationship between the two kinds of impurity was understood in dif-

analogies were drawn between dysfunctions or "impurity" at the physical/biological level and dysfunctions or impurity in the mind or soul.[43] Israel, at every level of its being, body and soul, was to emulate God's holiness as it was reflected in the creational order.[44]

These distinctions between clean and unclean, holy and common, are dynamically expressed in the worship at the temple. In the movement of a typical worship service, a chosen but sinful humanity moves toward the presence of God; sin and impurity are acknowledged and dealt with; this renewed human community offers thanksgiving, praise, and petitions in the presence of God; and they are blessed as they are sent back out into the world.

In such worship, the goal of laws concerning impurity and sin is not to exclude creatures from God, nor to take creatures out of the world, but rather that God's purity and holiness might be extended outwards from the temple into the entire world, in both body and soul. In the vision of Zechariah, on the great day of Lord when the kingdom of God extends into all the nations, "every cooking pot in Jerusalem and Judah shall be sacred to the LORD of hosts." Those cooking pots will be just as holy as the cooking pots in the temple and even the "bowls in front of the altar" (Zech. 14:20–21).

This vision of holiness is also a call to a profoundly ethical way of life. At the heart of the Torah is the "holiness code." YHWH through Moses says to Israel, "You shall be holy, for I the LORD your God am holy" (Lev. 19:2). Such holiness involves rising before the elderly (Lev. 19:32), treating the resident alien as fairly as the natural born citizen (Lev. 19:33–34), and conducting all

---

ferent parts of the Old Testament, later writers and schools in Judaism, and the New Testament. A difficulty he faces is that terms such as "clean" and "unclean" are sometimes used precisely and at other times more loosely or metaphorically throughout the Old Testament; thus the line between ritual and moral impurity is sometimes quite obvious, but in some cases more difficult to draw (Klawans, *Impurity and Sin*, 21–31). In contrast, Gordon Wenham, *The Book of Leviticus*, New International Commentary on the Old Testament (Grand Rapids: Eerdmans, 1979), 15–32, understands purity laws to form a much more integrated system.

43. Similar to Wenham's position in the note above, Balentine also sees ritual and moral impurity as part of an integrated whole. Drawing from the work of Mary Douglas, he writes: "the impurity laws seek to maintain the principles of righteousness and justice on which the entire cosmos depends. As she puts is, 'Everything in the universe shows forth the righteousness of the Lord.' In this sense, the summons to purity and cleanness is a summons to emulate the holiness of God." Balentine, *Torah's Vision*, 161.

44. See also chapter 7 on the daily celebrations below.

business and measurements honestly (Lev. 19:35–36). The ultimate goal is that all of creation—bodies, hearts, minds, spirits, and actions—would resonate with the holiness of God so that God might dwell closely with all his creation. In this way God's reign will finally extend from the heavens, to the temple, and throughout the earth.

4. Connections to Past and Future

First-century Jews knew the temple was part of an overarching narrative. That narrative started at creation—at the garden of Eden—and it reached into the future—to the day when God's purposes would be fully realized and God's reign would be finally and fully realized on earth. These connections form a fourth component in the Jewish understanding of the temple.

Put differently, one could say that the temple's connection to the kingdom of God, its eschatological significance, has several dimensions. The temple in part pointed backward to the garden of Eden. The temple also pointed "upward" to the heavenly temple where God reigns and is worshipped by the angelic court. The temple also pointed forward. In the visions of the prophets, in the prayers of the psalmists, and in intertestamental literature, the temple plays a central role in visions of the age to come, an age also connected to the past. Levenson writes, "The rabbis termed the coming era the 'Garden of Eden'; they saw protology as a prefigurement of eschatology as did their biblical predecessors."[45]

The temple was connected to the past in several ways in Jewish thought. The garden, the tabernacle, and the temple are typologically related to one another. They all are points at which "the divine powers emanate to the world," the points from which creation sprang forth.[46] For example, in Jubilees 8:19 (c. 170 BC), the author writes: "[Noah] knew that the Garden of Eden is the holy of holies, and the dwelling of the Lord, and Mount Sinai the center of the desert, and Mount Zion—the center of the Navel of the universe: these three were created as holy places facing each other."

In the future-oriented visions of several biblical prophets and in extra-biblical literature, the temple will be rebuilt, God will once more dwell with

45. Levenson, *Sinai and Zion*, 183.
46. Schiffman, *Reclaiming the Dead Sea Scrolls*, 79.

Israel, and Israel will be holy in all its ways. Ezekiel's vision of the temple to come (Ezek. 40–48) ends with these words: "And the name of the city from that time on shall be, The LORD is There" (Ezek. 48:35). It is a vision of God dwelling in the midst of his holy people in a renewed Jerusalem—similar to how God dwelt with Adam and Eve in the garden. This brings us back to Zechariah's vision in which the temple is rebuilt, the world is judged, and those who survive the judgment participate in a great banquet. Zechariah writes, "Then all who survive of the nations that have come against Jerusalem shall go up year after year to worship the King, the LORD of hosts, and to keep the festival of booths" (Zech. 14:16). Not only do people go up to the rebuilt temple, but the reign and holiness of God stream out from it. Zechariah writes, "The cooking pots in the house of the LORD shall be as holy as the bowls in front of the altar; and every cooking pot in Jerusalem and Judah shall be sacred to the LORD of hosts" (Zech. 14:20–21).[47]

In the Temple Scroll we find a similar vision. The Dead Sea sectarians expected God to create and consecrate a new temple when the Messiah came at the end of days: "And I will consecrate my [te]mple by my glory, (the temple) on which I will settle my glory, until the day of blessing on which I will create my temple and establish it for myself for all times, according to the covenant which I made with Jacob at Bethel" (11QT 29.8–10).

In another of their writings, an important twist occurs. At the end of days, their own sectarian way of life, a way of righteousness and justice, will replace the worship of the temple: "When the time comes that men such as these are in Israel, then the council of the Yahad will be truly established, an eternal planting, a temple for Israel, and a council of the Holy of Holies for Aaron; true witnesses to justice, chosen by [God's] will to atone for the land and to recompense the wicked their due. . . . a dwelling of the Holy of Holies for Aaron, all of them knowing the covenant of justice and thereby offering a sweet savour" (1QS 8:4–9).[48] "The council of the Yahad" refers to their community. The just and righteous life of the Qumran community will function as a new temple, a "place" in which God will dwell and the kingdom of God will break into the earth.

47. Geoffrey Wainwright, *Eucharist and Eschatology* (Akron, Ohio: OSL Publications, 2002), esp. 22–30, traces many of these traditions which looked forward to feasting with God on the holy mountain or at the temple in the coming age.
48. Discussed in Schiffman, *Reclaiming the Dead Sea Scrolls*, 85.

Similarly, later rabbinic traditions taught that the study of Torah and prayer, as well as the Jewish home, would function as replacements of the temple.[49] And as we will see, in Christianity the worship of the congregation centered on the Eucharist is understood similarly to be a new spiritual temple.

So, we see that the temple and its sacred services are not only a bit of heaven on earth. They are also a foretaste of the feast to come. In all these visions, at the end of time, Jewish people expected God once again to dwell with his people on the earth. Whether it is an actual building, or a "temple" built out of the stones of God's holy people, the promise symbolized by the temple itself is fulfilled: God's holy presence will once again fully dwell in the earth and God's kingdom will be extended throughout the creation.

---

49. Schiffman, *Reclaiming the Dead Sea Scrolls*, 85.

4

THE EUCHARIST IN THE EARLY CHURCH

Temple Themes Transformed

> Come to him, a living stone, though rejected by mortals yet chosen and precious in God's sight, and like living stones, let yourselves be built into a spiritual house, to be a holy priesthood, to offer spiritual sacrifices acceptable to God through Jesus Christ.
>
> —1 Peter 2:4–5

The temple was not a presumptive and futile attempt on the part of humanity to reach toward God. Instead, as recorded in Scripture, the idea, plans, and details of the temple were given to Israel by God. The temple was a gift. Contrary to many Protestant opinions, the temple and its worship services were a God-given means of encounter and relationship.

As a gift, the temple shaped the imaginations and lives of the Israelites. Its symbolism, its worship, and the larger narrative of which it was a part shaped their understanding of God and God's intentions. Accordingly, the central meanings associated with the temple—both the building itself and its central worship services—provide God-given theological foundations for understanding God's intended relationship with God's chosen, priestly, and holy people. This relationship was not simply a "religious" one. It encompassed every aspect of their lives: religious, political, socio-economic . . . everything. The modern tendency to see the temple simply as a place where the Israelites would negotiate forgiveness for their sins is a vast reduction of its fuller meanings.

When God became incarnate in Christ, it was not as if these ways and intentions of God were destroyed or replaced by an entirely different system of religion and way of interacting with God. Christ did not come to abolish that system. "I have not come to abolish but to fulfill," as Christ said about the Law and the Prophets (Matt. 5:17). It is true that Jesus was highly critical of the current leadership and practices at the temple. In fact, Jesus and his disciples in the early church formed what some scholars have called a "counter-temple movement."[1] But they were not counter to the purposes of the temple system, but rather to the way it was being stewarded. The temple, under the administration of the high priest and Jewish leaders in Jerusalem, was not fulfilling its goals.

Furthermore, the life, death, resurrection, and ascension of Christ created a new chapter in God's redemptive history. In and through Christ, the temple was not abolished, but transformed. As Jesus said, "Something greater than the temple [building] is here" (Matt. 12:6). The New Testament and the writings of the leaders of the early church witness to the fact that Jesus's relationship to the temple is a central way both Jesus and the early church understood who he was—his person—and what he came to do—his work. As the building itself relates to his person, so the practices of the temple relate to his work.

In turn then, just as the central meanings of the temple illuminate the person and work of Christ, so too they illuminate the being, worship, and mission of the church. Both the New Testament and the writings of the leaders of the early church understand the church, especially as it gathers in eucharistic worship, to be a new temple.

While we will look closer at the specific rites and worship services performed at the temple in the following chapters, this chapter focuses on the central meanings of the temple itself, particularly the four central meanings highlighted in the previous chapter. In the New Testament and in the writings of the leaders of the early church those meanings are first connected to Christ—he is the new temple—and then also to the church gathered in eucharistic worship—the church is a new temple built on the foundation stone of Christ. The type of the temple finds its fulfillment in Christ. This type is then extended to the church as Christ's body. This type looks upward and forward to the great day when the temple in heaven is fully joined to the temple on

1. See Nicholas Perrin, *Jesus the Temple* (Grand Rapids: Baker Academic, 2010), 12–13 for an explanation of this phrase.

earth—when God's kingdom is fully revealed and a loud voice will say, "See, the home of God is among mortals. He will dwell with them; they will be his peoples, and God himself will be with them" (Rev. 21:3).

The Temple Fulfilled and Transformed in Christ and His Disciples

The portraits of Jesus created over the centuries by artists and academics, portraits often quite dissonant with one another, are enough to fill several cluttered galleries. This fact is enough to give one pause before attempting to create and hang yet one more representation. I will not attempt that task here. Instead, I will describe, appreciate, and recommend a portrait of Jesus that has been carefully worked on for the last fifty years. It is a portrait that is attentive to the Gospels and the writings of the earliest Christians, helping us to read the Gospels better rather than obscuring or replacing them.

Here are the central claims of this portrait: Jesus's relationship to the temple was at the center of Jesus's sense of vocation. The temple formed the most important backdrop for his central symbolic actions during his earthly ministry, his claims about it provoked the Jewish leaders to call for his crucifixion, and it is a sure foundation upon which to base a theology of his person and work. Building on this portrait of Christ, the temple became an important typological framework in and by which the New Testament writers and early church theologians understood the being, eucharistic worship, and mission of the church.

Such claims are highly contentious. However, there is a growing body of New Testament scholarship that makes precisely these claims.

As discussed in chapter 1, since the mid-twentieth century, scholars have been re-evaluating Christianity's relationship to Judaism. New Testament scholars have offered revolutionary re-evaluations of both Paul and Jesus in relation to their Jewish heritage.[2] In theology, at least one Jewish philosopher,

---

2. As far as Pauline scholarship, Krister Stendahl's "The Apostle Paul and Introspective Conscience of the West," *Harvard Theological Review* 56 (1963): 199–215, and E. P. Sanders's *Paul and Palestinian Judaism* (Philadelphia: Fortress, 1977) mark such re-evaluations of Paul's letters and theology vis-à-vis Judaism, paving the way for various "new perspectives on Paul." A central theme in these new perspectives is that God has not abandoned the covenant made with the Jewish people, but rather the covenant has

viewing the Protestant theological landscape, thinks that this re-evaluation of the relationship of Christianity to its Jewish roots amounts to what might be called a "new Reformation."[3]

Within this larger re-evaluation of Christianity's relationship to Judaism, an important strand of New Testament scholarship has highlighted the connections between Jesus and the temple.[4] In this strand the works of N. T. Wright, Gregory Beale, and Nicholas Perrin stand out.[5] These scholars have argued that the Gospels are best understood in the context of a large-scale background story in which the covenant, the temple, and Christ are the key figures.[6] N. T.

<hr />

found fulfillment in Jesus and in the new community composed of both Jewish and gentile disciples of Jesus. See, for example, N. T. Wright, *Paul and the Faithfulness of God* (Minneapolis: Fortress, 2013).

3. Ochs, *Another Reformation*. Ochs shows how what might at first seem like two disconnected conversations dovetail together so well: the conversation about Christianity and its relationship to Judaism, and the conversation about modern and postmodern epistemology in which the concept of tradition began to be recovered (e.g., Gadamer, MacIntyre). This epistemological recovery of tradition provided a philosophical framework by which one could better appreciate Judaism, the tradition out of which Christianity emerged.

4. See, e.g., Ben F. Meyer, *The Aims of Jesus* (London: SCM, 1979), and Meyer, *Christus Faber: The Master-Builder and the House of God*, Princeton Theological Monograph Series (Allison Park, PA: Pickwick, 1992); E. P. Sanders, *Jesus and Judaism* (London: SCM, 1985); Levenson, *Sinai and Zion*; Meredith Kline, *Kingdom Prologue: Genesis Foundations for a Covenantal Worldview* (Eugene, OR: Wipf & Stock, 2006); Bruce Chilton, *The Temple of Jesus: His Sacrificial Program within a Cultural History of Sacrifice* (Philadelphia: Penn State Press, 1992).

5. Beale, *Temple and the Church's Mission*; Gregory Beale and Mitchell Kim, *God Dwells Among Us: Expanding Eden to the Ends of the Earth* (Downers Grove: InterVarsity Press, 2014); N. T. Wright, *The Climax of the Covenant* (Minneapolis: Fortress, 1991); Wright, *Jesus and the Victory of God* (Minneapolis: Fortress, 1996); Perrin, *Jesus the Temple*.

6. Perrin summarizes this story on pp. 9–13 of *Jesus the Temple*. Wright tells a similar story in *Jesus and the Victory of God*; see also N. T. Wright, *Pauline Perspectives* (London: SPCK, 2013), 384–89 for this larger story as the background of Col. 1:27. In Beale's work, *Temple and the Church's Mission*, he alerts us to the cosmic nature and grand scale of the role of the temple within the grand story underlying Scripture. He painstakingly works through the entire biblical witness, highlighting the important roles Adam, the garden, the temple, Christ, the church, and the New Jerusalem play in the larger story. He tells the beginning of the story this way: "Adam's failure led, in time, to the reestablishment of the tabernacle and temple in Israel. Both were patterned after the model of Eden and were constructed to symbolize the entire cosmos in order to signify that Israel's purpose as a corporate Adam was to extend its borders by faithfully obeying God and spreading his

Wright underlines the importance of this re-evaluation: "One of the chief gains of the last twenty years of Jesus-research is that the question of Jesus and the Temple is back where it belongs, at the centre of the agenda."[7]

One reason many scholars have gained a clearer perception of the centrality of this theme in the gospels is our increased knowledge of the hopes and fears of first-century Jews, including our better understanding of so-called counter-temple movements within Judaism in the first century BC, such as the community at Qumran.[8]

So, what are the most important features of this portrait of or story about Jesus?

First, the temple played a crucial role within the expectations, hopes, and fears of first-century Jews. The preamble of the covenant given to Israel on Mount Sinai is important background in this regard: "Now therefore, if you obey my voice and keep my covenant, you shall be my treasured possession out of all the peoples. Indeed, the whole earth is mine, but you shall be for me a priestly kingdom and a holy nation" (Exod. 19:5–6). We see in these verses that God's purpose for redeeming Israel from Egypt was not simply to give them freedom from oppression, but to establish Israel as a kingdom of priests—one that would worship God as God chose—and a holy nation—a nation that would shine forth with God's character through their actions. Worship and ethics, not simply deliverance, were central to God's plans for Israel.

Furthermore, proper worship and ethics were linked to God's desire to dwell among his people. We hear of this desire in the Song of Moses and Miriam (Exod. 15:1–21). In this song—probably one of the most ancient por-

---

glorious presence throughout the earth" (369). God's intentions for Adam in the garden, after Adam's failure, are taken up by Israel and its priests in Israel's temple worship. Due to the failure of Israel to execute the duties they had received in line with Adam, "Christ indicates that the old temple is becoming obsolete and that he is replacing it with the new one" (176). God's special presence, found in Christ, is extended to the church, which in turn has the commission to further extend that presence: "It was this divine presence that was formerly limited to Israel's temple and has begun to expand through the church, and which will fill the whole earth and heaven, becoming co-equal with it" (368).

7. Wright, *Jesus and the Victory of God*, 405.

8. Perrin, *Jesus the Temple*, also names two presuppositions that have prevented others from recognizing these connections to the temple: (a) an understanding of the meanings of the temple that reduces it to a place where sins are forgiven, and (b) the failure to see how Jesus's and Paul's teachings about resurrection depend upon and assume the underlying narrative that "the final goal of Israel's redemption was not merely freedom, but the opportunity to establish a proper temple and with it proper worship" (10; discussed in 6–13).

tions of Scripture—God chooses a place, a mountain, upon which would be a sanctuary, where he would dwell with his people and from which he would reign: "You brought them in and planted them on the mountain of your own possession, the place, O Lord, that you made your abode, the sanctuary, O Lord, that your hands have established. The Lord will reign forever and ever" (Exod. 15:17–18). These verses were important in Jewish writings during the Second Temple period where they not only were interpreted as referring to the temple in Jerusalem, but were also linked to hopes for a future eschatological temple. Visions of the eschatological temple pictured a time when all that the temple stood for would be fulfilled, when the heavenly temple and the earthly temple would be fully aligned or perhaps joined together. Such a temple would be constructed by God alone; it would be a temple "not made with human hands" (cf. Acts 7:48; 17:24; 2 Cor. 5:1). Perrin writes concerning the vision contained in Second Temple texts: "No, if Moses was to be understood aright, it was to be the divinely wrought eschatological temple that would prove to be the terminal goal of the Exodus and thus too, on analogy, the ultimate goal of all Yahweh's redeeming purposes."[9]

In contrast to this eschatological vision, it was alarmingly apparent to many Jews in the first century BC that the current temple was not fulfilling its purposes. Proper worship and ethics were not happening. As a result, the temple was defiled. And so, Jewish sectarian counter-temple movements formed in reaction.

Perrin examines three such movements: the sect associated with the Psalms of Solomon (written in the 60s BC), the Qumran sect behind the Dead Sea Scrolls, and the followers of John the Baptist.[10] He constructs "a rough phenomenology" of these movements, pointing out the following shared features: First, they all considered the ruling priesthood to be corrupt and defiled. Second, they believed that a great time of tribulation was underway for Israel as a whole and for their group in particular, as evidenced by their group's estrangement from the temple. Third, Perrin argues all these movements "embraced a vocation on behalf of the poor," and that the communities behind the Psalms of Solomon and the Dead Sea scrolls identified themselves with "the poor." Finally, such movements took upon themselves certain functions of the temple, understanding this to be a kind of emergency and temporary measure until

9. Perrin, *Jesus the Temple*, 10. For primary sources, see 10n21.
10. Perrin, *Jesus the Temple*, 17–45.

the coming of the messiah, who would both bring apocalyptic judgment and inaugurate the eschatological temple.[11]

Jesus lived in a time when several Jewish movements critical of the temple leadership flourished. The question then follows, were both Jesus and the early church counter-temple movements? Perrin's answer is a definite yes.[12]

Wright agrees with Perrin: "Jesus acted and spoke as if he thought he were a one-man counter-temple movement."[13] For Wright, Jesus did not simply aim to create a new temple, or to cleanse the old one. Instead, Jesus understood that in some way, the hopes for the eschatological temple were being fulfilled in and through him. God was coming back to his people in person, a new temple was being built, and in and through this new temple the kingdom of God was entering into creation in a new and powerful way.

In making this case, Wright asks the reader to focus attention on the symbolic acts Jesus performed. The words, parables, and riddles of Jesus are best understood against the backdrop of his symbolic actions. These symbolic acts are the deepest clues to Jesus's own sense of vocation.[14] For Wright, the two acts that provide the deepest insight into Christ's aims and intentions are, first,

11. Perrin, *Jesus the Temple*, 44–45.

12. Perrin, *Jesus the Temple*, 46. Perrin's larger argument involves an analysis of these counter-temple movements, the Gospels, Johannine literature, 1 Peter, Hebrews, Matthew, Luke-Acts, the various writings of Paul, and patristic writings, showing the importance of the temple for their self-understanding and activity.

13. The longer quotation: "Or suppose we approach the matter from another angle, vital and central but, remarkably enough frequently overlooked. Jesus' actions during the last week of his life focused on the Temple. Judaism had two great incarnational symbols. Temple and Torah: Jesus seems to have believed it was his vocation to upstage the one and outflank the other. Judaism spoke of the presence of her God in her midst, in the pillar of cloud and fire, in the Presence ('Shekinah') in the Temple. Jesus acted and spoke as if he thought he were a one-man counter-temple movement" (N. T. Wright, "Jesus and the Identity of God," *Ex Auditu* 14 [1998]: 53). This article draws in part from *Jesus and the Victory of God* (Minneapolis: Fortress, 1996), esp. chap. 13.

14. Wright, *Jesus and the Victory of God*, 86: "Historians do not live by sayings alone." Later in the same work, he writes, "We are in a position to study not merely isolated or detached *sayings*—which always tilt the balance towards skeptical non- or pseudo-reconstruction—but *actions* and *events*, which, freighted with symbolic significance, create a context in which stories and sayings can settle down and make themselves at home" (543). Similarly, Perrin writes, "Because the actions of Jesus (with a minimum of interpretive help from the words of Jesus) are sufficient for my case, I rely on little else. This is not to say that Jesus' teachings, conversations, and parables are not important" (*Jesus the Temple*, 15).

his cleansing of the temple, and second, his symbolic acts on the night before his death at the Last Supper.

The temple cleansing is significant in part because it led to Jesus's death. "Apart from one or two dissident voices, almost all scholars now writing in the field agree on two basic points: Jesus performed a dramatic action in the Temple, and this action was one of the main reasons for his execution."[15] But what were Jesus's intentions? Jesus's actions both in the temple (Matt. 21:1–22; Mark 11:1–25; Luke 19:28–48; John 2:13–17; 12:12–19) and at the Last Supper continue to undergo a variety of interpretations and are at the center of much disagreement among scholars.

Wright believes that by seeing both their relationship to the temple and their relationship to one another, the sense of not only the temple action, but also the Last Supper become clear. They are "mutually interpretive."[16] Wright claims, "However we 'read' the whole complex of Temple and Last Meal . . . it belongs together *as* a complex, an interconnected web of intentional events in which Jesus was enacting, or setting the scene to enact, the coming of the kingdom."[17] The Last Supper helps explain the reason for such an action—just as the temple cleansing helps us understand the Last Supper.

Wright connects the two acts in this way. He interprets Jesus's action at the temple as a symbolic act which symbolized the "imminent destruction of the Temple."[18] Its destruction was part of the climax of God's covenantal history with Israel. Israel was being judged by God; specifically, they were judged to have failed "to obey YHWH's call to be his people." More specifically, they failed to enact justice within their society, they were committed to national rebellion, and the present temple system was in disarray.

But Jesus's act of cleansing the temple was not only an act of judgment. It also showed the intention to replace the temple with a new one. But how?

This temple replacement is symbolized in the Last Supper. Wright sees it as a fitting culmination of all the symbolic acts of Christ throughout his ministry. Wright pulls these symbolic activities together in this way:

15. Wright, *Jesus and the Victory of God*, 405.
16. Wright, *Jesus and the Victory of God*, 438.
17. Wright, *Jesus and the Victory of God*, 438.
18. Wright, *Jesus and the Victory of God*, 417. This and the following points in this paragraph can be found in summary form on 417–18.

We get Jesus feasting with his motley group of followers, as a sign of their healing and forgiveness; Jesus implying that those with him are the true Israel; Jesus enacting the real return from exile, the new exodus; Jesus marking his people out with a new praxis which did for them what Torah did for the pre-eschatological Israel; Jesus forming a counter-Temple movement around himself. If we were to attempt to draw these pictures into one, the scene might look suddenly familiar. It might consist of a young Jewish prophet, reclining at table with twelve followers, celebrating a kind of Passover meal, constituting himself and them as the true Israel, the people of the renewed covenant, and doing so in a setting and context which formed a strange but deliberate alternative to the Temple.[19]

In this portrait of Jesus that Wright, Perrin, and other New Testament scholars paint, we see him and his followers taking on precisely the four central meanings of the temple as described in the previous chapter. In Jesus's counter-temple movement, those meanings are draped over them like a garment, and then transfigured.

Picking up the first central meaning, Jesus became a place where the presence of God dwelt. This is perhaps the most controversial but also ultimately the most foundational point. For Wright, Jesus understood that he was not only fulfilling the functions of the present temple, such as forgiving sins, but also embodying the traditions which predicted the presence of God coming to dwell among God's people. YHWH the King was returning to Zion in and through Jesus. Jesus fulfilled the traditions about the eschatological temple and the mysterious messianic figure who was also closely associated with God. Wright concludes: "I suggest, in short, that the return of YHWH to Zion, and the Temple theology which it brings into focus, are the deepest keys and clues to gospel christology. . . . He [Jesus] would be the pillar of cloud and fire for the people of the new exodus."[20]

Not only was God present in Christ, but in Christ we find a "place" where heaven and earth meet, the second meaning of the temple, and also where the reign of God is extended to the earth, the third. As Perrin argues extensively, we should see events such as the transfiguration as indications of the presence of God and the heavenly realms transfiguring earthly realities. But not only

19. Wright, *Jesus and the Victory of God*, 437.
20. Wright, *Jesus and the Victory of God*, 653.

that. We can also see the Jubilee-like ministry of Christ to "the poor" (Luke 4:18–19), his exorcisms, his healing miracles, and his inclusive and joyful meal ministry as indications of the reign of God coming to earth, and thus the inauguration of the eschatological temple in himself. "Jesus' concern for the poor was a function of his calling as the priestly founder of the new temple," claims Perrin.[21] "Both" his healing ministry and his meals "signal the in-breaking of the eschatological temple."[22]

Finally, we see embedded in Jesus's beliefs and actions pointers that he is connected to both the past and future. Jesus is the pivotal figure in the larger temple story that began in Eden and will end when the eschatological temple is fully extended throughout all of creation, when the distance between heaven and earth is finally overcome.

Temple Themes in Early Christian Thought and Practice

Not only was the temple a central image by which the Gospel writers articulated the person and work of Christ, the type of the temple was also important for the self-understanding of the early church.

The leaders of the early church saw that both the church and their worship centered in part on the Eucharist were new temples built on the foundation of Jesus Christ. They saw the church as fulfilling the type of the temple in Jerusalem, and also as a type of the eschatological temple yet to come.

The earliest Christians drew such connections in at least three different ways. First, these typological relationships provide the theological substructure of many of the theological writings of early Christian leaders. Second, the earliest Christian liturgies reflect these relationships, and third, these relationships also influence early Christian art and architecture.

Temple Imagery in Paul's Letters to the Corinthians

While there are many places in the New Testament that temple imagery occurs, the letters of Paul have always held an eminent place in the hearts and theologies of Protestants and evangelicals.

21. Perrin, *Jesus the Temple*, 14.
22. Perrin, *Jesus the Temple*, 14.

Paul's letters to the Corinthian churches are an important example of how the temple-church-Eucharist typology functioned. As is well known, these letters were written in large part to address problems in the church in Corinth, a mainly Gentile city. First Corinthians is perhaps best known for its images of the church as a body (1 Cor. 12), but alongside this metaphor, the image of the church as temple is also prominent. However, much of the scholarly literature has interpreted Paul's references to a temple as references to the pagan temples surrounding the Corinthian congregation, thereby overlooking Paul's appeals to the larger substructure of salvation history in which the Jewish temple looms large. Some contemporary exegetes—especially those who re-read the Corinthian letters in light of the new perspective on Paul, a perspective which recognizes his Jewish heritage much more clearly—have recognized these prominent connections to the Jewish temple.[23]

The following list of verses and phrases gives a sense of the way temple imagery is used by Paul in these letters. It is not meant to be exhaustive or definitive, but rather illustrative:

1 Cor. 3:9–17	v. 9: "You are . . . God's building."
	v. 10: "I laid a foundation."
	v. 11: "That foundation is Jesus Christ."
	v. 16: "You are God's temple."
	v. 17: "You are that temple."
1 Cor. 5:3–8	v. 4: "When you are assembled . . ."
	v. 7: "You really are unleavened."
	v. 7: "For our paschal lamb, Christ, has been sacrificed."
	v. 8: "Therefore, let us celebrate the festival . . . with the unleavened bread."

23. For example, Christopher R. A. Morray-Jones reads Paul's mention of his ascent into paradise as parallel to Jewish *Heikhalot* literature associated with proto-rabbinic mysticism. *Heikhalot* literature and *Merkavah* literature center on the mystical temples and thrones associated with the temple in Jerusalem—similar to the eschatological temple in Revelation. Morray-Jones, "The Ascent into Paradise (2 Cor 12:1–12): Paul's *Merkava* Vision and Apostolic Call," in Reimund Bieringer et al., *Second Corinthians in the Perspective of Late Second Temple Judaism* (Leiden: Brill, 2014), 245–85. Perrin, *Jesus the Temple*, 66–69.

1 Cor. 9:13–14	v. 13: "Those who are employed in the temple service get their food from the temple."
	v. 14: "In the same way, the Lord commanded that those who proclaim the gospel should get their living by the gospel."
1 Cor. 10:1–6	v. 1: "Our ancestors were all under the cloud, and all passed through the sea."
	v. 2: "All were baptized."
	vv. 3–4: "All ate the same spiritual food, and all drank the same spiritual drink."
1 Cor. 10:16–18	v. 16: "The cup of blessing that we bless, is it not a sharing in the blood of Christ? The bread that we break, is it not a sharing in the body of Christ?"
	v. 18: "Consider the people of Israel; are not those who eat the sacrifices partners in the altar?"
1 Cor. 11:25	v. 25: "In the same way he took the cup . . . saying, 'This cup is the new covenant in my blood.'"
1 Cor. 15: 20–23	v. 20: "Christ . . . the first fruits of those who have died . . ."
	v. 23: "Christ the first fruits . . ."
1 Cor. 15:51–53	vv. 51–52: "We will all be changed, in a moment . . . at the last trumpet."
2 Cor. 5:1–3	v. 1: "We have a building from God, a house not made with hands."
2 Cor. 6:14–7:1	6:16: "What agreement has the temple of God with idols?; as God said, 'For we are the temple of the living God. I will live in them and walk among them.'"
	7:1: "Let us cleanse ourselves of every defilement."
2 Cor. 12:2	v. 2: "I know a person who . . . was caught up to the third heaven."

Taken individually, these examples make it difficult to argue that Paul has the type of the Jerusalem temple and its liturgies in mind as he writes every one of these passages, and harder still to argue that each of those passages reflects the understanding that the church in Corinth is an inauguration of the eschatological temple. For example, 2 Corinthians 5:1 references the important phrase "a house not made with hands,"[24] and yet in that verse Paul refers to the individual believer rather than the church as a temple. The verses from 1 Corinthians 15 are also difficult to argue for any sort of direct connection. Could Paul's mention of first fruits and trumpets allude to the first fruits offering at the temple and the feast of trumpets which starts the final celebration of *Sukkot*? There are a variety of apocalyptic passages in the background, so whether or not he had in mind those particular passages or the feast in which those passages were liturgically celebrated is impossible to say.[25] But taken together, these passages suggest that temple imagery played a greater role in Paul's imagination than is often acknowledged.

Examining 1 Cor. 3:9–17 will help illustrate the import of temple imagery for Paul. It will also illustrate how recent interpreters, with a few exceptions, have often either passed over such temple allusions or overlooked their importance.

In 1 Cor. 3:5–17 Paul speaks about the church community using three metaphors. The church is God's "field" (vv. 5–9), God's "building" (vv. 10–15), and God's "temple" (vv. 16–17). One option for interpreting these metaphors is that they are simply convenient illustrations Paul is using to make his point; Paul is aware of his audience and finds everyday illustrations the Corinthian congregation would be familiar with in their own city—fields, buildings, and Greek temples. Most modern commentaries prefer this way of understanding Paul's use of these images. Even if they recognize the probability that Paul is referring to the Jerusalem temple, that allusion is of little consequence, Richard Hays's commentary being the clear exception.[26]

---

24. Cf. Acts 7:48; 17:24; Isa. 66:1–2. All of these passages reference a larger story of salvation in which the temple plays a central role.

25. But if so, it is interesting for this project to note that Paul creates allusions to aspects of all three pilgrim feasts, and transforms them in light of Christ's death, the giving of the new covenant, and the final judgment and resurrection. Passover is tied to his death, our new exodus, and Christ's firstfruits offering. One could argue there are allusions to Pentecost in the celebration of the new covenant, and that there are echoes of *Sukkot* in Paul's discussion of the final judgment and resurrection of the dead.

26. A few examples: David Garland, *1 Corinthians*, Baker Exegetical Commentary on the New Testament (Grand Rapids: Baker Academic, 2003), notes possible allusions to the temple in v. 12 but discounts them. In regards to v. 16: "Paul is not trying to make the case that they are the new spiritualized temple of the last days, replacing the Jerusalem temple"; instead, he is simply using it as "a metaphor of unity" (120). William

The other option is that Paul's arguments are created in light of his typological understanding that the church is the beginning of the fulfillment of the hopes surrounding the eschatological temple. Paul understood that the temple and related types in Scripture were meant "to instruct us, on whom the ends of the ages have come" (1 Cor. 10:11); they formed the most important substructure of his thought in this and other passages.

Four arguments can be mounted for this.

First, the initial images of field and building are common images for the people of Israel in the Old Testament. Israel is often described as God's field or vineyard or planting. Furthermore, this image is often combined with images of a house, building, or sanctuary situated in the midst of the field—similar to the way the tabernacle was positioned in the midst of the tribes of Israel during the exodus and the temple stood in the center of the promised land (Num. 2:1–2; cf. Ezek. 40).

A foundational text is Exodus 15:17–18, the final verses of the Song of Moses: "You brought them in and planted them on the mountain of your own possession, the place, O Lord, that you made your abode, the sanctuary, O Lord, that your hands have established. The Lord will reign forever and ever." Israel is a planting of God, like a field or vineyard; they were planted on the mountain, the mountain on which God's sanctuary abode is built. This text is referred to

---

F. Orr and James Arthur Walther, *1 Corinthians: A New Translation*, The Anchor Bible (Garden City, NY: Doubleday, 1976), do not mention the temple as a possibility for the building mentioned in vv. 10–15, and in v. 16 contend that Paul is interested in the temple only as a means of contrast: "The Jerusalem temple played no significant role in the life of the gentile Christian churches; so he could freely make a figurative contrast" (174). Raymond Collins, *First Corinthians*, Sacra Pagina (Collegeville, MN: Liturgical Press, 1999), touches on the possibility, but does so quite lightly: "It almost appears as if Paul is anticipating the identification of the community as the temple of God" (150). Gordon D. Fee, *The First Epistle to the Corinthians*, The New International Commentary on the New Testament (Grand Rapids: Eerdmans, 1987), criticizes interpreters such as Hans Conzelmann for being "too enamored by Greek sources" (140) and interpreting Paul's statement as a reference to pagan temples and buildings in Corinth, but Fee does not follow the implications of Paul's use of this image. It is only in Hays's commentary, of the ones that I surveyed, that the full ramifications of Paul's allusions to the temple in Jerusalem are given voice: "He is making a world-shattering hermeneutical move, decentering the sacred space of Judaism (cf. John 4:21–24)" (57). Richard B. Hays, *First Corinthians*, Interpretation (Louisville: John Knox, 1997). This brief survey indicates that the impact of new or fresh perspectives on Paul has not yet reached the standard commentaries—Hays being an exception.

by many writings during the Second Temple period, writings that are looking forward to God's action to bring to earth the "eschatological temple."[27] This vision of Israel as planted by God is also part of the blessing of Balaam on Israel as they near the promised land in Numbers 24:5-6.

In the visions of Isaiah and Jeremiah, the prophets use such images as they mourn the fact that Israel has not lived up to its true vocation. For example, Isaiah 5:1-7 describes a vineyard which is identified as Israel: "For the vineyard of the LORD of hosts is the house of Israel, and the people of Judah are his pleasant planting; he expected justice, but saw bloodshed; righteousness, but heard a cry!" (v. 7). Furthermore, it depicts a building in the midst of the field: "He dug it and cleared it of stones, and planted it with choice vines; he built a watchtower in the midst of it" (v. 2).

In Jeremiah, the double image of building and planting is a major theme throughout the book. Jeremiah's vocation is given in terms of this double image: "See, today I appoint you ... to build and to plant" (1:10). But throughout the book, it is truly God who does the building and planting, as the Lord tells Jeremiah in the well-known episode at the potter's house: "And at another moment I may declare concerning a nation or a kingdom that I will build and plant it, but if it does evil in my sight, not listening to my voice, then I will change my mind about the good that I had intended to do to it" (18:9-10). A stern warning to Israel! And while God will indeed bring disaster on Israel, in a later vision in which the remnant of Israel is likened to "good figs" (24:3-5), God declares concerning this remnant: "I will plant them, and not pluck them up. I will give them a heart to know that I am the LORD; and they shall be my people and I will be their God" (24:6-7).[28] And later, just before the new covenant is spoken of in 31:31-33, God vows to "watch over them to build and to plant" (31:28). And finally, in a warning not to migrate to Egypt, God promises that if they stay in the land, "I will build you up and not pull you down; I will plant you, and not pluck you up" (42:10).

27. "This Exodus verse was traditionally interpreted as an allusion to the eschatological temple erected in the final age by God himself ... an old well-known exegetical tradition." Devorah Dimant, *History, Ideology and Bible Interpretation in the Dead Sea Scrolls*, Forschungen zum Alten Testament 90 (Tübingen: Mohr Siebeck, 2014), 278. She cites 11QT 29.9-10; Jub. 1:17; 1 En. 90:29; *Mek. Masechta deShira*, 10; *Mek. de Rashbi*, 15, 17.

28. Cf. the final words of the prophet Amos: "I will plant them upon their land, and they shall never again be plucked up out of the land that I have given them, says the LORD your God" (9:15).

The point here is that not only are these images being used together, they are used together in the Law and Prophets to speak about both the judgment of Israel and the hope for a new start for Israel. After a period of judgment, God promised to rebuild the temple, to replant the field of God's people, and to give them a new covenant. Could it be that such images and passages, now applied to the church, were in Paul's mind as he wrote his letters to the church in Corinth?

Such a combination of images was being used in Paul's day by the counter-temple movement in Qumran, and applied to their own community. The Qumran sect's *Rule of the Community* talks about their community as "an eternal plant, a holy house" (1QS 8:5) and "a house of holiness for an eternal plant" (1QS 11:5).[29] Perhaps Paul's imagination was similar to theirs.

Second, the building materials of the structure in question allude back to the temple in Jerusalem. Paul writes, "Now if anyone builds on the foundation with gold, silver, precious stones, wood, hay, straw . . ." (3:12). Gordon Fee writes concerning this: "Finally, it is probably not irrelevant that 'gold, silver, and costly stones' recur regularly in the OT to describe the building materials of the Temple."[30] I agree, although I think his point is understated. All three of the good materials, gold, silver, and precious stones, are found in descriptions of the temple as it is being built in 2 Chronicles 3:1–5:1 as well as in Exodus 31:1–5 (here concerning the tabernacle). Significantly, the silver and gold of the temple are mentioned in Haggai 2:8, a passage about God's promises to rebuild the temple, contained in a larger prophecy that also mentions laying the foundation of the temple (Hag. 2:18). This backdrop likely shaped Paul's understanding of the church.

Third, Paul's mention of "the Day" when what has been built will be revealed with fire—"the fire will test what sort of work each has done" (1 Cor. 3:13)—has clear resonance with apocalyptic traditions. Hays notes this and calls attention especially to Malachi 4:1–2. He writes, "Paul's vision of final judgment is com-

29. Collins, *First Corinthians*, notes this (147) but then does not follow up on the implications. See also Sir. 49:7; Philo, *Alleg. Interp.* 1.15 §48; Odes Sol. 38:16–22. The Sirach reference is especially pertinent, as Jeremiah's vision of building and planting is applied to "the chosen city of the sanctuary" (49:6). The building in question in Philo is also "the altar of the Lord your God."

30. Fee, *First Epistle to the Corinthians*, 140, citing Hag. 2:8; 1 Chr. 22:14, 16; 29:2; 2 Chr. 3:6.

pletely consonant with this tradition, with the single exception that here he is applying the image of judgment by fire not to the fate of individuals but to the ecclesiological construction work done by different church leaders."[31] True, and yet if you expand the Malachi reference back to chapter 3, we find that the situation Malachi is referring to in fact precisely concerns leadership problems at the temple and not simply individuals: "See, I am sending my messenger to prepare the way before me, and the Lord whom you seek will suddenly come to his temple. The messenger of the covenant in whom you delight—indeed, he is coming, says the LORD" (Mal. 3:1). And when the Lord comes, what will he do? "He will purify the descendants of Levi and refine them like gold and silver, until they present offerings to the LORD in righteousness" (Mal. 3:3). Such a prophecy fits very well with the situation in Corinth. The typological "descendants of Levi," the leaders of the church, are being warned by Paul that their actions need to be fitting of the temple of the Lord.

Fourth, after all these possible connections of "field" and "building" imagery to the temple, Paul makes the connection explicit: "You are God's temple" (v. 16).

These three metaphors, field, building, and temple, all fit together for Paul. In this passage, Paul is viewing the church in Corinth in light of these typo-logical relationships and important prophetic traditions about the temple in Jerusalem.

Similar arguments can be made for the other temple passages in Paul's letters. For Paul, the church is the new planting/building/temple prophesied by the prophets and hoped for in Second Temple Judaism. Paul is furthermore guided in both his "ethics" and his understanding of proper worship by these typological relationships—but more on that in the following chapters.

Temple Imagery in Early Church Writings and Liturgies

Stepping away from these familiar Pauline texts and moving into early church practice and liturgies can be somewhat shocking to many Christian people. For many Protestants, the writings and liturgies of the early church are not what they expect. Many Protestants operate with—let me coin a phrase—the myth of original simplicity. They imagine that the early church was a period of original innocence (analogous to what Rousseau posited of humankind

---

31. Hays, *First Corinthians*, 55, citing Dan. 7:9–10; 2 Peter 3:7, and Mal. 4:1–2a.

in general) in which Christ's disciples celebrated informal *agapē* meals and worshipped in the free-form sort of fashion found at evangelical Christian camps. Only later, when Christians moved out of the catacombs and house churches into idolatrous cathedrals, and when the early prophetic "charisma" of the apostles was systematized and routinized into stultifying, rigid, and Spirit-stifling patterns produced by power-hungry priestly leaders (as Hume, Weber, and others down through Dan Brown have thought)—only later did the complicated prayers and liturgies we find in imperial Christianity emerge. I am, of course, creating a caricature, but one that I think deeply resonates with many Protestants' understanding of early church history.

In actuality, the earliest writings and liturgies of the church outside of the New Testament are not like that. They reflect what might be called a temple imagination. Early Christians viewed the church at worship as a new, spiritual, transformed temple. Images, themes, and direct terminology that have their home in the Jewish tabernacle and temple are applied to the Christian congregation in eucharistic worship and appropriately transformed. All four of the central meanings of the temple discussed in chapter 3 are applied to the church through temple imagery in known writings and liturgies from the first few centuries of the church.

For example, the temple as the place where God dwells, where the Name of God tabernacles, finds voice in the Didache, one of the earliest writings outlining aspects of early Christian worship. It is the central image that structures the prayer after the Eucharist: "And after you have had enough, give thanks [*eucharistēsate*] as follows: We give you thanks, Holy Father, for your holy name, which you have caused to dwell [*kateskēnōsas*; "tabernacle"] in our hearts, and for the knowledge and faith and immortality that you have made known to us through Jesus your servant; to you be the glory forever."[32] This passage indicates that Christians gathered in eucharistic worship embody a new kind of temple in which God has taken up residence.

Later, in chapter 14, the Lord's Day assembly is outlined: "On the Lord's day gather together and break bread and give thanks [*eucharistēsate*], having first confessed your sins so that your sacrifice [*thysia*] may be pure." The eucharistic rite is called a "sacrifice" four times (14.1, 14.2 and 14.3 twice)—again drawing imagery from the temple and applying it to the eucharistic rite.

32. Didache 10.1–2 (Holmes).

The eucharistic assembly is also understood to be a place where heaven and earth meet, like the temple. Quite early on, the Sanctus became a standard part of most eucharistic prayers.[33] The cry of the angels in Isaiah's vision of the temple—"Holy, holy, holy is the LORD of hosts; the whole earth is full of his glory" (Isa. 6:3)—was the worship of heavenly hosts in the heavenly temple where God dwells. This was echoed by the worshippers at the temple in Jerusalem. In the early church it was also connected to Christian worshippers gathered around the altar of the Eucharist.

Consider the eucharistic prayer of Addai and Mari, a prayer dating back to the third century in Edessa, Syria.[34] In it, the Sanctus sung by Christian worshippers is clearly connected with and joined to the worship of the angels in heaven:

> Thy majesty, O my Lord, a thousand thousand heavenly beings
> and myriad myriads of angels adore
> and the hosts of spiritual beings, the ministers of fire and of spirit,
> glorifying thy name with the cherubim and the holy seraphim,
> ceaselessly crying out and glorifying and calling to one another and
>   saying:
> Holy, holy, holy, is the Lord Almighty:
> The heavens and the earth are full of his glory.
> Hosanna in the highest! Hosanna to the son of David!
> Blessed is he who has come and comes in the name of the Lord.
> Hosanna in the highest![35]

Just as striking is the prayer said over the incense which is offered right before the Eucharist. This incense prayer may be a later addition to the earliest versions of the liturgy, but it utilizes and elaborates on the same imagery. In it once again the eucharistic rite is envisioned as a rite within "thy glorious temple." The prayer seems to imagine that in the Eucharist, the distance between God's reality and the worshipping assembly is overcome:

---

33. Spinks, *Sanctus in the Eucharistic Prayer*, 57–124.

34. A. Gelston, *The Eucharistic Prayer of Addai and Mari* (Oxford: Clarendon, 1992), 28, 65, 76.

35. Gelston, *Eucharistic Prayer*, 49, 51.

O our Lord and our God, may the pleasant savour which
we offer thee before thine holy altar within thy glorious temple
be acceptable unto thee and may it be for the joy of thy
holy name and for the pardon of thy servants and of thy flock,
O Father and Son and Holy Ghost, forever.[36]

Heaven and earth meet in this temple that the worshippers form during the rite of the eucharist.

Third, the idea of the kingdom being present or breaking into the world during eucharistic worship is also expressed in many liturgies and documents. For example, in the Apostolic Constitutions, another very early document (compiled around AD 375–380 in Syria, but drawing upon earlier materials, including the Didache), the prayer after the Eucharist is recorded in this way:

After the participation, give thanks in this manner: We thank thee, O God and Father of Jesus our Saviour, for Thy holy name, which Thou hast made to inhabit among us; . . . do Thou even now, through Him [Jesus], be mindful of this Thy holy Church, which Thou hast purchased with the precious blood of Thy Christ, and deliver it from all evil, and perfect it in Thy love and Thy truth, and gather us all together into Thy kingdom which Thou hast prepared. Let this Thy kingdom come.[37]

Such prayers for the church to be drawn, perfected, and gathered together look forward to an anticipated future but also ask God to accomplish such things "even now," in this way expressing the complex "now and not yet" inaugurated eschatology common in the New Testament.

Finally, in early church writings connections are drawn not only forward to the coming New Jerusalem, but also back to the garden. We find this connection beautifully expressed in this stanza from one of the hymns by Ephrem the Syrian (c. 306–373) from his collection titled "Hymns on Paradise":

---

36. F. E. Brightman, ed., *Liturgies Eastern and Western* (Oxford: Clarendon, 1896), 282.
37. *ANF* 7:470. And it continues: "Hosanna to the Son of David. Blessed be He that cometh in the name of the Lord—God the Lord, who was manifested to us in the flesh. If anyone be holy, let him draw near; but if anyone be not such, let him become such by repentance."

> The assembly of the saints
> > bears resemblance [alt. trans.: "is on the type of"] to Paradise.
> in it each day is plucked
> > the fruit of Him who gives life to all.
> In it, my brethren, is trodden
> > the cluster of grapes, to be the Medicine of Life.[38]

Here, the grapes, alluding to Christ who is the Vine, are squeezed and given to those assembled. For Ephrem, as the "assembly of the saints" gathers, a taste of Paradise is given.

In another of Ephrem's hymns a "breath" from that garden wafts into this world, this time at Pentecost:

> The breath that wafts
> from some blessed corner of Paradise
> gives sweetness
> to the bitterness of this region,
> it tempers the curse
> on this earth of ours.
> That Garden is
> the life-breath
> of this diseased world
> that has been so long in sickness;
> that breath proclaims that a saving remedy
> has been sent to heal our mortality.[39]

Apparently the garden is not only a reality of the past, but is in some way equivalent to the heavenly realms, the temple above. It at times breaks into, or to use Ephrem's more gentle imagery, "wafts" into our world, as at Pentecost, as during the Eucharist.

Examples from early church sources can be multiplied. We will see much more of this temple imagery in chapters below when we examine more spe-

---

38. St. Ephrem the Syrian, *Hymns on Paradise*, trans. S. P. Brock (Crestwood, NY: St. Vladimir's Seminary Press, 1990), 6.8.
39. St. Ephrem, *Hymns on Paradise*, 11.10.

cifically how the types of the sacrifices and pilgrim feasts are applied to the Eucharist. But let us turn now to another aspect of early church life in which this temple imagination is displayed: its architecture and art.

Temple Themes in Early Christian Art and Architecture

Connecting temple themes to early Christian architecture may at first seem odd. For, if the church is not a building but rather the people, why do the architectural shape and layout of the church building matter?

Even if the temple is the people, there are architectural expressions that allow the essential spirit of the community and its corporate worship to flourish better than others. I appreciate the way that Louis Bouyer approaches the topic of the connection between liturgy and architecture. He first makes a connection between the spirit of a community and its rites or liturgy. As he puts it, "'Spirit' always means, for Christians, some interior reality, one that tends toward incarnation, or rather cannot exist without being incarnate."[40] For Bouyer, the internal spirit of a community is expressed or made incarnate in its central rites. So, for Bouyer, in examining the churches "which were arranged or built on purpose to house the Christian liturgy," it is not "a series of fixed details, all taken in isolation or together, which is important." Instead, it is the "dynamic relation between some different focuses of the celebration, embodied in various elements and their coherent disposition."[41] In other words, the elements related to the foci of the community's celebrations and the ways these foci relate to the Christian community gathered in worship are of highest architectural importance. These are what matter most.

So, what do we find in early Christian architecture and liturgical art? Do we find connections to the temple or "figural performances" that are analogous to the temple in their configuration of space and art?

To answer this, let us first briefly consider the history of the development of church buildings during the first four centuries after Christ. This is important mainly to put away certain common inaccurate stories. Just as there is a myth of original simplicity concerning the liturgy, many people understand the his-

40. Louis Bouyer, *Liturgy and Architecture* (Notre Dame: University of Notre Dame Press, 1967), 1.
41. Bouyer, *Liturgy and Architecture*, 7–8.

tory of early Christian architecture in a similar way. The story is told that the early Christians consciously chose the house church form in part to avoid any resemblance to the idolatrous practices of pagan temples, and in part because Christianity primarily came from the poor and dispossessed, and so such unassuming spaces were both natural to and accessible to them. It is further assumed that there was little connection between these early Christian worship places and the basilica structures which were imposed on the Christian church after Christianity became the official church of the empire.

In contrast to such a story, L. Michael White's important work *Building God's House in the Roman World* traces Christian architectural development from the time of Christ until the fourth century, and in so doing overturns many of those common assumptions.[42] He develops a four-step typology of change for churches in various places around the Mediterranean world: from the house church, to the "*domus ecclesiae*," to the "*aula ecclesiae*," to the basilica structure that came to dominate Christian church structures from the fourth century onwards.

Early Christians first met in house churches. Initially these were people's homes in which no architectural changes were made. Over time we find evidence that structural renovations were made to existing structures: walls were knocked out, rooms enlarged, and yet the overall exterior of the building remained the same. But at some point the church communities rather than individuals became the "owners" of areas that were parts of larger buildings;

42. L. Michael White, *Building God's House in the Roman World: Architectural Adaption among Pagans, Jews, and Christians* (Baltimore: Johns Hopkins University Press, 1990). White's book is important in that it names many reigning assumptions about the development of Christian architecture that are common in the literature but are unsubstantiated by evidence. He builds on and yet critiques some of the assumptions made by Richard Krautheimer, probably the most important twentieth-century writer in this area until White. In White's words, these assumptions were as follows: first, that Christians met in houses to "avoid the idolatrous practices of Greek and Roman temples, and because the Christian movement came from among the poor and dispossessed"; second, that there is "little or no direct line from the *domus ecclesiae* to the basilica"; and third, "after [AD] 314 basilica form universally and almost immediately superseded all existing church buildings" (White, 21). Here he cites Richard Krautheimer, *Early Christian and Byzantine Architecture*, 4th rev. ed. (New Haven: Yale University Press, 1984), a key proponent of these assumptions. White's work is now published as vol. 1 of a two-volume work, *The Social Origins of Christian Architecture*, Harvard Theological Studies (Valley Forge, PA: Trinity Press, 1996).

the renovated areas were dedicated for use for church worship. This kind of structure is referred to as the *domus ecclesiae* (*domus* is Latin for "house" or "household," but here the house is owned in part by the church).[43] In the third century, even larger projects were taken on, and even exterior walls were remodeled in order to create what were typically larger rectangular halls for the church community to worship in. This arrangement is called the *aula ecclesiae* (*aula* is Latin for "hall" or "inner court"). White writes, "Well before Constantine introduced the basilica to Church architecture, the Christians had begun to move toward larger, more regular halls of assembly."[44] Eusebius, the early church historian, writes that this kind of church became suddenly more common in the middle to late third century—even before Christianity was officially decriminalized in AD 313 by the Edict of Milan.[45] Finally, under the aegis of Constantine, basilica-style churches were sanctioned and that architectural form quickly became the dominant church style until the twentieth century.

In short, White shows that even in spite of periods of persecution, there was a gradual development of form. This development was motivated by growing numbers of believers and desires for certain kinds of worship spaces, and yet restricted by finances and limitations of space in urban areas. Existing buildings were gradually adapted to a typical form—a large rectangular space with a raised platform at one end, with altars that were present in either moveable or fixed forms, and a separate baptistery. Such earlier forms endured even after Constantine.

What does this tell us about their worship spaces? First, their worship was organized around certain foci: the altar, the bema or raised platform in their main worship space, and a separate baptistery. Second, the way these foci

---

43. One important example is the earliest known Christian building at Dura-Europos in Syria. The church there renovated an existing building sometime between AD 232 and 256, taking out a wall to create a large hall with a platform at one end, and another room in which they created an elaborate baptistery with frescoes on the walls. In the meeting hall, which could accommodate 65–75 persons, "at the east end was a rhomboid shaped podium or *bema* about 0.97 meters from the wall, 1.47 meters long, and 0.20 meters high." Graydon F. Snyder, *Ante Pacem: Archeological Evidence of Church Life before Constantine* (Macon: Mercer University Press, 2003), 132.

44. White, *Building God's House*, 128.

45. White, *Building God's House*, 127. This was even before the Diocletian persecution of Christians in AD 303.

were positioned drew in larger part from Jewish precedents, especially typical synagogue layouts.[46]

The liturgical foci of synagogue were themselves based on the temple. For example, early Syrian synagogues often had the outer shape of a Roman basilica, a rectangular hall with an apse, a curved niche in the wall at one end. In the center of the hall we find a raised platform, or bema, upon which sat the seat of Moses, the place from which teaching in the tradition of Moses would come and upon which prayers would be offered to God. Also on this platform was a menorah which was placed in front of a veil. Behind the veil was a low-standing portable chest with Torah scrolls in it that symbolized the ark of the covenant.[47] In this we see clear representations of important symbols of the temple: the ark, veil, and menorah. The scroll chest and the teaching from them became the central symbols or means of God's presence, analogous to the ark of the covenant which functioned as both repository of the covenant and the throne of God from which he ruled. In the apse itself, Torah shrines came to be placed and veiled, and there Torah scrolls were also kept.[48] The apse pointed toward the temple in Jerusalem. This was so the assembly's worship and prayers were directed to Jerusalem, or more precisely to God's presence in the holy of holies. This direction of prayer was tied not only to God's presence in the holy of holies but also to messianic expectations. After the temple was destroyed, this direction was understood

---

46. In making these summaries, I draw especially upon the following: White for the general structure of the building; the helpful article by Jensen concerning placement of altars; Tigay for a more recent study of the ancient synagogues; the work of Louis Bouyer, which has been very influential in post–Vatican II discussions of liturgy and architecture, for his relation of the church to the synagogue; and the short article by Lang showing which parts of Bouyer's work have been accepted and which have been critiqued. Robin M. Jensen, "Recovering Ancient Ecclesiology: The Place of the Altar and the Orientation of Prayer in the Early Latin Church," *Worship* 89 (2015): 99–124. Jeffrey H. Tigay, "The Torah Scroll and God's Presence," in *Built by Wisdom, Established by Understanding: Essays on Biblical and Near Eastern Literature in Honor of Adele Berlin*, ed. Maxine L. Grossman (Bethesda: University Press of Maryland, 2013), 323–40. Uwe Michael Lang, "Louis Bouyer and Church Architecture: Resourcing Benedict XVI's The Spirit of the Liturgy," *Journal of the Institute for Sacred Architecture* 19 (2011): 14–17.

47. Tigay, "Torah Scroll," 332. R. Hachlili, "The Niche and the Ark in Ancient Synagogues," *BASOR* 223 (1976): 43–53.

48. Tigay, "Torah Scroll," 333.

as linked to hopes for the rebuilding of the temple, and to the coming of the new eschatological temple.

While synagogues are places of teaching, the typological relationships between synagogue and temple gave the reading and teaching from the Torah a sacramental quality. The presence and positioning of the menorah, veil, ark, and apse all allude to the temple, creating the expectation that in the reading and teaching of the Torah, God's presence also came and rested upon those gathered. In early rabbinic teaching up until the present day, both the Torah scrolls themselves and the act of reading them and hearing God's word are clearly tied to God's presence.[49] A well-known rabbinic saying makes this explicit: "R. Hananiah b. Teradion said: . . . When two sit together and there are words of Torah [spoken] between them, the *Shekhinah* (the presence of God) abides among them" (*m. Avot* 3:2; similarly 3:6).[50] In the gospels, Jesus makes a parallel claim about his own presence and the community gathered in his name (Matt. 18:20).

In early Christian Syrian churches, we find a similar layout.[51] In some reconstructions, the menorah, veil, and Ark are still retained on the raised bema in the center of the nave—remarkable in itself. But instead of a Torah shrine being placed in the apse, we find the altar around which the Lord's Supper was celebrated.

What does this mean? It seems to indicate—and the liturgical texts of early Christianity bear this out—that the altar becomes another key symbol that refers to the holy of holies, or rather, to that to which the holy of holies also referred: to God's heavenly presence and kingdom which meet earth in the place and time of the rite being performed around the altar.

For early Christians, their worship was centered on two sacramental places: the bema, from which scriptural readings, teachings, and prayers were offered, and the altar, around which the Eucharist was celebrated.[52] "The Jews in the

49. Tigay's chapter traces these connections from the earliest synagogues to the present day.

50. Quoted alongside similar sayings in Tigay, "Torah Scroll," 331.

51. "We have, as in the synagogue, the office of readings and prayers everywhere performed on a bema, which regularly occupies the center of the nave" (Bouyer, *Liturgy and Architecture*, 27).

52. Special baptisteries were also created quite early—so one could say there were three main sacramental foci, but two, the bema and the altar, that were part of the typical service.

synagogue, hearing the word of God, looked at the Ark and beyond the Ark at the Jerusalem Holy of holies which it evoked. The Christians in their churches, hearing the word, are led by it from the Ark to the altar. And beyond the altar itself, they look toward no other early place but only toward the rising sun as toward the symbol of the *Sol justitiae* they are expecting. The holy table, for them, is the only possible equivalent on earth of what was for the Jews their Holy of holies."[53]

Early church congregations were fully involved in the reading, teaching and praying and the Eucharist. They were not merely spectators. Bouyer writes: "There is not a worship of the clergy performed for the passive attendance of the congregation, but a congregational worship in which all pray together in the mediation of the word communicated by the ministers, and participate with them in a common eucharist."[54] While there was a kind of priestly hierarchy, there was no dualism. The ministers were the organic head or mouth of the body, but the body acted as a whole. In Syrian churches, the congregation even physically moved from gathering around the bema to gathering around the altar, further accentuating the active participation of all.[55]

Not all early Christian altars were placed in the apse, however. In Africa, altars were commonly placed in the middle or middle front of the nave, while the bema, the raised platform where elders and Scriptures were located, and where teaching and prayers were offered, instead occupied the apse area.[56] There is also evidence in Tyre and in some early Roman churches that the altar was placed not in the apse, but toward the center of the church. Even in Old St. Peter's Basilica in Rome the altar was movable, and it was typically placed in a location that was "common ground" for both clergy and laity, where it could be easily accessed by all.[57]

53. Bouyer, *Liturgy and Architecture*, 31.

54. Bouyer, *Liturgy and Architecture*, 35.

55. Bouyer, *Liturgy and Architecture*, 35. Bouyer notes that this was true in these churches for both men and women (38–39), different than the synagogue.

56. This evidence is contrary to commonly held opinions. "The centralized placement of African altars is commonly noted by architectural historians (e.g. Milburn, *Early Christian Art and Architecture*, 153). . . . Yet many modern commentators still follow Jungmann who says on p. 182 of his book, *The Mass of the Roman Rite* (New York: Benziger, 1959) "'that it is a striking fact that in the history of Christian architecture the altar is hardly ever placed in the center'" (Jensen, *Recovering Ancient Ecclesiology*, 104n19).

57. Jensen, *Recovering Ancient Ecclesiology*, 108. The comments about Old St. Peter's

So while the exact placement of the altar and the bema varied, the earliest architectural evidence we have indicates that Christian churches revolved around those two liturgical foci. To use more contemporary language, two of the internal pressures that influenced early Christian architecture were the dynamics of the liturgy of the Word and the liturgy of the Sacrament. Both of these were typologically related to the realities of the temple.

It is important to see that both of these main foci, the bema and the altar, are typologically related not to the altar of sacrifice in the temple court, not even to the holy place, but to the holy of holies. There is the symbolic understanding that in and through its interactions with Scripture and in and through the sacrament of the altar/table, the church at worship is invited into the holy of holies, the place where heaven and earth are connected and where the presence of God dwells. A sacramental reading of Hebrews 12, in which one assumes worship centered on the Eucharist is being envisioned, reflects such a scene, where the writer is comparing the old and new covenants: "But you have come to Mount Zion and to the city of the living God, the heavenly Jerusalem, and to innumerable angels in festal gathering, and to the assembly of the firstborn . . . and to God . . . and to the spirits of the righteous . . . and to Jesus, the mediator of a new covenant, and to the sprinkled blood" (Heb. 12:22–24).[58] Perhaps such an allusion to Eucharistic worship is also reflected in Revelation 4:1–2, when John is taken immediately to the throne where scrolls are read and a feast is eventually celebrated.

---

are based on work by Krautheimer; Jensen notes many older drawings and reconstructions of Old St. Peter's confuse the confessio with the altar.

58. This alludes to a much debated issue about the relationship between the epistle to the Hebrews and the Eucharist. I find Arthur Just's approach to this issue salutary. He writes that it is better not to try to "prove" that Hebrews is referring to Eucharist, but rather to say, "Eucharistic interpretation provides answers to many of the questions Hebrews raises" (Arthur Just, Jr., "Entering Holiness: Christology and Eucharist in Hebrews," *Concordia Theological Quarterly* 69 [2005]: 95). Earlier in that article, Just writes concerning Heb. 12:18–24: "When Hebrews' first-century hearers ask themselves, 'where is this place?' their immediate response must be where Christ speaks for his Father and acts for his Father. That place is the liturgy where Christ's performative word brings purification of sins through preaching and the Eucharist. The inaugurated eschatology of the New Testament encourages us to consider that our approach to God's presence in Jesus begins already now in the church's eucharistic life even as it will reach its consummation when we fully experience Christ's presence at the heavenly feast" (93).

The earliest surviving Christian art that decorated early churches also reflects this temple typology of the church gathered in eucharistic worship.

In Rome and Ravenna, Italy, in some of the earliest surviving Christian churches in the world, several of the beautiful and massive mosaics in the apses of those churches depict scenes that would be especially appropriate for such an understanding of the Eucharist. As Lang writes, "Their iconographic programmes are often related to the Eucharist that is celebrated underneath. These mosaics may well have served to direct the attention of the assembly whose eyes were raised up during the Eucharistic prayer."[59] In such mosaics, especially prominent are depictions of the risen Christ. In the grand sixth-century mosaic of the church of Sant' Apollinare in Classe, in Ravenna, several themes are complexly woven together, themes that would be highly appropriate as symbols of the eucharistic celebration.[60] In the larger mosaic, Christ, symbolized by a disk with a cross on it in the sky, is flanked by Moses and Elijah, and surrounded by three sheep, evoking the Mountain of Transfiguration. Immediately below the disk is bishop Apollinaris, who is portrayed as a good shepherd. He is surrounded by twelve sheep in a lovely scene reminiscent of both Psalm 23 and the garden of Eden. Given a eucharistic setting, Apollinaris, who is presiding, plays the role of Christ the good shepherd, who is above him in heaven, feeding the people of God gathered around him, in a foretaste of the peaceable kingdom that will come.

In Rome, in the church of *Santi Cosma e Damiano*, at the center of the mosaic we see the risen Christ on clouds. Below the largest part of the mosaic, there is a horizontal band in which Christ is portrayed as a sheep, the Lamb of God, who is standing on a mountain with four streams coming out of it.[61]

59. Lang, "Louis Bouyer and Church Architecture," 15.

60. For images, see for example: http://www.turismo.ra.it/eng/Discover-the-area/Art-and-culture/Unesco-world-heritage/Basilica-of-Sant%27Apollinare-in-Classe.

61. For images, see: http://www.cosmadamiano.com/. "Although heavily restored in the sixteenth and seventeenth centuries, this apse mosaic remains one of the finest and most historically significant examples of late antique Christian art in Rome" (Daniel C. Cochran, "Projecting Power in Sixth-Century Rome: The Church of Santi Cosma e Damiano in the Late Antique Forum Romanum," *Journal of History and Cultures* 3 [2013], 1). This scene became the pattern for other later mosaics, such as the apse mosaic in the church of San Clemente, created by Masolina da Panicale in the twelfth century, and the apse mosaic in the *Basilica di St. Praxedes*, commissioned by Pope Hadrian I in AD 780; both of these feature the motif of the Lamb of God on a mountain with four rivers flowing out of it. A similar apse mosaic is found in the church of San Marco Evan-

Here Christ is surrounded by twelve sheep, approaching in procession toward him. The mountain with four streams flowing out of it likens Mount Zion to the garden of Eden with its four rivers—an equation often made about the temple itself. Given the connection of the apse with the Eucharist, the Eucharist is likened to the temple which is likened to the garden which is likened to heaven above where Christ dwells in glory. And all this resonates well with a possible eucharistic reading of Psalm 23:

> The LORD is my shepherd, I shall not want....
> He leads me in right paths for his name's sake.... [as in Scripture
>   reading/teaching]
> You prepare a table before me ... [as in the Eucharist]
> You anoint my head with oil ... [as in baptism]
> I shall dwell in the house of the LORD my whole life long.

These apse mosaics illuminate the understanding of the eucharistic rite celebrated beneath them. They proclaim that in the Eucharist, heaven and earth are coming together in a new temple. At the eucharistic feast we are in the presence of the risen Christ who is in heaven, our Lamb and our shepherd. In the feast we are fed and gain a foretaste of the feast of the kingdom of God.

Perhaps I have lingered too long on this topic. But I think it is important for especially Protestants to see that there was no "original simplicity" in the early church. The earliest disciples of Christ did not invent a new simple style of worship that was later corrupted, routinized, and made hierarchical by unspiritual power-hungry Constantinian leaders. Rather, Spirit-filled disciples understood that as they gathered together around word and sacrament, the church became a new spiritual temple.

The witness of the New Testament, the writings of early church fathers, the earliest known liturgies, the architecture of the early church, and some of the earliest known Christian liturgical art all reflect this. As at the temple in Jerusa-

---

gelist (ninth-century Rome). In the Chapel of Saint Zeno, a side chapel located within the church of St. Praxedes (AD 817–824), we also see the symbols of the four rivers of paradise flowing from a mount upon which the Lamb of God stands. Here, however, there are four deer that are drinking from those streams, reminiscent of Psalm 42, which mentions the psalmist's longing for the festivals at the house of God. Thank you to Rev. Dana English for guiding me to some of these sites.

lem, so when the early church gathered God was really and personally present, heaven and earth met, and the kingdom of God was extended into the earth, as it was in the garden and as it will be fully in the great day of the Lord.

5

THE TABLE TODAY

The Presence of God and the Kingdom in the Eucharist

> The liturgy of the Eucharist is best understood as a journey or
> procession. It is the journey of the Church into the dimension
> of the Kingdom.
>
> —Alexander Schmemann,
> *For the Life of the World: Sacraments and Orthodoxy*

The temple. We first examined its central meanings for the people of Israel. We
then traced the typological connections the New Testament writers and the
early church made between the temple, Christ, and the church. We are now in
the position to ask: What kind of pressure do those typological connections
place on contemporary thought about and practice of the Eucharist?[1]

---

1. As mentioned in chap. 1, I take the term "pressure" from Christopher Kavin Rowe,
"Biblical Pressure and Trinitarian Hermeneutics": "The biblical text is not inert but instead exerts a pressure ('coercion') upon its interpreters and asserts itself within theological reflection and discourse such that there is (or can be) a profound continuity,
grounded in the subject matter itself, between the biblical text and traditional Christian
exegesis and theological formulation" (308).

Biblical Pressure on Contemporary Thought and Practice

Certainly these typological connections do not come with a pre-packaged, fully detailed eucharistic theology. And yet we want our sacramental theology and practice to have a profound fit or continuity with them. They pressure us into ways of thinking and practice that "fit" with them. This pressure is an important way Scripture functions as an authority.[2]

More specifically, we are pressured to picture the Eucharist as an event in which the church is being built into a new spiritual temple. Taking the major meanings of the temple and applying them to the Eucharist, we are pressured to understand that in the Eucharist: (1) God is really and personally present, (2) heaven and earth are meeting and overlapping, (3) the kingdom of God is being extended into the earth, and (4) what is happening now is connected to both past and future. Our sacramental theology and practice should fit with these meanings.

This way of understanding the Eucharist resonates well with important twentieth-century proposals in three different areas for the reform of sacramental theology and practice.

First, in the area of sacramental theology, this typological understanding of the Eucharist intersects with proposals for reforming our understanding of how God, Christ, and Spirit are present in the sacrament. It also intersects with proposals that highlight the relationship between the Eucharist and the kingdom of God. Showing how these temple themes resonate with these proposals and how an overarching temple typology provides a home for them is the focus of this chapter.

Second, in the area of Christian ethics and ecclesiology, understanding that in the Eucharist, the kingdom of God is being extended into the earth in and through the gathered community puts pressure on how one thinks about the relationship of our worship to the rest of our lives. In short, if in the Eucharist the kingdom of God is breaking into the world, the central practices and activities of eucharistic worship ought to become guiding practices for all our lives as the people of God and for our mission in the world. Around the table, the patterns of the kingdom are being revealed. Revealed in a concentrated way in

---

2. I understand the authority of tradition in part as a privileged "hermeneutical trajectory" for interpreting Scripture. See Stanley Grenz and John Franke, "Tradition: Theology's Hermeneutical Trajectory," in *Beyond Foundationalism* (Louisville: Westminster John Knox, 2001), 93–129.

eucharistic worship, these patterns of human life in proper relationship to God and one another should "roll down like waters" out of the church's worship into the rest of their lives and into the life of the world. As such, the practices involved in eucharistic worship can and should be guiding patterns for ecclesiology, mission, and ethics. These are precisely the claims of twentieth- and twenty-first-century proposals about how to reform our understanding of ecclesiology and its relationship to ethics and mission.

I have written of these connections in other places, one of them being an initiative toward "a liturgical-missional ecclesiology" within the PC(USA).[3] Combining insights from the liturgical renewal movement with those from the missional church conversation, this initiative deeply resonates with the temple themes under discussion. Indeed, I find temple typology to be the best way to biblically ground such an initiative. Stanley Hauerwas and Sam Wells suggest similar reforms, especially in *The Blackwell Companion to Christian Ethics*.[4] A Eucharist-centered ethics also fits well with the broader emerging tradition in ethics called "ecclesial ethics" by Ben Quash, Sam Wells and Rebekah Eklund in *Introducing Christian Ethics*.[5] And from a more evangelical and Baptist angle, what Robert Webber calls "ancient-future worship" and "ancient-future evangelism" fit with this overall way of conceiving God's action in and through the worship, life, and mission of the Church.[6] A temple typology pressures one to take these proposals for the overall shape of Christian ecclesiology, mission, and ethics seriously.

Finally, linking the central meanings of the temple to eucharistic worship puts pressure on how we think about our spaces for worship. These temple themes resonate with important recent proposals about how to think about, structure, and renovate worship spaces. Such implications will be treated in the final chapter in which concrete practical proposals for worship spaces and eucharistic liturgy are offered.

3. David Stubbs, "Locating the Liturgical-Missional Church in the Bible's Story," in *Liturgical-Missional: Perspectives on a Reformed Ecclesiology*, ed. Neal Presa (Eugene, OR: Wipf & Stock, 2016), 15–32. Stubbs, "Ending of Worship—Ethics," in *A More Profound Alleluia*, ed. Leanne Van Dyk (Grand Rapids: Eerdmans, 2005), 133–55.
4. Stanley Hauerwas and Samuel Wells, eds., *The Blackwell Companion to Christian Ethics* (Malden, MA: Blackwell, 2004).
5. Samuel Wells, Ben Quash, and Rebekah Eklund, *Introducing Christian Ethics*, 2nd ed. (Malden, MA: Wiley-Blackwell, 2017).
6. Webber, *Ancient-Future Worship*. Robert Webber, *Ancient-Future Evangelism* (Grand Rapids: Baker, 2003).

Pressure on Sacramental Theology

The twentieth century saw a great renewal of interest in sacramental theology. But "interest" is far too tame a word. Great movements swept through the Christian world in especially the last half of the twentieth century. These movements have included sweeping changes in practice as a result of Vatican II in the Roman Catholic world and the liturgical renewal movement in both the Catholic and Protestant worlds, increased hunger for ritual practices in the Protestant world, critiques of past thought forms, and retellings of the history of the Reformation. It has been an era of turbulence and renewal. These historic changes have prompted many divergent proposals and many debates about how to move forward as well as vigorous defenses of the old ways.

The central meanings of the temple discussed in chapter 3 intersect with two sets of proposals within sacramental theology. They intersect first with proposals about how best to understand God's presence in the Eucharist. Specifically, many scholars have expressed concern that the typical ways of understanding God's real presence in the Eucharist tend to undermine God's personal presence, and so they have proposed alternative understandings. The temple's central meanings also intersect with proposals that highlight the in-breaking of the kingdom of God in the eucharistic rite.

Intertwined with these sets of proposals are critiques of the typical way signs and symbols have been understood in the Christian West and applied to the Eucharist. These critique common ways of thinking about signs—our explicit semiotic theories—as deficient; they are part of the reason God's personal presence and connections to the in-breaking of the kingdom of God have been obscured.

Such proposals fit with the central meanings of the temple. But temple typology does not only resonate with them. It also provides a house for them, an organizational structure within which proposals for reform which at first seem unrelated can live together and take shelter. And it provides a biblically-based rationale for them—a throne of judgment and mercy, if you will, by which they might be judged and vindicated.

God Is Really and Personally Present in the Eucharist

How is God present in the Eucharist? Here we enter a minefield of arguments about the mode of the Father's, Christ's, and the Spirit's presence in the Eucharist, arguments that have been traditional points of division between Roman Catholic, Lutheran, Reformed, and Anabaptist traditions. Careful and respectful stepping is called for.

There are divisions between those who affirm or deny the real presence of Christ in the Eucharist. For those who affirm the real presence of Christ, there are further divisions regarding *how* Christ is really present.

If God's presence in the Eucharist has a typological relationship to God's presence in the temple, we are pressured to enter into the conversation in a certain way. As pointed out above, God's presence at the temple was both real and personal. So, given a temple typology combined with a Christian trinitarian understanding of God, we would expect that God, Christ, and the Spirit would be present in the Eucharist not only really but also personally.

But we can go further. At the temple God is present in the holy of holies, on the ark, enthroned between the cherubim. That is God's primary position; God is not primarily in any elements or sacrifices at the temple. So, where and how is God present in the Eucharist? Unlike many eucharistic debates which start with how Christ is present in the elements of bread and wine, we are pressured instead to begin by understanding that God is watching over and interacting with God's people, as an active personal giver and recipient superintending over the rite as a whole, just as he sat between the cherubim, receiving the sacrifices of Israel and extending his blessing to them.

However, given the transformation from the older Mosaic covenant to new covenant, things get more complicated. Given the vicarious or substitutionary work of Christ, a work empowered by the Spirit, we would also expect God's presence, through Christ in the Spirit, also in the position of the priest who sacrifices, as well as the sacrifice that is given. Christ, as the true human covenant partner of God empowered by the Spirit, takes the role of priest/true Israelite/true human. He is the righteous human who offers a proper sacrifice to God (Heb. 7:15–16). Not only that. He—his righteous and obedient life to the point of death—is also what is offered (Heb. 9:11–14). But given the "once for all" aspect of his work as sin offering (Heb. 7:27), Christ is not being resacrificed as sin offering, but rather we "remember" that aspect of Christ's work as we "enter the sanctuary" (Heb. 10:19).

Furthermore, through the Spirit we are united to this new humanity which Christ has pioneered (John 6:53; 1 Cor. 12:27; Heb. 12:2; cf. 1 Cor. 11:19–20, 28–29). We become one with him, so that we too might participate in the offering of our lives as a "living sacrifice" (Rom. 12:1). In this way, God is present through the Spirit also in the persons and actions of those gathered for the Eucharistic feast.

So, based on temple typology, we would look for God's Trinitarian presence as personal giver and receiver superintending over the rite as a whole, also in the bread and wine, as that which is offered and received, and also within the priestly congregation as they offer and receive gifts from God. God is really present in three different ways in these various roles. A temple typology pushes us beyond focusing solely on God's presence in the elements of bread and wine.

In twentieth-century eucharistic theology, some calls for reforming the way we picture God's presence in the Eucharist clearly resonate with this. In particular, scholars involved in eucharistic theology and ecumenical dialogue have desired to recover a fuller sense of God's *personal* presence in the rite. They argue that past understandings of God's *real* presence in the Eucharist have obscured God's *personal* presence.

In order to better understand what is being called for, let me take some time to carefully unpack what is meant by God's personal presence. "Personal" is not a technical term, but rather a helpful way of pointing to the mode of God's presence that is implicit in the biblical portrayals of God at the temple. "Person" and "personhood" are notoriously difficult concepts to precisely define, but for our purposes, I am using the term "person" to refer to beings capable of intentional action and who are able to form mutual relationships.[7] Both

7. Definitions have been philosophically problematic in the modern world; they are also implicated in technical discussions of trinitarian theology. The terms "person" and "personhood" also have a wide range of meanings in popular use. While this brief working definition is mine, I have in mind the combination of foci of John Macmurray's Gifford lectures published as *The Self as Agent* (New York: Harper and Brothers, 1957) and *Persons in Relation* (Atlantic Highlands: Humanities, 1996). Both of these were influential in many later reflections on "persons" within theology. My working definition also tries to capture the constitutive role of both a language community and agency one finds in Charles Taylor, *Human Agency and Language* (Cambridge: Cambridge University Press, 1985) and *The Language Animal: The Full Shape of the Human Linguistic Capacity* (Cambridge, MA: Belknap Press, 2016). It captures some of the emphases of Martin Buber's "I-Thou" understanding, which was influential for both Karl Barth and Abraham Joshua Heschel. In political philosophy, these poles balance the insights of modern individualism and the communitarian reaction to it. In trinitarian theology, I think communitarian emphases need to be balanced by the particularity of each person, as argued

poles of this definition are needed: one can engage in mutual relationships only if one can act intentionally, and acting with intention is possible only for beings that are part of a language community, a community of mutual relationships. So, "personal" here means interacting in a way "appropriate to persons" as opposed to ways appropriate to most animals, vegetables, minerals, or force fields.[8]

One danger in using the word "personal" is that it can also mean tailor-made or private. I do not want to suggest either of those meanings. Encounters between God and Israel at the temple are personal in the sense of being filled with intention and involving mutual relationship. But they were certainly not designed around the personal desires of each individual, as in the phrase "personal trainer." Nor were they personal in the sense of a private or interior encounter, one that is only understood and sensed by each individual person. Especially in the evangelical world, I fear the phrase "a personal relationship with God" rightly begins with the first emphasis but then often slips into the other two.

Such characteristics of human persons—their ability to act with intention, and their ability to form mutual relationships—are also posited of God. Personal transactions between God and Israel were centered at the temple.

We see this in biblical descriptions. God's presence at the temple is not simply a force, but a center of awareness: God listens, hears, and smells (Lev. 1:13) from the temple. God dwells and walks in the temple. In addition, God takes on higher modes of interaction with Israel. God is seated on the throne, and from there God reigns (Ps. 47:8; Isa. 6:1; Rev. 4:2). God judges from the temple. God hears and answers from the temple (Ps. 138:2–3). God speaks and is heard. God accepts, God reasons, God forgives the sins of Israel through the atoning or covering activities of the temple. God feasts with Israel (Deut. 12:7), and finally God blesses in and through the actions at the temple (Num. 6:27; Ps. 128:5; Ps. 134:3).

Not only was God understood to be a personal presence, but God was present to Israel in such a way that respected Israel's personhood. The major

---

by Nageed G. Awad in "Personhood as Particularity: John Zizioulas, Colin Gunton and the Trinitarian Theology of Personhood," *Journal of Reformed Theology* 4 (2010): 1–22.

8. Whether some animals, such as dolphins, dogs, apes, and elephants also have "personhood" defined in this way is a live question—see Alasdair MacIntyre, *Dependent Rational Animals: Why Human Beings Need the Virtues* (London: Duckworth, 1999).

modes of encounter between God and Israel were forms of symbolic communication that assumed and respected the personhood of the other. While there can be discussion about the extent to which descriptions of God's personal characteristics and interactions with Israel were metaphorical, I think one greatly distorts Scripture to say anything less of God or anything less of God's relationship to Israel. God is certainly more than a person, but God is at least a person.

We see this most centrally in God's desire for a covenant relationship with Israel. This covenant relationship, a relationship grounded upon intentionality and mutuality, is at the center of Israel's faith (Exod. 19:3–6; Josh. 24:1–28). Abraham Joshua Heschel emphasizes this personal aspect of the God of biblical religion. Such an understanding is reflected throughout his writings, and is implicit in this statement: "Biblical religion is the attempt to teach about the Creator of all things and the knowledge of his will. It does not intend to teach us principles of creation or redemption. It came to teach us that God is alive, that he is Creator and Redeemer, Teacher and Lawgiver."[9]

While God was related to all of Israel personally, this did not mean God's presence was centered on the person of each individual Israelite. The primary way that God is pictured as being involved with his chosen people is not through personal relationships with each individual of Israel wherever they happen to be; instead, individual and communal personal covenantal interactions between God and Israel are ritually focused at the temple.

Recognizing the personal aspect of God's relationship to Israel also guards against common misunderstandings of sacrifice. The sacrifices and worship at the temple are not pictured as magical or automatic in the sense of ritual manipulation of spiritual forces—even though they were sometimes misunderstood that way—but rather as means of personal encounter between God and God's people, both as a community and as individuals.

Psalm 50 is quite illuminating in this regard. In it, God mocks those who shortchange the personal dimensions of God's interactions with Israel through the temple. God first makes it clear that he does not want sacrifices because he is hungry: "If I were hungry, I would not tell you, for the world and all that is in it is mine" (Ps. 50:12). One should not understand sacrifices in a way

---

9. Abraham Joshua Heschel, *God in Search of Man: A Philosophy of Judaism* (New York: Farrer, Straus & Giroux, 1983), 16.

that implies God interacts with Israel at the level of animal nature—or even has an animal nature. God instead wants these sacrifices to be personal acts of "thanksgiving" (Ps. 50:14), to be part of a relationship that involves vow-making and vow-keeping and intercession (Ps. 50:14–15). God also rebukes those who present sacrifices and "take [his] covenant on [their] lips" but who do not follow his ways in their lives (Ps. 50:16–23). It is implied these "wicked" (v. 16) people see the covenant sacrifices as a ritual action that automatically results in the blessings and grace of the covenant. They treat the temple rites as sub-personal, automatic power transfer mechanisms. They perform sacrifices, expect to get the "stuff" of forgiveness and blessing, and then go and do wicked actions. Cheap grace indeed! Temple sacrifices should instead be means of personal and intentional interaction in which mutual relationships are formed and maintained.[10]

The crucial point here is that at the temple, as Israel performed its worship, the people were in the real presence of the living and personal God, who inter-

10. Having said this, however, I do not want to deny that God's presence and its effects at the temple are sometimes envisioned in a sub-personal, or perhaps super-personal, manner. There are places in Scripture where God's presence at the temple centered on the ark or throne of God seems to take on the mode of a sub-personal, automatic force-field-like presence. The "glory" and "holiness" of God at times seem like forms of energy that affect and pattern creaturely energy systems that they come into contact with, doing so with either life-giving or destructive results. For example, one thinks of the death of Aaron's sons, Nadab and Abihu, who offered "unholy fire before the Lord" and were consumed by fire (Lev. 10:1–2). It is unclear whether such destruction and blessing flowed from the presence of the Lord automatically or through intentional decisions of God.

Moving to the New Testament, consider Jesus, the temple made flesh. While not common, we do find an instance where healing power flows out of Jesus without a personal decision on his part when a woman who has been suffering from hemorrhages for twelve years touches the hem of Christ's garment and is healed (Mark 5:27–30; Matt. 9:20–21; Luke 8:44–46).

What is the mode of God's presence and power in such instances? Is there a substantial or material change that occurs in those places and with those objects that is then transferred to those who interact with them? God's presence in these instances might be understood more on the level of a "thing" or "energy" or merely as a "substance" (understood as less than personal) than as a person. Certainly there is not a carefully laid out theology of such holy "places" and "things" being "sacraments." So, while there are places in Scripture that suggest such sub-personal divine presence in and through such things—the ark, holy places, perhaps blood, and Christ's hem—they are the exception rather than the rule.

acted with them in a personal way. This pressures us to have a similar emphasis in our conception of God's real presence in the rite of the Eucharist and other Christian sacramental rites of the new covenant. Baptism and the Eucharist are not simply thankful remembrances of past events, not simply duties, not manipulations of materials that unleash divine power, not distributions of a divine substance. Above all, they are events of personal encounter between God and God's people.

As this relates to contemporary eucharistic theology, certain theologians argue we should reconceive sacraments most basically as rites. In doing so, they seek to bring the contributions of ritual theory to sacramental theology. By viewing the sacraments in this way—as rites and rituals—personal interactions between God and God's people are highlighted.

Peter Leithart's proposals are a good example.[11] Leithart is an influential contemporary Reformed and evangelical theologian whose publications are prolific and multifaceted. In several books and a series of articles he has reflected deeply on sacramental theology, posed important critiques of tendencies in the West, and strongly argued that sacraments should be reconceived above all as rites.[12]

What does this entail for Leithart? First, seeing sacraments as rites focuses on actions more than things and substances. Leithart writes, "The Supper is not merely bread and wine plus the word but bread-and-wine-eaten-and-drunk-by-the-church plus the word."[13] Furthermore, such actions are personal in the sense that they are intentional actions of the community as they interact with God. Thus the sacrament of the Eucharist refers to the intentional actions of

---

11. Peter Leithart, "Old Covenant and New in Sacramental Theology Old and New," *Pro Ecclesia* 14 (2005): 174–90; "Embracing Ritual"; "What's Wrong with Transubstantiation: Evaluating Theological Models," *Westminster Theological Journal* 53 (1991): 295–324; "Conjugating the Rites: Old and New in Augustine's Theory of Signs" *Calvin Theological Journal* 34 (1999): 136–47; "Marburg and Modernity," *First Things* (Jan 1992): 8–9; *A House for My Name* (Moscow, ID: Canon, 2000); *1 and 2 Kings* (Grand Rapids: Brazos, 2006).

12. Discussions of rites and rituals often rely upon Catherine Bell's seminal work, *Ritual Theory, Ritual Practice* (Oxford: Oxford University Press, 1992), in which she critiques earlier discussions of rituals by using the idea of practice, thus erasing any strong distinctions between thinking and doing.

13. Leithart, "Embracing Ritual," 18.

people and groups of people as they handle the elements, not just the physical and visible elements of bread and wine.[14]

Martha Moore-Keish is another liturgical theologian, also within the Reformed tradition, who seeks to draw from the insights of ritual theory and liturgical theology.[15] She emphasizes that at the heart of the sacramental rites are personal interactions with God. As such, the sacrament becomes the entire rite, not just the elements. She writes: "If the eucharist is regarded as ritual, then the sense of 'sign' itself is expanded to include the entire event, rather than solely the material objects of bread and wine."[16]

In this way the Eucharist comes to be understood as a series of "personal and covenantal exchanges" with God.[17] These exchanges are in fact its central meanings. In viewing sacraments as rites, one sees them as extended forms of dialogical communication and gift-giving between God and God's people, or forms of personal interaction.

Seeing sacraments as intentional interactions also highlights how they are effective. The sacramental rite brings about changes like other "performative utterances" and other "status-changing" rites.[18] Like a marriage ceremony or the inauguration of a president, sacraments really effect changes in relationships and statuses. As Leithart writes, "To call the sacraments rites is to emphasize that they actually accomplish and do things; God recognizes the baptized person as a baptized person, and a church that celebrates the Supper is considered by God as a church that has celebrated the Supper."[19]

There is a danger in this. An emphasis on the ritual character of sacraments could lead to a Pelagian understanding of what is happening, sacraments becoming human works that earn a right status before God. Leithart recognizes this, and in response he first underlines that these rites were given to us by God as gifts. The initiative for doing the rite in the first place comes from God. In addition, within the rite, it is not only the people who are acting, but also God. As the church in the Eucharist acts toward God, God is also acting toward the church, and God is also in the congregation empowering them in their activity:

14. Leithart, "Embracing Ritual," 18.
15. Moore-Keish, *Do This in Remembrance of Me*.
16. Moore-Keish, *Do This in Remembrance of Me*, 146.
17. Leithart, "Old Covenant and New," 189.
18. Leithart, "Embracing Ritual," 18.
19. Leithart, "Embracing Ritual," 19.

"It must be emphasized that God is giving gifts in, with, and under the performance of the sacramental rituals."[20] Not only are humans acting, but God is also acting in a complex way as Father, Son and Holy Spirit.

As a result, a central question becomes, What kinds of performative utterances and activities are taking place? What kinds of "personal and covenantal exchanges" are happening between God and God's people? What gifts are being given and received? In a ritual understanding of the Eucharist, such personal and covenantal exchanges become the main point; they are its central meanings.

Another danger lurks related to the first. An emphasis on the personal aspect of this encounter could obscure the interior work of the Spirit. But this need not result provided one recognizes that one important exchange happening in the Eucharist is a union with the person of Christ through the action of the Spirit. This in fact is the exchange or gift most highlighted by Leithart.[21] But it is not the only one. Seeing the Eucharist as a rite that consists of a series of personal and covenantal exchanges weaves the activity of God that unites the church with Christ through sacramental eating and drinking into the larger structure of the rite.

Rather than fully identifying all the interactions and exchanges that are part of the rite—that will be the subject of the following chapters—it is enough for now to see that viewing the Eucharist as a rite leads one to ask that question.

Notice too how this emphasis on personal interactions between God and people pushes one toward a full Trinitarian account of God's presence and activity in the sacrament rather than a merely Christological or pneumatological one. In other words, it is the Triune God whom the congregation is praying to and encountering and receiving from. The presence of the body and blood of Christ and the activity of the Spirit are part of a larger, more complex way in which God is present and active.

In sum, one way that temple typology puts pressure on eucharistic theology is by suggesting that, just as at the temple, God's presence is both real and personal. Peter Leithart, Martha Moore-Keish, and others who see the Eucharist as a rite emphasize the fact that God is personally present, engaging with those gathered in a way appropriate to persons. Such an approach affirms

20. Leithart, "Embracing Ritual," 20.
21. Leithart, "What's Wrong with Transubstantiation," 323–24.

that God is really present but presses on to ask, What is God here to do? More precisely, it pressures us to ask what kind of personal and covenantal exchanges are happening in this personal encounter between God and God's people.

Typical Ways Personal Presence Has Been Obscured:
Sign versus Reality and Sacraments as Things

Before addressing that question it will be worth pausing to address another question, namely, How did such a sense of God's personal presence become obscured? Within twentieth-century sacramental theology many scholars have critiqued two tendencies in the West that have obscured themes a temple typology would emphasize.[22] These two tendencies critiqued are (1) an understanding of signs which sharply divides them from reality, and (2) a focus on sacraments as objects rather than activities. Such tendencies obscure the *personal* encounter and communication with God that occur in the Eucharist. They also obscure one of the gifts given in the rite, namely, union with the full *person* of Christ (meaning here his way of life) through the Spirit. Finally, they obscure the in-breaking of the kingdom of God in the Eucharist, a point taken up in the next sections of this chapter.

These tendencies are fueled by a particular theory of symbolism greatly influenced by Augustine. Augustine is a towering figure in sacramental theology. In his writings, he develops the distinction between *signum* and *res*, between the sign and the thing which it signifies. He applies this distinction to the sacraments.[23] For Augustine, the goal of signs is to bring something to mind—some invisible and mental thing to which the sign points. For example, physical and visible letters on a page point to a spiritual and invisible idea, even though the physical ink and paper have no intrinsic relationship to it. As one applies this letter and spirit relationship to sacraments, the physical sacramental things are like letters. They point to something else, something invisible and spiritual that they signify. This spiritual "thing" has often been spoken of in the West as "invisible grace."

22. I draw upon especially Alasdair Heron and Peter Leithart to make these points. Alasdair Heron, *Table and Tradition: Toward an Ecumenical Understanding of the Eucharist* (Philadelphia: Westminster, 1983).
23. Leithart examines this distinction and its repercussions in Augustine's *De magistro, Christian Instruction,* and in book 15 of *The Trinity* in "Conjugating the Rites," 137–40.

Such ways of thinking about the relationship of *signum* and *res* can also be applied to the relationship between the divine and human natures of Jesus Christ. The Alexandrian leaders Clement and Origen, who came before Augustine, emphasized the divine nature of Christ as that which feeds the soul. Clement, for example, takes the symbolism of flesh and blood in the Eucharist as an allegory for the reception of the Holy Spirit and the Word. Clement relates the flesh to the Holy Spirit and the blood to the Word—it is these that we feast on in a spiritual manner.[24] Origen similarly "distinguishes very clearly between the material elements and the spiritual reality of Christ the Word of God, and insists that what matters is not simply the physical eating of the bread, but the reception of the Word, of Christ, in faith."[25]

While there is truth to be found here, one wonders with Alasdair Heron about the "danger of driving such a wedge between the physical and the spiritual that they can no longer really be held and seen together."[26] This presents a challenge for understanding Jesus Christ (though it also applies to the sacraments, as will be seen shortly). Is the humanity of Christ really just a sign with no intrinsic relationship to what it signifies?[27] Is not a central point of the incarnation the re-forming of the humanity of Christ into a proper covenant partner with God? A strong distinction between sign (humanity of Christ) and thing signified (divine Word) undermines this goal of Christ's saving work.

While Augustine is often critiqued for this way of understanding signs, his thinking is more complex than the synopsis presented here. At points in *Christian Instruction* he regards certain signs as embodiments of what they signify.[28] Nevertheless, a strong division between sign and thing signified is often what gets picked up in those who follow Augustine, especially given the

24. Heron, *Table and Tradition*, 68.
25. Heron, *Table and Tradition*, 69.
26. Heron, *Table and Tradition*, 69.
27. "All [solutions proposed in the Reformation] to some degree at least point to a crucial difficulty in Augustine's position. It risks drawing such a sharp and clear divide between Jesus' humanity and divinity, this physical presence and the outreach of his divine power, and with it, between the reality and the sacramental sign, that it is not in the end apparent that he has really succeeded in overcoming the problems we noticed above in Origen" (Heron, *Table and Tradition*, 73).
28. See Rowan Williams, "The Nature of Christian Formation," in *On Augustine* (London: Bloomsbury Continuum, 2016), 41–58, esp. 57. Williams himself mentions debates of interpretation and draws on Carol Harrison, *Beauty and Revelation in the Thought of Saint Augustine* (Oxford: Clarendon, 1992), esp. chapter 2.

fact that at points he explicitly "insists on the arbitrary nature of the relation of words to things."[29]

A strong division between sign and the thing signified combined with the focus on the sign as an object (as opposed to an activity) is allied in many Western sacramental theologies with the common description of sacraments as "means of grace." The sign aspect of the sacrament—the bread and wine for the Eucharist, water for baptism—is the means by which the thing (notice thing, not activity) pointed to, something called grace, is communicated. Similarly, the description of sacraments as "visible words" can suggest a similar kind of division between the visible "letter" or "word" and the invisible thing pointed to.

Leithart critiques all three of these typical ways of describing sacraments: "means of grace," "signs and symbols," and "visible words." He certainly admits that such umbrella phrases do not necessitate any particular end result; a nuanced understanding of these phrases may overcome their problematic tendencies. However, these phrases, these metaphors, and the ways of thinking upon which they are based tend to push one's sacramental theology in certain directions.

All these typical ways of describing sacraments have the tendency to reduce the sign, means, or visible part "to a secondary and somewhat unfortunate necessity."[30] Augustine even at one point suggests that "there is no necessity of chewing and digesting. Believe, and you have eaten (*crede, et manducasti*)."[31] The connection between the heavenly and earthly realities can seem a bit arbitrary, as Heron points out: "This is perhaps the fundamental problem to be faced by any approach to the Eucharist via the category of 'sign': there is always the danger that the two sides thus correlated, the physical and the spiritual, visible and invisible, may appear to fall apart—or, what is little better, to be held together only in a quite arbitrary fashion."[32] Such a division even raises the question, Is the Eucharist itself really all that important? Historically, the

---

29. Williams, "Nature of Christian Formation," 42.

30. Liethart, "Conjugating the Rites," 137.

31. Augustine, *Tractates on the Gospel of John*, 25.12. Cited in Heron, *Table and Tradition*, 71.

32. Heron, *Table and Tradition*, 73. Heron argues that Augustine was not very successful in holding these two together, especially given his Platonic and neo-Platonic frameworks of thought (73).

infrequency with which Protestants have celebrated it suggests that they have thought not.

Besides this problematic relationship between creaturely sign and divine reality, the sign of the sacrament is often reduced to simply the bread and wine. This further obscures the understanding that the rite itself is a symbolic way of personally communicating with God.

And finally, the "thing" communicated often is reduced to a single depersonalized entity. The dynamic is easy to spot: if you understand sacraments as visible signs of invisible grace or as a means of grace, there is a tendency to see "grace" in terms of a sub-personal thing which is communicated through the sign object—as opposed to a renewed relationship with a personal God which includes a union with the full personal humanity of Christ through the power of the Spirit. As T. F. Torrance writes, grace "came to be thought of in sub-personal fashion as pneumatic power."[33] Such a grace—whether the Holy Spirit himself or an infused principle of charity[34]—is thought to be given to us through the channel of the signs of bread and wine. Hugh of St. Victor famously compared the grace we receive in the sacrament to a liquid in a vessel.[35] Similarly to how we drink wine, we "drink" grace. Some "thing" fills us and changes us. Other eucharistic theologies have emphasized that the "substance" of Christ's body and blood saves us, where his "substance" is talked about as if it is a sub-personal thing. This is the thing communicated through the creaturely signs of bread and wine.

Certainly theologians have understood these problems and have posited nuanced understandings of "substance" and "grace" that avoid them; however, the recurrent misunderstandings at least raise the question whether these umbrella phrases and frameworks are the best tools to explain what is happening.

For example, Thomas Aquinas as well as the leading Reformation figures, Luther, Zwingli, and Calvin, all sought to push back against the tendency to depersonalize "substance" and "grace" within Western sacramental theology.

---

33. T. F. Torrance, *The Doctrine of Grace in the Apostolic Fathers* (Edinburgh: Oliver & Boyd, 1948), 140. Cited also in Leithart, "Embracing Ritual," 9n11.

34. For discussion, see Geertjan Zuijdwegt, "'*Utrum Caritas Sit Aliquid Creatum in Anima*': Aquinas on the Lombard's Identification of Charity with the Holy Spirit," *Recherches de Théologie et Philosophie Médiévales* 79 (2012): 39–74.

35. *On the Sacraments of the Christian Faith* 1.9.4.

They all sought to emphasize that in the sacraments we are encountering the whole person of Christ and not simply a power or thing. Max Thurian argues that the basic emphasis in Thomas's teaching about transubstantiation is the reality of the presence of Christ. He writes, "The dogma of transubstantiation has a protective and defensive purpose," namely, "to express the mystery of the real presence [of the person of Christ] in an understandable way to the men of this period."[36] But in his appropriate efforts to contextualize Christian doctrine, the categories he used for thinking about the sacraments hindered him. As a result, Thurian argues that Thomas sometimes "deprived certain truths of their proper evangelical savor, substituting insipid Aristotelianism."[37]

Likewise, Leithart argues that in spite of the fact that all these figures wanted to maintain that we are encountering the whole person of Christ, the categories used (i.e., *signum* and *res* as well as the more specific categories used in transubstantiation) were unwieldy and created problems for such affirmations.

Of these Reformation figures, Leithart argues that Calvin most genuinely broke with such unhelpful ways. Calvin emphasized that in the Eucharist we are encountering and being united to the personal presence of Christ: "Calvin was challenging, in a more fundamental way than Luther had done, the liturgical and religious straightjacket in which the scholastic framework had bound Eucharistic theology. For Calvin, the Supper is not a theatrical miracle at which the people of God are spectators, but a living encounter with the glorious person of the ascended Christ."[38] I agree. And for Calvin, a central point of this encounter at the Supper is that through the Spirit we are united to or participate in the *life* and righteousness of Christ, a life renewed in Christ's humanity.

"Life" is a word that Calvin often uses to describe the point of the sacrament. For example, he writes: "The flesh of Christ is like a rich and inexhaustible fountain that pours into us the life springing forth from the Godhead into itself. Now who does not see that communion of Christ's flesh and blood is

36. Max Thurian, "Toward a Renewal of the Doctrine of Transubstantiation," in *Christianity Divided*, ed. D. J. Callahan (New York: Sheed & Ward, 1961), 197–98.

37. Thurian, "Toward a Renewal," 198. Cited in Leithart, "What's Wrong with Transubstantiation," 298n13.

38. Leithart, "What's Wrong with Transubstantiation," 318. And again, "Calvin's emphasis was on the presence of Christ in the communion, rather than the presence of Christ in the elements" (322).

necessary for all who aspire to heavenly life?"[39] And similarly, "The flesh of Christ gives life . . . the same flesh breathes life into us, or to express it more briefly, because ingrafted into the body of Christ by the secret agency of the Spirit we have life in common with him. For from the hidden fountain of the Godhead life was miraculously infused into the body of Christ, that it might flow from thence to us."[40]

Life—meaning a way of human life filled with intentions and relationships, empowered by the Spirit, shaped according to the patterns of the Word, to the glory of the Father, roughly sketched in the Law, incarnated in Christ, flowing from heaven to earth through the Eucharist like a stream of life-giving water. This image of heavenly life flowing from the Godhead into the earth through the humanity of Christ, through the Eucharist, is common in Calvin. It begins to answer the question raised earlier: What is God here to do? This image and this question also open up another temple theme: that in the Eucharist, the kingdom of God meets and flows into the earth.

The Kingdom Meets and Breaks into the Earth in the Eucharist

In addition to God's real and personal presence, a second renewed emphasis in eucharistic theology is the in-breaking of the kingdom of God into the world. This was a central meaning of the temple, and so such an understanding makes sense given that in the Eucharist, the church becomes a new spiritual temple.

But what is the kingdom of God? While this question can and should be debated, I have come to appreciate the way that Nicholas Wolterstorff talks about the kingdom of God by drawing upon the biblical image of shalom. This image of shalom, rooted as it is in the Old Testament, is especially appropriate to the understanding of the kingdom of God as it is linked with the temple.[41] Wolterstorff defines shalom as a picture of the world that is marked

39. John Calvin, *Institutes of the Christian Religion*, Library of Christian Classics 20, ed. John T. McNeill (Philadelphia: Westminster Press, 1960), 4.17.9.

40. "Exposition of Heads of Agreement," in *Calvin's Tracts and Letters* (Carlisle, PA: Banner of Truth, 2009), 2:238. See also larger discussion in Charles Partee, *The Theology of John Calvin* (Louisville: Westminster John Knox, 2010), 271–89.

41. Ulrich Mauser, *The Gospel of Peace: A Scriptural Message for Today's World* (Louisville: Westminster John Knox, 1992), argues that the idea of shalom is an important but underappreciated part of the New Testament as well.

above all by the quality of the relationships of creatures with one another and God. Shalom involves humans "dwelling at peace in all their relationships: with God, with self, with fellows, with nature."[42] As Wolterstorff describes it, these relationships of shalom are first of all relationships of justice—where each is given their due. Shalom does not stop with justice, but includes relationships of love. He defines *agapē*, the most important Greek word for love in the New Testament—somewhat against the stream, but convincingly—as care, as a positive and willful care for the other. But shalom does not even stop with love/care; it also includes delight. Delight means taking positive pleasure and joy in the other. Shalom "is perfected when humanity acknowledges that in its service of God is true delight."[43]

To these three, I would add and perhaps start with wisdom. Shalom involves creatures wisely participating in the creational cycles set up by God in such a way that creatures flourish with life and health in ways appropriate to each creature. Squirrels, trees, skin, ants, and people all can be "wise" in their own way. Such creaturely wisdom is often pointed to in the book of Proverbs. Wisdom is also related to the Old Testament distinction between clean and unclean—clean, unblemished people and animals represent this kind of wise participation in God's creational order that leads to flourishing.[44]

In the Eucharist, the in-breaking kingdom is revealed in the interactions between the gathered people and God, within themselves, with one another, and with nature that wisdom, justice, love, and delight. These interactions also imply the people involved have the related virtues, namely, wisdom, justice, love, and joy.

Given this understanding of the kingdom of God, how does it break into our world in the Eucharist? An important part of the answer is that it does so precisely as the creaturely dimensions of the Eucharist—the people, their activities, and other elements such as bread, wine, and other offerings—are taken up, empowered, and shaped by Word and Spirit into fitting symbols of those kingdom patterns and relationships.

Within twentieth- and twenty-first-century theology, such a way of viewing the Eucharist richly connects with many proposals for eucharistic reform.

42. Nicholas Wolterstorff, *Until Justice and Peace Embrace: The Kuyper Lectures for 1981 Delivered at the Free University of Amsterdam* (Grand Rapids: Eerdmans, 1983), 69.
43. Wolterstorff, *Until Justice and Peace Embrace*, 70.
44. More will be said about this in the following chapter.

Below we will consider such contributions by Alexander Schmemann, the ecumenical scholar Alasdair Heron, the ecumenical document *Baptism, Eucharist and Ministry*, Vatican II documents, and the analyses of early church worship by the liturgical scholar Paul Bradshaw. We will also consider reasons this understanding of the Eucharist has been obscured in the West.

Let us begin with the work and proposals of Alexander Schmemann (1921–1983). He was born in Estonia, became a Russian Orthodox priest, taught in Paris from 1946 to 1951 at the St. Sergius Institute and spent the final part of his career at St. Vladimir's Seminary in New York. His work in liturgical theology has influenced and inspired many, not only within Eastern Orthodoxy but also within the Protestant and Roman Catholic worlds. A major desire of his was to reform and renew Orthodox worship by stripping away some of its excesses in order to reveal its true inner structure, a structure rooted in the worship and theology of the early church, while at the same time showing its great relevance and ethical import for our contemporary world.

A key critique Schmemann makes of the Western sacramental tradition is the way signs and symbols are understood—similar to the critiques Leithart levels. In perhaps his most well-known book, *For the Life of the World: Sacraments and Orthodoxy*, he argues that the West has created a problematic dichotomy between what is considered real and what is considered symbolic. He suggests this division was first "provoked by the encounter of Christianity with Hellenism." In the eucharistic debates of the twelfth century we see this division further solidifying as Christ's presence was argued to be *either* real *or* symbolic.[45] He argues that in the modern world, this division finally metastasized into secularism—an age in which there is a very strict division between what is natural and what is supernatural.[46]

For Schmemann, the real things Christians encounter in the Eucharist are God and God's kingdom, the heavenly realm where God dwells. He argues that the early church understood the things and actions of Christians in their

---

45. Schmemann, *For the Life of the World: Sacraments and Orthodoxy* (Crestwood, NY: St. Vladimir's Seminary Press, 2000), 135–36.

46. Schmemann, *For the Life of the World*, 128–29. He also sees the Thomistic distinction between *causa prima* and *causae secundae* as a cause of secularism (129). I would argue instead we should keep the distinction, but understand that some secondary causes can also shine with and participate in the forms of the Word through the power of the Spirit.

worship, in their liturgy, as symbolic. But they understood "symbolic" to mean that the realities of the kingdom are revealed by and in some way overlap with those symbolic things and practices. Schmemann uses the word "sacrament" to refer to things and practices in which this overlap or transparency between heaven and earth occurs and in which kingdom realities are revealed in earthly things. For Schmemann, what are often called sacramental signs are not arbitrarily connected to kingdom realities.

It is not difficult to see that what Schmemann is arguing for bears strong analogies to how the Israelites viewed the temple. In the temple, and for Schmemann in the Eucharist, heaven and earth meet in this way.

Schmemann speaks of the natural sacramentality of all things—all things bear in themselves part of the Word by which all was created. And so the world has a kind of sacramental structure, of which the sacraments of the church are special instances.[47] But the symbols and thus sacraments in the Eucharist are above all intentional actions or patterns of activity.[48] While he does not stress this as a separate point, his discussion of the meaning of the word "liturgy" demonstrates his focus on activity: "It meant an action by which a group of people become something corporately which they had not been." He goes on to say, "It also meant a function or 'ministry' of a man or of a group."[49] In both *For the Life of the World* and *The Eucharist* the sacraments named are specific parts of the liturgy, specific intentional activities.

Such activities are ways of living and acting that are symbols of life in the kingdom of God. In fact, Schmemann uses the word "life" in his title and throughout his book to point to a pattern of activity, a way of life, energized by the Spirit and patterned on God's own life as embodied in Christ. Later in

47. Schmemann, *For the Life of the World*, 139–42. See discussion of this aspect of Schmemann in David Schindler, "'In the Beginning Was the Word': Mercy as a 'Reality Illuminated by Reason,'" *Communio* 41 (2014): 759–62.

48. I say "above all" because he does, rightly to my mind, also hold out the possibility of things, such as holy water, being sacraments, in so far as they find their proper function within a larger order or pattern of activity in which God and God's kingdom are revealed. For example, he writes, "By being restored through the blessing to its proper function, the 'holy water' is revealed as the true, full, adequate water, and matter becomes again means of communion with and knowledge of God" (Schmemann, *For the Life of the World*, 132). But such illustrations tend to obscure the point of Christian sacraments such as baptism and Eucharist—the goal is that people, not objects, become real symbols.

49. Schmemann, *For the Life of the World*, 25.

his concluding section of another essay in *For the Life of the World*, "Symbol and Sacrament," we get perhaps his clearest statement about this point: "The proper function of the *'leitourgia'* [the liturgy of the Eucharist] has always been to *bring together*, within one symbol, the three levels of the Christian faith and life: the Church, the world, and the Kingdom; that the Church herself is thus the sacrament in which the broken, yet still 'symbolical,' life of 'this world' is brought, in Christ and by Christ, into the dimension of the Kingdom of God, becoming itself the sacrament of the 'world to come' . . . the Temple of the Holy Spirit."[50]

Thus, there are two related points of reform. First, Western sacramental theology has not understood sacramental signs and symbols to be those "things" in and through which the kingdom of God is revealed. Instead they have forgotten this kind of intimate relationship between our liturgical signs and the kingdom itself. Second, the most important sacramental signs are not merely objects, but rather the intentional actions and relationships of humans and God that together compose the liturgy. In its liturgy, the church itself, shaped into the patterns of the Word through the power of the Spirit, manifests the kingdom of God in its symbolic activity in the presence of God.

In *The Eucharist: Sacrament of the Kingdom*, Schmemann names many "sacraments" that are part of the eucharistic liturgy (which includes everything from the gathering of the people to their sending back into the world). Among them are the sacrament of the Word (God speaks through the reading, preaching, and hearing of Scripture), the sacrament of the offering (putting gifts into the offering baskets or plates and presenting these and bread and wine to God), the sacrament of thanksgiving (the beginning of the eucharistic prayer), the sacrament of remembrance (another part of the eucharistic prayer), the sacrament of the Holy Spirit (this refers to the calling on and receiving of the Holy Spirit in the Eucharist), and the sacrament of communion (the actual partaking of bread and wine).[51] In each of these, the sacramental "elements" he highlights most clearly are the activities in which the people interact with God and each other. For example, by calling the offering a sacrament, Schmemann argues that as humans offer up gifts to God, the kingdom of God is present and

---

50. Schmemann, *For the Life of the World*, 151.
51. Alexander Schmemann, *The Eucharist: Sacrament of the Kingdom* (Crestwood, NY: St. Vladimir's Seminary Press, 2003), 5.

revealed. Offering up our gifts, tithes, talents, and selves to God is an activity in which those who are present at the liturgy are caught up into and joined together with heavenly patterns of being and acting.

Schmemann's central point, that in the Christian eucharistic liturgy the kingdom of God is extended into the earth as heaven and earth meet, has clear analogies to a central meaning of the temple. As we will see in the following chapters, under the pressure of the major celebrations and feasts at the temple, I arrive at a list of central meanings of the Eucharist that are only slightly different from Schmemann's *The Eucharist.*

Other twentieth-century proposals for eucharistic reform have also focused on the church's actions in the Eucharist.

For example, Alasdair Heron, a Reformed theologian involved in ecumenical work, in *Table and Tradition: Toward an Ecumenical Understanding of the Eucharist,* structures the central meanings of the Eucharist around the activities of offering, *anamnesis* (remembering), and *epiclesis* (calling upon God). All of these are seen as fitting human responses to God's prior activity—human actions that correspond to divine actions. Heron's framework explicitly names human activities (offering, remembering, calling upon), yet implies a series of paired interactions between God and God's people. He finds this framework in early church traditions. As he comments on *The Apostolic Tradition* of Hippolytus:

> Just as the Jewish thanksgiving for bread was not a prayer for blessing *on the bread,* but one of praise *to God* who gives food, so too here attention is not concentrated chiefly upon the bread and wine, nor indeed on what the speaker and the congregation are doing, but on what *God has done.* . . . In *anamnesis,* the church looks back to Christ and sets its own offering of bread and wine in the context of that remembrance; in *epiclesis,* it asks for the gift of the Holy Spirit to take hold of both of the elements and of the worshippers. . . . These two moments are thus integrated within the overall pattern which centres on the mighty acts of God in Christ. We shall see later how subsequent liturgical developments in the West tended to fragment and disrupt this framework.[52]

52. Heron, *Table and Tradition,* 63. While I agree with Heron's emphasis on God's activity in relation to God's people, I think Heron's statement can be improved. The eucharistic prayer of *The Apostolic Tradition* and other early eucharistic prayers are not

Such a framework for understanding the Eucharist as a multifaceted response to what God has done, a response involving interactions with God and each other, is also found in *Baptism, Eucharist and Ministry*, hereafter *BEM*.[53] *BEM* is perhaps the most important ecumenical document of the twentieth century. In that document five "aspects" or "meanings" of the Eucharist structure its understanding. All these are spoken of as aspects of the one complex gift which God has given us: "The eucharist is essentially the sacrament of the gift which God makes to us in Christ through the power of the Holy Spirit."[54] The Eucharist is to be seen and celebrated as "Thanksgiving to the Father," "Anamnesis or Memorial of Christ," "Invocation of the Spirit," "Communion of the Faithful," and "Meal of the Kingdom."[55]

Here again it is the responses to and transactions between God and his people in the Eucharist that are the key to its meaning. This emphasis is quite different from traditional debates about the "meaning" of communion in the form of how and if Christ's body is present.

As far as the structure of the five meanings, they have a Trinity-church-kingdom flow. In the detailed explanations of each of those aspects we get the sense they somewhat parallel God's redemptive history. Father, Son, and Holy Spirit act, the church is brought into communion with God and each other, all with the goal of anticipating and welcoming the coming kingdom.

While I deeply appreciate this document, I do have a few points of concern. First, it is not clear how the five aspects and "the gift" of Christ through the Spirit are related to one another. If one understands the gift to be God's self-constitution as triune, plus the gift of creation, plus the gift of God's relationship to Israel and the Church through Christ and the Spirit, then perhaps all are related, but these connections are not clarified. Second, I do not think those five meanings reflect some of the most central meanings of the Eucharist as well as they might, especially the theme of the new covenant. Christ's words, "This cup is the new covenant in my blood" (1 Cor. 11:25; cf. Luke 22:20) or

---

structured around only what "God has done," but what God has done, is doing, and will do. Human activity is a fitting response to divine activity in past, present, and future.

53. World Council of Churches, *Baptism, Eucharist and Ministry*, Faith and Order Paper No. 111 (Geneva: World Council of Churches, 1982).

54. *BEM*, Eucharist II.2.

55. These are the titles of sub-sections II.A, B, C, D, and E that are part of section II, "The Meaning of the Eucharist."

"my blood of the [new] covenant" (Matt. 26:28; Mark 14:24; some manuscripts have "new"), place the covenant theme at the center of the celebration. Accordingly the covenant should be emphasized more in our understanding of and teaching about the Eucharist.[56] I also think the flow of God's activities in redemptive history, including the people of Israel, should be made more transparent. And finally, there is not a clearly given rationale for approaching the idea of meaning or aspect in this way, nor are the meta-reasons given for those five meanings or interactions with God rather than others. Certainly each of those five aspects on their own makes sense in light of both Scripture and tradition, and I understand the limitations of a document such as this, but the reasons for the overall thought patterns could and should be made clearer.

Nevertheless, the fact that the meanings of the Eucharist are intentional interactions is quite important to note. My own list of central meanings based on the temple shares much in common with *BEM*.

Within *BEM* one can discern another important feature. The Eucharist not only involves important interactions between God and the people, but also important interactions among the people. A community is being revealed and formed in, under, and through the horizontal interactions between and relationships within the gathered community. In these interactions and relationships, the kingdom of God is being symbolized and revealed. In the words of *BEM*, the Eucharist is not only a communion between individuals and God, but also "the communion of the faithful," a communion "within . . . the Church."[57]

Such an emphasis on the revelation and formation of the community of the church is another important feature of many proposals for reform within twentieth-century Eucharist theology, proposals that come from quite divergent corners of the church and larger academy.

In one of these corners is the work of several important Roman Catholic theologians who laid the groundwork for Vatican II, culminating in the official documents of Vatican II themselves, above all *Lumen Gentium*, the Dogmatic Constitution on the Church. In this groundbreaking document, official Roman Catholic ecclesiology is set forth.

---

56. For this critique, see John Witvliet, "Covenant Theology in Ecumenical Discussions of the Lord's Supper," in *Worship Seeking Understanding* (Grand Rapids: Baker Academic, 2003), 67–90.

57. *BEM*, Eucharist II. D.19.

Lumen Gentium emphasizes that the Eucharist is bound up with the formation of the visible yet mystical community, the church. In the church community the life of the kingdom of God is revealed, witnessed to, and partially manifested. In the opening paragraph, it declares, "The Church is in Christ like a sacrament or as a sign and instrument both of a very closely knit union with God and of the unity of the whole human race."[58] The linking of vertical and horizontal dimensions, that in the Eucharist both union with God and unity within the church and even within the whole human community are both manifested and brought about, is a leitmotif throughout.

In this way *Lumen Gentium* corrects an all-too-common tendency in the traditions of the West to see the Eucharist as having little to do with the church community. It has often been seen primarily as an action, a sacrifice, that is performed by the priest. As a result, the laity have often merely viewed the Eucharist rather than participated in it. In *Sacrosanctum Concilium*, the Constitution on the Sacred Liturgy, a sister document that brought about many sweeping changes to eucharistic practice, this older tendency is explicitly combatted. *Sacrosanctum Concilium* encourages active and conscious participation of everyone, "not . . . as strangers or silent spectators."[59] They participate in order that "they should be drawn day by day into ever more perfect union with God and with each other."[60] Many reforms to various parts of the liturgy were proposed in order that the people could more actively participate in the texts and rites, in order that they might "understand them with ease and take part in them fully, actively, and as befits a community."[61]

In *Lumen Gentium*, the Church is explicitly pictured as the community in which the kingdom of God is inaugurated and begins to take shape: "The Church, or, in other words, the kingdom of Christ now present in mystery, grows visibly through the power of God in the world."[62] The Eucharist is in part an instrument and sign of this unity: "In the sacrament of the eucharistic

58. Second Vatican Council, "Dogmatic Constitution on the Church, Lumen gentium, 21 November, 1964," in Flannery, *Vatican Council II*, sec. 1 (hereafter cited as *LG*).
59. Second Vatican Council, "Constitution on the Sacred Liturgy, Sacrosanctum concilium, 4 December, 1963," in Flannery, *Vatican Council II*, sec. 48 (hereafter cited as *SC*).
60. *SC*, sec. 48.
61. *SC*, sec. 21.
62. *LG*, sec. 3.

bread, the unity of all believers who form one body in Christ is both expressed and brought about."[63]

Thus, the kingdom of God is seen in, first, the unity of the church. This unity is revealed and symbolized as the church actively partakes of the Eucharist together. The church is "the visible sacrament of this saving unity."[64] Guided by the four adjectives that describe the church in the Nicene Creed ("one, holy, Catholic, and apostolic"), this kingdom is also seen in the holiness of the church, a holiness that consists in part "in the fruits of grace which the Spirit produces in the faithful,"[65] a holiness that takes its primary shape from the life of Christ, "the Model of all perfection."[66]

In pointing out that the church is a mystical body created through the union of humans with the triune God and each other, and that the Eucharist is both a sign of and an instrument of this community, the framers of Vatican II realized that they were recovering emphases that had not been prominent for centuries; however, these emphases were true to the practice and theology of the early church: "Our Constitution restores strength to a doctrine that is central in our faith, a doctrine which the Latin tradition has received from the Fathers and on which it had long insisted, which St. Thomas accepted when he said that the mystical body, the Church, is the *res* of the eucharist; in recent centuries it has become less prominent."[67]

The unified and holy church is the *res*, the real thing that the sacrament manifests—I find that to be an amazing statement. How such unity and holiness of the church are seen and modeled in the celebration of the Eucharist is not elaborated on in depth, yet it is quite significant that *Lumen Gentium* focuses on the community of the people of God, and even the "common priesthood of all the people of God."[68]

---

63. *LG*, sec. 3.
64. *LG*, sec. 9.
65. *LG*, sec. 39.
66. *LG*, sec. 40.
67. Henri de Lubac, S. J., "Lumen Gentium and the Fathers," in *Vatican II: An Interfaith Appraisal* (Notre Dame: University of Notre Dame Press, 1966), 156. He cites various texts from Aquinas's *Summa Theologia*, including 3.73.2–3. These connections between the document and the larger theological movements of the twentieth century are also highlighted in the chapter by Canon Charles Moeller, "History of Lumen Gentium's Structure and Ideas," in *Vatican II*, 123–52.
68. *LG*, sec. 10.

This emphasis on the importance of the eucharistic community, and more specifically on the kinds of relationships and interactions manifested between the gathered people, is similarly stressed in discussions about the origins of the Eucharist by New Testament and liturgical scholars.

Paul Bradshaw, a contemporary liturgical scholar, has critiqued a common way of narrating the origins of the Eucharist.[69] In this common way of telling the story, a single highly standardized eucharistic practice developed early on in the Christian church. This fairly uniform practice was based on Christ's words and actions at the Last Supper. Bradshaw calls this "the Dixian hypothesis" after Dom Gregory Dix. Dix was instrumental in making this the standard story through his influential book *The Shape of the Liturgy*.[70] Bradshaw argues in numerous books and essays that instead there were at least two points of origin, the meal ministry of Jesus and the Last Supper. Drawing from John's Gospel, the *Didache*, Ignatius of Antioch, Justin Martyr, and Irenaeus, he argues that some parts of early Christianity understood their eucharistic meals not against the background of "the Last Supper nor . . . the impending passion,"[71] but rather the meal ministry of Jesus. Christ's life-giving "flesh" rather than sacrificed "body" was being remembered, and "an eschatological anticipation of God's Kingdom" was being celebrated, one in which "the hungry are fed" and in which "tax-collectors and sinners" are being welcomed.[72]

Bradshaw argues that the loss of this other emphasis over time, especially as eucharistic liturgies became more standardized in the fourth and fifth centuries, led in part to a decrease in the frequency of reception of the elements of bread and wine by members of the church. The greater emphasis on the "sacrifice" of the Eucharist accomplished by the priest in remembrance of the sacrifice of Christ's "body" made the reception and co-celebration of the people less central. As Bradshaw puts it, there was "a disproportionate emphasis, if you like, on altar rather than table."[73]

Bradshaw and others have done a great service by pointing out the variety of emphases and eucharistic themes in these early Christian sources, the strong ties of these eucharistic theologies to the in-breaking of the kingdom

69. Bradshaw, *Eucharistic Origins; Reconstructing Early Christian Worship.*
70. Bradshaw, *Eucharistic Origins*, viii.
71. Bradshaw, *Eucharistic Origins*, 9.
72. Bradshaw, *Eucharistic Origins*, 18–19.
73. Bradshaw, *Eucharistic Origins*, 19.

of God in the meal celebrated by all, as well as the ways this in-breaking of the kingdom was seen in and in part modeled on the meal ministry of Jesus. However, the interpretation of "sacrifice" and the implied contrasts between altar and table present in these proposals are problematic. Was it not at the temple that the greatest feasts of Israel were joyfully celebrated around the altar of sacrifice? Were not the new ways of covenant life celebrated through the sacrifices of *Shavuot*—a life characterized by the inclusion of outcasts and oppressed classes such as the "resident alien" (cf. Exod. 23:9) and by remembrance of the feeding ministry of God (God "fed [them] in the wilderness" [Deut. 8:16])? And do not almost all of the patristic sources mentioned—the *Didache*, Ignatius, Irenaeus—see the Eucharist as typologically linked to the worship of the temple?

The points Bradshaw and others make by linking the Eucharist to the meals and feasts of Jesus during his ministry themselves echo and fulfill the main feasts of the temple. Rather than setting altar and table in opposition, Jesus in his life as well as sacrificial death fulfills the several meanings of the temple and its principal feasts—all celebrated around the temple's altar-table. No need to oppose these emphases; one should simply include them in a larger whole. All this will be argued more extensively in the chapters below on the feasts of *Shavuot* and *Sukkot*.

That being said, Bradshaw and others rightly draw our attention to these neglected themes that characterize Jesus's meal ministry.[74]

These emphases on the formation and revelation of a new covenant community in the Eucharist also resonate with important work done by biblical scholars on a much disputed eucharistic passage, 1 Cor. 11:27–29. Paul, directly after handing on what are called the words of institution (1 Cor. 11:23–26), warns the Corinthian congregation not to eat the bread or drink the cup "in an unworthy manner" and warns them that those "who eat and drink without discerning the body, eat and drink judgment against themselves." In many traditions, such warnings were understood as Paul telling people that they must have a proper understanding of Christ's bodily presence within the eucharistic elements in order to partake worthily. But starting with Gerd Theissen's im-

---

74. These recovered emphases are in fact picked up in *BEM* in the opening section, "The Institution of the Eucharist," which connects the meal ministry of Jesus and the "fellowship of the Kingdom" to "the imminence of Jesus' suffering." *BEM*, Eucharist 1.1.

portant 1974 article on the passage,[75] scholars have become more and more convinced the "body" Paul speaks of here is that of the community as the body of Christ (cf. 1 Cor. 12). Paul is addressing their activity which reveals and furthers social divisions within the body, namely, the divisive practice of the rich of the Corinthian congregation eating separately, more sumptuously, and before the poor of the congregation (cf. 1 Cor. 11:17–22).[76] Eating the supper worthily involves understanding and acting in a way fitting the communal and ethical implications of the supper.

So, how do these emphases—which come from quite different scholarly directions—find places within this way of seeing the Eucharist as a "new temple"? They all helpfully point to the communal and ethical aspects of the kingdom of God and life of the new covenant community that are being revealed in the eucharistic rite. This kingdom of God does not consist of a disembodied individual spiritual experience between the believer and God. No. It is a kingdom in which God's shalom is extended into the earth, resulting in renewed relationships of the gathered people with God, with each other, and even with the nonhuman creation. As the kingdom comes and is revealed in a preliminary way, it consists of a new covenant way of life as a community, as the Body of Christ, which takes the form of the visible church in this life before Christ's second coming. This community is one in which "tax collectors and sinners" are welcomed (Luke 5:29–32), and in which the walls between classes, genders, and people groups are visibly broken down (Gal. 3:27–29; cf. 1 Cor. 11:21–22, 27–29). The central symbol of this community is the eucharistic feast in which all eat together before and with God in unity, holiness, and shalom, in which they, as a new spiritual temple, form a community in which God is present and God's kingdom meets and breaks into the earth.

Typical Ways Connections to the Kingdom of God Have Been Obscured

Typical ways that sacraments have been spoken of in the West not only tend to obscure the "personal" nature of God's presence, but also tend to obscure connections to the kingdom of God. As pointed out above, questions about

75. Gerd Theissen, "Soziale Integration und sakramentales Handeln: Eine Analyse von 1 Cor 11:17–34," *Novum Testamentum* 16 (1974): 179–206.

76. This has now become a standard interpretation in many, if not most, of the standard scholarly commentaries.

presence in the Western eucharistic tradition have centered not so much on the personal presence of God as God interacts with persons of the community in the eucharistic celebration, but on the real and local presence of Christ's body and blood, their substance, or alternatively, the invisible grace being given, and its relationship to the eucharistic elements of bread and wine. Those elements become means of grace or means of partaking of the substance of Christ. The substance or grace received is often limited to a kind of interior reality. In this way, the gracious coming of the kingdom of God in the Eucharist is often missed.[77]

In many Protestant traditions, the grace of the Eucharist is talked about as "Christ and his benefits." One could interpret that phrase quite broadly: given that Christ is the kingdom in himself, if a person receives Christ, they receive the kingdom. But this expansive understanding of Christ and his benefits is not typical. The connection between *the celebration of the sacrament* and *the in-breaking of the kingdom of God* is certainly not prominent.

Take for example the *Westminster Confession of Faith*, an influential document within many Protestant traditions such as my own Presbyterian tradition. In it the new covenant of grace is explained using the following images: "Under the gospel, when Christ, the substance [Col. 2:17], was exhibited, the ordinances in which this covenant is dispensed are the preaching of the Word, and the administration of the sacraments of baptism and the Lord's Supper."[78]

While this statement can be interpreted in a variety of ways, its images tend toward the problems of "de-personalized" and "de-kingdomized" grace that are being highlighted here. In this passage, Christ is called "the substance" of the new covenant which is "dispensed" to us through word and sacrament. Such wording is difficult to relate to the idea that in the Eucharist the kingdom of God is breaking in. Instead, it is more readily interpreted as meaning that in

---

77. Leithart ties the tendency to imagine grace as an interior reality to Augustine's ways of understanding signs: "In *de Magistro, de doctrina Christiana,* and Book 15 of *de Trinitate,* Augustine imports questionable notions into his definitions of *signum* that have the double effect, when applied to sacramental theology, of reducing the sign to a secondary and somewhat unfortunate necessity and, conversely, of interiorizing the 'thing' or reality signified by the sacrament." Leithart, "Conjugating the Rites," 137.

78. "Westminster Confession of Faith," in *Book of Confessions: The Consitution of the Presbyterian Church (U.S.A.) Part I* (Louisville, KY: The Office of the General Assembly, 2016), 7.6 (hereafter cited as *WCF*).

the new covenant a kind of "invisible grace" is being dispensed through word and sacrament.

Westminster even bends Scripture toward that kind of interpretation of the Eucharist. In the quote above, Colossians 2:17 is cited as background to the word "substance." But under closer inspection, this passage in Colossians calls for a different interpretation. In this section of Colossians, a typological understanding of the ceremonies of the Old Testament is evident; those ceremonies are called "shadows" (Col. 2:17). But the "substance" which these shadows point to in the Colossians passage is not precisely "Christ," but instead the substance is something which "belongs to Christ" (Col. 2:17). In the context of Colossians, this more substantial reality which belongs to Christ is a pattern of activity, a "life," a kingdom way of life (Col. 1:13; 3:4) which is contrasted with another way of life (Col. 3:7). Our rescue from the "power of darkness" to "the kingdom of his Son" forms the larger framework for the letter as a whole (Col. 1:13).[79] But these connections to this kingdom way of life do not get picked up in Westminster. Rather, the language of being "dispensed" indicates some sort of impersonal and individualized transaction, thereby obscuring these connections.

Later, when sacraments are defined in the Westminster Confession, it states, "Sacraments are holy signs and seals of the covenant of grace, immediately instituted by God, to represent Christ, and his benefits; and to confirm our interest in him."[80] But what is the substance of this covenant of grace? Different parts of the catechism link this covenant of grace to life in the kingdom of God. Receiving such signs confirms our union with Christ and leads to a nourishment for "the duties which they owe unto him,"[81] which elsewhere are considered "good works," understood as the evidence of a "true and lively faith."[82] So, by drawing from these different sections and using their terms "duties" and "good works," connections to the kingdom of God can be made in Westminster. But one must work hard to do so. Such a kingdom way of life is not explicitly considered part of the eucharistic rite or imaged in it in any

79. For a contemporary treatment of the letter in which these contrasting ways of life are emphasized, see Bryan Walsh and Sylvia Keesmaat, *Colossians Remixed: Subverting the Empire* (Downers Grove, IL: InterVarsity Press, 2004).
80. WCF, 27.1.
81. WCF, 29.1.
82. WCF, 16.2.

way. Rather, Westminster's emphasis in the explanation of the Eucharist is that "Christ and his benefits" are represented and "dispensed" to the believer.

Other examples of this disconnect between the sacrament and the kingdom in the Western tradition of sacramental theology can be multiplied.

In contrast to these common tendencies, if we see the Eucharist as a typological extension and transposition of the worship at the temple, we will instead see the Eucharist as a rite in which several kinds of personal interactions between God and God's people take place. These interactions are activities in, under, and through which the life of the kingdom of God is revealed and embodied. As will be elaborated in the following chapters, we will focus on the sacrifice of thanksgiving and offering made by the community to God in partial fulfillment of our calling as the human priests of all creation—this is the "substance" of the daily, weekly and monthly temple liturgies. We will focus on our remembrance in the presence of God of the great Passover sacrifice of Christ—this is the "substance" of the feast of Passover. We will focus on God's action to unite the community together and to himself in Christ through the Holy Spirit as we open ourselves anew to the realities of this new covenant relationship, one that was opened to us at Pentecost—this is the "substance" of the temple feast of Pentecost. And we will also focus on our celebration of this eucharistic feast as a kind of meal together with God, one that is a foretaste of the great feast to come—this is the "substance" of the feast of Booths. In all these different ways God is really and personally present to his people. In all these different ways, the ways of heaven are being extended into the earth, and the ways of earth are being aligned with the ways of heaven. In these activities, the earthly elements, especially the people, are becoming real figures of the worship of heaven—with the ascended Christ at the center of it all.

Conclusions

I vividly recall the first time I heard this oft-quoted line from C. S. Lewis: "I believe in Christianity as I believe that the sun has risen: not only because I see it, but because by it I see everything else."[83] It was at a Christian rock con-

---

83. C. S. Lewis, "They Asked for a Paper," in *Is Theology Poetry?* (London: Geoffrey Bles, 1962), 165.

cert when I was in high school in Los Angeles.[84] That line struck me then and has stuck with me ever since. As a young person I was trying to fit together a coherent view of the world, and like Lewis, I was finding—and to this day continue to find—that Christianity is a way of thinking and living that opens up the world and is able to make sense of it all. As Lewis writes, all the truths around us can be "fitted into" or allowed for within the Christian tradition's basic way of seeing things.[85]

There is a similar point to be made about viewing the church's eucharistic worship as a typological extension of Israel's temple worship: it throws light on so much else. In this chapter I have shown the temple's central meanings pressure one toward ways of thinking about sacraments that are not necessarily new. Others have come to similar places but by different routes. But the way the temple themes make sense of and organize these conversations is quite intellectually satisfying. It shows the "progressive" nature of this particular "research programme" of temple typology, to borrow Imre Lakatos's terminology. But the greatest virtue of temple typology is that the temple and its worship provide an expansive typological framework that grounds all these discussions in the narrative center of Scripture and in a central way that God has chosen to encounter God's people in both old and new covenants.

Having provided a foundation by considering the central meanings of the temple itself, we can now move forward to consider the central meanings of its major celebrations. Once one sees the temple as the place where God is present in a special way, present to personally encounter God's people in order to shape and form them in such a way that the ways of heaven are being extended into the earth, it raises the question: What are the central kinds of interactions that God desires with and within God's people? The answer is found in plain

---

84. Leslie Phillips, who later went by the name Sam Phillips, was singing and referred to this line as she introduced a song.

85. I have since found more sophisticated expressions of this way of thinking about truth and rationality in Alasdair MacIntyre's idea of tradition-based rationality and Imre Lakatos's methodology of scientific research programmes, but Lewis makes the point with poetic flair. Alasdair MacIntyre, "The Rationality of Traditions," in *Whose Justice? Which Rationality?* (Notre Dame: University of Notre Dame Press, 1988), 349–69. Imre Lakatos, *The Methodology of Scientific Research Programmes: Philosophical Papers, Vol. 1* (Cambridge: Cambridge University Press, 1978). These ways of thinking are powerful enough to save one from post-modern relativism and perspectivalism once one tires of the universal pretensions of much of Enlightenment-based modern thought.

sight, in the central worship rites God commanded Israel to observe in the Mosaic Covenant at Sinai: the daily, weekly, and monthly liturgies and the three yearly pilgrim feasts. These central kinds of encounter are taken on and transformed by Christ in his person, and then extended to God's new covenant people in the Eucharist.

PART THREE

Table Practices in Light of Temple Practices

6

CENTRAL PRACTICES AT THE TEMPLE

From Daily Worship to the Three Pilgrim Feasts

The catechism of the Jew is his calendar.

—Rabbi Samuel R. Hirsch

At the temple, God was present to meet with his chosen people. Further, at the temple the heavenly realms, the kingdom of God, met and broke into the earth. But what happened at those meetings? How did the kingdom of God break in? To answer these questions we must examine the central meanings of the rites and practices at the temple.

While individual Israelites did come to the temple to worship on their own and to offer offerings, prayers, petitions, and sacrifices of various kinds, what interests us here are the principle *corporate* worship rites. In these rites Israel as a whole worshipped and interacted with God. The central meanings of these principal communal worship services of the people of the Old Testament foreshadow and provide a foundation for understanding the eucharistic worship of the people of the New Testament.

These principal corporate celebrations were clearly laid out in the covenant given to Israel at Mount Sinai. Israel was commanded by God concerning these rites in several places in Scripture where that covenant is recorded: Exodus 20:22–26; 23:10–19; 29:38–46; and Leviticus 23:1–44. They are summed up again in Numbers 28:1–29:40 and Deuteronomy 16:1–17.

Which celebrations were commanded? The main ones are listed in what is called "the book of the covenant" (Exod. 24:7; 20:22–23:33), which is included

TABLE PRACTICES IN LIGHT OF TEMPLE PRACTICES

in the first part (Exod. 19–24) of all the Sinai covenant material (Exod. 19:1–Num. 10:10).[1] It is written that Moses read this earliest block of material to the people, and then after he read it, the covenant was ratified in the rite involving "the blood of the covenant" (Exod. 24:8). Following that, the leaders of Israel went up and "ate and drank" together with God (Exod. 24:11). The rest of the Sinai material elaborates on and adds to this early material.

In this book of the covenant, instructions concerning sabbatical years and Sabbath observance are given, followed by instructions for the three yearly festivals, Passover, the Feast of Weeks, and the Feast of Booths or in Hebrew, *Pesach, Shavuot,* and *Sukkot.* Thus, Sabbath rites and the three yearly festivals are at the heart of Israelite worship.[2] Sabbath worship is supplemented later in Exodus and in Numbers by commands concerning daily and monthly worship, rites which bear similar meanings to the Sabbath offerings.[3]

While there are minor variations in these foundational texts, in them we see a clear picture that Israel's corporate worship was structured around the regular daily, Sabbath, and monthly services together with the three yearly pilgrim feasts. The central meanings of these central feasts sum up many of their beliefs and structure their main regular interactions with God. As Rabbi Samuel Hirsch (d. 1888) famously put it, "The catechism of the Jew is his calendar."[4]

The formative power of this "calendar," this regular pattern of worship, must be emphasized. The worship practices of God's people formed them and gave them a "counter-imagination of the world," of who and what God, the creation, and humanity are, how they should be, and how they should relate to one another.[5] It should be reiterated that this system of practices and beliefs not

1. For source critical background, see Balentine, *Torah's Vision of Worship,* 121–22.
2. See discussion about the structure and meaning of the worship practices in the book of the covenant in Balentine, "The Liturgy of the Covenant," in *Torah's Vision of Worship,* 119–47.
3. In Exod. 29, further instructions are given concerning daily worship. In Leviticus, the various "holy convocations" (*miqra qodesh*) of Israel are given: all of Israel is commanded to come together, to "convoke," every Sabbath day and then at various points during the three great gatherings of Israel. In Numbers, the calendar of appointed feasts and the offerings to be made includes daily, Sabbath, and monthly celebrations as well as the three pilgrim feasts. Deuteronomy only lists the three pilgrim feasts.
4. Hayyim Schauss, *The Jewish Festivals: A Guide to Their History and Observance,* trans. S. Jaffe (New York: Schocken, 1962), ix.
5. Balentine, *Torah's Vision of Worship,* 31–32, 235–36.

only formed "Old Testament" people, but also Jesus and his disciples. Jesus and his disciples went to Jerusalem for the pilgrim feasts: "The Passover of the Jews was near, and Jesus went up to Jerusalem" (John 2:13). And even after Christ's death, resurrection, and ascension, new converts daily "spent much time together in the temple" (Acts 2:46). Jesus and his disciples were "good Jews." The work of Christ transforms this background system of beliefs and practices; it does not abandon it.[6]

What were the central meanings of these celebrations? In the following chapters, I will walk through the liturgy and activities of these celebrations, and then reflect on those activities in order to answer that question. Once a person gets these central meanings clearly in mind and gains a better feel for the details of these rites it becomes easier to spot how these Jewish ceremonies at the temple "rhyme" with the early Christian Eucharist. Throughout my work on this project I have often been surprised at how clear the resonances, allusions, and direct references to these temple celebrations are in early eucharistic texts and practices.

The second part of each of the following chapters examines those early church connections. And then each chapter concludes by asking how such connections might pressure our contemporary eucharistic theology and practice.

Looking in detail at these complex and beautiful rites provides a needed antidote to all-too-common reductions of the meanings of worship at the temple. Too often temple worship is reduced to one thing, sacrifice, and the meaning and purpose of sacrifice is further reduced to one thing, the forgiveness of sins. Old Testament worship is grossly misunderstood as a result. We will follow a different path.

---

6. N. T. Wright writes, "And, so as not to keep you in suspense, my somewhat unoriginal proposal is that when we look at the Spirit and worship in the New Testament we find that the early Christians believed that their Spirit-led worship was the new-covenantal form of that synagogue and Temple worship, worshipping the same creator God but filling that worship with new content relating specifically to Jesus crucified and risen—and believing (as, interestingly, did the community at Qumran) that the promised Holy Spirit was leading them in that worship." "Worship and Spirit in the New Testament," in *The Spirit in Worship—Worship in the Spirit*, ed. Teresa Berger and Bryan Spinks (Collegeville, MN: Liturgical Press, 2009), 6.

Regular Celebrations and Yearly Pilgrim Feasts

The corporate worship calendar of the temple had two main components: the regular celebrations—meaning the daily, weekly, and monthly liturgies—and the three pilgrim feasts.

These regular or ordinary rites celebrated the fundamental relationships between God and all creation, relationships and orders which are to a certain extent cyclical. Humanity, as priests of all creation, took their proper place within the regular rhythms of the world and gave voice to all the created order, lifting thanks to God for God's creation, providence, and continued sustenance. But they also prayed that the ways of God's kingdom and shalom would come more fully into our enchanted yet fragile and distorted earth and into human life and society, transforming them all into the kingdom of God. Thus there is a forward-looking, non-cyclical aspect to these celebrations; in them Israel anticipates, commits themselves to, and prays for the full realization of the coming kingdom of shalom, an event that will happen at a particular time in history. Even so, in these celebrations creation, with its regular, healthy, life-giving patterns, takes center stage.

The three pilgrim festivals, three major festival sequences when many Israelites made a pilgrimage to Jerusalem, punctuated Israel's year. In them one can see a shift of emphasis from creation to history. There is no strict dichotomy here, but rather a shift of emphasis.[7] Rather than focusing only on God's more regular creational and providential activity, they highlight the grand story of salvation and covenant between God and his chosen people.[8] These festivals mark God's action in Israel's exodus from Egypt, the covenant made at Mt. Sinai, and the journey to and anticipation of the promised land. These events

---

7. In modern thought and scholarship, however, a strong division between "nature" and "history" has often been made and should be resisted—itself being based on a dichotomy between the supposed freedom of the human spirit and the supposed determinism and regularity of the rest of "nature." See Joseph Cardinal Ratzinger, *The Spirit of the Liturgy* (San Francisco: Ignatius Press, 2000), 24–25 for statements against such strong divisions.

8. There was an older scholarly consensus that these feasts were initially nomadic feasts (the Passover) or agricultural feasts (Unleavened Bread, Weeks, Booths) which only later came to be associated with aspects of Israel's history; however, there is no evidence for this. See J. G. McConville, *Deuteronomy* (Downers Grove, IL: InterVarsity Press, 2002), 270–71. Instead, there is good evidence that Passover and Unleavened Bread are linked directly to the exodus. John Hartley, "Massot," *New International Dictionary of Old Testament Theology and Exegesis* (Grand Rapids: Zondervan, 1997), 2.1065–68.

together with the specific proper human responses related to them are the figures or types that structure Passover (*Pesach*), Pentecost (*Shavuot*), and Booths (*Sukkot*), the Jewish liturgical year, and the history of salvation. Certainly there are creational aspects of these feasts; creation is the stage upon which this redeeming and covenant history takes place and the shalom of all creation is the final goal of it. Still, in these feasts history, with its singular historical events, takes center stage.

There is a related shift of emphasis as one considers the typological connections between these temple rites, the work of Christ, and the Eucharist. In the following chapter, we will see that certain patristic authors relate the Eucharist to the regular temple liturgies, liturgies that emphasized "creational" themes. These leaders of the early church also linked the Eucharist to recurring events in Christ's ministry emphasized in the first half of the Gospels: to his miraculous feedings, meals, and healings. Those aspects of Christ's ministry highlight his concern for the regular, life-giving patterns of human life.

In contrast, other patristic writers drew typological connections between the Eucharist and the pilgrim feasts at the temple. These writers also connected the Eucharist to the more singular historical events in the last half of the Gospels: to Christ's death and resurrection, to the outpouring of the Spirit at Pentecost, and to Christ's anticipated second coming. Furthermore, these connections are often tied back to the Last Supper.

Temple typology provides one way to unite these different emphases, all of which inform the Eucharist. It unites creation and history, as well as the first and last halves of the Gospels. It will be helpful to keep these shifts of emphasis in mind when reading the following chapters.

While the central meanings of these Jewish festivals, their connections to the Eucharist in the early church, and their implications for today will be examined in detail in the coming chapters, here I provide an overall snapshot of the yearly pilgrim festival cycle at the temple. This overview of the pilgrim feasts will lead into a discussion of how the movement of their key themes is recapitulated in the accounts of the Last Supper in the New Testament.

The Pilgrim Feasts

The three yearly pilgrim feasts—*Pesach* or Passover, *Shavuot* or Pentecost, and *Sukkot* or the Feast of Booths—were central events that structured the national life of Israel. In Exodus 23:17, God commands Moses, "Three times in the year all your males shall appear before the Lord GOD." This command had a profound effect on the lives of Jews at the time of Christ. As Oskar Skarsaune writes, "This Torah commandment to visit Jerusalem on the three festivals . . . is the key to understanding life in Jerusalem in the Second Temple period."[9]

During the first century AD, approximately 5 million Jews lived in the diaspora around the Mediterranean. While not all of them fulfilled that commandment literally, all Jews did so vicariously. They participated in temple worship through the yearly half-shekel tax that was collected and sent to Jerusalem and used to fund the temple system and the corporate sacrifices. It is estimated that around one percent of the diaspora Jews would make the pilgrimage to attend a given pilgrim festival (*hag* in Hebrew). But even that small percentage would swell the population of Jerusalem to at least double its regular size. This obviously had great economic significance.[10] It also had great cultural and theological significance; the pilgrim feasts were the central means by which the theology, identity, and worldview of Israel were shaped.

These three main worship festivals centered on seven "holy convocations,"[11] times when the entire nation would gather at the temple for worship. The festivals were the highest expression of Israel's life together as a people. They formed Israel's understanding of God and their identity in part by recalling their history with their saving Lord, just as the regular liturgies centered on their relationship with God as their Creator. While there are symbolic ties to the yearly seasons and harvest calendar—for example, the Passover is appropriately celebrated in the spring, the season of new life—the ties back to Israel's history are central to their meanings.

The Passover festival—which includes the Passover sacrifice and meal, the Feast of Unleavened Bread, and the presentation of a firstfruits offering—most centrally remembers the redemption of Israel from Egypt.

The *Shavuot* festival, Pentecost, followed fifty days after the Passover firstfruits offering, just as, according to some traditions, the covenant on Sinai

---

9. Skarsaune, *In The Shadow of the Temple*, 89. The following section on the festivals draws from Stubbs, *Numbers*, 99–104, 214–26.
10. Skarsaune, *In the Shadow of the Temple*, 91.
11. See Stubbs, *Numbers*, 216.

followed fifty days after Israel's deliverance from Egypt.[12] Themes concerning the covenant are central.

Sukkot, the Feast of Booths or Tabernacles, was a festival cycle that looked forward to God's future judgment, mercy, and final victory as King. It occurred in the seventh month and was the final festival season of the year. It centered on the holy convocations of Trumpets, the Day of Atonement, and the final great feast. *Sukkot* was an eschatological festival, meaning that many of its themes and images were connected with God's coming at the close of the year or even at the close of the age. The booths themselves recalled the temporary dwellings Israel lived in during their journey to the promised land (Lev. 23:43). That historic journey became a type of Israel's continued corporate journey and each individual's journey toward God's good future for them.

The following is a calendar of these feasts with their convocations, based on the calendars in Leviticus 23, Numbers 28, and Deuteronomy 16:

Pilgrim Feast (*Hag*)	Date	Holy Convocations (*) and Assemblies
Passover (*Pesach*)	Nisan 14	Passover (*Pesach*)
	Nisan 15	*Unleavened Bread
	Nisan 15–21	Seven-day Feast of Unleavened Bread
	~Nisan 16	Offering of Omer of Firstfruits
	Nisan 21	*Final Convocation of Unleavened Bread
Pentecost (*Shavuot*)	~Sivan 6	*Pentecost or Weeks (*Shavuot*)
Booths (*Sukkot*)	Tishri 1	*Trumpets (*Rosh Hashanah*)
	Tishri 10	*Day of Atonement (*Yom Kippur*); Great Fast
	Tishri 15	*Booths (*Sukkot*)
	Tishri 15–21	Seven-day Feast of Booths
	Tishri 22	*Eighth Day Final Feast

12. This connection between covenant making and Pentecost is made explicit in the book of Jubilees and Qumran literature. It fits with timing of Israel's travels in the book of Exodus and is alluded to in the use of Pss. 50 and 81, in 2 Chr. 15 and in Acts 2. Elior, *Three Temples,* 142n22. Moshe Weinfeld, "Pentecost as Festival of the Giving of the Law," *Immanuel* 8 (1978): 7–18. Stubbs, *Numbers,* 221–222. McConville, *Deuteronomy,* 377–80.

Together, these three festival times created a sweeping portrait of God's history with and plans for Israel. Israel remembered God's deliverance of them and longed for a future and final messianic deliverance, celebrated and recommitted themselves to the goodness of God's covenants with them as a people, and prepared themselves for and anticipated the day of the Lord, a day of judgment and final atonement, which would be followed by a great banquet after the final eschatological harvest. All these meanings were common understandings of the temple and its worship for first-century Jews. Together, the three feasts formed Israel into a people of remembrance of God's gracious deliverance, covenantal communion with God, and hope.

Connections Between the Feasts and New Testament Accounts of the Last Supper

These same three central themes of the pilgrim feasts can be mapped onto the passages in the Synoptic Gospels and in 1 Corinthians that address Jesus's words at the Last Supper.

Were Jesus and the writers who recorded that event intentionally alluding to those three festivals in these passages? Perhaps they were. Or perhaps, as with the pilgrim feasts themselves, the structure of God's saving work with Israel was in the imaginative background. Whatever the case, these passages containing the words of institution bear a typological relationship to the pilgrim feasts, a relationship that ties them back to the full scope of God's saving activity with Israel symbolized and celebrated in the cycle of Israel's three pilgrim feasts.

The New Testament passages that relate those words and the details of the Last Supper are, in the Synoptic Gospels, Matthew 26:17–30, Mark 14:12–26, and Luke 22:7–39, and Paul's discussion of the Lord's Supper in 1 Corinthians 11:17–34. While more detailed comments about these passages and connections will be made in the following chapters, here I will simply chart the phrases and images in those passages that connect to the themes of each pilgrim feast and make a few introductory comments and explanations.

	Pesach themes	*Shavuot* themes	*Sukkoth* themes
Matt 26:17–30			
vv. 17–19	"Unleavened Bread" "Passover" (x3)		
v. 26	"this is my body"		
v. 28		"my blood of the covenant"	
v. 29			"never again drink …" "drink it new with you in my Father's kingdom"
v. 30			"Mount of Olives"

	Pesach themes	*Shavuot* themes	*Sukkoth* themes
Mark 14:12–26			
vv. 12–16	"Unleavened Bread" "Passover lamb is sacrificed" "Passover" (x3)		
v. 22	"this is my body"		
v. 24		"my blood of the covenant"	
v. 25			"never again drink …" "drink it new in the kingdom of God"
v. 26			"Mount of Olives"

	Pesach themes	*Shavuot* themes	*Sukkoth* themes
Luke 22:1–39			
v. 1	"Unleavened Bread" "Passover"		

	Pesach themes	Shavuot themes	Sukkoth themes
v. 7	"day of Unleavened Bread, on which the Passover lamb had to be sacrificed"		
vv. 8–13	"Passover" (x3)		
vv. 15–16	"Passover"/"before I suffer"		"I will not eat it until it is fulfilled in the kingdom of God"
v. 18			"I will not drink . . ." "until the kingdom of God comes"
v. 19	"this is my body"		
v. 20		"the new covenant in my blood"	
vv. 29–30			"I confer on you . . . a kingdom" "eat and drink . . . in my kingdom" "judging the twelve tribes"
v. 39			"Mount of Olives"
	Pesach themes	**Shavuot themes**	**Sukkoth themes**
1 Cor 11:17–34			
v. 19			"who among you are genuine"
v. 24	"this is my body that is for you"		
v. 25		"this cup is the new covenant in my blood"	

v. 26	"you proclaim the Lord's death until he comes"
vv. 27–32	"judged" "judgment"

In Matthew, Mark, and Luke, the setting of the meal is clearly the Passover festival and the meal they eat is almost certainly the Passover meal. As Matthew writes, "So the disciples did as Jesus had directed them, and they prepared the Passover meal" (Matt. 26:19; cf. Mark 14:12–16; cf. Luke 22:7–13). As mentioned above, there have been questions about the historical accuracy of this reporting, and also about whether the meal eaten was a transformed Passover or simply another meal Jesus ate with the disciples during that larger festival. Joachim Jeremias makes a strong case for the former in his appropriately-titled chapter "The Last Supper—a Passover Meal!" and provides rebuttals to various counter-arguments.[13]

But within this Passover meal, transformed into something more by Jesus, there is a reference to the "blood of the covenant" as recorded in Matthew and Mark. This is not a central Passover theme. Rather, the phrase "my blood of the covenant" refers back to the original covenant celebration on Mount Sinai.[14] When Christ says "Do this," he is asking his disciples to do something that resonates clearly with the covenant ceremony on Mount Sinai, a ceremony celebrated at *Shavuot* or Pentecost. This connection to Pentecost makes further sense of the phrase "new covenant" in Luke and 1 Corinthians, a phrase that alludes backward to the "new covenant" prophesied by Jeremiah (31:31–34)

13. Joachim Jeremias, "The Last Supper—a Passover Meal!" and "Objections," in *Eucharistic Words of Jesus*, 41–61, 62–83.

14. Jeremias tries, unsuccessfully in my opinion, to connect the phrase "the blood of the covenant" to the blood of the Passover lambs through a rather obscure rabbinic interpretation of Zech. 9:11 (Jeremias, *Eucharistic Words of Jesus*, 225–26). But the phrase most obviously connects to Exod. 24. And in Zech 9:11, the phrase "the blood of my covenant" also has Exod. 24 in the background, as Carol Meyers and Eric Meyers note: "The association of 'blood' with 'covenant' occurs elsewhere only in Exod. 24:3–8, which describes the covenant ceremony that took place at Sinai." Carol Meyers and Eric Meyers, *Zechariah 9–14*, The Anchor Bible (Garden City, NY: Doubleday, 1993), 139. Other commentators who deal with this phrase in the words of the Last Supper have little to say about how it connects to the Passover sacrifice itself.

and Ezekiel (11:14–25; 36:16–38) and forward to the figural performance of the firstfruits of that new covenant relationship being poured out at Pentecost in Acts 2:1–42.

The eucharistic words of Jesus also contain several images, phrases, and actions that point forward to the coming of the kingdom of God, a coming most fully celebrated in the Festival of Booths. The Passover celebration itself during Jesus's time anticipated the coming of the Messiah—we see this in the recitation of the Hallel Psalms and in several prayers. But the themes and images of the coming of the Lord, judgment, the Day of Atonement, and the following great banquet on the eighth day, all find their fullest expression in the Feast of Booths.

Even the Mount of Olives, which is mentioned at the end of all the synoptic accounts, is connected to the Feast of Booths. Zechariah prophesies that the Lord will come to judge and then says, "On that day his feet shall stand on the Mount of Olives" (Zech. 14:4). After the judgment, all nations shall come to Jerusalem "to keep the festival of booths" (Zech. 14:16). And on that day, "there shall no longer be traders in the house of the LORD of hosts" (Zech. 14:21). Zechariah is the only book in the Old Testament that mentions the Mount of Olives. Because of Zechariah's prophecies, the site became an important burial area for the Jews and had eschatological connotations for the New Testament writers.[15] Zechariah 14:21 as well as Jeremiah 7:11 were in the background of Jesus's temple action in the Synoptic Gospels (Matt. 21:13; Mark 11:17; Luke 19:46), the action that precipitated his death. Since the Old Testament connects the Mount of Olives to themes anticipated in the Festival of Booths, the deliberate recording that Jesus and his disciples went to the Mount of Olives after the supper might also resonate with these themes.

The movement from thankful remembrance for deliverance, to celebration of and commitment to the new covenant, to a hopeful anticipation of the coming kingdom seen in the eucharistic words of Christ is parallel to the thematic movement of the three pilgrim feasts at the temple.

There is an important result. The three pilgrim feasts encapsulate Israel's entire story of redemption, from the new birth of Israel remembered in Passover, to the giving of the Law and to the covenant commitment made at Sinai celebrated in Pentecost, to the eschatological fulfillment of the covenant promises

15. Meyers and Meyers, *Zechariah 9–14*, 420–24.

anticipated in the Feast of Booths. This entire story of Israel's redemption then becomes a type of Christ's life. The pattern is recapitulated in his exodus-like baptism in the Jordan (Passover), in his renewed teaching of Law, especially in the Sermon on the Mount, and his fulfillment of it in his life and ministry (Pentecost), and in his judgment, atoning death, and joyful resurrection in which the final end of human life is seen (Booths). And because of Christ's death and resurrection and the pouring out of the Spirit at Pentecost, other humans can also enter into that way paved by Christ. We do so first in baptism and then regularly in the Lord's Supper. This pattern can again be seen in the overall flow of the Eucharist, as well as tightly encoded in the dense collation of words and images in the "words of institution."

In the Eucharist, the full gospel is preached, and an altar call is given. The Spirit and the bride (Rev. 22:17) are present, and say "Come." The Eucharist is a fractal, a microcosm, in which the entire history of God's redemptive work with humankind is remembered, presented and entered into by those who take part in the feast.

7

FOUNDATIONAL MEANINGS OF THE DAILY, WEEKLY, AND MONTHLY CELEBRATIONS

Thanksgiving for Creation and Providence

The Eucharist is at the very center of our worship. And our sin toward the world, or the spiritual root of our pollution, lies in our refusal to view life and the world eucharistically, as a sacrament of thanksgiving, as a gift of constant communion with God on a global scale.

—Patriarch Bartholomew I, quoted in
Chryssavgis, *Cosmic Grace, Humble Prayer*

We begin our detailed exploration of the worship practices at the temple with the daily, Sabbath, and monthly rites.

There is no clear-cut biblical summary of the central meanings of these complex rites. Only disconnected bits and pieces of the daily and Sabbath celebrations at the temple are described in Scripture. So, we best understand the main liturgical movements and meanings of the daily, Sabbath, and monthly rites at the time of Christ by putting those bits and pieces in conversation with the rabbinic tractates *Tamid* and *Menahot,* and other intertestamental sources.[1] By examining these details, their core meanings become clear.

---

1. I should clarify, in line with earlier comments about rabbinic sources in chap. 2, that I am not claiming the rabbinic sources give us knowledge of the exact temple liturgies in

Daily, Sabbath, and Monthly Rituals: Foundational Meanings

Every day at the temple, morning and evening services were celebrated. They together were called the *tamid* (meaning "continual" or "perpetual" for *olah tamid*, perpetual burnt offering), and they were quite similar to one another. Preparations began well before dawn. Priests stood watch in several chambers in the temple during the night. As dawn approached, those who wished to be eligible to participate in cleaning the altar and preparing its fires would go down a staircase into the Room of Immersion, where they would immerse themselves in a pool of water, a *mikvah*. The need for everyone and everything to be ritually clean was an important part of temple worship. While it was still before dawn, the supervising priest would then gather all the priests on duty at the temple and cast lots to assign priests to each of the preparatory tasks.[2] Then the priests on duty would divide into two groups, enter into the court-yard, proceed in different directions around it, and check to make sure all the vessels and utensils for the morning rites were in order. They would then meet at the place where the *chavitim* would be made.

The *chavitim* were loaves or cakes of bread, made out of flour and oil and baked in a pan, which would be part of the offerings made during the service.

---

use at the time of Christ, but simply that they, when triangulated with biblical and extra-biblical sources, give us reasonable knowledge of the main liturgical movements and central meanings of those services. Joshua Schwartz is representative of some scholars who are extremely cautious about rabbinic sources in "Sacrifice without the Rabbis," *The Actuality of Sacrifice: Past and Present* (Leiden: Brill, 2014), 123–49: "It is far from certain today that these sources provide reliable information" (146). However, David Instone-Brewer's work on the rabbinic materials argues that the earliest strands of the rabbinic materials do reflect pre-AD 70 worship practices, and that the overall movement of the rites is typically considered pre-AD 70. The later strands of these documents are often comments and disagreements about details of the services and descriptions of minor liturgical details added later; these do not concern us, so we can be confident in our description of the central movments and actions that composed the rites. Furthermore, the non-rabbinic sources J. Schwartz and others draw from fit within the lines of interpretation presented here.

2. According to Alfred Edersheim's classic text *The Temple: Its Ministry and Services at the Time of Christ* (1874; repr., Peabody, MA: Hendrickson 1995), "casting lots" took this form (113): The priests stood in a circle, one priest took off his head-gear to mark where the counting would start; each priest would hold out one or more fingers; the president would name some number; and each finger was counted until the number was reached, in this way marking the person who won that lot.

Some priests would be appointed to make the bread. Another priest would clean the ashes from the altar. He would make both a main and a smaller pyre of wood—the greater one for the burnt offerings and the lesser one for burning incense during the rite.

After all these preparations, the priests would meet in the Chamber of Hewn Stones, one of the several chambers just off the Court of Priests. They would cast lots a second time to determine who would perform different roles in the service: those who would carry the bread, the wine, and the different parts of the lamb in the Court of Priests, and those who would cleanse the menorah and the altar of incense in the holy place during the first part of the service. They would then wait for the watchman, who would announce at sunrise, "The eastern sky is shining, it is dawn."[3]

When the morning sun lit up the sky as far as Hebron, the chosen priests would retrieve a lamb from the Chamber of Lambs, give it water to drink out of a golden bowl, re-inspect it to make sure it was ritually clean with no blemishes, and take the lamb to the place of slaughtering. This was an area within the Court of Priests with short pillars and hooks used to hold the animals while they were being slaughtered and marble tables on which they would be skinned and dressed.[4] Others would gather the utensils and vessels and other offerings they would use for the service. At that point all was ready.

The service began with great fanfare. As the gate of Nicanor was opened, it made a great noise. The *magrefah* was played, while a priest announced the beginning of the service. The *magrefah* was most likely an organ consisting of ten pipes, each with ten holes, activated by a keyboard much like the modern organ.[5] The basin of water in the court was noisily filled as a large wooden wheel was turned, shofroth were sounded, and eventually flutes and cymbals were played while the choir of Levites began their singing or saying of the daily psalm. The *Tamid* says of all these, "From Jericho they would hear the sound of the Great Gate being opened. From Jericho they would hear the sound of the *Magrefa*. From Jericho they would hear the sound of the wood that *Ben Katin*

---

3. m. Tamid 3:2.
4. m. Tamid 3:5.
5. Cyrus Adler and Judah David Eisenstein, "Organ," *Jewish Encyclopedia* (New York: Funk & Wagnalls, 1906).

made for the wheel of the laver. From Jericho they would hear . . ."[6] Probably an exaggeration, but certainly this was not a quiet, contemplative service.

The service itself consisted of three parts. In the first part, several actions took place simultaneously. The great gate of Nicanor that separated the Court of Israel from the Court of Women was opened to the playing of three blasts on silver trumpets. Representatives from the people of Israel gathered at the gate of Nicanor to witness and participate in the service. The gates to the holy place were opened as well. The sacrifices were prepared in the priests' court, while the menorah and altar of incense were tended to in the holy place.

As for the preparation of the sacrifices, during the morning and evening service, a single lamb, flour, bread, and wine would be offered. At a particular point in the service the lamb was prepared by slaughtering it in a manner prescribed in detail. As its throat was cut, a priest collected the blood in a vessel. He then went to two corners of the altar in succession and sprinkled blood on the four sides of the altar. He poured any remaining blood out at the southern base of the altar. The lamb was hung without breaking its legs, skinned, and then cut into pieces.[7] These pieces were given to six priests, who stood in a line, while a seventh priest carried a meal offering of fine flour, an eighth carried the *chavitim*, and a ninth carried the wine offering. They would then carry these to the ramp of the altar, salt them, and then place them there for use later in the service.

Meanwhile, two appointed priests entered the holy place. One priest removed the ashes from the altar of incense. The other tended the menorah by cleaning the ashes from all its lamps except the few that were left burning at all times.

The second part of the service consisted of a second round of casting lots and prayers. All the priests would go back to the Chamber of Hewn Stones and there they would say prayers, recite the Ten Commandments, and recite the Shema (which was composed from Deut. 6:4–9; 11:13–21; and Num. 15:37–41). Then they would cast lots to determine which priest would offer incense. Offering incense in the holy place was a special task, marked by the fact that only those who had never done so before were included in this casting of lots, unless every priest present had already had the privilege. Then lots were cast for the other roles at the altar of sacrifice and in the holy place.

6. m. Tamid 3:8.
7. m. Tamid 4:2.

The third and culminating part of the service began as the priests emerged from the Chamber of Hewn Stones. As they appeared the *magrefah* was sounded again. This signaled the high point of the service. Three priests entered the holy place. One priest was responsible for the menorah. During the morning service that priest filled the lamps with oil, all except the few that had been left burning, and prepared them to be lit. During the evening service the priest responsible for the menorah lit all its lamps. A second placed coals in the altar of incense. When these tasks were finished, they left so that the third priest was alone in the holy place. This priest offered incense on the coals, bowed, and offered prayers before God.

When the priest finished offering prayers in the holy place, all five priests who had been in the holy place during the whole service gathered at the top steps leading into the holy place, lifted their hands in a gesture of blessing[8] and blessed the nation using the familiar words, "The LORD bless you and keep you; the LORD make his face to shine upon you and be gracious to you; the LORD lift up his countenance upon you and give you peace" (Num. 6:24–26).[9]

Meanwhile, at the altar of sacrifice, the pieces of lamb, the fine flour, the *chavatim*, and the wine were all offered. As they were offered, trumpets would sound, and the Levites sang the psalm appointed for the day.[10] At each "chapter" or division within the psalm, the trumpets would sound again and all the people would bow. After the singing finished and the priestly blessing was given, the service ended.

Given this reconstruction of the daily rite, what were its central meanings? I will summarize the central meanings of this elaborate service as a whole, and then reflect on some of its most important symbols.

Taking all the actions together, the service can be seen as an exchange of gifts between Israel and God. The service highlights God's role as creator, sustainer, and restorer of the order of creation and the gifts God gives in these

---

8. The fingers were splayed, except that the fourth and fifth fingers were kept together and the second and third fingers of each hand were kept together as well. Those familiar with Star Trek—apparently the Vulcans were familiar with the Jewish temple—or who have visited Jewish graveyards will readily recognize this hand position for blessing.

9. m. Tamid 7:2.

10. In m. Tamid 7:4, the daily psalms are given: for Sunday, Ps. 24; Monday, Ps. 48; Tuesday, Ps. 82; Wednesday, Ps. 94; Thursday, Ps. 81; Friday, Ps. 93; and on Saturday, the Sabbath, Ps. 92.

roles. Israel, who at this service was acting as a representative of all humanity, even the priest of all creation, would come into God's presence and offer thanksgiving to God for those gifts through words, offerings, and sacrifices. The offerings and sacrifices were also symbols of tribute to God and God's ways. They were tokens of their willing commitment of their entire being to God, a commitment to play their proper role in that creational order. That creational order, pictured as full, complete, and without sin or disorder, was called shalom. Shalom describes the order of the kingdom of God realized on earth. That order includes human justice and righteousness as well as the proper movements of the stars in the sky. Israel prayed that God's order, way, or kingdom would increasingly reorder the rebellious earth, prone to chaos and sin, and realign it with God's heavenly kingdom. And the Israelites, as they lived in accordance and harmony with that order, were blessed by God. They experienced the fruits of knowledge and life that come from God's ways.

This perpetual exchange between Israel and God in these regular acts of temple worship symbolized God's intended relationship with all his creatures. God's kingdom, God's shalom, God's creational order was being extended into the earth through their worship. Israel's thanksgiving, commitment to God, prayers, and joyful reception of God's presence and blessing was their participation in that order.

In short, in and through these rites, Israel was saying, "We remember and give thanks for God's creation and providence; we commit ourselves to wisely participate in God's creational order." And in and through these interactions with God, they received God's blessing.

All the central symbols of the daily ceremonies pointed to those primary meanings.

The sacrifices of the lamb and of the flour, cakes, and wine, were symbols of these meanings. The lamb was an *olah* or burnt offering, one of the four main kinds of corporate sacrifices.[11] The Hebrew word *olah* means "to go up, to ascend." In *olah* offerings an animal is presented, the offerer lays their hands on the animal, and the entire animal is turned into smoke on the altar and lifted

---

11. See Lev. 1–6 for descriptions of the sacrifices. The four corporate offerings are the burnt offering (*olah*), the grain offering (also called a loyalty offering or *minhah*), the sin offering (*hattat*), and the well-being offering (*shelamim*). The guilt offering (also called a restitution offering or *asham*) was typically the sacrifice of an individual, not Israel as a whole.

up to the Lord. In describing this offering, the emphasis in Leviticus is not the death of the animal. Instead, the emphasis is that the entire animal (except for the skin) is turned "into smoke" (Lev. 1:9), smoke itself a fitting symbol of the transferral of the offering from the offerer to God since smoke goes up or ascends and disappears into the sky. Its blood is specially handled, and as Lev. 17:11–14 states, blood is a symbol of life.

The meaning of the *olah* or burnt offering remains a subject of debate. I take Alfred Marx's careful and recent work on the sacrificial system as my standard.[12] He emphasizes that the Jewish sacrificial system changed over time; however, while the nuances of meaning and even practice are not immutable, there are certainly constants.[13] The *olah* is the most common and perhaps the most important of the offerings.[14] The *olah*, the *minhah*, and the *shelamim* are presented to God as meal or food offerings, allowing the two parties to "draw near" to one another.[15] While the lordship of God and the servanthood of the human are the primary parts of this relationship—Marx speaks of this as a "feudal" relationship—the details of the service as a whole, the fact that the sacrificial system has both compulsory and voluntary sacrifices, and the details especially of the *shelamim* sacrifice show that the relationship goes beyond command and obedience to something that could involve willing service, care and even delight.[16]

---

12. Alfred Marx, *Les systèmes sacrificiels de l'Ancien Testament: Formes et fonctions du culte sacrificiel à Yhwh* (Leiden: Brill, 2005); "The Theology of the Sacrifice According to Leviticus 1–7," in *The Book of Leviticus: Composition and Reception*, ed. Rolf Rendtorff and Robert Kugler (Leiden: Brill, 2003), 103–20. Other important studies on Old Testament worship and sacrifice include H. H. Rowley, *Worship in Ancient Israel: Its Forms and Meanings* (London: SPCK, 1976); Hans-Joachim Kraus, *Worship in Israel: A Cultic History of the Old Testament* (Richmond: John Knox Press, 1966); Gary Anderson, "Sacrifice and Sacrificial Offerings," *Anchor Bible Dictionary* (New York: Doubleday, 1992), 5:870–86; Walter Brueggemann, *Worship in Ancient Israel: An Essential Guide* (Nashville: Abingdon, 2005); and Jacob Milgrom, *Leviticus: A Book of Ritual and Ethics* (Minneapolis: Fortress, 2004), and *Leviticus 1–16: A New Translation with Introduction and Commentary* (New York: Doubleday, 1991).

13. Marx, *Les systèmes sacrificiels*, 46–49.

14. Marx, *Les systèmes sacrificiels*, 47.

15. There is a strong line that can be drawn between these and the *hattat* and the *asham*. These "offerings of pleasant aroma" show that the primary sense of the sacrificial cult is to establish communion with God; atonement is important but secondary (Marx, "Theology of the Sacrifice," 111).

16. Marx, *Les systèmes sacrificiels*, 202, 221–22.

The meaning of the laying on of hands is also debated. Marx takes it as expressing "the negative aspect of the gift, the giving up by the offerer of what had belonged to him."[17] I am drawn to the possibility that this act indicates an even stronger identification of the offerer with the animal. On the first interpretation, the offerer is showing their willing, even if costly, subjection to God; on the latter, the offerer is going beyond that to present God with a representation of an obedient and faithful life wholly given to God by the worshipper. Baruch Schwartz writes, "The lay person's private burnt offering would then be one way of symbolically offering oneself to God."[18] In public sacrifices, both interpretations suggest the dedication and self-giving of Israel to God.

The daily offerings of flour and cakes are the *minhah* offerings, which are variously called grain, cereal, tribute, or loyalty offerings. Both the name and the ingredients of these offerings are suggestive of the covenant relationship between God and Israel. The word *minhah* means "tribute"—which indicates that the sacrifice is a gift symbolizing both loyalty to and dependence on God. Leviticus instructs Israel to make cakes or wafers for the offering using flour mixed with oil, incense, and "the salt of the covenant," while honey and leaven are specifically excluded from the mixture (Lev. 2:11–13). The exclusion of honey and leaven seems to symbolize being on the journey toward the promised land but not yet having arrived; the promised land was filled with "milk and honey" and unleavened bread was associated with the exodus from Egypt. Portions of the cakes were burnt or turned into smoke and offered to God, while the other portions were eaten by "Aaron and his sons" (Lev. 2:10). The symbolism of the elements and actions suggests that the offerer is thanking God for the sustenance he gives Israel on their continued journey. The offerer acknowledges the fruits and blessings of covenant experienced thus far, while also loyally recommitting himself or herself to that covenant, to "the initial covenant allegiance exhibited by Israel in the exodus."[19] The wholehearted dedication to God symbolized by the burnt offering is given greater specificity in this offering suggesting covenant rededication—these offerings are typically made together.

---

17. Marx, "Theology of the Sacrifice," 113. Also Rendtorff, *Leviticus 1, 1–10, 20* (Neukirchen-Vluyn: Neukirchener Verlag, 2004), 32–48.

18. Baruch Schwartz, *The Jewish Study Bible* (New York: Oxford University Press, 2004), 207.

19. Nobuyoshi Kiuchi, *Leviticus*, Apollos Old Testament Commentary (Downers Grove, IL: InterVarsity Press, 2007), 71. Marx, "Theology of the Sacrifice," 114.

Looking more closely at this connection between Israel's covenant with God and the creational order, the precepts of the covenant, "the law," can be understood as describing and commanding a pattern of life in which God's original intentions for an ordered creation are pictured and in part realized. The law serves as a contextual sketch of kingdom life. Contextual, because different parts of the law pertain to different contexts: nomadic life and settled agricultural life, both in the ancient Near East. A sketch, because God's intentions for every detail of Israel's way of life in that context are not fully captured. However, those precepts were expansive, in that they dealt with Israel's worship of and relationship to God, their relationships with one another, and their actions toward the rest of the creation. As Israel commits to and lives according to those precepts of the covenant, the order of creation is being restored.

This order was disrupted in part by the evil inclinations of the human heart, as told in the story of Noah (Gen. 6:5). However, those evil inclinations began to be righted in that same story. In the description of Noah's sacrifice and God's response to it in Gen. 8:20–22, we see that "God's creational designs may yet be realized in a fragile world."[20] The covenant at Mount Sinai continued this trajectory. Many of Israel's writings tie Israel's worship commanded by the covenant back to the sacrifice of Noah—the tabernacle and temple sacrifices were understood to be based on the type of Noah's sacrifice. The commands for those regular sacrifices were given in part to help "reorder" Israel, to help Israel live in alignment with God's intended patterns within the created order. As Balentine writes, "The Torah envisions the Sinai pericope to begin not simply with a traditional covenant ceremony as might be common elsewhere in the ancient world, but with a *liturgy of covenant* that is peculiarly shaped by Israel's understanding of God's cosmic design."[21] That cosmic design included humanity's worship of God, an enactment of the proper inclinations of the human heart: "The covenant at Sinai also makes clear that the requirements of obedience not only recall the primordial design for an ordered world, they also renew the creational summons to worship God."[22]

Given that Israel's regular worship was part of God's reordering of the creation, it is important to see that the entire nation of Israel, not only the priests, was understood to participate in this daily rite at the temple. A half-shekel

20. Balentine, *Torah's Vision of Worship*, 102.
21. Balentine, *Torah's Vision of Worship*, 123.
22. Balentine, *Torah's Vision of Worship*, 136.

tax was instituted in Exodus 30:11–16 and continued to be paid in the Second Temple period; through this important yearly contribution all of Israel, both those who lived in Jerusalem and those in the diaspora, participated in the daily and Sabbath sacrifices.[23] The tax was announced on the first day of the month of Adar and had to be paid by the fifteenth. Every Israelite, rich or poor, paid this half-shekel—no more and no less.[24] Also, representatives from the twenty-four parts of Israel took part in service. These divisions of Israel were represented through the rotation of twenty-four courses of priests. In addition, lay people from each part of Israel, referred to as the *ma'amad*, would come to Jerusalem on a specific rotation. They would be present at the gate of Nicanor for the Sabbath services, for the presentation of their firstfruits, and for the daily sacrifices.

In these ways all of Israel was represented at these daily and weekly sacrifices.[25] Thus, the sacrifices, prayers, and blessings were understood to be those of Israel as a corporate body, or, as Philo argues, to represent the worship of all of humankind:

> And since of the sacrifices to be offered, some are on behalf of the whole nation, and indeed, if one should tell the real truth, in behalf of all mankind, while others are only in behalf of each individual . . . we must speak first of all of those which are for the common welfare of the whole nation. . . . For some of them are offered up every day, and some on the days of the new moon . . . each of them being a sacrifice of thanksgiving; the one for the kindnesses which have been bestowed during the day, and the other for the mercies which have been vouchsafed in the night, which God is incessantly and uninterruptedly pouring on the race of men.[26]

In this text, Philo summarizes these daily rites as a "thanksgiving" to God, made by Israel, who functioned as a priest of all of humanity, for the mercies which God gives continually to all humankind.

The timing of these sacrifices, namely, that they were to follow the daily, weekly, and monthly patterns of the earth's natural systems in a perpetual pat-

---

23. Josephus, *Antiquities* 3:193–196.
24. m. Sheqal. 1:3.
25. m. Tamid 5:6. Also mentioned in the War Scroll, 1QM 2:3–5. The *ma'amad* and their role in presenting the firstfruits are described in m. Bik. 3:2.
26. Philo, *Spec. Laws* 1:168–69.

tern, also fit with their character as thanksgivings for the gifts of God's providence, for the life and blessings of God's creational order, and as symbols of their commitment to live in harmony with that order.

The manufacture and symbolism of the incense used in the services point in similar directions. The incense was a carefully prescribed formula of thirteen spices, taken from all parts of the earth and sea. As Josephus describes its meaning, he writes: "But the altar of incense, by its thirteen kinds of sweet-smelling spices with which the sea replenished it, signified that God is the possessor of all things that are both in the uninhabitable and habitable parts of the earth, and that they are all to be dedicated to his use."[27] It was as if all the earth were being gathered and brought before God and offered back up to him in thanksgiving and praise.[28]

The prayers said during the service also participated in these dynamics. The overarching theme of these prayers is a call for God's kingdom, God's shalom, God's creational order to be extended fully into the earth. Several of the eighteen benedictions, a well-known group of prayers, were most likely said during the daily services.[29] The first benediction begins with praise to God as "owner of heaven and earth," and the final one includes a prayer for and blessing to God for "shalom."[30] Here is one early version of this final prayer:[31]

27. Josephus, *J. W.* 5.218.

28. Philo further interprets the incense as a representation of the rational part of humanity, paired with the lamb which represents our body: "The most fragrant of all incenses are offered up twice every day in the fire . . . so that the sacrifices of blood display our gratitude for ourselves being composed of blood, but the offerings of incense show our thankfulness for the dominant part within us, our rational spirit, which was fashioned after the archetypal model of the divine image" (*Spec. Laws* 1:171).

29. m. Tamid 5:1. At the very least the seventeenth and eighteenth were said.

30. While the eighteen benedictions only reached their fixed final form at Javneh after AD 70, fairly stable forms were developed before this, a representative pre-AD 70 version being Solomon Schechter's Geniza Palestinian fragment (T-S K27.33b in the Cambridge University Library). Comparison with other versions shows a conservatism and a relative stability in the transmission of these important prayers, so a prayer very close to this was likely regularly said at the temple. See David Instone-Brewer, "The Eighteen Benedictions and the Minim Before 70 CE," *Journal of Theological Studies* 54 (2003): 25–44.

31. Instone-Brewer, "The Eighteen Benedictions," 32.

> Place your peace [*shalom*]
> upon Israel your people,
> and upon your city,
> and upon your inheritance.
> And bless us all as one.
> Blessed are you, maker of peace [*shalom*].

The familiar Aaronic blessing (Num. 6:24–26) given by the priests, standing on the steps leading into the holy place, also ends with the word "shalom" or peace: "The LORD bless you and keep you; the LORD make his face to shine upon you, and be gracious to you; the LORD lift up his countenance upon you, and give you peace [*shalom*]."

Summing up these details, the daily services are an enacted yearning for God to bless Israel, even all of humanity, as Israel enters into and recommits itself to creational patterns of shalom. The patterns and order of the kingdom of God, realized in heaven, meet the earth and attune the earth and all creation, including humans, to God's creational patterns of peace in and through the rites of this service.

The service held on the new month or new moon was similar to these daily rites, but apparently grander.[32] The offerings were larger (Num. 28:11–14), and in addition, "one male goat for a sin offering" (Num. 28:15) was also offered to the Lord.

We do not know much with certainty about the monthly offerings during the first century, but we do know that it was of great importance during biblical times.[33] As for its meanings, in this beautiful prayer from the third century AD attributed to Rabbi Judah, God is praised for the creation and renewing of the months or moon, suggesting this service also revolved around the central meanings of the daily sacrifices discussed above:

> Blessed be He who created the Heavens with His word, and all their hosts
> with the breath of His mouth. He appointed unto them fixed laws and times,
> that they should not change their ordinance. They rejoice and are glad to do

---

32. The Hebrew phrase, *rosh hodesh*, can be translated as new month or new moon; Israelite calendar months are based on the lunar cycle.
33. 1 Sam. 20:5–24; 2 Kings 4:23; Isa. 1:13; 66:23; Ezek. 46:1–3; Hos. 2:11.

the will of their Creator. They work truthfully, for their action is truth. The moon He ordered that she should renew herself as a crown of beauty for those whom He sustains from the womb, and who will, like it, be renewed in the future, and magnify their Maker in the name of the glory of His kingdom. Blessed art Thou, O Lord, who renewest the moons.[34]

Themes of creational order are readily seen. The "fixed laws and times" of the celestial hosts, created by "His word," are part of "His kingdom."

The service on the Sabbath day was also similar to the daily and monthly rites—or perhaps it is better to say that the daily and monthly rites reflect the Sabbath service.[35] The Sabbath burnt offerings were larger in number than the daily offerings. In addition, the Sabbath rite included important ritual actions involving the twelve loaves of bread in the holy place called "the bread of the Presence." These twelve loaves of bread were kept on the golden table in the holy place. On the Sabbath, these were replaced with new bread, while the older loaves were taken out and then eaten by the priests.

Since the Reformation era, these loaves have often been called the "shewbread" or "showbread." But the Hebrew name is *lechem happanim*. In Hebrew, *panim* means "face" or "presence." Literally translated, it means "the bread of the face" or "the bread of the Presence."

The table of the bread of the Presence was one of the four most important symbols in the holy of holies and holy place, alongside the ark of the covenant, the altar of incense, and the menorah. Among these holy objects, the table and the ark hold a special place. Both had to be wrapped in three layers of protection while being transported (Num. 4:5–8) while the other holy objects were wrapped only in two.

It is also clear that flagons of wine were placed on or next to the table. In Exodus, it is written: "You shall make its plates and dishes for incense, and its flagons and bowls with which to pour drink offerings; you shall make them of pure gold. And you shall set the bread of the Presence on the table before me always" (Exod. 25:29–30). Texts in Numbers (4:7; 15:5–7; 28:7) indicate those flagons were filled with wine. Parallels to the eucharistic table of bread

34. b. Sanh. 42a.
35. The book of the covenant in Exodus only mentions the Sabbath, while daily and monthly rites are outlined in the book of Numbers, which as a literary composition is dated later; so, at least based on literary history, the Sabbath seems to have priority.

and wine are clear—especially given this was one of the two holiest pieces of furniture in the temple.

During the Sabbath celebration, eight priests would enter into the holy place. Two of them would carry an arrangement of six loaves of bread each, and two priests would carry a bowl of incense each. The other four would carry out the previous week's bread and incense.[36] All of these items were prepared earlier and temporarily placed on a marble table outside of the holy place. During the service, the priests with the new loaves would stand on the north side of the table in the holy place, and as loaves of bread were taken off by the two priests standing on the south side of the table, the priests on the north side would place the new loaves. The bowls of frankincense were handled similarly. All this was done carefully so that there would always be bread on the table. Then the older loaves were taken out and placed on the gold table in the antechamber to the holy place. The bread would then be eaten by all the priests within that courtyard.[37]

So, every Sabbath the bread of God's presence would be eaten, accompanied by the drinking of wine. This rite bears great resemblance to the original covenant celebration on Mount Sinai in the presence of God:

> And Moses wrote down all the words of the LORD. He rose early in the morning, and built an altar at the foot of the mountain, and set up twelve pillars, corresponding to the twelve tribes of Israel. He sent young men of the people of Israel, who offered burnt offerings and sacrificed oxen as offerings of well-being to the LORD. . . . Then Moses and Aaron, Nabad, and Abihu, and seventy of the elders of Israel went up, and they saw the God of Israel. . . . They beheld God, and they ate and drank. (Exod. 24:4–5, 9–11)

36. m. Menah. 11:1–9. For descriptions of the Sabbath liturgy we must rely almost solely on the Mishnah without corroboration from non-rabbinic sources; Josephus only mentions that trumpets were blown for the Sabbath sacrifice. See J. Schwartz, "Sacrifice without the Rabbis," 136.

37. The Mishnah says that "there were two tables in the antechamber at the entrance to the sanctuary, one was made of marble and the other of gold. They would place the *lechem happanim* on the marble [table] upon its entry into the sanctuary and on the golden [table] upon its exit, because we increase sanctity and we do not reduce sanctity" (m. Menah. 11:7). So, being in the presence of God throughout the week, the bread of the Presence gained holiness.

Notice the parallels between the twelve pillars, representing Israel, and the twelve loaves, as well as the sacrifice at the base of the mountain and the feast at the top.

The meaning of these loaves of bread is also illumined by their connection to the phrase *berith olam*, or eternal covenant. Leviticus 24:8 states: "Every sabbath day Aaron shall set them [the *lechem happanim*] in order before the LORD regularly as a commitment of the people of Israel, as a covenant forever [*berith olam*]." Most other uses of the term *berith olam* point to a covenant that involves symbols of shalom, fruitfulness, and life.[38] The rainbow that God set in the sky after Noah's sacrifice is a symbol of God's *berith olam* between God and every creature (Gen 9:16), a sign of God's ongoing providence, care, and commitment to bless. The observance of the Sabbath itself, the completion and crown of creation, is also called a *berith olam* (Exod. 31:16).

Malachi 2:4–5 indicates that this covenant is intended to bring forth shalom, and that Israel's worship is a response to that gift of shalom: "Know, then, that I have sent this command to you, that my covenant with Levi may hold, says the LORD of hosts. My covenant with him was a covenant of life and well-being [*shalom*], which I gave him; this called for reverence and he revered me and stood in awe of my name."

The bread rite shares elements of both the *minhah* (tribute offering) and the *shelamim*. In general, the *shelamim* or "sacrifice of well-being" was usually the final offering in a sequence of offerings. For this sacrifice, an animal was killed, and certain fatty portions of the animal were turned "into smoke" on the altar and offered "as a food offering by fire to the LORD" (Lev. 3:11). The other portions were eaten by the priests, the offerer, and other invited guests. It was a meal shared between God and humans (Deut. 12:7; 1 Sam. 1; 1 Kgs. 8:62–66). The meal celebrated an occasion when the blessings of God and the longed-for harmony or shalom between God, humans, and all of creation were partially experienced here and now. Corporate *shelamim* were regularly celebrated at harvests and at *Shavuot*, and all Israel celebrated through *shelamim* at the inauguration of the temple (1 Kgs. 8).[39] In these celebrations, worshippers

38. Gen. 9:16; 17:6–7, 13, 19; Exod. 31:16; Lev. 24:8; Num. 18:19; 2 Sam. 23:5; 1 Chron. 16:15–17; Isa. 55:3; 61:8; Jer. 32:40; 50:5; Ezek. 37:26; Ps. 105:8; 111:5. Cf. conversely, Deut. 28:46; Isa. 24:5; Ezek. 16:60.

39. Scripture also records it being celebrated for the blessings of the promised land (Deut. 12:5–7), and at the birth of a child given in response to a vow (1 Sam. 1:24–25).

joined "together with the priests in a sacred meal at which God himself was perceived to be an honored guest."[40] In a certain type of *shelamim* rite, the *todah*, bread and wine were eaten as well as the meat (Lev. 7:12–13; m. Menah. 7; cf. 1 Chron. 16:3). The Sabbath eating of the bread of the Presence takes a similar form to these sacrifices.

The name of the bread, *lechem happanim*, also recalls God's close dealings with Moses: "Thus the LORD used to speak to Moses face to face (*panim al-panim*), as one speaks to a friend" (Exod. 33:11). The connection suggests that God, in the holy place where the bread is kept and in this Sabbath rite in which the bread is handled, is coming face to face with Israel, to speak as a friend, or in this rite, to feast together. Such connotations were picked up in the rabbinic tradition. In one place, it is written: "In this world you offer before me Bread of the Presence and sacrifices, but in the world to come I shall prepare for you a great table," here referring to the table of Psalm 23.[41] And in the Talmud, there is a comment that on the days of the major festivals, priests would take the table out and show it to the people and say, "Behold, God's Love for you!"[42]

Finally, it should not be missed that bread itself is a typical symbol for life and sustenance. As pointed out above, the table in the holy place represented the abundant life and the menorah represented the light and illumination that God's presence brought to Israel and the whole creation as God dwelt in their midst. Bread, a symbol of life, combined with wine, a symbol of life abundant, together create a fitting symbol of the shalom that results from God's presence.

In sum, in the Sabbath celebrations—as in the daily and monthly rites—the Israelites give thanks for, celebrate, and recommit themselves to God's cre-

---

40. Baruch Levine, *Leviticus*, JPS Torah Commentary (Philadelphia: Jewish Publication Society of America, 1989), 14.

41. Num. Rab. 21.21.

42. b. Menah. 29a. I interpret this saying as the priests pointing to God's love in his willingness and desire to "eat" together with his people Israel, to be present to them in this way. There is another rabbinic tradition in which God's love is seen in this instance in the miracle that the bread was just as hot and fresh on that day as on the day it was baked (b. Menah. 29a). In my opinion, that explanation seems a bit too homey to fit the solemnity of the occasion and the profundity of the statement. An image of Mom's fresh cookies hot out of the oven after school comes to mind: "Behold, Mom's love for you"— though this interpretation has a loveliness of its own. In contrast, no special miracle is needed for the bread to be a symbol of God's steadfast love.

ational order. Partaking of bread and wine, they feast with God and celebrate God's abiding presence. These rites were a memorial of, a partial realization of, and an anticipation of the blessings of God's eternal covenant of creational shalom. They remembered, celebrated, and looked forward to the life and well-being that come from living in the presence of God and in harmony with God's ways.

Connections to the New Testament and Early Church

In what way were these themes from these regular practices at the temple carried over into the images and practice of the Eucharist in the early church? Or, put differently, did the early church understand the themes of these regular temple celebrations to be typologically extended into the Eucharist? Did early Christians think of the Eucharist as a rite in which they gave thanksgiving for God's providence, committed themselves to and prayed for shalom, and in which God's blessing and shalom were being received first into the community of God's people and then extended outward into the world?

Indeed, such themes are highlighted in some of the earliest texts outside of Scripture that record discussions of the Eucharist.

In 1873, an ancient church order, the Didache, was discovered and published in 1883. It has since been at the center of much discussion and controversy, principally because it presents "a challenge to the view that all eucharistic practice was derived from the actions of Jesus at the Last Supper and recalled that event."[43] Its date has been debated; it was written sometime between the mid-first century and the mid-second century. Even whether it describes an actual Eucharist has also been debated—in part because its prayers do not seem to fit well with common understandings of what a Eucharist entails.[44]

---

43. Bradshaw, *Eucharistic Origins*, 25. Bradshaw discusses the Didache in *Eucharistic Origins*, 24–40, and in *Reconstructing Early Christian Worship*, 38–45, and discusses its dating and provenance in *The Search for the Origins of Christian Worship*, 2nd ed. (Oxford: Oxford University Press, 2002), chap. 4, 73–98. See also Kurt Niederwimmer, *The Didache: A Commentary* (Minneapolis: Fortress, 1998).

44. Some saw it as "only ancillary" to the eucharistic prayer, others claimed that it was a different kind of Eucharist, one which was related only to the meal ministry of Jesus and unrelated to the Pauline tradition of remembrance of the Last Supper, others claimed it described an *agapē* meal, a meal distinguished from the Eucharist. Bradshaw

But since the 1960s, "The majority of liturgical scholars . . . have come round to the view that the rite in Didache 9–10 is itself a form of the Eucharist . . . and have modified their own theories about early eucharistic development accordingly."[45]

In the *Didache* there are many parallels to regular forms of worship at the temple, and yet the significance of these connections has not been fully recognized in the literature, even though they are sometimes mentioned in passing. Instead, the connections both to Jesus's meal ministry and to the Jewish prayer after meals, the *Birkat ha-Mazzon*, have occupied scholars' attention during the last decades.[46] Perhaps because it was assumed that the Jewish background to the Eucharist was a Jewish meal at home rather than worship at the temple, those temple connections are often passed over or downplayed.[47]

Three chapters of the Didache (9, 10, and 14) contribute to our understanding of the Eucharist.[48] Starting with chapter 14, let us consider these short chapters in light of the regular services at the temple.

In chapter 14, the author almost explicitly says that the Eucharist is a weekly Christian typological extension of the regular sacrificial services at the temple. He writes that "every Sunday," the church assembles to "break bread and give thanks" and that this celebration is "your [i.e., the church's] sacrifice" (14:1–2). Then, quoting Malachi 1:11 and 14 freely, he writes, "This is [the meaning] of what was said by the Lord: 'to offer me a pure sacrifice in every place and time, because I am a great king,' says the Lord, 'and my name is held in wonder among the nations'" (14:3). In other words, the Eucharist is what Malachi was

and others propose instead that it was a Eucharist. See discussion of these options in Bradshaw, *Eucharistic Origins*, 1–32.

45. Bradshaw, *Eucharistic Origins*, 30.

46. See Bradshaw's discussion of these comparisons, *Eucharistic Origins*, 32–35. His conclusion about the importance of the *Birkat ha-Mazzon*: "Yet the truth is that the parallels exist only in the very broadest of terms, and in any case are of dubious value" (*Eucharistic Origins*, 33).

47. Bradshaw, *Eucharistic Origins*, 32n36 lists the sources that began this discussion in the early twentieth century. See further discussion above in chap. 1.

48. I use the translation found in Niederwimmer, *Didache*, changing only "broken bread" in chap. 9. See also Bradshaw's updated translation, *Eucharistic Origins*, 24–25, and R. C. D. Jasper and G. J. Cuming, *Prayers of the Eucharist: Early and Reformed*, 3rd ed. (New York: Pueblo, 1980), 23–24. Online versions are typically the older translation by J. B. Lightfoot.

prophesying about, the restoration and purification of the temple's regular sacrificial practices.

Let us consider the context of this Malachi quotation more carefully. Malachi 1:6–2:9 addresses problems at the temple. The temple priests are not discharging their sacred duties. Instead they are offering impure sacrifices by keeping the better lambs while offering blind, lame, and sick ones (1:8, 13), ones that even their governor wouldn't accept (1:8). Plus, the priests consider the entire system a nuisance (1:13). In all these ways they despise and profane "the LORD's table" (1:7; cf. 1:12: "the Lord's table"). Yes, the phrase, "the Lord's table" is found in Malachi. In contrast to these corrupt practices, Yahweh through Malachi says, "For from the rising of the sun to its setting my name is great among the nations, and in every place incense is offered to my name, and a pure offering; for my name is great among the nations, says the LORD of hosts" (v. 11). While not explicit, this general reference to incense and offerings from the sun's rising to setting most likely alludes to the regular daily, Sabbath, and monthly sacrifices.

Malachi 1:11, which from the *Didache* forward gets linked to the Eucharist by many in the early church,[49] could mean a variety of things in its context in Malachi. Under a present interpretation, Malachi claims the nations that surround Israel are doing a better job of offering pure sacrifices to God than Israel is (i.e., God's name is presently great among the nations but not in Israel).[50] Another option, an eschatological option, interprets the verse as offering a vision of what will be; the prophet sees a day when God's name is great and pure offerings are offered among the nations, a day that by contrast puts to shame what is happening at the temple currently.[51] I find this eschatological interpretation of Malachi convincing in part because the book as a whole envisions a coming messenger (1:10; 3:1) who will "prepare the way before me,

---

49. E.g., *Apostolic Constitutions* 6.4.23; Justin, *Dial. Trypho* 42; Origen, *Homilies on Genesis* 13.3; Chrysostom, *Discourses Against Judaizing Christians* 5.12.3, and *Demonstration Against the Pagans* 43; Augustine, *City of God* 18.35; *In Answer to the Jews* 9; *Letter 185*, 5; and *Sermon 228B*, 1.

50. Andrew Hill, *Malachi*, The Anchor Bible (New York: Doubleday, 1998), 188–89, and some others prefer the present option on grammatical grounds, even "despite the difficulties theologically" (188).

51. Ralph Smith presents five different options, including the two I mention. Smith, *Micah-Malachi*, Word Biblical Commentary 32 (Waco, TX: Word Books, 1984), 313–17.

and the Lord whom you seek will suddenly come to his temple" (3:1).[52] And when the Lord comes, he will bring both judgment and a renewal of worship, not an end to it: "Then the offering of Judah and Jerusalem will be pleasing to the LORD as in the days of old and as in former years" (3:4).

The Didache interprets Malachi in this eschatological fashion, seeing the Eucharist as this pure sacrifice "among the nations" prophesied by Malachi, and ultimately brought about through the coming of the messenger, John, and the Messiah, Jesus. But in this messianic age, there is still a danger of impure sacrifices. Instead of impure lambs, however, either lack of confession beforehand (14:1) or divisions or blemishes in the community taint this sacrifice: "Let no one engaged in a dispute with his comrade join you until they have been reconciled, lest your sacrifice be profaned" (14:2).[53]

So what are the central meanings of this eucharistic sacrifice according to the Didache? In chapters 9 and 10, we find themes similar to the regular sacrifices at the temple. Here is part of the prayer recorded in chapter 10:

> When you have had your fill, give thanks [*eucharistēsate*] this way:
> We thank you, holy Father,
> For your holy name, which you made dwell in our hearts,
> And for the knowledge and faith and immortality, which you made
> known to us through Jesus your servant.
> To you be glory forever.
> You, almighty Lord, created all things for the sake of your name,
> and you gave food and drink to human beings for enjoyment,
> so that they would thank you;

---

52. Smith also prefers this option, for the same reason.

53. Cf. Matt. 5:23-24. Most interpreters of the Didache see 14:1-2 as calling for necessary preparations before an offering, similar to the ritual cleansing required of the priests. But there is a deeper interpretation that fits better with the textual context of Malachi, in which it was the lamb itself that was unclean: just as the *olah*, the OT daily lamb sacrifice, represented the people as a whole, divisions and impurity in the "body" of the church can render it as an impure sacrifice. Understanding the *olah* as a type of the Eucharist, the church itself is caught up in and participates in the total gift of self seen in Christ. This coheres with the more recent interpretation of what "discerning the body" means in 1 Cor. 11:27-34 (see chap. 5); it is not implausible that the author of the Didache is making similar theological connections.

> But you graced us with spiritual food and drink and eternal life
> through Jesus your servant.
> For all things, we thank you, Lord, because you are powerful.
> To you be glory forever.
> Be mindful, Lord, of your church. . . . Gather it . . . into the
> kingdom.

Themes of the daily, Sabbath, and new moon celebrations are present and yet taken up and transformed in light of the work of Christ. Those assembled give thanks to God first for his creational providence for the body, including food and drink, and then for his spiritual food and drink given through Jesus. Such spiritual nourishment is surely related to God's "holy name, which [he] made dwell in our hearts"—a New Testament extension of how God's name is placed upon Israel through the priestly blessing at the temple. As it is written, "So they shall put my name upon the Israelites, and I will bless them" (Num. 6:27).

In chapter 9, the cup and bread are spoken of as follows:

As for the thanksgiving [*eucharistias*], give thanks [*eucharistēsate*] this way:
First, with regard to the cup:
"We thank you, our Father, for the holy vine of David your servant, which you have made known to us through Jesus your servant. To you be glory forever."
And with regard to the broken bread [*klasmatos*]:
"We thank you, our Father, for the life and knowledge which you made known to us through Jesus your servant. To you be glory forever.
And as this broken bread [*klasma*] lay scattered upon the mountains and became one when it had been gathered, so may your church be gathered into your kingdom from the ends of the earth."

A few comments are in order. First, note the stress throughout the Didache on the Eucharist as a thanksgiving. The discovery of the Didache has in fact changed the preferred term from the Lord's Supper, Mass, or Communion to Eucharist in many traditions in the West, as the title of the ecumenical document *Baptism, Eucharist and Ministry* itself indicates.[54] Thanksgiving to God is also the central theme of daily, Sabbath, and monthly temple worship.

54. "Eucharist" has always been the preferred term for the Eastern Orthodox churches.

Second, in this chapter, Jesus is considered in primarily two ways: as a kingly messiah in the line of David (symbolized in the cup), and as "life and knowledge" (symbolized in the broken bread). It is not implausible that the author sees Jesus in light of the central features of the temple: the ark as a kingly throne, the table of the bread of the Presence as life, and the menorah as knowledge—all fulfilled in Christ, our king and priest. In any case, key Old Testament themes and offices are being fulfilled as Christ gathers the church into the kingdom.

Third, the Greek word for "broken bread" is *klasma* rather than the usual term for bread, *artos*. The same word is found twice in John's feeding narrative in John 6 (vv. 12–13), a key background text for the Eucharist. Those verses are the probable background for this way of describing the bread. John's feeding narrative also fits with the theme in the Didache of "gathering" (Didache 9:4; 10:5). In John 6:12–13 "gathering" results in twelve baskets of pieces, while in the Didache "gathering" results in "your church gathered together from the ends of the earth into your kingdom" (Didache 9:4).[55] Thus the feeding and meal ministry of Jesus seems to be the controlling background image for the Didache's vision of the Eucharist, one that ties feeding together with the work of gathering the church together into the kingdom.

Summing up, the Didache understands the Eucharist in light of a typological extension from the pure sacrifices of regular temple worship through Jesus's feeding and meal ministry into the Eucharist. The Eucharist is a thanksgiving for God's work in bringing the realities of the kingdom into the earth, through the conduit of the church, as a result of the work of Christ. In and through this meal of thanksgiving, God is present to bless the church by extending God's presence and name into the hearts of the assembled church. Note that these kingdom realities are tied to God's creational work. This coming of the kingdom can be seen as a renewing and realigning of humanity and the creational order, described in terms of the bodily health and sustenance that come from food and drink (Didache 10:3), combined with the spiritual work of God gathering the church and God's name dwelling in the hearts of the church (Didache 9:4, 10:5, 10:2).[56]

55. C. F. D. Moule, "A Note on Didache 9.4," *JTS* 6 (1955); 240–43, for one comparison of the two.
56. An emphasis on the change from old to new covenant, from an "outer" to "inner" work is found in Origen, *Homilies on Genesis* 13.3, in which he quotes Mal. 1:11.

We find similar typological extensions in the early church writings of Irenaeus and Justin Martyr.

In *Against Heresies*, Irenaeus does not link the Eucharist back to sin offerings, or even to the Passover. Instead, he uses the image of the firstfruits sacrifice repeatedly (almost solely) to express what the Eucharist is and does.[57] He writes:

> Again, giving directions to His disciples to offer to God the first-fruits of His own, created things—not as if He stood in need of them, but that they might be themselves neither unfruitful nor ungrateful—He took that created thing, bread, and gave thanks, and said, "This is my body." And the cup likewise, which is part of that creation to which we belong, He confessed to be His blood, and taught the new oblation of the new covenant; which the Church receiving from the apostles, offers to God throughout all the world, to Him who gives us the means of subsistence the first-fruits of His own gifts in the New Testament, concerning which Malachi . . . spoke beforehand. . . . [58]

Justin Martyr in his *Dialogue with Trypho* understands Christ's entire life as a fulfillment of the type of the Passover lamb.[59] But in his reflections on the Eucharist, he likens that rite to the grain or *minhah* offering at the temple given after one is cured from leprosy:

> "And the offering of fine flour, sirs," I said, "which was prescribed to be presented on behalf of those purified from leprosy, was a type of the bread of the Eucharist, the celebration of which our Lord Jesus Christ prescribed, in remembrance of the suffering which He endured on behalf of those who are purified in soul from all iniquity, in order that we may at the same time thank God for having created the world, with all things therein, for the sake of man, and for delivering us from the evil in which we were, and for utterly overthrowing principalities and powers by Him who suffered according to His will.[60]

57. Irenaeus, *Against Heresies* 4.17.5; 4.18.1, 4.
58. Irenaeus, *Against Heresies* 4.17.5.
59. Justin, *Dial. Trypho* 40.
60. Justin, *Dial. Trypho* 40.

Justin further argues the Eucharist, understood in this way, is a fulfillment of Malachi's prophecy, similar to what we found in the *Didache*: "Hence God speaks by the mouth of Malachi. . . . He then speaks of those Gentiles, namely us, who in every place offer sacrifices to Him, i.e., the bread of the Eucharist, and also the cup of the Eucharist, affirming . . . that we glorify His name."[61]

Why does Justin understand the Eucharist is like the thanksgiving offering given for the curing of leprosy? This type might seem a bit "small," since the leprosy offering was not a central Old Testament sacrifice made on behalf of all of Israel, and so it does not seem to fit well with the centrality of the Eucharist for Christians nor its communal nature. Yet, the offering for cleansed leprosy opens up a central Old Testament theme: the change from unclean to clean. A bit of background is helpful.

In Leviticus 10:10–11, God tells Aaron, "You are to distinguish between the holy and the common, and between the clean and the unclean; and you are to teach the people of Israel all the statutes that the Lord has spoken to them through Moses." This was a central task of the priests of the temple.

This distinction between "the clean and the unclean" is a distinction between that which exemplifies God's creational designs for order, integrity, and health, and that which temporarily or permanently does not. Creational order is linked to life; its breakdown leads to death.[62] These purity laws stipulated that no one with a skin disease, no one who was leaking or had recently leaked fluids that symbolized life (such as semen or menstrual fluid), no one who had had recent contact with decomposing corpses would be allowed to take part in worship at that time (Num. 5:1–4). In all three cases, the "skin" or boundaries of a person's body were temporarily or permanently breaking down. Their body was lacking integrity and order.

These purity laws and regulations often strike modern people as exclusionary and hierarchical as well as primitive. They in fact do exclude people temporarily from being able to worship at the temple. And yet, one can also see

---

61. Justin, *Dial. Trypho* 41.

62. There is some debate about the purposes and intentions of purity laws. See, for example, Mary Douglas, *In the Wilderness: The Doctrine of Defilement in the Book of Numbers* (Sheffield: Sheffield Academic, 1993), 23, in which she states, "The underlying principle is that death and life are opposed."

them as creating a visual representation at the temple of God's concern for life, for the health of his people, and for the integrity of creation as a whole.[63]

While purity codes for the temple tended to stay at this more physical or outer level, the concept of cleanness extended into the moral realm for the Israelites. Thus the cries of the psalmist "Create in me a clean heart, O God" (Ps. 51:10) and "Cleanse me from my sin" (Ps. 51:2) are not merely metaphors, but also recognitions that not only bodies but also souls, spirits, and hearts can fall out of line with God's desired creational patterns and become distorted. Sin points not only to wrong actions, but also to a disordered state of the soul that needs cleansing or healing.

Jesus's ministry to the unclean and sinners both carries forward and also transforms God's concern for wholeness, integrity, and health. Jesus, as the temple made flesh, continues God's concern for the cleanness of the creation, but instead of excluding people in unclean states, he reaches out, touching and healing those with "unclean spirits" (Mark 1:21–28), lepers (Mark 1:40–45), those with unnatural discharges (Mark 5:25–34), and the dead (Mark 5:21–43). Similarly in Jesus's meal ministry, God addressed sin not through exclusion, but rather through compassionate invitation, engagement, calls for repentance, and healing presence. In response to the Pharisees' critique, "Why does he eat with tax collectors and sinners?" Jesus replied, "Those who are well have no need of a physician, but those who are sick; I have come to call not the righteous but sinners" (Mark 2: 16–17).

Given this background, Justin Martyr fittingly sees that in the Eucharist, we meet with the presence of Christ, the one who touched and ate with those who were unclean. Rather than excluding the unclean, in the Eucharist he extends to them his nourishing, compassionate, challenging, and healing presence.

Summing up some of these early church connections, we find many of the earliest eucharistic sources do not center their thinking on the Last Supper and the death of Christ. Instead, Jesus's meals, feedings, and healings serve as the central images and events in Jesus's work that are linked to the Eucharist.[64] Only later, as the New Testament took full shape, did the connection with the Last Supper, the words of institution, and the death of Christ become more prom-

---

63. Stubbs, *Numbers*, 52–57.

64. Geoffrey Wainwright, *Eucharist and Eschatology*, 51–52, points out that the images in the catacombs associated with the Eucharist are not the cross but instead the feeding miracles of Jesus.

inent. Paul Bradshaw sums up this development as follows: "It was only much later, as the New Testament books gained currency and authority, that it [early Christianity] began to shape both the catechesis and the liturgy of the churches, and to shift the focus of eucharistic thought from feeding to sacrifice."[65]

However, if the healing and feeding ministry of Christ is a linking step in a typological extension from the regular worship services at the temple to the Eucharist, Bradshaw's dichotomy of *feeding* and *sacrifice* does not fit so well. After all, the main sources Bradshaw works with in what he calls the "feeding" trajectory all refer to the Eucharist as a sacrifice. More likely, these different ways of thinking about the Eucharist, both Bradshaw's "feeding" and "sacrifice," are instead different ways early Christians made typological connections between the Eucharist, Christ's work, and the temple. They were all unified in this fundamental typology, but pointed to different facets of the liturgies, sacrifices, and meanings of both temple worship as well as the saving work of Christ.

In this particular early strand of eucharistic thought, the background story of God's creating, sustaining, and renewing of creation looms large, just as it did in the regular daily, Sabbath, and new moon worship services of the temple.

In the Eucharist, according to the Didache, Irenaeus, and Justin Martyr, the gathered church gives thanks for and celebrates God's work through Christ to bring about creational shalom. The church gives thanks for God's work through Christ who has come to those who have been unclean and sinners, and has begun cleansing them, gathering them back into God's household, kingdom, and presence. The church—as forerunners of all creation—receives God's blessing and eats a meal together with God who is present. God feeds his church with spiritual food that brings health and shalom just as God in Christ fed the crowds in his ministry. As the eucharistic bread is raised, the church proclaims—as the Jews did as they raised the bread of the Presence—"Behold, God's love for you!"

Temple Pressure: Recovering Creational Themes
in Contemporary Eucharistic Theology and Practice

We have seen that the central themes of the regular worship services at the temple are thanksgiving to God for God's provision of blessings through the

65. Bradshaw, *Reconstructing Early Christian Worship*, 19.

created order, commitment to God and God's created order, and prayer for the full reordering of ourselves, human society, and the creation in accordance with the life-giving patterns of God's kingdom of shalom. These themes are taken up and transformed in Christ's feeding and healing ministry and surface in early church writings about the Eucharist. How do these themes pressure current theology and practice?

First, they most obviously pressure us to incorporate such themes into our eucharistic rites, both in words and actions. I will offer a few practical sugges-tions and point to resources below, especially in regards to the eucharistic prayer and the offering.

But incorporating such themes into our practice runs into several concep-tual and imaginative roadblocks, roadblocks that someone like Irenaeus did not face. Perhaps the largest overarching issue is that most current eucharistic practices are not guided by an integrated vision of God's work in creation, reconciliation, and redemption, a vision which formed a basic part of the larger theological visions of first-century Jews and the early church.

An Integrated Vision of God's Work

In our present context, these creational themes appear at odds with what we might consider more "traditional" Eucharist practices. Incorporating such themes might seem to risk eclipsing the centrality of remembering the atoning work of Christ accomplished through his life, death and resurrection. Indeed, some churches might welcome such an eclipse, preferring an emphasis on the goodness of creation over against Eucharistic practices that emphasize human sinfulness and the substitutionary suffering and death of Christ. Such an ap-parent conflict of interests likely factored into the lively debates regarding the Didache after its discovery. But isn't this a false dichotomy? How might these themes related to the created order be best integrated with sacrificial emphases within the Eucharist?

Temple typology pressures us to integrate these themes rather than to di-vide, contrast, or privilege one over the other. The daily, Sabbath, and monthly rites provide a continuous "bass line" in relation to which the melodies of the three pilgrim feasts are integrated. Those feasts highlight God's particular sav-ing acts in the Exodus, in the giving of the law, and God's final actions at the end of this age. That saving activity finds its place within the broader narrative of God's creation and restoration of the cosmos. Conversely, God's particular saving work gives insight into the general character of the created order. Such a full, integrated theology is reflected in Israel's temple worship.

As a Christian, Irenaeus takes up this Jewish heritage and transforms it in light of God's work in the incarnation of the Son and sending of the Spirit. The Eucharist is an "announcement" of "the fellowship and union of the flesh and the Spirit."[66] He understands God desires to fully dwell in the midst of creation, in Christ, in the bread, and finally in the sanctified life of all created things. For Irenaeus, the Eucharist itself argues against the gnostic story that the created order is not good and is something we need to be saved from:

> But how can they [the Gnostics] be consistent with themselves, [when they say] that the bread over which thanks have been given is the body of their Lord, and the cup His blood, if they do not call Him the Son of the Creator of the world, that is, His Word, through whom the wood fructifies, and the fountains gush forth, and the earth gives first the blade, then the ear, then the full grain in the ear (Mark 4:28).[67]

Such themes concerning the relationship of the Word to all of creation and its relevance to God's saving work in Christ have not been fully integrated within eucharistic thought and practice in the West, or at least not integrated convincingly or powerfully enough to effectively form the imaginations of the majority of Christian people. This results in an impoverished vision of humanity's relationship to and vocation toward the rest of creation. Most do not see that creation care practices are important parts of Christian discipleship and part of what we are committing ourselves to in our eucharistic celebration. At best we have an ambiguous eucharistic heritage.

The same might be said of Western theology more broadly. Paul Santmire's *The Travail of Nature: The Ambiguous Ecological Promise of Christian Theology* examines Western theological traditions in light of the "unexamined position espoused by scores of ecologists, philosophers, poets, nature writers, political activists, and even some theologians" who claim that "the Western theological

---

66. Irenaeus, *Against Heresies* 4.18.5.
67. Irenaeus, *Against Heresies* 4.18.4.

tradition is ecologically bankrupt."[68] Starting with Irenaeus and Origen and ending with the twentieth-century theologians Karl Barth and Pierre Teilhard de Chardin, Santmire examines motifs and thought forms of Western theology as they relate to the created order. While disagreeing with the extreme claims of many, Santmire sees this tradition as filled with "ambiguities," "uncertain" voices, and "unspoken ecological promise."[69] For example, in the medieval period, he examines the influential visions of Bonaventure and Dante, whose leading metaphors for the spiritual life led people to see Christianity as providing a "ladder to heaven" out of the earth, and contrasts them with the words and life of Francis, who fully embraced nature and understood God desired to dwell in, sanctify, glorify, and transform the world rather than rescue human souls from it.[70]

While such an integrated vision can only be worked out fully in the details of systematic theologies and in the details of the lives of Christians, typological connections between temple and Eucharist push us to see the need for and value of such an integrated theological vision.[71]

One finds good examples of such an integrated vision in much of contemporary Eastern Orthodox thought and eucharistic theology. In contrast to the West, Eastern Christianity has had a much less ambiguous heritage in

---

68. Paul Santmire, *The Travail of Nature: The Ambiguous Ecological Promise of Christian Theology* (Minneapolis: Fortress, 1985), 1. He uses, as many do, the 1967 article in *Science* by Lynn White, Jr., "The Historical Roots of our Ecological Crisis," as an important historical summary of such opinions.

69. Santmire, *Travail of Nature*, viii-ix.

70. Santmire, *Travail of Nature*, 97–120.

71. For an excellent argument for ecological themes within Christian theology, and a critical evaluation of various environmental movements from a Reformed evangelical Christian perspective, see Steve Bouma-Prediger, *For the Beauty of the Earth: A Christian Vision for Creation Care*, 2nd ed. (Grand Rapids: Baker Academic, 2010). From my Reformed perspective, I see both ecological promise as well as some ambiguities in both Calvin's and Barth's larger theological perspectives, some of which Santmire treats in his book. I also find great promise and also some issues within the larger Dutch Reformed tradition of "common grace." David Kelsey's recent theological anthropology, *Eccentric Existence: A Theological Anthropology* (Louisville: Westminster John Knox, 2009), is an important recent work that draws from the best of both Calvin and Barth while developing further the importance of God's creational work. His particular treatment of the creation of the world through "Wisdom" is an important contribution to this general topic. See David Stubbs, "Kuyper's Common Grace and Kelsey: Polishing a Reformed Gem," *Journal of Reformed Theology* 10 (2016): 314–39.

regards to the created order. Creational themes are found throughout their liturgies and woven into their theologies. In fact, Bill McKibben, a leading Western environmentalist, in his foreword to a recent and important collection of Orthodox essays about creation and the environment, asks the question, "Why has Bartholomew, the Ecumenical Patriarch and spiritual leader of Orthodox Christians worldwide, been such a standout among religious leaders in his call for environmental care?" His own answer to the question is that Bartholomew's "forthright activism is simply an expression of an underlying spiritual tradition with deep connections to the natural world and remarkable gifts to offer to the rest of the world."[72] Given this, Eastern Orthodox theology and eucharistic practice can provide at least one example of how these creational themes from the temple might be extended into our contemporary world and our celebrations of the Eucharist.

Two additional details of such an integrated vision can be touched on here. The first is what might be called an enchanted, or for Christians, a sacramental vision of the cosmos. The second common feature is the extension of our salvation to include a restored vocation in relation to the created order. A common way of naming this vocation of humanity is that we are called to be "priests of all creation."

Let us examine these two features more fully.

The Enchanted, Sacramental Cosmos

Modern thought, by which I mean the main currents of philosophical and scientific thinking based on the assumptions and ideals of the Enlightenment, has led most modern people to view the world as "disenchanted."

"The disenchantment of the world" is a phrase used to describe the profound change that occurred in modernity when people ceased to believe there were "inner principles" or "spirits" operative within the things of this world with the exception of humans.[73] People no longer understood crickets, stones,

---

72. Bill McKibben, "Foreword" in *Toward an Ecology of Transfiguration: Orthodox Perspectives on Environment, Nature, and Creation*, ed. John Chryssavgis and Bruce V. Foltz (New York: Fordham University Press, 2013).

73. One source of the term is Max Weber: "Hence, it means that principally there are no mysterious incalculable forces that come into play, but rather that one can, in principle, master all things by calculation. This means that the world is disenchanted." Weber,

kernels of wheat, and mighty oaks as having inner animating principles that humans should try to discern and respect. Nor are inner animating principles understood to reflect further spiritual or heavenly realities. Instead, humans decide what things are for. They organize and purpose things—now pictured as raw materials—through their own calculations and ideals.

T. S. Eliot mourned this disenchantment in his well-known poem *The Wasteland*, published in 1922. In the following lines he mourns how the world has become "a heap of broken images" to modern humanity:

> What are the roots that clutch, what branches grow
> Out of this stony rubbish? Son of man,
> You cannot say, or guess, for you know only
> A heap of broken images, where the sun beats,
> And the dead tree gives no shelter, the cricket no relief,
> And the dry stone no sound of water. [74]

Eliot's expression "broken images" suggests that the things of this world used to be seen as images. Images of what?

For the Hebrew people, the things of earth imaged the things of heaven. The temple, especially in its regular sacrificial practices, was understood to be a place where earth and heaven aligned. As clean and holy people, animals, and things properly align with the ways of heaven in both form and activity, the glory of God and "the glorious splendor of [his] kingdom" (Ps. 145:12) shine in and through them. Proper internal and relational ordering and proper connection between heaven and earth, this kind of imaging, are the very definitions of shalom and what it means for God's kingdom to extend into the earth.

In the Old Testament and extra-scriptural wisdom literature, this connection between heaven and earth is understood in part through the idea of the creation of the world through God's "Word" (Gen. 1) or alternatively through

---

"Wissenschaft als Beruf," in *Gesammelte Aufsätze zur Wissenschaftslehre*, 7th edition, ed. Johannes Winckelmann (Tübingen: J. C. B. Mohr, 1988), 594. Translated in Anthony J. Carroll, S. J., "Disenchantment, Rationality and the Modernity of Max Weber," *Forum Philosophicum* (2011): 133. See also Charles Taylor, *A Secular Age* (Cambridge: Harvard University Press, 2007).

74. T. S. Eliot, *The Wasteland*, lines 19–24.

God's "Wisdom."[75] Proverbs 8:22–36 is one of the key canonical texts.[76] From this larger passage:

> Ages ago I [Wisdom] was set up, at the first, before the beginning of the earth.... When he [the LORD] assigned the sea to its limit, so that the waters might not transgress his command, when he marked out the foundations of the earth, then I was beside him, like a master worker; and I was daily his delight, rejoicing before him always, rejoicing in his inhabited world and delighting in the human race. (Prov. 8:23, 29–31)

This Wisdom is intimately related to the being and character of God, and the created order reflects the ways and form of Wisdom. Wisdom can be "heard"— "Does not Wisdom call?" (8:1)—in and through the created order, discernable in the patterns of the creation and activities of creatures that Proverbs and other wisdom literature reflect on.

In John's Gospel such thinking is taken up and transformed. Jesus is understood as the "Word" through which "all things came into being" (John 1:3) and which then "became flesh and lived among us" (John 1:14)—claims that have Genesis 1 and Proverbs 8 in the background.

Such connections between the ways and forms of earth and heaven are reflected on more fully in other writings in the New Testament as well as in the theology of the early church using Hellenic forms of thought.[77] In this trajectory of thinking, with roots in Plato and Stoic thought and stretching from Philo, Origen, and Maximus forward into contemporary Eastern Orthodox theology, everything has its own *logos*. In patristic literature, "The *logoi* are the 'inner essences' of things, the value and significance they have in the

---

75. For extra-scriptural wisdom literature, see, for example, the references to Wisdom throughout the book of Sirach.

76. The proper relationship between Wisdom and the second person of the Trinity, and the relationship between the second and the first persons as implied in this passage were much debated during the formation of Christian Trinitarian doctrine. See Hans Boersma, "The Sacramental Reading of Nicene Theology: Athanasius and Gregory of Nyssa on Proverbs 8," *Journal of Theological Interpretation* 10 (2016): 1–30.

77. See the excellent discussion of the best recent understandings of these Hebrew and Hellenic thought forms in Kelsey, *Eccentric Existence*, 171–73, 215–41. There are many New Testament passages that reflect this understanding, such as Col. 1:15–20.

eyes of the Creator rather than in our faulty human estimation."[78] These inner essences are all understood to be related to each other and each in some way reflective of God, whose *Logos* created it all, and in whom all things find their purposes and meaning.

Rather than speaking of such a world as enchanted, contemporary theology has preferred to speak of a "sacramental vision of the world" or a "sacramental worldview." For example, in the official teaching of the US Conference of Catholic Bishops, the sacramentality of the world refers to the potential "transparency" of all things to divine activity or presence.[79] Transparency means that one can "see" the activity or presence of God in some way in, under, or through the activity of a part of creation, similar to the way that one can see a pane of glass and also what lies beyond the glass. Some evangelicals have also spoken of recovering a sacramental worldview.[80] A sacramental worldview is certainly part of some evangelicals' renewed interest in Celtic Christianity's creation-affirming spirituality, expressed in these lines of a larger poem:

> There is no plant in the ground
> But is full of His virtue,
> There is no form in the strand
> But is full of His blessing.
> Jesu! Jesu! Jesu!
> Jesu! meet it were to praise Him.[81]

Certainly, one must be careful to guard against the dangers of forms of natural theology, as the twentieth-century theologian Karl Barth has warned. Certainly, one must also be careful to keep clear the difference between creature

78. David Bradshaw, "The *LOGOI* of Beings in Greek Patristic Thought," in *Toward an Ecology of Transfiguration*, 23.

79. "Sacramentality means that all physical matters and actions have the potential to become transparent vehicles of divine activity and presence in our world. This being the case, we are also aware of the transformative character of the sacraments." United States Conference of Catholic Bishops, *Sacramental Catechesis: An Online Resource for Dioceses and Eparchies* (Washington, DC: US Conference of Catholic Bishops, 2012), 12.

80. For example, Hans Boersma, *Heavenly Participation: The Weaving of a Sacramental Tapestry* (Grand Rapids: Eerdmans, 2011).

81. Alexander Carmichael, *Carmina Gadelica* (Edinburgh: Oliver and Boyd, 1928), 1.14, 39.

and creator—a line that some, but not all, forms of nature spirituality, revivals of Celtic Christianity, panentheist thinking, and ecotheology tend to blur. As Richard Bauckham puts it, the creation is "sacred" in the sense of "dedicated to or associated with" God, but not "divine."[82] In addition, distinctions must be made between the world being simply "enchanted" by inner principles, the sacramentality of the world in which the Word and Spirit shine through aspects of creation, and "sacraments" proper.[83]

However, a worldview offering these features (inner principles, sacramentality and sacraments proper) and these distinctions is part of the common heritage of Christianity. In my own tradition, John Calvin and Jonathan Edwards are often seen as promising figures in this regard.[84] Such a worldview is needed to fully appreciate the early Christian understandings of the Eucharist as found in the Didache, Irenaeus, and Justin Martyr. Such a worldview is also needed to fully appreciate and incorporate the creational themes we have been discussing into contemporary celebrations of the Eucharist.

A few aspects of this vision are particularly significant. First, it is holistic. The world is not a heap of broken images. Instead, creation, including humanity, has a purpose and an order to it; within it all things have smaller purposes and orders that are connected to one another and the greater whole. In most premodern Western visions of the world, people recognized some kind of "ladder of nature" or "great chain of being" in which smaller systems found both their purposes and aspects of their "form" or way of being through their partial determination by larger, "higher," or more comprehensive systems or

82. Richard Bauckham, *Bible and Ecology: Rediscovering the Community of Creation* (Waco, TX: Baylor University Press, 2010), 86. Steve Bouma-Prediger carefully articulates a Christian theology and ethic of the creation in *For the Beauty of the Earth*.

83. See for example, the review of Boersma's book by Nicholas J. Healy, Jr., "Evangelical Ressourcement," *First Things* (May 2011); https://www.firstthings.com /article/2011/05/evangelical-ressourcement.

84. While Calvin's theology of the created order is complex, Susan Schreiner claims this in her conclusions: "In the course of these discussions Calvin formulated an essentially Irenaean vision of creation and redemption. In Calvin's theology, God is the Lord of nature and of history and is reclaiming his creation so that nothing of its original substance will be lost or destroyed." Susan E. Schreiner, *The Theater of His Glory: Nature and the Natural Order in the Thought of John Calvin* (Grand Rapids: Baker Academic, 1991), 115. For Edwards, see for example his essay, "Images of Divine things," in *A Jonathan Edwards Reader*, ed. John E. Smith, Harry S. Stout, and Kenneth P. Minkema (New Haven: Yale University Press, 1995), 16–21.

powers. In Christian versions, ultimately the highest form or system was the *logos* or Wisdom of God.[85]

Second, those purposes and orders are fully known only by God, and yet humans are capable of understanding them in part. Humans did not create them, nor are humans autonomous in the sense of being able to create our own law and order without regard to this larger order. Rather, we must listen to and gain wisdom in order to understand the world and participate in it as we should.

For early church writers, being able to discern these purposes and order required "an education of the senses," an education involving both ascetic and liturgical components. We develop an ear for wisdom and eyes for the *logoi* of things through the proper ordering of ourselves and by placing ourselves in proper relationship to God through worship.[86] The perception of the sacred order we find ourselves in is also an important source of our moral empathy for the creatures around us.[87]

Such an understanding created the conditions needed for the flourishing of science. Christianity saw the creation as a good creature with a knowable yet mysteriously deep order that could reflect the being of God. Because of this particular understanding, Christianity could, on the one hand, avoid denigrating the creation through denying the body leading to an unhealthy asceticism

---

85. See, for example, Arthur Lovejoy, *The Great Chain of Being: A Study of the History of an Idea* (Cambridge: Harvard University Press, 1971).

86. David Bradshaw summarizes Maximus the Confessor's thought on this: "In summary, it would seem that for Maximus there are two fundamental forms of the education of the senses: liturgical (discussed above all in the *Mystagogy*) and ascetical (discussed in *Ambigua* 21). Each provides the essential context for the other, for without regular practices of self-denial and obedience, liturgical worship is little more than a form of aesthetic enjoyment, and without liturgical worship, asceticism is merely what St. Paul (coining a marvelous word) calls 'will-worship,' *ethelothrēskeia* (Col. 2:23)." David Bradshaw, "The *LOGOI* of Beings," 21. We find this also in John Calvin's thought: "This gradual internal restoration of the soul enables the believer to find again a richer knowledge of God from the contemplation of nature." Schreiner, *Theater of His Glory*, 113.

87. Or so argues John Anthony McGuckin: "In other words, using ancient patristic terms, once the observer no longer sees the sacral connection between the observing self and the observed order of the Cosmos (namely, the *logos* behind the connection between sentient and insentient life forms, which is the substructure and the 'value' of consciousness, that is, its valency, *eudaimonia*, *phronesis*, or purpose, *telos*), then there can be no moral empathy." "The Beauty of the World and its Significance in St. Gregory the Theologian," in *Toward an Ecology of Transfiguration*, 36.

such as you find in certain forms of gnostic thought, and on the other hand, move beyond the admiration of the surface beauty of creation that was mixed with fear of the "gods" underneath its surface such as you find in paganism. Such is the argument of Bruce Foltz, drawing from the work of the Russian philosopher and theologian Florensky. "This relation to nature," he maintains, "became conceivable only when people saw in creation not merely a demonic shell, not some emanation of Divinity, not some illusory appearance of God, like a rainbow in a spray of water, but an independent, autonomous, and responsible creation of God, beloved of God and capable of responding to His love."[88] In this way nature was seen as fully real, truly lovable, and ultimately intelligible.

Finally, such a cosmos is one that is full of beauty and glory. "The heavens declare the glory of God," as the psalmist cries. In response, humans are called to delight in creation as Wisdom did in the very creation of it. Such splendor, beauty, and delight are integral aspects of creation's purposes. For example, St. Gregory the Theologian understood such human delight in beauty not as an extra, not a nice addition to more serious matters—like arts programs in our schools—but rather a central reason for our existence. The Eastern Orthodox scholar McGuckin says this of Gregory: "What we see here, quite explicitly, is what for me stands as the quintessential patristic contribution to ecological thought: that the perception of the beauty of the world is a sacred and priestly matter that is the core rationale of why things exist at all."[89]

Through our proper worship of God as the source of the beauty around us and the final goal of the deep longing that the beauty of the world produces in us, our relationship to the creation can be rectified and purified. Proper worship protects us from improper worship of creation, from cheap enticement by its beauty, and from the desire to use it for self-indulgence.

Such a vision of the cosmos is not only premodern or Eastern Orthodox. One finds it in many contemporary ecological and political visions in the West.[90]

88. Elizabeth Theocritoff, "Liturgy, Cosmic Worship, and Christian Cosmology," in *Toward an Ecology of Transfiguration*, 327–28, quoting Pavel Florensky, *The Pillar and Ground of the Truth: An Essay in Orthodox Theodicy in Twelve Letters*, trans. Boris Jakim (Princeton: Princeton University Press, 1997), 210.

89. McGuckin, "Beauty of the World," 40.

90. One such vision is found in the writings of Wendell Berry. For example, in his oft-quoted essay, "The Two Economies," Berry understands that all our man-made "small economies"—our systems of life and exchange—should find their place within

Such an enchanted, sacramental vision of the world is not only possible. It is needed to fully celebrate the Eucharist today, if our goal is to fully continue the trajectory started at the temple and extended through Christ into the early church.[91]

The Priests of All Creation

A second typical aspect of this more integrated vision of God's action in creation and salvation is an understanding of salvation which entails a vocation and calling with respect to the created order.

And what is this calling? Particularly important biblical touchstones for pursuing this question are the Genesis accounts of creation and humanity's

---

the "Great Economy." The Great Economy is a transcultural equivalent phrase he substitutes for "the Kingdom of God" in that essay. Wendell Berry, "The Two Economies" in *Home Economics* (New York: Farrar, Straus & Giroux, 1987), 54–75.

91. But one might ask, is such an enchanted view of the world true? While obviously a full argument is out of the question here, let me point in two suggestive directions. First, the modern disenchanted vision has created philosophical problems it cannot solve. No comprehensive philosophical vision has arisen within the modern world that has satisfactorily replaced the systematic comprehensiveness of such a premodern Hebraic/Hellenic vision. Instead, the most important conundrums in contemporary philosophy continue to be insolvable precisely because of the rejection of such "first principles" and "final ends" found in such an enchanted world, as Alasdair MacIntyre argued in *First Principles, Final Ends, and Contemporary Philosophical Issues*. Second, "science" itself no longer has a single way of viewing the world, as many people assume, nor do most practitioners of science subscribe to a fully disenchanted vision of the world. Instead, many reigning theories within the scientific world contain a more complex, layered vision of the world around us. In them principles of causation are talked about as internal to systems rather than exterior laws—such principles are like the "spirit" of a system. These principles are in turn layered within other principles of causation, like wheels within wheels. This, for example, is how causal explanations are made in contemporary biological psychology. To give one example, Huib Looren de Jong describes the situation in this way: "In comparison with the philosophy of mind, the philosophy of biology has developed more subtle and complex ideas about functions, laws, and reductive explanation than the stark dichotomy of autonomy or elimination. It has been argued that biology is a patchwork of local laws, each with different explanatory interests and more or less limited scope. This points to a pluralistic, domain-specific and multi-level view of explanations in biology." Huib Looren de Jong, "Levels of Explanation in Biological Psychology," *Philosophical Psychology* 15 (2002): 441. Many models within contemporary science are quite open to an enchanted, sacramental interpretation.

place in the garden of Eden (Gen. 1–3), the creation of the world through Wisdom and Wisdom's call to humanity (esp. Prov. 8–9), and various images of humanity at worship with the rest of creation (e.g., Pss. 19, 148). In the West, the idea and image of humanity as having "dominion" over creation has been common—and much abused. The image of humanity as "steward" is also common. Another particularly promising approach is to think of humans as "priests" of all creation, a calling symbolized by and most fully realized in the Eucharist. It finds biblical roots in Genesis 2:15: "The Lord God took the man and put him in the garden of Eden to till it and keep it." Given that these words—which can also be translated as "to serve and protect" or "to serve and preserve"—are also used to describe the vocation of the priests in the temple in Numbers (3:7–8; 8:26; 18:5–6), it appears that God intended humanity to have a priestly or quasi-priestly role in the "garden," in creation as God intends it.[92]

This image of humanity as priests of all creation provides a fruitful context for understanding the significance of the creational themes in both the temple and in the early church and can open our contemporary eucharistic celebrations to such themes.

This model is common in Eastern Orthodoxy, but is becoming more common in the West.[93] James B. Torrance writes: "But God made men and women in his own image to be the priests of creation and to express on behalf of all creatures the praises of God, so that through human lips the heavens might declare the glory of God. When we, who know we are God's creature, worship God together, we gather up the worship of all creation."[94] John Zizioulas similarly describes this model of the human in relationship to the rest of creation: "The priest is the one who freely, as himself an organic part of it, takes the world in his hands to refer it to God and who, in return, brings God's blessing

92. Gordon Wenham, "Sanctuary Symbolism in the Garden of Eden Story," in *"I Studied Inscriptions from Before the Flood": Ancient Near Eastern, Literary and Linguistic Approaches to Genesis 1–11*, ed. Richard Hess and David Tsumura (Winona Lake, IN: Eisenbrauns, 1994), 401. See also McBride, "Divine Protocol," 3–41.

93. See, e.g., Mark Clavier, *Stewards of God's Delight: Becoming Priests of the New Creation* (Eugene, OR: Wipf & Stock, 2009); David Buller, "To Serve and Preserve—Genesis 2 and the Human Calling," Jan. 2, 2013, www.biologos.org.

94. *Worship, Community and the Triune God of Grace* (Downers Grove, IL: InterVarsity Press, 1996), 13.

to what he refers to God."[95] The phrase "refer it to God" means to see, use, and relate to the world in a certain way. It means to see the ends and purposes of all creatures—people, trees, squirrels, bread, and wine—in terms of their relationships to God, and thus to see all of creation precisely as a gift from God that is also meant to be an offering back to God.[96]

In the Eucharist such a vocation is both symbolized and fulfilled. Humans take the stuff of the earth—bread and wine—see and name it for what it is, give thanks for it, acknowledge God as source and giver, and offer it back to God. The words of the old familiar hymn summarize it well:

> We give thee but thine own,
> Whate'er the gift may be.
> (William How, "We Give Thee but Thine Own")

In doing so, humans become aligned with the ways of God, and God's presence and blessing are extended into the earth and rest upon all these symbols of human life and culture. It is as if the whole creation in and through these representative humans gathered in eucharistic celebration reaches up toward God, opening themselves to him as he descends and dwells in and among them.

The "priests of all creation" model of humanity deserves comment at several points. At the outset, one can see how different this picture of humanity's relationship to the creation is from typical modern understandings. For example, Descartes, Bacon, and even Kant picture humanity as the masters or possessors and/or judges of nature—not priests.[97]

The steward model, by contrast, has more in common with the "priests of all creation" model. But while stewards may simply conserve a thing or resource, this idea of humans as priests, through its links back to Adam's quasi-priestly role in the garden, suggests that humans are to also to "till the garden," to cultivate and develop the created order, of which they are a representative

95. John Zizioulas, "Proprietors or Priests of Creation?" in *Toward an Ecology of Transfiguration*, 187.

96. Alexander Schmemann uses the word "refer" in a similar way as he explains what is happening in a separate Eastern Orthodox rite of preparation of the Eucharistic elements before the service: "For the essence of this preparation lies in referring the bread and wine, i.e., our very selves and our whole life, to the sacrifice of Christ, their conversion precisely into *gift* and *offering*." *The Eucharist*, 110.

97. Zizioulas, "Proprietors or Priests," 183–84.

part, in order to present it as a gift back to God.[98] Like the servants in Jesus's parable of the talents, we are to make good, creative use of what we have been given (Matt. 25:14–30). Similarly in the Eucharist, we present bread and wine, the fruit of human labor and culture, not simply wheat and grapes, to God. They are fitting symbols that our relationship to the created order is not simply conservation but also cultivation and development.

The idea of cultivation and development impacts every aspect of human life and so many areas of human research and action. Developing the world well requires a conscious commitment to wisely participate in God's providential order.

In my Reformed tradition, especially the Dutch branches, Genesis 2:15 is interpreted to mean that humans have been given a "cultural mandate" by God to enter into God's creational order and to develop a culture that fits within it.[99] But discerning such "orders of creation" in economics, sexuality, politics, and ecology is fraught with peril and has been much abused in the past when people claim something is "natural" or unnatural—yet we have no choice but to try.[100] Andy Crouch, a contemporary theologian and writer who draws from this tradition, writes: "What is most needed in our time are Christians who are deeply serious about cultivating and creating but who wear that seriousness lightly—who are not desperately trying to change the world but who also wake up every morning eager to create."[101] We are called to "till," to creatively engage with the world, as well as to "keep," to discern and protect the order of the world.

Seeing humans as priests also ties our role within creation to worship. Here, there is a healthy disagreement about the extent to which human as priests "mediate," which could imply that the rest of creation needs our voice for its praise to reach God, or simply "represent" the worship of all creation to

98. Zizioulas, "Proprietors or Priests," esp. 190.

99. Abraham Kuyper's writings on common grace are often cited as the source for this way of putting the point. Kuyper, *Common Grace: God's Gifts for a Fallen World* (Bellingham, WA: Lexham, 2015).

100. Stubbs, "Kuyper's Common Grace and Kelsey," 314–39. "Orders of creation" is a theological point of discussion in Lutheran and Reformed traditions, but also was critiqued in the twentieth century by theologians such as Karl Barth and Dietrich Bonhoeffer.

101. Andy Crouch, *Culture Making: Recovering Our Creative Calling* (Downers Grove, IL: InterVarsity Press, 2008), 12.

God.[102] Do not the "angels" and "sun and moon" praise God without the help or mediation of humanity (Ps. 148:2–3)? Elizabeth Theokritoff argues that in the tradition of the church, it was understood that humans not so much led, but joined in the worship of all creation during the Eucharist. Drawing from Psalms as well as the mystical experiences of saints throughout the ages, she points to the worship that was understood to be happening in the three "estates" of the creation: the angelic hosts, the rest of visible creation, and humanity.[103] She interprets the call to "lift our hearts on high" in the eucharistic prayer as a call to "aspire" to hear the praise of all creation, "the usually unseen and unheard context within which we offer our own thanks and praise."[104] Not only that, but in the liturgical and written tradition of the East, it is often assumed that "creation may not only guide fallen man to recognize his Lord but also have a surer instinct for His purposes."[105] In other words, humans often fail where other creatures more faithfully worship God in their own ways.

Is such talk of mountains and birds praising God mere poetry? John Chrysostom reflected on this, and suggests that creatures glorify God through appearance, through life and activity, and through words.[106] Thus mountains, birds, and humanity all glorify God, but do so in different ways. And it is assumed as well that these different kinds of "words" are not simply for our benefit: "The 'words' of creation really are addressed to its Creator, not just to us. Our conscious response does not create cosmic worship, yet it plays a crucial part in the total 'symphony.' If we want a metaphor for our own role in cosmic worship, we might say that the nonhuman creation 'speaks' in a sort of 'vacuum of consciousness'; our conscious response fills that vacuum with a medium that allows creation's own 'word' of praise to resonate."[107] Thus humanity does have its particular and important priestly part to play, but does so within a larger chorus. The eucharistic rite becomes a living symbol of what

102. Richard Bauckham is critical of especially Zizioulas precisely on these grounds, preferring to see humanity's role within the worship of creation as part of and representative of the community of creation without implying that the rest of creation needs humanity as a mediator. *Bible and Ecology*, 83–86.
103. Elizabeth Theokritoff, "Liturgy, Cosmic Worship and Christian Cosmology," in *Toward an Ecology of Transfiguration*, 299.
104. Theokritoff, "Liturgy, Cosmic Worship and Christian Cosmology," 300.
105. Theokritoff, "Liturgy, Cosmic Worship and Christian Cosmology," 304.
106. John Chrysostom, *On Psalms*, PG 55:486.
107. Theokritoff, "Liturgy, Cosmic Worship and Christian Cosmology," 305.

all creation is doing and a particular place where such worship resonates and comes to verbal expression.

To sum up, the creational themes of the Eucharist are most intelligible within a fully integrated understanding of God's creating, reconciling, and redeeming actions. We live in an "enchanted" and "sacramental" world, a world filled with beings whose purposes and ends are intended by God to in some way echo God's own *logos* through the power of the Spirit. Humanity is in a special way called to be a priest of all creation, to serve, cultivate, and preserve it, to offer it up to God, and to join in creation's worship of God. This calling was perfected in Christ, the *logos* incarnate, who offered himself back to God as a living sacrifice and through whom God's blessing and presence are poured out to the world. The Eucharist exemplifies the priestly calling of all humanity in an act which draws together and in which resonates the worship of all creation. Such a vision of human vocation symbolized in the Eucharist is well encapsulated in these words of Bartholomew I:

> Gift (*dōron*, in Greek) and gift in return (*antidōron*, in Greek) are the terms by which it is possible to signify our Orthodox theological view of the environmental question in a concise and clear manner. Nature is the *dōron* of the Triune God to humankind. The *antidōron* of humankind to its Maker and Father is the respect of this gift, the preservation of creation, as well as its faithful and careful use. The believer is called upon to celebrate his or her daily life eucharistically, that is to say, to live and to practice daily what he or she confesses and proclaims at each Divine Liturgy: "We offer to you your own of your own, in all things and for all things, and we give thanks to you, Lord!"[108]

Suggestions for Eucharistic Practice

How might these insights and ways of seeing God's activity in the creation, the place of humanity in it, and our eucharistic response to God be better symbolized in our practice of the Eucharist?

Perhaps the first thing that must be said is that simply changing the forms

---

108. From "Toast during the Banquet in Constanza" given in 1997. *Cosmic Grace, Humble Prayer*, 200–201.

and words of the eucharistic rite is not enough. There is also a need for what is called mystagogy, a proper explanation of the meanings of the Eucharist and other church rites and practices, which in parts of the Christian tradition are called "mysteries." Classes for new members, catechesis before baptism, Christian education classes, sermons, book studies, blogs, and even explanations in worship bulletins are all possible ways of doing this work. While the symbols and words of the Eucharist communicate much, they are complex. People are well-served by a good explanation of these rites. An explanation of meanings and movements in a complex piece of music cultivates greater appreciation for its intricacies. Knowing the rules of a game like soccer or football allows a higher level of participation and understanding. Likewise, an explanation of the Eucharist's central movements and meanings will allow people to understand, appreciate, and participate more fully in the rite.

The typological connections between temple and table have offered the following teaching points: The bold lines of connection with the temple itself remind us that God is really and personally present; the Kingdom of God is breaking in. Now, connections with the regular temple services direct us to remember and give thanks for God's creation and providence. They commit us to wise and creative participation in God's created order.

Such teachings open up a variety of important conversations. Topics such as God's relationship to the world, humanity's place within it, and the purposes of human work and culture can be explored through an examination of the Eucharist. The claim that in the Eucharist we commit ourselves to wisely and creatively participate in God's creational order opens up many questions about the creation and human culture.

At the very least, we can in our teaching and preaching give people these two simple eucharistic intentions to contemplate as they participate in the Eucharist:

God is really and personally present; the Kingdom of God is breaking in.

We remember and give thanks for God's creation and providence; we commit ourselves to wisely and creatively participate in God's creational order[109]

109. Three more summary "intentions" based on the central meanings of the Eucharist will be discussed in the following chapters.

Beyond explicit teaching, there are other ways of making these central themes apparent in our eucharistic practice.

The most obvious one is to include such creational themes in our eucharistic prayers. There are wonderful prayers available that already do so—no need to reinvent the wheel. In the Reformed tradition, the Iona Community in Scotland as well as the Calvin Institute for Christian Worship in Michigan provide many resources for worship that highlight the theme of "creation care," including eucharistic prayers.[110] Most Protestant denominations and the Roman Catholic Church have similar resources. *Toward an Ecology of Transfiguration* includes liturgical suggestions in its appendix. Many of them are most appropriate in Orthodox churches, but they provide models and ideas that could be tailored for other traditions and contexts.

My concern in using such "creation care" resources is that some see them as colorful additions, or an optional theme dealt with only on certain Sundays, perhaps around Earth Day. I hope instead that creational themes become integrated more fully into all our eucharistic celebrations, that they become part of a larger integrated vision of God's entire creating and saving action toward us that calls for our thanksgiving and commitment. At the temple, creational themes were woven together with God's saving action toward Israel. As we have seen, they were also woven into early church celebrations of the Eucharist. I wish the same for contemporary Christian celebrations.

One eucharistic prayer in the PC(USA) *Book of Common Worship* is exemplary for gracefully including such themes within a larger integrated whole.[111] It includes a beautiful and quite poetic *Eucharistia* section[112] describing the creation of the world and our human calling within the created order that leads into the *Sanctus*. Here is the final part of that section, along with the *Sanctus*:

110. See, e.g.: http://www.ionabooks.com/e-liturgies-prayers/creation-environment .html; http://worship.calvin.edu/resources/resource-library/worship-resources-for -creation-care/.

111. "Great Thanksgiving E," prepared by the ecumenical International Commission for English in the Liturgy, in PC(USA), *Book of Common Worship*, 142–145 (hereafter *BCW*).

112. For those unfamiliar with traditional structures of Eucharistic prayers, the *Eucharistia* section is the opening "thanksgiving" section after the *Sursum Corda* (Latin for "Lift up your hearts," referring to the opening dialogue).

When the times at last had ripened
and the earth grown full in abundance,
you created in your image man and woman,
the stewards of all creation.
You gave us breath and speech,
that all the living
might find a voice to sing your praise,
and to celebrate the creation you call good.
So now, with all the powers of heaven and earth,
we sing the ageless hymn of your glory.

The people respond with the *Sanctus*:

Holy, holy, holy Lord, God of power and might,
heaven and earth are full of your glory.
Hosanna in the highest.
Blessed is he who comes in the name of the Lord.
Hosanna in the highest.[113]

While the model of humans as "stewards of all creation" is highlighted, notice how the priestly task of giving voice to the larger created order is also clear to see.[114]

When placed within the larger context of the prayer, the words of the *Sanctus* itself, that "heaven and earth are full of your glory," speak of the enchanted, sacramental nature of this "good" created order that we inhabit. God's glory shines in and through the earth as well as in heaven. While a commitment to wisely and creatively live within such a created order is not explicit, the very act of recognizing that other members of the created order, the "powers of heaven and earth," are not raw material but rather fellow creatures tasked with giving God glory and praise implies this.[115]

---

113. *BCW*, 142.

114. In my Reformed context, perhaps it would be wiser in public worship settings to use "steward" language and broaden it to include priestly themes than to directly use "priest" language. Ironically, the Reformation stress on the priesthood of all believers has led to a general suspicion of priest language, at least for the time being.

115. Tony Campolo argues this in his more popular and evangelical-targeted book

The attention paid to the creation here begins to reunify the creating and redeeming work of God. This goes far in implying a Christian "ecological ethic," namely that "care for the earth is an integral feature of authentic Christian discipleship."[116]

The Lutheran theologian and ethicist Paul Santmire in his book *Ritualizing Nature* calls attention to another part of traditional eucharistic prayers, the *Sursum Corda*. He argues that the Western tradition is built upon a "theology of ascent," the understanding that in worship we transcend the physical creation in order to be with God in heaven in our spirits. The architecture of medieval gothic cathedrals is an important symbol of this for him. As a result, "The more the faithful aspired to transcend matter in order to be with God above the heavens, the more they also, in this era, engaged themselves with the earth below as 'mere matter,' as a world at their disposal, as an 'It.'"[117] Western prayers, rites, and hymns emphasize human souls ascending to be with God in heaven, rather than heaven and earth meeting and the kingdom of God breaking into the earth. For Santmire, this theology and imagery need to be better balanced with a "theology of descent," the understanding that God has come down, and continues to come down, to dwell in our midst and throughout creation.

And so, as he examines our eucharistic practice in detail, he suggests a change to the *Sursum Corda*, the opening dialogue that begins most traditional eucharistic prayers. One contemporary version of the *Sursum Corda* is this:

Celebrant: The Lord be with you.
People: And with your spirit.
Celebrant: Lift up your hearts.
People: We lift them up to the Lord.
Celebrant: Let us give thanks unto the Lord.
People: It is meet and right so to do.

How to Rescue the Earth without Worshipping Nature (Nashville: Nelson, 1992).

116. Bouma-Prediger, *For the Beauty of the Earth*, 135. Calvin DeWitt also sees the similar implications of "reuniting the creative and redemptive work of our Lord" in *Caring for Creation: Responsible Stewardship of God's Handiwork* (Grand Rapids: Baker, 1998), 58.

117. Paul Santmire, *Ritualizing Nature: Renewing Christian Liturgy in a Time of Crisis* (Minneapolis: Fortress, 2008), 98.

Santmire suggests a small but significant change to the third and fourth lines:

> *Celebrant*: Open your hearts.
> *People*: We open them to the Lord.[118]

For Santmire, it frames the eucharistic celebration in a way that opens the congregation to descent-oriented understandings of God's action. The United Church of Canada has changed their liturgy and adopted similar language, perhaps as a result of Santmire's arguments for this change.[119]

While I appreciate the historic continuity of the traditional *Sursum Corda*, and realize that the traditional expression "Lift up your hearts" can be interpreted in a number of ways, I think Santmire's proposal is worth consideration. Like the ladder of Jacob, the Eucharist involves both ascending and descending, and in our context perhaps an emphasis on the descent is needed.[120]

One final suggestion concerns the offering—which in some traditions involves bringing the bread, wine, and monetary offerings forward to the table. It is an important part of the eucharistic celebration that is quite open to such creational themes.

The offering is seen by some in the contemporary church as an awkward intrusion of worldly business into an otherwise spiritual service—"We've got to pay the electricity bill, so help us out." But at the temple, the daily, weekly, and monthly offerings were part of the point, not an intrusion.

Or, as in some Reformed circles, the offering might be distinguished from the Eucharist in this way: the offering is our gift of gratitude in response to the good news proclaimed in Scripture and sermon; in contrast, the Eucharist is God's gracious gift to us.

While there is truth to be found in both of these approaches, both temple

---

118. Santmire, *Ritualizing Nature*, 162.

119. See discussion in Santmire, *Ritualizing Nature*, 292n12.

120. For a wonderful discussion of these metaphors, see Julie Canlis, *Calvin's Ladder: A Spiritual Theology of Ascent and Ascension* (Grand Rapids: Eerdmans, 2010). While appreciative of Calvin's Christological focus on ascent, as am I, Canlis also senses the need to supplement Calvin with an extended journey into Irenaeus's theology in order to guard against a denigration of the flesh and the physical world. Canlis claims that Irenaeus stresses that "flesh is not the antithesis of the Spirit but is his magnum opus" much more clearly than Calvin (211).

worship and early church approaches to the Eucharist suggest an asymmetrical cycle of gift-giving and blessing.

Picture this as a possible practice. As part of the eucharistic liturgy, offering plates or baskets are passed through the congregation and the collection taken. This offering is processed up to the table-altar along with the gifts of bread and wine which will be used for the Eucharist. The pastor or priest presiding at the Eucharist takes all these offerings, and lifts them up toward God while offering this or a similar prayer:

> "Powerful and gracious God,
> You have created the world, made it good and fruitful, and called us
>   to be stewards and cultivators of your world.
> We offer back to you from what you have first given us.
> These offerings are symbols of the fruitfulness of your creation and
>   the fruit of our own work, creativity, and culture. We offer
>   them and ourselves back to you with gratitude, committing
>   ourselves anew to wisely care for and creatively live within
>   your world.
> [At this point, the pastor or priest lays the gifts on the table and
>   raises his/her hands over the gifts, in a sign of blessing.]
> We pray that you would bless these gifts, including this bread and
>   wine. May they be used to build up your church so that we
>   might be the body of Christ, and may they strengthen and
>   empower us to participate in your mission in this good but
>   hurting world.
> We ask this in the name of Christ our Lord, through the power of
>   the Spirit. Amen."

The presider then takes the offering plates and hands them to one or two deacons, people appointed and known to be in charge of different ministries of the church, who take them to some safe place where they will eventually be counted. Then the presider arranges the bread and wine as needed to prepare for the eucharistic prayer.

Such a brief rite clearly names and attends to what is happening between God and God's people. It also integrates God's creating and saving work. It creates hooks for a deeper theology of culture, work, and mission, as is appropriate for the offering. And it also helpfully extends the type of the daily, Sabbath, and monthly rites at the temple into the church.

Speaking of culture, the elements of bread and wine present a further opportunity. Churches might get the bread from a local bakery known for good and just practices, or have it produced by volunteers at the church using ingredients that show creativity, care, and respect for the world around us. The wine should be of a quality that one would be proud to serve guests at home. The same standards should apply in cases of gluten-free and non-alcoholic alternatives. The bread and wine should be "unblemished" symbols of the creation and our human culture—so that God's complaint in Malachi will not apply to us: "You bring what has been taken by violence or is lame or sick, and this you bring as your offering! Shall I accept that from your hand? says the LORD" (Mal. 1:13). The bread and wine which will become the body and blood of Christ should be fitting symbols of the firstfruits of creation and human culture.

Such are a few possibilities for changes in practice that would highlight the creational themes of the daily, Sabbath, and monthly services of the temple as they are transformed and find their home in the Eucharist.

8

Passover

Remembrance, Faith, and Deliverance through the Sacrifice of the Firstborn

Clean out the old yeast so that you may be a new batch, as you really are unleavened. For our paschal lamb, Christ, has been sacrificed. Therefore, let us celebrate the festival, not with the old yeast, the yeast of malice and evil, but with the unleavened bread of sincerity and truth.

—1 Corinthians 5:7–8

The Passover. Most Christians know of it. Most even have some mental images of its primary ritual actions. Whether they are images of the original Passover meal eaten in haste before Israel's exodus from Egypt, or images of contemporary Seder meals, at least a few of the central rituals and meanings of the feast will come to mind when Passover is mentioned. Besides being the most familiar of the festivals, this celebration is also the part of Israel's worship that Christians most readily link to the celebration of the Lord's Supper. Variations on the words of Paul in 1 Corinthians 5:7–8 are incorporated into many Eucharist celebrations.

And yet, even though the basic link is there, people seldom ponder its significance. In what way is Christ's death and resurrection like the sacrifice of the Passover lamb? Or, going a bit deeper, in what way is our eucharistic celebration like the Feast of Unleavened Bread?

In recent years, some churches have taken up the practice of hosting a

Jewish Passover Seder or a "Christian Seder." This meal is often celebrated on Maundy Thursday, the Thursday before Easter. Perhaps their experience was like my own when I participated in one several years ago. On the one hand, the many links between this Passover rite and the Eucharist were enriching. But on the other hand, many aspects of both celebrations did not seem to line up well. Why? What is the relationship between the two rites?

Passover Foundations: Remembrance of Past Deliverance

In the following, I hope to clarify the ways the central meanings of the Passover celebration at the temple and the meal in Jewish homes can help us better understand and ground some, but not all, of the central meanings of the Eucharist. I begin by unpacking the ritual form and the central meanings of the Passover celebration as practiced by the people of Israel at the temple in the first century AD.

The Passover festival at the temple in the first century, distinguished from the original celebration of the Passover by the Israelites at the time of the exodus, provides the most immediate background to the meal ministry of Christ culminating in the Last Supper as well as the early church's eucharistic celebrations. While the original Passover in Egypt and the temple celebration centuries later are closely related, certain details of the rites are different. For example, the ritual action of sprinkling blood on the lintels and doorposts of the house as recorded in Exodus 12:7 is not repeated in later celebrations, nor is the original celebration a weeklong festival, since it looks forward to God's action rather than remembers it. However, most of the central meanings and symbols of the feast remain constant from the original celebration as recorded in Exodus 12 to contemporary celebrations in Jewish homes today.

Similar to earlier chapters, I will first examine the central forms and meanings of the Passover, and then look to New Testament and early church writings to see how the ritual forms and meanings of the Passover are taken up into the forms and meanings of the Last Supper and the Eucharist. Finally, I will ask to what extent the forms and meanings of the Passover celebration currently shape our working theologies and practice of the Eucharist, and how they might better do so.

Israel's Passover Practice

Our knowledge of Israel's Passover festival practice in the first century rests on firm foundations.[1] Many biblical and extra-biblical texts and traditions give insight into the main practices and symbols of the feast.[2] While some details are disputed, the festival's overall shape and key symbols are not under debate.[3] The Passover was not celebrated regularly throughout Israel's history.[4] Yet, both biblical and extra-biblical evidence indicate that the Passover and other festivals were celebrated regularly at the temple throughout the Second Temple period, from the fifth century BC until AD 70.[5] While there is much controversy about the details of the origins and development of Passover, it

1. This is not to say that we have detailed temple liturgies, nor exact liturgies of the Passover Seder meal, but simply solid knowledge of the main ritual actions at the temple. See for example, discussion in Paul Bradshaw and Maxwell Johnson, *The Origins of Feasts, Fasts and Seasons in Early Christianity* (Collegeville, MN: Liturgical Press, 2011), 39–43, and Joshua Kulp, "The Origins of the Seder and Haggadah," *Currents in Biblical Research* 4 (2005): 109–34, who argue strongly against earlier assumptions that rabbinic literature gives us the precise words and practices of the Passover Seder meal before AD 70. I agree. I am instead making claims primarily about temple practice, not the Seder meal, using primarily extra-rabbinic sources. I do, however, rely on Instone-Brewer's confidence that there is some continuity between core elements of rabbinic materials and pre-AD 70 practices.

2. Many biblical texts give rules for the feast: Exod. 12:1–51; 23:14–17; 34:18–25; Lev. 23:4–14; Num. 9:1–14; 28:16–25; Deut. 16:1–8. Other biblical texts give snapshots of Passover celebrations over the years and prophetic visions of future idealized celebrations: Num. 33:3; Josh. 5:10–12; 1 Kgs. 9:25; 2 Kgs. 23:21–23; 2 Chr. 8:12–13; 29:3–30:27; 35:1–19; Ezra 6:19–22; Ezek. 45:21–25; Gospels, passim; 1 Cor. 5:6–8; Heb. 11:28. Extra-biblical materials give further snapshots of celebrations as well as discussions of its meanings: Elephantine ostraca and papyri; 1 Esdr. 1:1–22; Jubilees; Ezekiel the Tragedian, *Exagōgē* l. 132–92; Wisdom of Solomon 10:18–20; 18:8–9; Philo, *Special Laws* 2.144–75; *On the Life of Moses* 231–32; Pseudo-Philo; Josephus, *Antiquities* 2.14.6, 3.10.5, 9.4.8; *B. J.* 6.9.3. Rabbinic materials discuss the Passover in detail. Core elements of those rabbinic materials can be traced back to the pre-AD 70 era: m. Pesah., m. Zebah, m. Menah.

3. The largest discrepancy, in my opinion, is that Jubilees 49:20–21 imagines, in contrast to most other sources, that the Passover sacrifice is eaten only at the temple, not in people's homes. Whether eaten at the temple or at home, the central symbols are the same.

4. 2 Kings 23:22: "No such Passover had been kept since the days of the judges who judged Israel."

5. J. B. Segal, *The Hebrew Passover: From the Earliest Times to AD 70* (London: Oxford University Press, 1963), 1–41.

is also clear that the main ritual aspects and central meanings of the festival achieved a stable form during that time.[6]

So, what would observant Jews in the century preceding the destruction of the temple have seen and experienced when they came to Jerusalem to celebrate the Passover festival?

The preparations for this festival, during which the city swelled to over twice its typical size, would have been begun long before the festival. At one point in the first century, the "crowded" Passover of Agrippa (AD 41–44) included over 300,000 sacrifices made at the temple for Passover, which conservatively would mean three million people were present.[7] The celebration itself lasted eight days. It included four key events that took place at the temple: the Passover sacrifice (Lev. 23:5; Num. 28:16) followed by a ritual meal, two other "holy convocations" that marked the first and last days of the weeklong Feast of Unleavened Bread (Lev. 23:6–8; Num. 28:17, 25), and the offering of the firstfruits of the grain harvest, "the omer" (Lev. 23:9–14).[8] The days of the festival with the central actions and symbols are as follows:

Day		Rituals/Symbols
14 Nisan	Passover Eve	Search for and destruction of leaven in homes
		Sacrifice of Passover lamb (or goat) at the temple

---

6. See, for example, Segal, *Hebrew Passover*, 78–113. Segal narrates the many modern theories about the origin of the Passover. Jon D. Levenson, *The Death and Resurrection of the Beloved Son: The Transformation of Child Sacrifice in Judaism and Christianity* (New Haven: Yale University Press, 1993), is an important recent contribution to the discussion about the origins and central meanings of the Passover sacrifice.

7. Instone-Brewer, *Feasts and Sabbaths*, 199. m. Pesah. 4.15. Josephus, *J. W.* 2.280, 6.425 gives similar numbers for two Passover celebrations in Jerusalem.

8. The basic calendar for this festival is laid out in Exod. 12:1–16; 23:14–17; 34:18–25; Lev. 23:4–14; Num. 28; and Deut. 16:1–8. While the basic structure is fairly clear, the timing of the Passover sacrifice continued to cause confusion among the Jewish people and rabbis because of disagreements about lunar and solar calendars, Passovers that fell on a Sabbath, and the biblical phrase "between the evenings." See m. Pesah. 5:1–4 and commentary on this in the Talmud. See Instone-Brewer, *Feasts and Sabbaths*, 126–43. Such issues may play a part in discrepancies in the Gospels about the timing of the crucifixion of Christ in relationship to the Passover festival.

Day		Rituals/Symbols
15 Nisan	Passover/first day of Feast of Unleavened Bread	Passover meal eaten at home (wine, lamb, bitter herbs, unleavened bread, three questions, Hallel psalms)
		Temple convocation
		No work allowed
		Unleavened bread eaten Nisan 15–21
		Daily and special offerings at temple Nisan 15–21
16 Nisan	Day of Offering of the Omer	Offering of firstfruits omer at temple
17–20 Nisan		Intermediate days of Passover
21 Nisan	Final day of the Feast	Temple convocation of Unleavened Bread/Passover
		No work allowed

The first important ritual actions took place on the day before the Passover sacrifice, on Nisan 14, which was called "the day of preparation" or "Passover Eve." On this day, people searched for any kind of leaven (Heb. *hametz*) or products that contained leaven throughout their homes. This included not only bread and yeast or leaven itself, but many items ranging from beer to makeup, anything that contained yeast. They started at night and then finished by noon, when they removed and burned the leaven. On Jewish reckoning, the calendar day begins when the first stars appear in the sky, a practice based upon Genesis 1:5: "And there was evening and there was morning, the first day."

On the day of preparation, the regular daily sacrifices were offered before the Passover sacrifices. That ceremony would be scheduled earlier if Passover or Passover Eve was on a Sabbath.[9]

For the Passover sacrifice itself, people who were going to celebrate the Passover divided themselves into a company or household with a minimum of ten adult males. The company would later eat the Passover meal together in a home, a meal which would include eating parts of the animal sacrifice. The sacrifice was typically a male lamb, but it could also be a male goat. Represen-

9. Instone-Brewer, *Feasts and Sabbaths*, 127.

tatives from the company went to the temple with their sacrificial animal in the afternoon, and then, with the help of the priests, would sacrifice the animal.[10] The animals would be killed and then flayed. For the flaying, the animal was either attached to prepared hooks, or if there were not enough hooks, they would be hung from slender poles held up by the household representatives. Their blood and fat portions were collected by priests and then taken to the altar where the blood would be tossed, sprinkled, and the fat burned. The other parts of the animal were then prepared for the meal, which was celebrated away from the temple by the household or company.

Given the large crowds, there would often be three groups of sacrifices—similar to the way that large churches in our day schedule more than one service.[11] The first group would fill the temple court and prepare their animals for the sacrifice, the priests would blow their shofroth, and then the sacrifices were made while the Levites sang the Hallel psalms (Pss. 113–118). After one group finished, the next group would come in and the short liturgy would be repeated.

The Passover meal, now called the Seder (a Hebrew word simply meaning "order" or "arrangement," so originally referring to the ritual ordering of the meal), would be celebrated that night, the night at the start of the calendar day of Nisan 15.

Passover Seder liturgies became quite elaborate over time. While many of those traditions have roots in the first century or earlier, they did not become standardized until later. It is clear, however, that the central ritual actions during the first century involved these things: cups of wine, bitter herbs, unleavened bread, the Passover lamb or goat, asking three questions, and reciting the Hallel psalms.

The ritual part of the meal was structured around three or four cups of wine.[12] The first cup was poured and mixed with water, a typical custom for drinking wine at that time. Blessings for the wine as well as for the particular celebration—

---

10. Instone-Brewer, *Feasts and Sabbaths*, 127. Joseph Fitzmyer, *The Acts of the Apostles* (New Haven: Yale, 1998) notes that the tradition in the first century was between 2:30pm and 5:30pm—an interpretation of Exod. 12:6.

11. m. Pesah. 5.5–10. See Instone-Brewer, *Feasts and Sabbaths*, 143–47.

12. It seems the fourth cup was added sometime in the first century (Instone-Brewer, *Feasts and Sabbaths*, 176–91).

here the Passover—would be said over the first cup.[13] After those blessings, the bitter herbs, the unleavened bread, and the Passover lamb were eaten.

Then the second cup would be mixed, and the host's youngest son (who would be helped if needed) would ask three questions. In the following version those three questions about the distinctive elements are in the form of a single question with three qualifications:

> Why is this night different from all [other] nights? For on all [other] nights we eat leavened or unleavened bread [but on] this night all of it is unleavened bread. For on all [other] nights we eat other vegetables [but on] this night [we eat] bitter herbs. For on all [other] nights we eat roasted, stewed or boiled flesh [but on] this night all of it is roasted.[14]

These questions would prompt a retelling of the Exodus story as it is given in Deuteronomy 26:5, typically ending at verse 8. At this point, people sang either one or two Hallel psalms (Ps. 113 and sometimes Ps. 114) and a member of the group would give a benediction centered on the theme of redemption.

The household would then eat the rest of the meal, concluding with the third cup, which is called "the cup of blessing." Ritual meals at the Sabbath and other feast days typically ended with this cup as well. At that point those gathered would sing the final Hallel psalms (Pss. 114–118 or 115–118) and someone would give the final blessing. At some point pre-AD 70 a fourth cup was added to the Passover tradition. How this began is a bit unclear, but it seems to be a "final" cup, a kind of limitation to the amount of drinking that might occur after the end of the meal.[15]

The Festival of Unleavened Bread would then begin the next morning—still Nisan 15. The festival stretched from Nisan 15 to 21 and was marked by holy convocations on the first and last days. On the first day, no work was to be done. After the regular morning sacrifice, certain public sacrifices were made—"two young bulls, one ram, and seven male lambs a year old," accompanied by *minhah* or grain offerings, and "one male goat for a sin offering, to

---

13. Jubilees 49:6 mentions wine as part of the celebration.

14. m. Pesah. 10.4 in Instone-Brewer, *Feasts and Sabbaths*, 181.

15. See Instone-Brewer, *Feasts and Sabbaths*, 185–91 for discussion. The fourth cup may have been related to Jesus's statement that he would not drink any more wine after the "cup of blessing" (188).

make atonement for you" (Num. 28:19–22). Then the people brought their own personal sacrifices—a prescribed burnt offering, a prescribed *hagigah* or festivity offering that was a type of *shelamim*, and a final sacrifice of joy, another *shelamim* that was chosen "according to the blessing which the Lord had given" to the offerer (Deut. 16:17).[16] The corporate offerings were repeated throughout the week. The final day of the feast was also marked by no work and a special convocation.

At some point during this festival, "on the day after the sabbath" (Lev. 23:11, 15), which was interpreted as the day after the Passover and so Nisan 16, a sheaf or an omer (a unit of measurement, between two and four liters) of the newly harvested grain was offered to the Lord at the temple. It was accompanied by whole burnt offerings. This offering marked the beginning of the harvest season. It consisted of an omer of grain-meal from one of the first sheaves of grain that were harvested that year in Israel. That presentation to the Lord started the countdown to Pentecost, which occurred precisely fifty days later.

Passover: Central Meanings

Reflecting on the many symbols and rituals of this entire pilgrim festival, several stand out as most important: the Passover sacrifice; the practices concerning leaven and unleavened bread; the Passover meal with its main symbols of bitter herbs, unleavened bread, wine, and the Passover lamb; the Hallel psalms; and the presentation of the firstfruits omer. All of these point to central meanings of this complex festival. But the three questions asked by the youngest son guide us quickly to the heart of the Passover through its three symbols: the bitter herbs, the unleavened bread, and the Passover lamb.[17] Let us examine these first.

---

16. See m. Hag.

17. See Exod. 12:8: "They shall eat the lamb that same night; they shall eat it roasted over the fire with unleavened bread and bitter herbs." For those skeptical about the dating of Seder practices, these three symbols are also the central symbols in the biblical account of the Egyptian Passover meal. Bradshaw and Johnson agree these were the key parts of the meal: "The primary act prior to this time [the year AD 70] was the sacrifice of the Passover lambs . . . each of which was consumed by a group of participants. . . . That meal would have included the eating of *matzah* (unleavened bread) and bitter herbs, and often also the drinking of wine." Bradshaw and Johnson, *The Origins of Feasts*, 40.

During the Passover celebration meal, bitter herbs are eaten.[18] They symbolize the bitterness, oppression, and affliction Israel experienced in Egypt—eating them caused Israel to ponder this bitterness. Why might Israel be required to perform this ritual? During their sojourn toward the promised land through the wilderness, rebellious Israel often looked back with wistful eye to that time of slavery (Num. 11:5, 18, 20; 14:3; 21:5). "We remember the fish we used to eat in Egypt for nothing, the cucumbers, the melons, the leeks, the onions, and the garlic; but now our strength is dried up, and there is nothing at all but this manna to look at" (Num. 11:5–6). Their new situation of freedom required a lot from them, and they longed for their old way of life which seemed easier to them, one in which—at least in their nostalgic memories—food was readily available. They forgot the bitterness of their slavery and longed to return to Egypt.

In fact, in Numbers, which records Israel's journey to the promised land, the central sin of God's people appears to be sloth. The people of God rejected the journey toward God's good future and instead embraced what they perceived as an easier life. In Numbers 13–14, the dramatic center of the book, Israel sends twelve spies to scout the promised land. While Joshua and Caleb interpret it as "an exceedingly good land" (14:7), the ten other spies reject it, even after bringing back a grand cluster of grapes, pomegranates, and figs (13:23)—food even more appetizing than cucumbers and onions. But instead of rejoicing, they interpret God's good plan for them as a bad one, and the people weep, complain, and say, "Would it not be better for us to go back to Egypt?" (14:3) Yes, remembering the bitterness of slavery is necessary. Eating bitter herbs is a significant action of right remembering.

The unleavened bread has two central, related meanings. The first meaning is tied to the haste with which Israel had to leave Egypt. The bread is unleavened because Israel did not have time for the typical rising process. It is thus a reminder not of the slavery of Egypt, but of Israel's hasty and precarious departure that the Lord brought about. Deuteronomy 16:3 is often quoted in this regard: "For seven days you shall eat unleavened bread with it—the bread of affliction—because you came out of the land of Egypt in great haste, so that all the days of your life you may remember the day of your departure

18. See Stubbs, *Numbers*, 219–21. This section draws from and elaborates on those pages.

from the land of Egypt." The phrase "the bread of affliction" is thus best interpreted as good, healthy bread made quickly in a situation of affliction—not as bread that is in itself bad tasting or a source of affliction. Similar to manna, it is good but not yet the full, risen bread of the promised land. It is the bread of precarious freedom, bread for the journey. It symbolizes God's provision of a new beginning for Israel.

A different but related meaning of the unleavened bread comes from the emphasis on no leaven. "For seven days no leaven shall be found in your houses," the Lord tells Moses in Exodus 12:19 (cf. Exod. 12:15, 20; 13:7; Deut. 16:4). Leaven is a powerful symbol of something unseen that has great effects. Furthermore, given the practice of saving leaven from one batch of dough to the next—as people still do today with sourdough bread—it is also a wonderful symbol for a long-term tradition or habit. The ritual of cleaning out the leaven from a house and then burning it right before the start of the festival represents a new start in a household's habits, practices, and inner principles. This new start is linked to the new start of Israel, as they left behind the ways and practices of Egypt: "For on this very day I brought your companies out of the land of Egypt" (Exod. 12:17). The punishment for eating leaven is being "cut off from the congregation of Israel" (12:19). This keeps the "leavened" person away from the fresh dough of Israel. This interpretation of cleaning out the leaven is emphasized in later Jewish traditions and spoken of by Jesus and Paul. Evil intentions and evil persons, like "bad apples," and conversely, the holy intentions and patterns of the kingdom of God are all likened to leaven (Matt. 13:33; 16:6, 11–12; Mark 8:15; Luke 12:1; 13:21; 1 Cor. 5:6–8; Gal. 5:9). They are to carefully cast out the old patterns, habits, and spirit of Egypt as they begin their new life with God.

Leaving behind the old, starting fresh, God's deliverance, and God's providing a new start: these are the central meanings wrapped up in the symbol of unleavened bread. Embracing such a new start, committing to leaving behind old patterns and ways, joyfully remembering and giving thanks for God's strong deliverance, and God's providence for the beginning of a new journey toward the promised land: these are the central meanings that participating in the Feast of Unleavened Bread would have for the Jewish people.

The Passover lamb and its blood is a complicated symbol. It is also a unique form of sacrifice, sharing characteristics of several Israelite sacrifices.[19] The

---

19. Rowley, *Worship in Ancient Israel*, 118, writes that the Passover is a unique sacrifice.

original Egyptian Passover lamb functioned in part like a sin offering (*hattat*) in that the animal was given, killed, and its blood used to provide a kind of covering so that the judgment of God would pass over. But unlike a sin offering, the people also ate its flesh. In contrast, in the Passover celebrations of succeeding generations, the Passover sacrifice is closer in form to the *shelamim* offering.[20] The animal is eaten in a celebratory meal shared by God and God's people. Finally, there are resonances with the *olah* or burnt offering, something totally given over to God, in that the Passover sacrifice has similar meanings and there are scriptural allusions back to the binding of Isaac, who was to be an *olah* sacrifice (detailed below).

Though the Passover lamb sacrifice is a complicated symbol, its various threads can be combined into a coherent whole when they are understood in light of ideas connected to the firstborn, an image that plays a key role in the exodus story.[21] In that story, God tells Moses: "Then you shall say to Pharaoh, 'Thus says the LORD: Israel is my firstborn son. I said to you, "Let my son go that he may worship me." But you refused to let him go; now I will kill your firstborn son'" (Exod. 4:22–23). In this passage firstborn themes are linked not only to the Passover sacrifice, but also to Israel's deliverance and to their vocation to be a priestly people. These in turn draw upon the story of the binding of Isaac by Abraham in Genesis 22:1–19.[22]

20. See m. Pesah. 9.5 for distinctions between the Passover in Egypt and the Passovers of succeeding generations.

21. The original meaning or understood efficacy of the Passover sacrifice is greatly disputed. See Cornelis Houtman, *Exodus*, Historical Commentary on the Old Testament, 4 vols. (Kampen: Kok Publishing House, 1996), 2:176–77 for a good list of options, including "apotropaic power," "strengthening household gods," "a reconciling act," and "an act of purification." Segal's review of older scholarly opinions reveals the multitude of divergent reconstructions of the origins and meanings of the Passover festival and sacrifice that historical critical methods led to. Segal, "Modern Theories on the Origins and Early Development of the Passover," in *Hebrew Passover*, 78–113. We are in a period where a hermeneutic of trust of the biblical and Jewish source materials holds greater sway—Levenson's work being a prime example. As will be seen below, my interpretation based in part on Levenson has both "reconciling" and "purification" aspects to it.

22. "In the case of Judaism, the *Aqedah* [the binding of Isaac] has played a central role in two of its most defining sacred occasions, Passover and Rosh Hashanah (New Year's), and to this day it reverberates revealingly in the liturgy not only of the latter holiday but also much other Jewish prayer." Jon D. Levenson, *Inheriting Abraham: The Patriarch in Judaism, Christianity and Islam* (Princeton: Princeton University Press, 2012), 66. Jubilees 18 clearly sees the *Aqedah* as the foundation of the seven-day festival.

Firstborns were seen as especially precious. The Hebrew word for the first-born of people and animals, *bekor*, shares the same root as the word for the firstfruits of crops, the *bikkurim*. Firstborn sons, firstborn male animals, and the firstfruits of plants and crops all held a special place in Israel—and they are all to be dedicated to God. In Exodus 13:12, God tells Moses, "You shall set apart . . . all that first opens the womb," both animals and people, for God. Lesser animals are sacrificed to God, but larger animals can be and people are commanded to be "redeemed"—returned from the ownership or power of someone else by some payment or action. In the case of large animals, they are redeemed by the gift of a smaller animal, and in the case of humans, by a token amount of money (Num. 3:44–51). The payment acknowledges that they are rightly God's, but they are returned nonetheless. They are rightly God's in Exodus 13:15 because of God's action in saving the firstborn when he brought Israel out of Egypt. The rationale seems to be that because God rescued the firstborn, all the firstborn are his. This is true; however, there are also deeper reasons.

Throughout the Hebrew Scriptures, the proper and ideal response of humanity to God is understood to be the giving of the gift of one's faith, trust, fear, obedience—even one's very self—back to God. We are rightly God's because God is our creator. The most basic sacrifice at the temple, the *olah* or burnt offering, can be interpreted as a symbol of this. Baruch Schwartz writes that the *olah* is "the gift-offering par excellence," a token of "love and reverence" for the Lord.[23] Turning the entire gift into smoke represents the total self-giving of the one offering the sacrifice to God. The gift or token represents the offerer. What symbolic token best fits this meaning? For Israel, and for many other peoples, it is one's firstborn son.

Giving one's all to God is also reflected in the practice, continued to this day in Jewish communities, of "redeeming" one's firstborn son for five pieces of silver (Num. 3:44–51). One's duty is to give God one's firstborn, but then one is also commanded to redeem him back. There was also a parallel ancient practice: every firstborn son in Israel was to be given to God to be a priest. This practice was performed by Hannah in 1 Samuel 1:19–28. This understanding is reflected in the substitution of the priesthood of the Levites for the priesthood of all the firstborn males of Israel in the aftermath of the golden calf incident

---

23. B. Schwartz, *Jewish Study Bible*, 206–7.

(Exod. 32:29).²⁴ At first, all firstborn males were to be priests, but the Levites were substituted for them because of their zeal and dedication.

The epicenter of this ideal total sacrifice through the giving up of one's firstborn in Hebrew Scripture is the *Aqedah*, the binding of Isaac by Abraham. While this powerful story has received numerous and contradictory interpretations, I find Jon Levenson's interpretations and arguments most compelling.²⁵ For Levenson, a central meaning of the story is that it is a test of Abraham's total self-dedication to God: "Psychologically, what is asked is not only an inexpressibly painful act of sacrifice; it is also an act of *self*-sacrifice."²⁶ While Abraham is praised for his obedience in Gen. 22:18, for his faith in God's promises in Heb. 11:17, and for both obedience and faithfulness in Jubilees 18:16, underlying all of them is this total self-dedication. We see this in part because the type of sacrifice Abraham is intending to make is a burnt offering, an *olah* (Gen. 22:2), which as discussed above is itself a sign of self-dedication to God.

And Abraham offers this gift: "Abraham passes his great test only because he refuses to hold back his beloved son, only because he is willing to make even that donation, painful beyond words."²⁷ As a result of this: "The great paradox is that because he proves willing to donate Isaac, he not only retains him but to some degree merits the extraordinary promises that rest on his only/favored son."²⁸ Levenson uses the word "merit" intentionally. In Jewish traditions, the saying of Genesis 15:6 "and it was reckoned to him as merit [righteousness]" becomes associated not primarily with Abraham's belief in God's promises, but with his faithfulness proven through this test. As written in 1 Maccabees 2:52: "Was not Abraham found faithful when tested, and it was reckoned to him as righteousness?" (cf. Sir. 44:20).

The Passover is connected to this archetypal event in early Jewish tra-

---

24. As the Lord says to Moses in Numbers: "I hereby accept the Levites from among the Israelites as substitutes for all the firstborn that open the womb among the Israelites. The Levites shall be mine, for all the firstborn are mine; when I killed all the firstborn in the land of Egypt, I consecrated for my own all the firstborn in Israel, both human and animal; they shall be mine" (Num. 3:12–13).

25. Levenson, "The Test," in *Inheriting Abraham*, 66–112. This is a fresh and condensed restatement of many of the arguments and findings in his earlier *Death and Resurrection*.

26. Levenson, *Inheriting Abraham*, 69.

27. Levenson, *Inheriting Abraham*, 84.

28. Levenson, *Inheriting Abraham*, 84.

ditions. In Jubilees, Abraham's near-sacrifice is connected to, or better, the foundation for the Passover. Abraham's action occurs in the afternoon of the fourteenth day of the first month, and as a result, "It is ordained and written in the heavenly tablets concerning Israel and his seed to observe the festival seven days with festal joy" (Jub. 18:19).[29]

This connection makes sense. In both the heart-wrenching story of the *Aqedah* as well as in the story of the Passover, the great tension is between giving and withholding. The angel of the Lord tells Abraham, "You have not withheld your son, your only son, from me," and later reiterates the promise of blessing "because you . . . have not withheld your son, your only son" (Gen. 22:12, 16). In contrast, in Exodus 11:10, Pharaoh's heart was hardened, and as a result, "He did not let the people of Israel," God's firstborn, "go out of his land." He is hard-hearted and thus tightfisted. Similarly in Exod. 13:15, it explains, "When Pharaoh stubbornly refused to let us go, the LORD killed all the first-born in the land of Egypt, from human firstborn to the firstborn of animals. Therefore I sacrifice to the LORD every male that first opens the womb, but every firstborn of my sons I redeem."

Read in light of the *Aqedah*, this sacrifice of the firstborn in Exodus no longer looks like a strict tit-for-tat payback for a somewhat arbitrary historical action. One should not settle for this shallow interpretation: "God saved us by killing the Egyptian firstborn and saving our firstborn, and so we give him our firstborn, but in a different way." Instead, the deeper roots of this story in-dicate God desires a particular kind of human heart and life—one that rightly opens one's hand, one that offers the best, a token of all, to God, rather than stubbornly refusing and trying to find life through taking what is not rightly one's own and holding onto it tightly.

Israel is saved from the grasping and tightfisted ways of Egypt.[30] Israel is

29. Discussed in Levenson, *Inheriting Abraham*, 91–92; Segal, *Hebrew Passover*, 236.

30. This contrast between the ways of Egypt and the ways that God wishes for his people is encoded in the Ten Commandments, the Law given to them after their res-cue. The prohibitions on murder, adultery, and stealing all reflect this. The historical background to the commandment "You shall not steal" seems in fact to be practices of slavery, as argued by Patrick Miller, "Property and Possession in Light of the Ten Com-mandments," in *Having: Property and Possession in Religious and Social Life*, ed. William Schweiker and Charles Mathewes (Grand Rapids: Eerdmans, 2004), 17–50. By enslaving another, one steals their life to use for one's own purposes—the very opposite of self-giving love for the other.

called to be self-offering children of Abraham, as symbolized in the Passover sacrifice. "The blood of the lamb" becomes both a symbol of God's gracious deliverance—God provides something they have not yet lived into—and a reminder of their vocation to be a people totally offered to God. In later celebrations of the Passover, this sacrifice becomes a *shelamim* celebration. God dwells with and joins in the feast of his firstborn people, a feast which reminds them they are called to be a "priestly" people (Exod. 19:6), a people who offer themselves—like Abraham—and who thus model a different way of life.

What must not be lost in this play of symbols is this: the Passover sacrifice is not about atonement for sin. Instead, it is a celebration of being saved from powers of oppression and being saved for a specific vocation, to be a priestly people modeled on Abraham. Richard Hays says precisely this in his commentary on 1 Corinthians: "To repeat what has been said above, the Passover festival has nothing to do with atonement for sin and everything to do with deliverance from the powers of oppression. This fact has wide-ranging implications for the way we think about christology and about our own communal identity."[31] It also has wide-ranging implications for our celebration of the Eucharist.

Putting these three symbols all together—the bitter herbs, unleavened bread, and Passover sacrifice—we find that Passover certainly recalls the redemption of Israel by God from the bitter slavery of Egypt. But it is not a simple military victory party. Given the right remembrance of the bitterness of Egypt, the removal of leaven, and all the meanings and symbols that swirl around this Passover lamb including the background story of the binding of Isaac by Abraham and Israel's dedication of their firstborn to God, the Passover celebration is a feast celebrating the fact that God is creating a people who, saved from the powers of oppression, are called to live a different way of life.

Israel's new way was a life of total dedication to God, a life of self-giving—even if it involves great loss—rather than the hard-hearted and tightfisted holding back of Pharaoh. Such a hard-hearted way of life is politically manifested in the bitter slavery and oppression that Israel was subjected to. Israel was freed from both their political subjugation as well as the leaven of Egypt in order to become a priestly people. The political and the spiritual are not separated. Israel's way of self-giving symbolized and enacted in their worship life should

31. Hays, *1 Corinthians*, 90–91.

also spill out into all their ways as a holy nation. In so doing they will fulfill their vocation to be God's firstborn.

Christians should recognize this new way. It is in fact the deepest way of God, a way that becomes incarnate in Christ, the Passover lamb. In him the type is both grounded from all eternity and also fulfilled in time. In the Eucharist, we are called to remember "Christ our Passover Lamb," provided by God for us. In him are both our deliverance and our door into a different way of life.

Other aspects of the festival fit seamlessly with these themes.

The giving of an omer of the very first crops harvested in Israel on Nisan 16 is a firstfruits offering. While the major feast of tithing one's harvest occurred at Pentecost, fifty days later, this offering, like that of Abraham, was yet another indication that everything that Israel had was from God and to God. In the springtime of the year, in the first month, at the beginning of the harvest, it was a time of thanksgiving for this yearly new beginning—brought about by God. Their offering was an appropriate response.

The Hallel psalms were another important part of this celebration. In them—as well as in many of the recorded prayers associated with that feast— we find first of all praises to God for past deliverance. Psalm 114 recalls Israel's deliverance from Egypt by God (v. 1), the parting of the Reed Sea (v. 3) and God's bringing water from a rock (v. 8).

But along with this remembrance is a call for ongoing blessing. The God who delivered and blessed Israel in the past will continue to do so: "The LORD has been mindful of us; he will bless us" (Ps. 115:12).

And in Psalm 118 especially, we have passages that were given an explicit Messianic interpretation. "The stone that the builders rejected has become the chief cornerstone" (v. 22), and "Blessed is the one who comes in the name of the LORD. We bless you from the house of the LORD" (v. 26), were understood by Jews to picture the coming of God's anointed to the temple and the people blessing the Messiah from that place.

Israel continued to celebrate this feast even though the promises of God had not been fully fulfilled. And so, Israel looked forward to the day that, out of God's "steadfast love" for them (Ps. 118:1–4), God would send a Messiah who would bring those promises to fulfillment.

In the first century, the Passover celebration was linked to heightened expectations of a coming Messiah, who would again deliver Israel from her captivity to the powers of oppression, most obviously the empire of Rome, and inaugurate the coming Messianic age. It was a time of remembering God's redemption, and a time of hope for God's future redemption.

Passover Connections to the Table in the New Testament and Early Church

In the New Testament connections are clearly made between the Eucharist, Christ's death on the cross, and Passover. We see them in the Passover setting of the Last Supper and crucifixion in the Synoptic Gospels (e.g., Mark 14:12). In the Gospel of John, we see them in the positioning of Christ's own crucifixion to correspond with the sacrifice of the Passover lambs (John 19:14). Paul makes them explicit in this statement: "For our paschal lamb, Christ, has been sacrificed. Therefore, let us celebrate the festival" (1 Cor. 5:7–8).

Similar connections are clearly made in a variety of patristic statements about the Eucharist. But over time, these connections became less frequent; they were mostly "passed over" in the church's later liturgies and thinking. If they were mentioned, they had little effect on eucharistic thought or practice. In contemporary eucharistic theologies, connections between the Eucharist and Passover are sometimes noted, but the themes and meanings of Passover do little work in shaping either theology or practice. Such connections must be argued for again in order to be recovered.

One way a few contemporary scholars have sought to make such a reconnection starts with the prayers used by Jews at the Passover meal, as far as these are known. They then make the case that the earliest liturgies and prayers we have on record in the early church are literary developments of them. Such attempts at making literary connections are enlightening in their own way, but the results are fraught with challenges. I do not find this way of making connections tremendously compelling or enlightening. Usually at the end of the argument one is left with a possible case *that* the eucharistic prayers developed out of Passover prayers.[32] Instead, I am more interested in tracing typological

32. A good example of this is Skarsaune's chapter "Passover and Eucharist," in his book, *In the Shadow of the Temple*, 399–422. In the end, the result of his arguments is

connections, the development in the use of similar images, symbols, and practices, as these connections prompt more fruitful questions.

In the following discussion, I will first examine such typological connections and their impact in the letters of Paul. Following that, I will look at Passover connections in the Gospel of John and other Johannine works. Finally, I will consider other connections between Passover, Easter, and the Eucharist in the early church—all with the goal of seeing how the early church understood the Eucharist to be in part a transformation of the Passover celebration.

Paul

In 1 Corinthians 5, Paul writes: "Do you not know that a little yeast leavens the whole batch of dough? Clean out the old yeast [leaven] so that you may be a new batch, as you really are unleavened. For our paschal lamb, Christ, has been sacrificed. Therefore, let us celebrate the festival, not with the old yeast, the yeast of malice and evil, but with the unleavened bread of sincerity and truth" (1 Cor. 5:6-8).

The first thing to note is simply that Paul thinks of the Eucharist in light of the Passover. While his focus here is not on the celebration itself, he makes an argument that the Corinthian church should act in light of the fact that they are a people formed by the Eucharist, which for him is understood in light of Passover symbols—the Passover sacrifice and leaven.

Second, Paul uses these symbols and applies them to the Eucharist in ways fully in line with the Jewish interpretations of them. Paul sees the Eucharist as a typological extension of this Jewish feast in a way that does not negate or overturn the central meanings, but rather extends them into the Eucharist.

In 1 Corinthians 5, Paul is advising the Corinthian congregation how to deal with an incestuous man (1 Cor. 5:1). Members of the church are for certain reasons proud of his activity. Paul in response repeatedly calls the Corinthian people to remember their high vocation, that they should be a contrast-community, a community of "saints" (1 Cor. 1:2) that is "unleavened"

---

simply *that* there is a connection, not *how* this might change our understanding of or practice of the Eucharist: "This confirms the proposition made in chapter nineteen: each Eucharist is a small, weekly Passover celebration, even when the meal was eliminated and the Eucharist itself transposed to Sunday morning rather than evening" (421). See discussion above in note 1 of this chapter.

(1 Cor. 5:7). He tells them this involves exercising communal self-discipline, as Israel did symbolically in the Feast of Unleavened Bread as they threw out and burned the leaven before the festival. Here, the "leaven" they must "clean out" (1 Cor. 5:6) is a person—at least at first glance. The man is to be excluded from the community for now, cleaned out from the household of faith like a lump of leavened dough. Paul writes: "You are to hand this man over to Satan for the destruction of the flesh, so that his spirit may be saved in the day of the Lord" (5:5). He is to be "handed over," given over to the powers outside the household. In the Passover in Egypt, for households without the blood of Passover lambs on their lintels, the destroyer (Exod. 12:23) came and killed their firstborn. Paul through his use of imagery seems to make this claim: the world outside the Christian community is a world under the control of Satan; it is a world that functions according to the ways of the "flesh."[33] This man's "flesh" will be destroyed in the day of the Lord, but his spirit saved.[34] Thus the "leaven" which must be cast out is ultimately the man's "flesh" or the principles of action within him that are themselves part of the ways of the world under Satan's power.[35] Paul's community discipline is typologically based on the Passover practice of destroying leaven.

A similar pattern is found in 1 Corinthians 11. Paul again sees the Eucharist as an occasion that involves community self-discipline. There, however, the actions that the community should "judge" (1 Cor. 11:31) are practices in which the rich are humiliating those with less. Such actions are of "the world" (1 Cor. 11:32) and do not belong in the body of Christ.

Paul's understanding of Christ as Passover lamb in 1 Corinthians 5 and throughout the letter also fits with the interpretation given above. Christ's Passover sacrifice frees us from an old way of life and enables a new community to emerge, one that lives a new way of life with God. The "therefore" in his phrase "Therefore, let us celebrate the festival, not with the old yeast" implies that Christ's death as the paschal lamb frees the new community from an old life and enables it to begin anew an "unleavened" way of life. As a result of

33. For "flesh" as a system or power that operates in us, see, e.g., 1 Cor. 3:1, where Paul contrasts those who are "of the flesh" with those "of the spirit."
34. Paul is thinking similarly in, e.g., 1 Cor. 1:18 and 2:6. Those to whom the cross is foolishness "are perishing," living in the "world" or part of creation that is being or will be destroyed.
35. For a similar interpretation of this passage, see Hays, *1 Corinthians*, 84–88.

Christ's death, "We are set free from the power that held us captive, and sent out on a journey toward a promise."[36]

The powers of oppression from which Christ's sacrifice frees the new community are the "wisdom . . . and rulers of this age" (1 Cor. 2:6). In contrast, the new way of life, hinted at in Abraham's binding of Isaac, is ironically seen most clearly in Christ's giving himself over to death. What Abraham's sacrifice symbolized, Christ lived, especially as he died. Paul describes this way of life as the embodiment of an alternative wisdom, one at odds with the wisdom of this world (1 Cor. 1–2). This way of life, this Wisdom, this Word made incarnate in Jesus Christ, ultimately reveals the way and shape of God's inner life. As Paul writes, we see "the glory of God in the face of Jesus Christ" (2 Cor. 4:6). There are more facets to Christ's work for Paul than this, but the way Paul references the paschal sacrifice in 1 Cor. 5 points to these themes throughout his letters.

John

We find similar relationships between Christ's work, the Passover Lamb, and the Eucharist in the Gospel of John. In John, however, there is no mention of unleavened bread—instead, the bread associated with the Passover feasts in John is manna, the bread come down from heaven.

Similar to Paul, John considers God's people enslaved. Rather than being enslaved to Pharaoh and the Egyptians, people are enslaved to sin, which is part of the system of this world, a world under control of the "ruler of this world" (John 14:30) who is "the devil" (8:44). Jesus's conversations with the Jews in 8:31–58 evidence this theological understanding of slavery.[37] While this slavery is not directly connected in John to either the Passover or the Eucharist, like the Israelites tasting "bitter herbs," this situation must be contemplated and understood in order to fully appreciate God's Passover action.[38]

---

36. Hays, *1 Corinthians*, 91.

37. Melito of Sardis (second century) also draws connections between this situation of slavery and that of Egypt in *On Pascha and Fragments*, ed. Stuart Hall (Oxford: Clarendon, 1979), §§35, 37, 67–68.

38. Connections between these passages and the Passover are argued for in Paul Hoskins, "Freedom from Slavery to Sin and the Devil: John 8:31–47 and the Passover Theme of the Gospel of John," *Trinity Journal* 31 (2010): 47–63. However, such

Into this situation of slavery, Jesus comes. Jesus's activity is explicitly seen as a new or typological fulfillment of the sacrifice of the Passover lamb. John the Baptist announces this theme at Jesus's baptism: "Here is the Lamb of God who takes away the sin of the world" (John 1:29). This verse has had an immense impact on Christian iconography and imagination. But oddly, given its importance, it is difficult to know with certainty which "lamb" John is referring to. Some link this lamb to Isaiah 53:7, in which God's servant is likened to a lamb and a sin offering.[39] While that is a possibility, several considerations suggest the Passover lamb is a more likely referent.

First, the climax of John's Gospel is the crucifixion of Christ, which John takes great pains to point out happens at Passover. The entire second half of John occurs during the week before the Passover feast (11:55 onward), and the crucifixion for John occurs during the day of preparation (19:14, 31), in the afternoon, during the time when the Passover sacrifices would have been slaughtered in the temple. The quote in John 19:36, "None of his bones shall be broken," directly likens Christ to a Passover sacrifice. Thus, a Passover connotation would not be out of place in the Baptist's earlier statement about Christ as lamb.

Second, other related Johannine references to Christ as "the Lamb" (Rev. 5) and to Christ as the one who "takes away sins" (1 John 3:5) are more closely tied to Passover themes than to sin offering themes—or other possible references.[40] In 1 John 3:5, John writes that Christ appeared in order "to take away sins, and in him there is no sin." The description that in him "there is no sin" could describe any unblemished sacrifice. But in the larger passage the result of Christ's work is not best described as forgiveness—the result of a sin of-

---

connections are indirect and thematic and, as suggested here, provide more of a Passover-themed backdrop.

39. See the discussion of nine possibilities that have been suggested in Leon Morris, *The Gospel According to John*, rev. ed., NICNT (Grand Rapids: Eerdmans, 1995), 126–31. Morris concludes, "The fact is that a lamb taking away sin, even if it is distinguished as God's Lamb, is too indefinite a description for us to pinpoint the reference" (129). However, if one recognizes that connections to both the Lamb of Rev. 5 and to Gen. 22 can be integrated with the Passover theme, then the interpretational weight of most contemporary commentators is fully behind this way of interpreting the Lamb.

40. Commentators have puzzled over this rather rare way of talking about sins— rather than forgiving or atoning for sins, they are taken away here. See, e.g., discussion of possibilities in Morris, *Gospel According to John*, 130–31.

fering—but rather that those who abide in him also do not sin. As a result of Christ's work they are transferred from the household of the devil (3:10) and become "children of God" through being born of "God's seed" (3:9). The point here is that "taking away sins" in 1 John 3:5 does not seem to be envisioning the forgiveness of sins, the taking away of guilt, nor even their atonement or "covering."[41] Instead the context suggests "taking away" means the complete removal of the power of sin from the human subject and the beginning of a new way of life, a way that involves "laying down" one's life (3:16). It is in this way that the "works of the devil" are "destroyed" (3:8); this is how sin is "taken away." All this fits with the Passover themes discussed above.

In Revelation, John enters into the worship of the heavenly temple (Rev. 4:1) and soon sees the triumphant resurrected Lamb "standing as if it had been slaughtered" (5:6). The song of the living creatures and elders that follows speaks of the result of the Lamb's sacrifice: "You ransomed for God saints from every tribe and language and people and nation; you have made them to be a kingdom and priests serving our God" (5:9–10). Like at the Passover feast, in heaven there is a celebration of the freeing of God's firstborn people so that they might be "a priestly kingdom and a holy nation" (Exod. 19:5–6).

All these Johannine references support the understanding that the Gospel of John both starts and ends by viewing Christ as a new Passover lamb. In light of this, how is Christ's sacrifice as Passover lamb linked to the Eucharist in John's Gospel?

Key images surrounding the crucifixion have clear links to the Passover sacrifice and are also greatly suggestive of the Eucharist. John writes: "But when they came to Jesus and saw that he was already dead, they did not break his legs. Instead, one of the soldiers pierced his side with a spear, and at once blood and water came out. (He who saw this has testified so that you also may believe. His testimony is true, and he knows that he tells the truth.) These things occurred so that the scripture might be fulfilled, 'None of his bones shall be broken.' And again another passage of scripture says, 'They will look on the one whom they have pierced'" (John 19:33–37).

A few things to note about this passage.

First, the narrator underlines the historicity of these details regarding Je-

---

41. Heb. *kippur*, the word we translate as "atonement." See Stubbs, *Numbers*, 84–86, in which I argue the most basic sense of *kippur* is a "covering" for sin.

sus's legs and the blood and water coming out from his side. Why? The best explanation is that he regards these details as important and as typological fulfillments of Old Testament images and prophecies; he understands this would strengthen someone's faith.

Second, Christ's body is clearly linked to the Passover lamb in 19:31–36. John interprets Christ's death in light of two provisions about the Passover lamb. Exodus 12:10 says of the lamb, "You shall let none of it remain until the morning"—which parallels the fact that Jesus's body was not left hanging overnight (19:31–32). But more strongly, the narrator makes clear that Jesus's legs were not broken, in fulfillment of the instruction in Exodus 12:46, "You shall not break any of its bones." Numbers 9:12 also states, "They shall leave none of it until morning, nor break a bone of it." The type of the Passover lamb is fulfilled in Christ's body.

Third, the piercing of Jesus's side and the flowing out of blood and water at the crucifixion also connect to Passover (John 19:34–35, 37). The scripture that John quotes about the "pierced" one is Zech. 12:10, which is part of a larger oracle about the coming day of the Lord: "I [God] will pour out a spirit of compassion and supplication on the house of David and the inhabitants of Jerusalem, so that, when they look on the one whom they have pierced, they shall mourn for him, as one mourns for an only child, and weep bitterly over him, as one weeps for a firstborn." Zechariah follows this image with another: "On that day a fountain shall be opened for the house of David . . . to cleanse them from sin and impurity" (13:1). The imagery of the Gospel, understood against these background passages, suggests that Christ is a new Passover lamb, a new firstborn, whose "blood and water" are likened to Zechariah's fountain that will cleanse the people of God from sin and impurity. This image of blood and water coming from Jesus's side has been interpreted in several ways. However, given the Passover setting and the linking of Christ to the Passover lamb, the image may connect with the wine and water mixed in the cups that mark the Passover meal.[42] John seems to be saying, as Paul said, "Christ our paschal lamb is sacrificed for us."

How then does one receive or partake of this Passover sacrifice and benefit from this fountain? The answer is found earlier in the Gospel: through eating and drinking . . . and believing.

---

42. m. Ber. 7.5 mentions the mixing of wine with water at the Passover.

In John 6:22–71, his great "bread of life" discourse, Jesus speaks of the need to eat his body and drink his blood. Christ says, "Very truly, I tell you, unless you eat the flesh of the Son of Man and drink his blood, you have no life in you. . . . Those who eat my flesh and drink my blood abide in me, and I in them" (6:53, 56). Much of the Christian tradition has linked John 6 to the Eucharist. However, there are a nest of interpretational issues here, including whether or not Christ or even the author, John, intends such a connection.[43] A fairly safe interpretation is that in this passage Christ refers to spiritual realities that later are most fully celebrated and entered into through the Eucharist.[44]

That being said, the setting of John 6 supports connecting Jesus's words to the Eucharist and seeing the Eucharist through the typology of the Passover. The setting of John 6 is the Passover feast (6:4), and the original exodus event that the Passover remembers is in the background.[45] Mountains are climbed (6:3, 15), crowds are fed in wilderness places (6:4–14) and bodies of water are miraculously crossed (6:16–21). Christ's speech at the synagogue "the next day" (6:22) begins to explore the significance of all this. In his question and answer sessions with first the crowd (6:25–40), then the Jewish leaders (6:41–59), and finally his disciples (6:60–71), Jesus explains himself and his work through several symbols, including manna.

---

43. See discussion in Pitre, *Jesus and the Last Supper*, 194–97.

44. This way of putting it is what Morris calls a "mediating" position, the one he prefers, between seeing John 6 as referring first and foremost to the Eucharist and the opposite position which denies any such links, understanding Jesus to be merely speaking of spiritual realities. Morris, *Gospel According to John*, 313. In n. 57 he approvingly cites C. F. Nolloth, who "speaks of Jesus as having in this discourse 'laid down the meaning and necessity of that union with Himself of which the Sacrament was to be the chief effectual sign and means'" (*The Fourth Evangelist* [London: John Murray, 1925], 120). I would agree, and would add that John intends his readers to see those links as well.

45. In the Gospel of John, the Jewish feasts of Passover, Booths, and the Feast of the Dedication (of the temple) have great symbolic importance. In these settings, Jesus often reinterprets symbols associated with such feasts in light of himself. Raymond Brown's commentary was groundbreaking for making such connections. *The Gospel According to John I-XII* and *XIII-XXI*, Anchor Bible 29 and 29A (New Haven: Yale Univ. Press, 1966, 1970). Other examples include: Hoskins, *Jesus as the Fulfillment*; Mary Coloe, *God Dwells with Us: Temple Symbolism in the Fourth Gospel* (Collegeville, MN: Liturgical Press, 2001); Sofia Cavalletti, "Memorial and Typology in Jewish and Christian Liturgy," *Letter & Spirit* 1 (2005): 69–86.

Manna, Unleavened Bread, and the Eucharist

Jesus repeatedly references "manna," or "the bread that came down from heaven," in John 6 (vv. 31, 32, 38, 41). While manna is not one of the three main symbols of the Passover, manna traditions are nonetheless deeply connected with the unleavened bread of the Passover.

In Exodus 16:3, directly after the miraculous escape from Egypt, the people complain and long for the bread and meat of Egypt: "If only we had died by the hand of the Lord in the land of Egypt, when we sat by the fleshpots and ate our fill of bread." Part of the symbolism of the unleavened bread of the Passover they have just celebrated—that this new unleavened bread symbolized a new way of living, a bread free from the old "leaven" of Egypt—seems to be lost on the Israelites! Nonetheless, in response to their complaints, God sends both manna as well as quails to care for his people on their journey. "I am going to rain bread from heaven for you," God tells them.[46] God continues to send manna to feed them for forty years.

The manna thus replaces the unleavened bread they brought from Egypt after it had run out. Likewise, after the people make it to the promised land forty years later, the manna stops and is replaced in part by unleavened bread made from the firstfruits of the grain of the promised land. This happens at the Passover festival, probably on the day of the presentation of the *omer*, as Joshua 5:11–12 relates: "On the day after the Passover, on that very day, they ate the produce of the land, unleavened cakes and parched grain. The manna ceased on the day they ate the produce of the land, and the Israelites no longer had manna; they ate the crops of the land of Canaan that year."

So, manna substitutes for the unleavened bread during their journey, providing Israel with physical sustenance, and then is replaced again with unleavened bread.

It also carried with it many of the same connotations of the unleavened bread. The unleavened bread was a symbol of a new way of life—a life without the "leaven" of Egypt. The manna went further and carried an additional positive connotation about this new way of life: Israel is now living a life in

46. The heavenly origin of manna is also stressed in Ps. 78:24–25 where it is called "the grain of heaven" and "the bread of angels." Wis. 16:20 calls it "the food of angels" and "heavenly food" in 19:21.

which they are cared for and provided for by God, a way of life miraculously sustained by God's daily care. The manna is first of all miraculous—it shows forth God's glory (Exod. 16:7) and is described as "the grain of heaven" and "the bread of angels" (Ps. 78:24–25).[47] It is also a daily phenomenon—one that stresses the need for constant dependence upon God. One could not hoard it, but had to harvest it each day (Exod. 16:19–20). It is also a "just enough" kind of sustenance that is neither too much nor too little: "Those who gathered much had nothing over, and those who gathered little had no shortage; they gathered as much as each of them needed" (Exod. 16:18). The point seems to be reliance upon and contentment with the fatherly care of God who gives us just what we need, rather than reliance upon human strength and striving for more. Jesus relates such a way of living to the new life of the kingdom of God in Matthew 6:25–34 in his teaching about not worrying about tomorrow but striving instead for the kingdom of God.

So, it is not surprising that in traditions that look forward to a new Passover, the time when the Messiah will come to deliver God's people in a new exodus event, an event in which the kingdom of God will be inaugurated, that manna is expected to be given again. We find hints of this understanding in a text from Qumran[48] and the Sibylline Oracles,[49] but the clearest statement is in the Apocalypse of Baruch:

> And it shall come to pass . . . that the Messiah shall then begin to be revealed. . . . And those who have hungered shall rejoice: moreover, also, they shall behold marvels every day. For winds shall go forth from before Me to bring every morning the fragrance of aromatic fruits, and at the close of the day clouds distilling the dew of health. And it shall come to pass at that self-same time that *the treasury of manna shall again descend from on high*, and they will eat of it those years, because these are they who have come to the consummation of time. (2 Baruch 29:3–8)[50]

47. See Pitre, *Jesus and the Last Supper*, 150–51.
48. 4QSongs of the Sage [4Q511] frag. 10:9.
49. Sibylline Oracles 2:344–47.
50. It is intriguing that the following verses describe the resurrection—this parallels the development of thought in John 6 as well. "Then all who have fallen asleep in hope of Him shall rise again. And it shall come to pass at that time that the treasuries will be opened in which is preserved the number of the souls of the righteous" (2 Baruch

Thus, manna traditions at the time of Christ looked forward to the giving of manna from heaven when the Messiah came—a coming hoped for at Passover because the Messiah's coming would be like a new exodus or Passover event. Christ, the Messiah, however, not only *brings* the bread from heaven or "opens the treasury" of manna in the words of Baruch. He *is* the bread come from heaven. Jesus claims this in John 6: "Your ancestors ate the manna in the wilderness, and they died. . . . I am the living bread that came down from heaven. Whoever eats of this bread will live forever; and the bread that I will give for the life of the world is my flesh" (6:49–51). So, in order to be sustained by this bread, one must eat Christ. And Christ, like unleavened bread, like manna, sustains and embodies in himself a new way of life, a life which gives true life to the world.

At this point in Jesus's speech, the metaphors switch. Instead of bread, Jesus now speaks of his flesh and blood: "Those who eat my flesh and drink my blood abide in me, and I in them" (6:56). While the mention of "flesh" could seem to allude to the feeding of Israel by quails in the wilderness, the combination of flesh and blood resonates more with the sacrifice of the Passover lamb itself.[51] The manna, which is Jesus, combined with the flesh and blood of Jesus parallel the major symbols of Passover: unleavened bread and the Passover lamb.

These images of flesh and blood circle back to the crucifixion scene in John 19, when both Christ's body and blood are emphasized by the author. And it is indeed the crucifixion which seems to be the sign asked for by the crowd in that earlier chapter: "What sign are you going to give us then, so that we may see it and believe you?" (6:30). The author who witnessed the crucifixion subtly suggests this as he writes, "He who saw this has testified so that you also may believe" (19:35).

In John's Gospel, Christ takes up and wraps these two central Passover symbols around himself—both the Passover lamb sacrifice and the unleavened bread are messianically transformed. He then says, "Take, eat, and drink." John's Gospel emphasizes that Christians participate in these spiritual realities

---

30:2). See Craig Keener, *The Gospel of John: A Commentary* (Peabody, MA: Hendrickson, 2003), 1:681. Pitre, *Jesus and the Last Supper*, 155–59.

51. See Jeremias, *Eucharistic Words of Jesus*, 220–25 for precedents for "flesh and blood" referring to sacrifices, specifically the Passover lamb.

by "eating and drinking" Christ—an act most centrally ritually embodied in the lives of Christians in the Eucharist.

We will consider in more detail what this might mean for contemporary understandings of and practice of the Eucharist below.

But before doing so, we should note a final way that images of the Passover are picked up in the early church, and connected to Christ and the Eucharist.

Passover, Easter, and the Beginnings of Disconnection

Most of the meditation of the early church fathers on the connection between Christ's death, the Eucharist, and the Passover occurs not so much in treatises having directly to do with the Eucharist, but indirectly through writings about the celebration of Easter—which they called the Christian Passover. Every year the ancient custom was that churches would gather on Nisan 14 for their holiest celebration of the year, which was called by Melito of Sardis "the mystery of the Passover," or "the paschal mystery."[52] They celebrated the passion, death, and resurrection of the Lord, culminating in a eucharistic celebration often at midnight, seeing all of it in light of its typological connections to the Jewish Passover.

The midnight celebration had eschatological overtones. Christians looked forward to the second coming of Christ at the Christian Passover, just as the Jews anticipated the Messiah at Passover. After waiting for Christ's return, and seeing that he did not return, Christians would celebrate the Eucharist as another way of meeting their Lord.

This practice of celebrating the Christian Passover on Nisan 14 caused one of the most heated controversies in the early church, the Quartodeciman controversy (Lat. *quarta decima* = fourteenth, referring to those who celebrated on Nisan 14 as the "fourteeners"). In the mid–second century, many churches followed this custom, a custom handed down by John the Apostle (fitting, given the above interpretations of the Gospel) to Polycarp his disciple and then to the bishops who followed him in Asia Minor. Their way of celebrating Easter diverged from the traditions of the West, more associated with Peter and Paul who celebrated Easter always on a Sunday, the day of the week associated with Christ's resurrection.

52. Melito of Sardis, *On Pascha*, §2.

While the controversy is revealing for many reasons, one can see in this excerpt from a letter from the bishop Polycrates, a bishop in Asia Minor, to Victor, the bishop of Rome, that their Easter eucharistic celebration was based on strong typological links to the Passover:

> We observe the exact day; neither adding, nor taking away. For in Asia also great lights have fallen asleep, which shall rise again on the day of the Lord's coming. . . . All these observed the fourteenth day of the Passover according to the Gospel, deviating in no respect, but following the rule of faith. And I also, Polycrates, the least of you all, do according to the tradition of my relatives, some of whom I have closely followed. For seven of my relatives were bishops; and I am the eighth. And my relatives always observed the day when the people put away the leaven.[53]

Notice both the reference to John's Gospel and to the putting away of leaven. Such a practice, however, did not win the day. Later a definitive ruling on the controversy was given by Constantine at the Council of Nicaea in AD 325 that favored the Sunday, rather than Passover, practice. Here is part of Constantine's ruling and reasoning:

> And first of all, it appeared an unworthy thing that in the celebration of this most holy feast we should follow the practice of the Jews, who have impiously defiled their hands with enormous sin, and are, therefore, deservedly afflicted with blindness of soul. For we have it in our power, if we abandon their custom, to prolong the due observance of this ordinance to future ages, by a truer order, which we have preserved from the very day of the passion until the present time. Let us then have nothing in common with the detestable Jewish crowd; for we have received from our Savior a different way.[54]

While part of the rationale for the decision was to make sure that all Christians would end their Lenten fast and join together in glad celebration on the same day, one can also spot harsh anti-Semitism in Constantine's ruling. He shunned

53. Polycrates. *Letter to Victor*, quoted in Eusebius, *Ecclesiastical History* 5.24 (*NPNF2*, 1:242–44).

54. Eusebius, *Life of Constantine* 3.18 (*NPNF2*, 1:524–25).

any typological connections back to Jewish practices. Such attitudes became more and more common and sadly began to obscure all these typological connections—between Passover and the eucharistic celebration of Easter, and also between Passover and the Eucharist more generally.

Passover Pressure on Today's Table

Reconnecting the Eucharist back to its roots in the Passover will affect our theology and practice in important ways. Let us first consider in general how it will pressure us to tell the story of salvation, and second, how it will more specifically pressure our atonement theologies. Third, moving from theology to practice, we will consider how it will pressure specific elements of our eucharistic rites.

Telling the Story of Salvation

Temple typology pressures us to tell the Christian story of redemption in light of the Israelite exodus from Egypt. This deeply affects how we tell "the gospel" both during and outside of the Eucharist. Certainly one can preach the gospel of Christ in many ways, but the Passover can and should provide a primary, centering plotline that organizes other images and metaphors. Furthermore, the larger system of temple typology places this new "exodus" within a larger story—one that includes creation, the new covenant, and the new creation—so the central meanings of the Eucharist include Passover themes, but are not exhausted by them. In other words, the Eucharist seen in this light is not only a Christian Passover feast. It is more than that. It is a Christian Sabbath/Passover/Pentecost/Booths feast. That is crucial to see.

Let us examine its Passover connections in more detail. As mentioned above, the central meanings of the Passover can be told in relationship to the three central Passover symbols: bitter herbs, the Passover lamb, and unleavened bread (and manna).

Bitter herbs reminded the Jews of the slavery of Egypt. The New Testament speaks of a different kind of slavery—rather than being slaves to Egypt, this slavery is spoken of in terms of sin, the flesh, the world, and the devil, which are also related to death. Note too the corporate aspect to this—salvation is not primarily about the spiritual journey of an individual. Rather, *we* are enslaved and caught by powers that are larger than us and from which we are unable to free ourselves; powers that affect the way that we live and make decisions; powers that distort our human lives and society in ways that go against God's ways.

How are we rescued? The Passover lamb symbolizes God's answer. It is a symbol of what God desires from his firstborn people and from all humanity: total self-dedication to God. It is a symbol of loving God and obediently serving him, offering to him all our heart and minds and strength. But as the mysterious story of Genesis 22 hints at when Abraham says God will see to and provide a lamb, the total self-giving that Abraham pointed to is finally a gift of God. Thus the Passover lamb, in association with the *Aqedah*, is a symbol both of what God desires and of what God provides. The people of Israel, in applying the sign of the Passover lamb onto their houses, announce their faith in, trust in, and commitment to the God who will rescue them. God sees that sign and God's judgment passes over.

What is hinted at in these Old Testament types is clearly seen in Jesus Christ. What we are unable to do, God sees to and provides through the incarnation. Jesus Christ is the Passover Lamb, the firstborn true covenant partner. In his obedient human life, a life given to God even unto the point of great suffering and death, he offers to God the sacrifice humans are called to give but cannot. In his obedient life, totally given over to the will of the Father, he conquers sin, he conquers the flesh, he overcomes the world, he resists the devil, and in the resurrection he is victorious over death. He, in his human aspect, provides the seed of a new humanity. In his divine aspect, we see the love and condescension of God who becomes incarnate to give to us the gift that we should offer to God. As Christians, we take on the sign of this new way, the sign of the cross, onto ourselves and our households first through baptism and then through participation in the feast of the Eucharist—acknowledging our need for and identification with this way.

The symbols of unleavened bread and manna have two main facets. Unleavened bread is first of all a symbol of the community's rejection of certain ways of being, the ways of Egypt. The Passover and the Eucharist instruct us to "clean out the old leaven," the ways of the flesh, the world, and the devil which lead to death. But unleavened bread is also a symbol of sustenance. Especially as unleavened bread is changed into manna, we see that, in our situation of journeying toward the promised land, we need not only bread alone, but also the care, guidance, and providence of God. God not only provides a path through the waters, but also bread in the wilderness. In the Eucharist, the bread symbolizes our daily spiritual feeding by God that gives us strength for the next steps on our journey.

The full story of how we become united to or participate in this new seed of humanity and what we are journeying toward is best told using the symbols and images of the feasts of Pentecost and Booths—and so for that we must wait.

Pressure on Atonement Theology

Those versed in Christian theology will readily link the above way of telling the story of salvation to what are called "Christus Victor" themes and atonement theories. This is an important and far-reaching result of the pressure of temple typology. It would re-center the dominant atonement metaphors and language associated with the Eucharist, because Christus Victor themes are not common in eucharistic celebrations in the West, nor in much of traditional Protestant theology.

As the foundational action of God to save and create the people of God is the exodus event, so this Passover imagery should have priority of place in our thinking and celebrations.

This is a serious matter. In fact, if the claims of this entire project are accepted, this is one of the most important results of this book. It could require in many cases new liturgies and ways of thinking about the cross—and I would welcome such changes.

A few questions will help to unpack this. First, what images and atonement theories have most formed our eucharistic imaginations and liturgies? Second, what precisely is the "atonement theory" of the Passover sacrifice? And third, is such a re-centering a good thing? All complicated questions.

To answer the first question, one needs to examine the liturgies, prayers, songs, and imaginations that have been part of eucharistic practice. In my own experience, I have participated in, witnessed, and examined the liturgies of many types of Eucharist services ranging from non-denominational, to classic Presbyterian and Reformed, to Anglican and Roman Catholic. In these services, the lens of a sacrifice for individual sins, a sacrifice often interpreted in a penal-substitutionary manner, has been the dominant way of viewing Christ's work. Such an understanding runs deep within the West, especially within my own Reformed tradition.

For example, this Roman Catholic prayer from 1520 pictures the Eucharist as a sacrifice paying for sin: "Holy Father, almighty, everlasting God, accept this unblemished sacrificial offering, which I, thy unworthy servant, make to thee, my living and true God, for my countless sins, offenses, and neglects, and on behalf of all who are present here; likewise for all believing Christians, living and dead. Accept it for their good and mine, so that it may save us and bring us to everlasting life. Amen."[55]

During the sixteenth century, Protestants vigorously debated with Roman Catholics about whether the Eucharist *was* a sacrifice or whether it simply *remembered* or perhaps *participated* in Christ's once-for-all sacrifice. But common to all sides in these debates was the assumption that Christ's work was an atoning sacrifice—or more precisely, a sin sacrifice, usually understood in a penal-substitutionary way, in which Christ's punishment substituted for and thus saved us from the penalties of our "sins, offenses, and neglects."

This is changing, especially given new liturgies from the liturgical renewal movements beginning in the 1960s that have drawn extensively from the early church; however, I think the majority of people still view the Eucharist and the work of Christ in this way.

While this sin-offering lens is a valid and biblical way of viewing Christ's work (see below and esp. chapter 10), it can create problems if it forms the center of one's understanding of God's saving work and one's practice of the Eucharist. We'll examine such problems below.

In contrast, in the Passover sacrifice and feast there is an alternative implicit atonement theology. The Passover celebration and sacrifice symbolically call humanity to act as a proper "firstborn"—a priestly creature who worships God with total self-giving and faithfully lives according to God's good order for them. But given our inability to do so, God acts on our behalf.

More specifically, the Passover sacrifice and related rites are a complex symbol (a) of God's defeat of powers that hold humanity from achieving God's desires for them, (b) of the way those powers are defeated—both by God's action and by ascetic effort ("cleaning out the leaven"), (c) of what God desires

55. Michael Driscoll, "The Roman Catholic Mass (1520)," in *Twenty Centuries of Christian Worship*, ed. Robert Webber (Peabody, MA: Hendrickson, 1994), 177.

from humanity, namely, a self-giving, obedient, "sacrificial" movement toward God, as seen in the *Aqedah*, (d) that God will "see to" or "provide for" that end, and (e) that is also a covenantal sign taken on by God's people, a sign that "covers" them by God's forgiveness and patience—God's wrath passes over them—until God's purposes for them are finally achieved.

In the Gospels, we see that Christ fulfills this symbol. He is our Passover Lamb. In Christ, God sees to or provides for the fulfillment of God's purposes for humanity by taking on humanity in the incarnation. God has "recapitulated" humanity—given it a new "head" (Lat. *caput*) or a new start. In that priestly and holy human life of Jesus Christ, God has defeated sin, flesh, the world, and the devil precisely because Jesus, throughout his life and culminating in his death on the cross, has lived the way God desires for humanity to live. He is the prototype of the humanity that God desires as his firstborn, his true covenant partner. In the resurrection, God declares that Jesus is the firstborn son God intended, and the last enemy of humanity, death, is defeated. Those who follow Christ take on "the blood of the Lamb" and are marked as God's holy, chosen, and "covered" people, and their sins are not reckoned to them.

The feasts of *Shavuot* and *Sukkot* will further clarify the inner workings of the new covenant relationship between Christ, the Spirit, and God's people and the final ends toward which we and all creation are moving.

Thus, re-centering our understanding of Christ's work on the Passover emphasizes precisely this exodus-based "atonement theory" or understanding of Christ's work. This understanding focuses on the Christus Victor, incarnation, and recapitulation themes. But as Israel takes on the sign of the lamb, their sins are passed over as God considers them to be part of his household. In this Passover typology, there are substitutionary, representative, and declarative aspects to it as well.

But is this shift from the common tendency to see Christ's work in terms of a substitutionary punishment for sins to a more Passover-based understanding a good thing? A full answer would move in four directions: show that the kind of sacrificial act and saving action in the Passover corresponds well to the most central ways God's saving work is understood in both Old and New Testaments (Scripture); show that it corresponds well to the early apostolic tradition of the church before it was divided (tradition); answer questions about justice that emerge when certain penal-substitutionary atonement models are de-centered (ethics); and finally, show that such a vision opens up our understanding of

God's work in such a way that even more light shines on important aspects of our lives and the world around us (explanatory power).

I cannot hope to do full justice to this question here, but I will begin by making a few points in all four directions.

First, as far as the Old Testament, my comment above, that exodus typology provides a primary, centering plotline that organizes other images or metaphors for God's saving action, argues that a similar exodus-like atonement model should also be central within Christian theology, and thus also within our eucharistic celebrations.

Another kind of argument is based on the structure of the public sacrifices of Israel.[56] In Leviticus 1:1–6:7, five basic categories of sacrifices are listed: the *olah* (burnt offering), the *minhah* (grain, tribute, or loyalty offering), the *shelamim* ("shalom" celebration offering), the *hattat* (sin offering), and the *asham* (guilt offering). Only the first four are public offerings. Is there a logic to these? I take the first, the burnt offering, to be a symbolic description of what all humans owe God—the willing gift of themselves back to God. The second, the *minhah*, is similar, but gets more specific in referencing the covenant relationship between God and his people—we owe tribute, loyalty to God and obedience to the covenant relationship. One can see in these first two offerings descriptions of "primary justice," of intended, right relationships of people toward God.[57] The next, the *shelamim*, is a symbolic description of the goal of life together with God—it is a banquet where people feast with one another and God in which not only is justice fulfilled, but love and delight are also expressed.[58] Built upon but exceeding the meanings of the first two sacrifices, it is fitting that the *shelamim* is always the last in any sequence of performed sacrifices. The final one, the sin offering, is a symbolic description of "rectifying justice," of what needs to happen to make things right again if and when "primary justice" is not fulfilled. Here we see the need for "covering" over sin in order for the relationship between God and God's people to be

56. See discussion of these sacrifices above in chapter 7.

57. For this distinction between "primary" and "rectifying" justice, see Nicholas Wolterstorff, *Justice: Rights and Wrongs* (Princeton: Princeton University Press, 2008), ix–x, 71–72. He calls "rectifying" justice "corrective" justice in Wolterstorff, *Justice in Love* (Grand Rapids: Eerdmans, 2011), 86.

58. See Nicholas Wolterstorff, "For Justice in Shalom," in *Hearing the Call* (Grand Rapids: Eerdmans, 2011), 109–13, for this understanding of shalom.

restored so that the normal or right relationships described in the first three sacrifices may continue.

Given this, it seems that the center of the relationship between God and God's people is symbolically described in the first three sacrifices. The sin offering, while absolutely crucial when things go awry, is not the most basic. Like in a marriage relationship, justice, care, and delight are at the center— forgiveness is absolutely crucial, but needed only when the center is damaged (which may be often!). Based on this logic of the Old Testament sacrifices, I would argue that it is fitting that Passover sacrifice themes—highlighting the self-offering of the "firstborn" priestly human people of God as the basic justice due to God—are more basic than the sin-offering; and so a eucharistic practice in which such themes are also more basic is appropriate. Given this logic, the shift of emphasis is a good thing.

In the New Testament, I argued above that at least the Gospel of John centers its understanding of Christ's work precisely on this Passover typology. But what about Paul?

I am intrigued and persuaded by the work of New Testament scholars, such as N. T. Wright, who offer "new" or "fresh perspectives" on Paul's theology. For more than a quarter-century, they have argued against a simple penal-substitutionary understanding of Christ's sacrifice on the cross as the center of Paul's theology, even though that is the traditional Lutheran reading of Paul and the most common way of understanding Paul's "atonement theory" since the Reformation. They instead argue that for Paul, Christ's sacrifice and its logic are firmly located within the narrative, typological logic of the story or stories of Israel.

For example, in one of N. T. Wright's many essays, he argues that Paul's understanding of the cross is multifaceted.[59] Each facet of meaning corresponds to the way Christ's death on the cross functions within what Wright calls "seven interlocking narratives which form the backbone of all his thought" (301). But among these narratives there is a primary narrative at the center of his thinking: "Standing over all the stories that make up the narrative substructure of Paul's thought, we find frequent reference to the Exodus" (301). Wright does not offer a thorough interpretation of the Passover sacrifice in this chapter—in fact he

---

59. N. T. Wright, "Redemption from the New Perspective? Towards a Multi-layered Pauline Theology of the Cross," in *Pauline Perspectives*, 292–316. Additional references to this source will be given as page numbers in parentheses.

points out that the logic of sacrifice "is bound to remain a question mark within this chapter as a whole" (302).[60] But he points out that the logic of Christ's sacrifice and the word "redemption" itself finds its home within the story retold in the pilgrim feast of Passover: "For Paul this [redemption] was a word which spoke of promise fulfilled, of freedom attained, of the faithful love of God and the journey home to the 'inheritance'—in other words, of exodus" (316). All this to say that the event of the Passover, the exodus, is arguably the controlling typological center in Paul's thought about the saving work of Christ, a work remembered in the Eucharist. Shifting our emphasis toward such an exodus typology and away from sin offering or penal-substitutionary images in our eucharistic celebrations moves us closer to Paul as well as John; it is a good thing.[61]

As far as connections to the early church, let it suffice to say that since Gustaf Aulén's 1930 work, *Christus Victor*, much attention has been drawn to the fact that early Christians did not operate principally with a view of Christ's saving work that centered on Christ offering a substitutionary punishment or penalty for our sins.[62] Their understandings were not so much theories about forgiveness but rather typological understandings of God's work that centered on the redemption of God's people from slavery and their movement to God's full plans for them. Thus seeing the Eucharist in light of the Passover moves us closer to the thinking of the apostolic traditions of the early church.

What about justice? In my experience, anytime the centrality of a penal-substitutionary theory is called into question, this is one of the first objections expressed. It is a valid concern. In response, it should be clarified that the question is a question of corrective justice—actions that must be done to "right the scales" once things go awry (once primary justice, the state in

---

60. "Our difficulty here is not so much in recognizing that Paul sees Jesus' death as a sacrifice as in working out what he might have meant by this, since our knowledge of how second-Temple Jews understood the theology of sacrifice is remarkably thin" (302). Thin—in part because long-ignored and in part because of distrust that later rabbinic interpretations were projections back in time. My thorough description of the central meanings of the Passover by carefully working through the sources and the resulting portrayal of the logic of the Passover lamb is my response to this observation.

61. Similarly, in *Justification: God's Plan and Paul's Vision* (Downers Grove, IL: IVP Academic, 2009), Wright argues the center of Paul's thought is a "covenant theology" that fits well with the theology presented here, e.g., p. 250.

62. Gustaf Aulén, *Christus Victor: An Historical Study of the Three Main Types of the Idea of Atonement* (New York: Macmillan, 1960).

which everyone is given their due, has been upset). My two points of reply are, first, that typologically, the sin offering is the primary focus within the rites of *Yom Kippur*, the Day of Atonement, which is part of the Feast of Booths. So, corrective justice is not forgotten but takes its rightful place within the larger cycle of Israel's worship. Based on these typological relationships between Israel's temple worship and the Eucharist, it should also find its place within our eucharistic worship—even if it is not at the center (see chapter 10).

Second, again based on typology, we should pay close attention to the meanings of Israel's *hattat* or sin offering as we think through what is required to "right the scales." Not all interpretations of the sin offering are strictly penal-substitutionary in the ways that people often understand that term. And so, we should examine our own reasons for saying "justice is done" in light of Scripture, precisely in light of the sin offering. We will examine the logic of the sin offering further in chapter 10 as well.

Finally, we should ask about some of the implications a shift to a more exodus-centered view of Christ's work has on the larger contexts of our theology, life as a church, and culture.

Robert Webber, an influential evangelical Baptist author, has worked to change the dominance of this model or theme in worship. He writes:

> The same theme [creation-sin-redemption] was introduced by Augustine ... continued by Calvin and was handed down to evangelicals during the Enlightenment. It still prevails today as the major way of thinking about the Bible as a whole.
>
> There is nothing wrong with the Western model itself. The problem is the way it has been interpreted and applied. The popular approach, at least in my background, is to place the accent on sin in its personal and moral dimensions, thus not dealing adequately with the principalities and powers. . . . This emphasis led the West to a nearly exclusive concentration on the sacrificial view of the atonement without a strong connection to the resurrection and the triumph of Jesus over sin, death, and the powers of evil. The exclusive preoccupation with the satisfaction theory of the cross has failed to adequately see the unity that exists between creation, the incarnation, and ultimately the restoration of all God's creation. It fosters instead an individualistic form of Christianity.[63]

63. Webber, *Ancient-Future Worship*, 169–70.

There is much in this statement to notice. While several historical and terminological imprecisions and problems can be pointed out in Webber's words—including in my opinion a much too narrow understanding of what "sacrificial" means and what Jewish sacrifice was—this shift has many positive aspects.[64] This shift helps to address Christ's work in relation to "principalities and powers" of our world, to open our eyes to the political implications of Christ's work, to deal with creation (since the renewal of creation can be incorporated into this framework as opposed to simply the forgiveness of sins), and to foster a more corporate understanding of the implications of Christ's work. These are important ramifications.

But rather than treat these directly here—these topics are treated in other places in this book as well as argued for clearly by others who seek to promote "Christus Victor" understandings of Christ's work—let me suggest one further topic this shift resonates with that might be rather unexpected: evolutionary theory.

Sarah Coakley, in her 2012 Gifford lectures titled "Sacrifice Regained: Evolution, Cooperation and God," quite suggestively puts the self-dispossessing sacrifice we see in Christ in conversation with the latest deliverances of evolutionary biology and mathematical game theory. Coakley redefines "sacrifice" as "self-dispossession." Such a definition resonates with Christ's sacrifice as a Passover sacrifice as opposed to a sin offering, and also resonates with evolutionary biology.

Older versions of evolutionary theory highlighted the need for creaturely selfishness and a certain kind of sacrificial behavior—the sacrifice of weak individuals for the good of the whole—as necessary for progress. Nature was "red in tooth and claw." A bloody and competitive behavior was necessary—sacrifices needed to be made—in order for the species to progress. Such competition was needed in order for the fittest to mate and pass on their genes. The extension of this thinking into human society, social Darwinism, called into question the ultimate goodness or meaningfulness of much altruistic and charitable behavior. The virtues of such evolutionary competition were

64. Webber, *Ancient-Future Worship*, 170–73. I recommend Webber's "Conclusion: My Journey toward an Ancient-Future Worship," 168–78, as a concise, accessible, and eye-opening statement by a prominent evangelical about the journey that he and other evangelicals have made in their thinking toward an appreciation of early church and Eastern Orthodox paradigms of reading Scripture and understanding the narrative we find ourselves in as Christians.

often seen as needing to be extended into human society, politics, and market systems, putting a question mark over much traditional teaching in ethics and religion.[65]

Evolutionary biology and mathematical game theory have moved beyond this story, however. Coakley describes the radical "implosion" in evolutionary discussions caused by findings in both mathematical game theory and observed instances in biological populations that certain "cooperative" and "altruistic" options succeed better than selfish and non-cooperative ones in some circumstances.[66] Sacrifice understood as self-dispossession turns out to be part of the grain of the universe.

Such findings dramatically change the evolutionary stories that seem to best fit with the world around us. While there is so much of interest in Coakley's lecture and the greater discussion of evolutionary theory, the point here is that perhaps Christ's sacrifice, understood after the type of the Passover sacrifice as an act of total self-offering to and love of God and neighbor,[67] might be a key to the deepest wisdom of the world.[68] In contrast to the so-called wisdom

---

65. I take the popularity of Ayn Rand's writings as both a key indicator and influencer of this in twentieth-century American culture.

66. The work of Martin Nowak and E. O. Wilson are examples. Coakley worked alongside Martin Nowak for several years and herself cites Martin A. Nowak, "Five Rules for the Evolution of Cooperation," *Science* 314 (2006): 1560–63; *Evolutionary Dynamics* (Cambridge: Belknap, 2006); "Evolving Cooperation," *Journal of Theoretical Biology* 299 (2012): 1–8. Careful definitions are crucial in these discussions. She and Martin Nowak define cooperation as "a form of working together in an evolutionary population, in which one individual pays a cost (in terms of fitness, whether genetic or cultural) and another gains a benefit" (Coakley, "Lecture 2," 6–7). Altruism is similar, but a subset of cooperation. Altruism accounts for intention and motivation; one acts altruistically when one acts out of good will or love for another. Both slimes and humans can act co-operatively; humans but not slimes can act altruistically. And certain slime and human populations that exhibit cooperative behavior are predicted to have better evolutionary success in certain circumstances.

67. Penal substitutionary models also suggest Christ's actions are motivated by love and altruisism, but they involve a different kind of self-offering, namely the offer to be a payment or punishment for sin.

68. What I find exciting here is that Christianity no longer looks like a call to be "other-worldly" in an unhelpful way, a call to a good that is "right" but that does not work, but rather is instead a call to live in harmony with deeper aspects of our world that our current world-systems reject. Similarly, in Coakley's words, Christianity involves "*not* an arcane Gnosticism—not a piece of special *information* imparted to the spiritual élite, but rather the epistemological deepening and integration of capacities already given to us at

of this world, which is often understood to have a Nietzsche-like survival of the fittest form to it, perhaps aspects of the evolutionary process might reflect the deeper wisdom by which the world was created, which became incarnate in Jesus.

Shifting the primary metaphors by which Christ's work is understood and celebrated in the Eucharist might have rather unexpected and, in my opinion, beneficial results in the way it forms our imaginations and helps us to see the world around us. In this way, too, I would argue the shift in our primary metaphors for Christ's saving work is a good thing.

Pressure on Practice

These typological connections between Passover and Eucharist not only put pressure on our theology, but also cause us to ask, how might our eucharistic practices better reflect Passover connections?

First, the figurative performances of eating bitter herbs and cleaning out the leaven connect to practices of lament and confession of sin in our worship. The bitter herbs reference the situation of slavery in Egypt while leaven references hidden but formidable powers that affect us. We have seen how oppression and leaven are transformed in the New Testament into discussions of the power of sin, flesh, the world, the devil, and death. These Passover practices alert us to the fact that rightly remembering, lamenting, confessing, and rejecting sin should be parts of our eucharistic celebration, just as they were parts of the Passover feast. Such actions might be woven into the eucharistic prayer or other parts of the service.

There are several subtle dynamics to notice here. One of these is that seeing the situation that Christ saves us from through the type of Egyptian slavery takes the primary focus off of the individual and their particular sins. We live in a world in which all of humanity is enslaved to distorted forms of human life—

---

birth but yet to be further sensitized and transfigured through grace. The epistemological circle, however, is here open: you do not have to have trained your spiritual senses *already* to begin to be drawn towards this truth, already to 'catch the halo' of the saint or mentor; but in that catching is already a further invitation—to go deeper, to go in fact into a journey which itself partakes of a form of epistemological sacrifice in darkening and stripping and remaking our very capacity to see and hear and respond to the divine around us" ("Lecture 6," 14–15).

unjust and distorted aspects of the political, cultural, economic systems are part of the "world."[69] These should be recognized, lamented, and rejected. At the individual level, Christ has come to free us from enslavement to the powers of sin and the flesh which function in our lives not simply as bad choices but more powerfully as habits, vices, and addictions that are not fully within our conscious control. Certainly we have individual responsibility and culpability for the particular sins we have committed, and these should be confessed and disowned by us. But the Jewish practices of eating "bitter herbs" and "cleaning out the leaven" directs us to consider these larger corporate and political dynamics and incorporate similar movements into our eucharistic practice.

Another dynamic to notice is that such a practice would open us to not simply confession but also lament in our worship. There has been a renewed call for practices of lament within eucharistic worship from a variety of people and sources in the past decades.[70] Perhaps the most central biblical argument for doing so is the fact that Jesus took a psalm of lament, Psalm 22, onto his lips during his own Passover.[71] Lament comes from a heart that breaks from the situations of evil that still fill our world; calling on God to act quickly to save us from such evil that is both outside and inside us is not a sign of lack of faith in God's providence, but rather is a proper expression of one who wrestles with God. Gail Ramshaw, a contemporary writer of hymns, reflecting on the place of lament within eucharistic worship, sees the recovery of an exodus typology as a central resource: it "gives to the faithful community a revolutionary method of reflecting on past, present, and future by interpreting human chaos with the hope of grace."[72] Resources for doing so have long been part the Black church tradition in the United States, a tradition that has

69. John Howard Yoder, Walter Wink, and Hendrikus Berkhof are examples of authors who have sought to bring attention to the New Testament language of "powers" and relate them to aspects of our contemporary world.

70. Philip Gardner, "'A House for Sorrow and a School for Compassion': Recovering Lament in Contemporary Worship," *Touchstone* 20.1 (2007): 16–28. Gardner points out that both Luther and Calvin were not proponents of lament in worship, Luther subordinating lament to confession and Calvin seeing lament as antithetical to trust in God's providence.

71. Patrick D. Miller, "Heaven's Prisoners: The Lament as Christian Prayer" in *Lament,* ed. Sally A. Brown and Patrick D. Miller (Louisville: Westminster John Knox Press, 2005), 20.

72. Gail Ramshaw, "The Place of Lament Within Praise: Theses for Discussion," *Worship* 61 (1987): 317.

long meditated on exodus typology.[73] John Bell and the Iona Community, a contemporary community in Scotland dedicated to both the renewal of worship and social action, have also produced thoughtful and artful resources for prayers, songs, and practices of worshipful lament.[74] Lament in worship, combined with confession of individual sins as we see our own culpability and participation in such distortions of God's world, is a natural outgrowth of such a Passover typology.

Passover typologies also pressure us to remember the work of Christ in a particular way. Worship leaders could provide simple guides to help us remember the work of Christ modeled on Passover images, such as:

> In the Eucharist we remember Christ, our Passover Lamb. Through the gift of Christ's sacrificial life and death, God shows that he hears our cries and opens a way for us out of sin and the distorted ways of our world toward abundant and eternal life. We receive that gift in faith. As we eat and drink we are marked as a community who follows in Christ's way. And as God fed Israel in the wilderness, we are fed on our journey by Christ, the true bread from heaven.

Similar words might be part of a larger statement in a bulletin, form an outline for teaching or catechesis about the Eucharist, or be incorporated into a eucharistic prayer.

The eucharistic prayer specially written for Easter in the PC(USA) *Book of Common Worship* is a wonderful example. In the *Eucharistia* section, the story of our salvation is told. It includes these words, which graft us into the story

73. Forrest E. Harris, Sr., "The Children Have Come to Birth: A Theological Response for Survival and Quality of Life," in *Walk Together Children: Black and Womanist Theologies, Church and Theological Education* (Eugene, OR: Cascade, 2010), 26–41.

74. Norman Shanks, "The Iona Community and Its Global Impact," in *Worship and Liturgy in Context: Studies and Case Studies in Theology and Practice*, ed. Duncan Forrester and Doug Gay (London: SCM, 2009), 230–56. C. Michael Hawn, "The Wild Goose Sings: Themes in the Worship and Music of the Iona Community," *Worship* (2000): 504–21. Located in Scotland and part of the Reformed tradition, the Iona Community has long been engaged in writing music, prayers, and worship resources that breathe fresh life into traditional forms. Their contemporary resources are informed by their work for justice and among the poor in the city of Glasgow, their life in community, their drawing from certain aspects of Celtic spirituality, as well as their drawing from the depths of early church and biblical resources.

of Israel: "When we were slaves in Egypt, you broke the bonds of oppression, brought us through the sea to freedom, and made covenant to be our God." And then in the *Anamnesis* section after the *Sanctus*, it describes the work of Christ with these words:

> You are holy, O God of majesty,
> and blessed is Jesus Christ, your Son, our Lord,
> whom you sent to save us.
> He came with healing in his touch,
> and was wounded for our sins.
> He came with mercy in his voice,
> and was mocked as one despised.
> He came with peace in his heart,
> and met with violence and death.
> By your power he broke free from the prison of the tomb,
> and at his command the gates of hell were opened.
> The one who was dead now lives.
> The one who humbled himself is raised to rule over all creation,
> the Lamb upon the throne.
> The one ascended on high is with us always, as he promised.

Notice both the confrontation of one way of life over another and the victory brought about through the resurrection of the Lamb.

Other examples of Easter prayers could be multiplied that bring to the fore such Passover and Christus Victor themes. I hope, however, that such themes become more central to all our eucharistic prayers; I will offer an example below in chapter 11.

One final practical way that Passover types might guide our understanding and practice of the Eucharist is by linking the Eucharist more strongly to the waters of baptism. Passover types provide part of the background to both sacramental practices. Similar to how the Eucharist in part looks back to the type of the Passover lamb, baptism remembers the new birth of Israel as they crossed the Reed Sea and the defeat of the Egyptian forces in those waters. In the lives of Christians, baptism marks their own initial departure from "Egypt," from a life under the power of sin, through God's forgiving, cleansing, and delivering work.

So how might one emphasize this link between baptism and Eucharist in practice? In the exodus event, the Israelites marked their doorposts with the blood of the Lamb, a sign that they were part of the household of Israel. In baptism, Christians are marked with the sign of the cross on their bodies showing they are part of the household of faith. In the Eucharist, one could recall such signs and symbols in many ways.[75]

For example, at my seminary, in our weekly eucharistic services on Fridays, the worship leader often stands next to the baptismal font as they lead prayers of lament and confession. During the assurance of pardon, they pour water from a pitcher into the font as a way of reminding the congregation of their baptism—of the fact that they have been marked with the sign of the cross and adopted into God's household. Then, during communion, the congregation passes by the font, located on the way to the stations where bread and wine are distributed. Often people will dip their finger or hand into the water and mark themselves with the sign of the cross. Such an action has several meanings. It might be an enacted prayer for God's mercy and forgiveness. It might symbolize a recommitment to the way of Christ as one places the sign of the cross on one's body. It can also be a reassurance of God's love for them as they actively remember their baptisms on the way to the bread and wine.

In these and other ways Passover and Exodus typology are brought to mind, remembered, and actively entered into as part of the eucharistic feast.

75. For further suggestions for practices related to the baptismal font, see the work of the sacramental study committee of the PC(USA), *Invitation to Christ: A Guide to Sacramental Practices* (Louisville: PC[USA], 2006).

9

PENTECOST

The Covenant Renewed in the Present

The fires, that rushed on Sinai down
In sudden torrents dread,
Now gently light, a glorious crown,
On every sainted head.

—John Keble,
"When God of Old Came Down from Heaven"

While connections between the Eucharist and Passover are easy to spot, connections between the Eucharist and the Israelite Feast of Pentecost or *Shavuot* at the temple are not as obvious. However, when one considers that "the new covenant sealed in [Christ's] blood" is a central reality celebrated in the Eucharist and that the covenant sealed on Mount Sinai was the central reality celebrated at *Shavuot* or Pentecost, the typological lines of connection become apparent. Add to this the fact that according to Acts 2 the sending of the Holy Spirit occurred during the Feast of Pentecost. The coming of the Spirit to write God's law or *torah* onto the hearts of God's people was a key reality hoped for in prophecies about the new covenant. From early on, the Eucharist incorporated a similar calling for the Holy Spirit to come down again in what is called the *epiclesis* (Gr. *epiklēsis*, "calling upon" or "invocation"). In light of all this, the lines of connection become bolder.

Pentecost Foundations: Central Meanings of *Shavuot* at the Temple

As in previous chapters, let us begin by first considering what the Feast of Pentecost was like in the first century, both its practices and its central meanings. A first thing to note about this pilgrim feast is that it has more than one name. It is most commonly called the Feast of Weeks (*hag hashavuot*); hence the common Jewish name for the feast, *Shavuot* or Weeks (Exod. 34:22; Num. 28:26; Deut. 16:10, 16; 2 Chr. 8:13; cf. Lev. 23:16–21). The term "weeks" refers to the fact that the feast occurs a "week of weeks" (forty-nine days) plus one day after the omer offering of barley grain was presented at the Passover festival. Our English word "Pentecost" comes from the Greek word for "fifty" (*pentēkonta*).[1] In Scripture it is also called "the festival of the harvest" (Exod. 23:16) and "the day of the first fruits" (Num. 28:26). As these other names suggest, this festival was in part centered on the agricultural year and the firstfruits offerings that individual Israelites and Israel as a nation brought and offered to the Lord.

There are two levels of meaning to the feast: the agricultural and the historical. This is similar to a phenomenon of the Hebrew language itself, in which root words often have a more substantive meaning paired with an abstract idea. Take for example the noun *rosh*, which has the primary meaning of "head." That substantive thing, a physical "head," is paired with the more abstract idea of "beginning," as in *bereshit* ("in the beginning") or *rosh hashanah* (the "head" or "beginning" of the year). In a similar way there are two complementary levels of meaning to the Feast of Pentecost.

At the substantive level *Shavuot* was an agricultural celebration. It was a harvest festival in which firstfruits from the promised land were brought and the harvest was dedicated to God. For this, individuals from all parts of the nation and even beyond the bounds of Israel brought the actual firstfruits of seven species of their crops to God. In addition, the distinctive corporate offering of the feast, a "wave-offering" of two loaves of leavened bread made of the finest wheat, was in part a firstfruits offering.

---

1. The number fifty is also suggestive of new beginnings. Similar to the number eight, it is one after seven sevens. Given the "completed" aspect of the seven days of creation and the seven days of the week, it is suggestive of new start, a new beginning—just as the year of Jubilee, the fiftieth year in which debts were cancelled and lands restored, was a year of new beginnings.

But linked to the agricultural meaning was another meaning. At *Shavuot* Israel remembered and celebrated the revelation on Sinai, the gift of the law to Israel, and the covenant made between Israel and the Lord fifty days after the Passover from Egypt. In that covenant, God committed the promised land to Israel and stipulated the way of life Israel was to live in it. So Pentecost was also a time of remembering and recommiting to that covenant, and a celebration of the "fruits" of that covenant relationship between God and Israel.

The historical development of the feast is debated. Most important for this project is the question of when the covenant and the fruits of the covenant were central meanings of it. Specifically, was it a feast in which the law and covenant at Sinai were celebrated in the first century? Later Jewish tradition clearly emphasized *Shavuot* as a celebration of the giving of the law. For example, Maimonides, the revered twelfth-century Jewish sage, tells the meaning of the feast this way:

> The Feast of Weeks is the anniversary of the Revelation on Mount Sinai. In order to raise the importance of this day, we count the days that pass since the preceding festival, just as one who expects his most intimate friend on a certain day counts the days and even the hours. This is the reason why we count the days that pass since the offering of the Omer, between the anniversary of our departure from Egypt and the anniversary of the Lawgiving. The latter was the aim and object of the exodus from Egypt, and thus God said, "I brought you unto myself" (Exod. 19:4). As that great revelation took place only on one day, so we keep its anniversary only one day.[2]

Notice how he emphasizes both the counting and the relationship to the Passover. Counting is emphasized in the biblical instructions for the feast: "You shall count seven weeks" (Deut. 16:9; cf. Lev. 23:16). The careful counting from the presentation of the *omer* of barley at Passover to this festival links the two festivals together; what was begun at Passover reaches its conclusion at Pentecost. Maimonides emphasizes that the covenant relationship between Israel and God was the "aim and object" of their deliverance from Egypt. He likens that relationship to an "intimate" friendship, the law or covenant being the structure of that relationship.

While such connections between the festival and the giving of the law are

---

2. Maimonides, *Guide for the Perplexed* 3.43.

not explicitly made in Scripture, they are hinted at. Israel arrives in the wilderness of Sinai about forty-four days after the Passover: "On the third new moon after the Israelites had gone out of the land of Egypt, on that very day, they came into the wilderness of Sinai" (Exod. 19:1). After an initial contact between Moses and the Lord and several days of preparation, they worshipped God and sealed the covenant there—so this event would have taken place around fifty days after the Passover according to Exodus.

Given this "coincidence," it is reasonable to imagine that Israel understood the feast to be in part a celebration of the Sinai covenant. Another indication of this connection is the covenant renewal ceremony in King Asa's reign that took place when "they were gathered at Jerusalem in the third month" (2 Chr. 15:10–12).[3]

Whatever the case may be regarding the older history of these connections, the understanding that *Shavuot* was in large part a celebration of the law and the covenant was firmly interwoven into the rites and imaginative understanding of the feast in certain Jewish communities, such as the one at Qumran, by the time of Christ.[4] The important pre-first-century Jewish text Jubilees, written around 160–150 BC, relates that every important covenant in Scripture was made or celebrated at Pentecost. Evidence suggests leaders of temple worship in Jerusalem read and were influenced by that book.[5] As will be discussed below, the writer of Luke-Acts made connections between

3. Pss. 50 and 81 also contain such hints. Elior, *Three Temples*, 142n22. Moshe Weinfeld, "Pentecost as Festival of the Giving of the Law," *Immanuel* 8 (1978): 7–18. James C. VanderKam, "Covenant and Pentecost," *Calvin Theological Journal* 37 (2002): 239–54. Stubbs, *Numbers*, 221–22. McConville, *Deuteronomy*, 377–80.

4. The first three columns of their Community Rule describe a covenant renewal ceremony, see esp. 1QS I, 16–II, 25. Here are a few excerpts from these columns: "All those who embrace the Community Rule shall enter into the Covenant before God to obey all His commandments so that they may not abandon Him during the dominion of Belial because of fear or terror or affliction. On entering the Covenant, the Priests and Levites shall bless the God of salvation and all His faithfulness, and all those entering the Covenant shall say after them, 'Amen, Amen!' . . . Thus shall they do, year by year, for as long as the dominion of Belial endures." See discussion in Elior, *Three Temples*, 145–46. This ceremony is celebrated in the third month according to the Damascus Document, 4Q270 7 2.11–12. The community also had fifteen copies of Jubilees on hand, an indication of the importance of that document to them.

5. The book of Jubilees was known and used by the Hasmoneans and priestly circles (James Kugel, *A Walk through Jubilees* [Leiden: Brill, 2012], 167), the leaders of the temple in Jerusalem.

the coming of the Spirit at Pentecost and the covenant made at Sinai.[6] All this makes it likely that such connections were highlighted in the temple liturgy at the time of Christ.

Details of the Feast and Its Rites

Let us examine some of the details of the feast. The most important symbols and symbolic acts of *Shavuot* are the bringing and presentation of the firstfruits offering, the individual recitation and actions that accompany this offering, and the making, presenting, and eating of the two leavened loaves by the priests.[7]

Regarding the firstfruits offering, at the beginning of the harvest season, Israelites would ritually mark off the firstfruits of the seven species of plants and food mentioned in Deuteronomy 8:8, namely, wheat, barley, vines, fig trees, pomegranates, olives, and honey (perhaps meaning dates).[8] These were seen as evidence of the goodness of "the good land that [God] has given you" (Deut. 8:7). Each Israelite would decide how much of each kind he, or she, would mark, harvest, and bring to the temple. No specific amount is named in Scripture; instead, it is to be a "freewill offering" that is "in proportion to the blessing that you have received from the LORD your God" (Deut. 16:10). While it is typically assumed that the one bringing the offering would be a man, there

6. The understanding that Pentecost was in part a celebration of the covenant has not always been recognized by scholars, and so interpretations of Pentecost in Acts 2 have often overlooked such typological connections. However, with the discovery of the Dead Sea Scrolls in the twentieth century which greatly illuminated first-century Jewish traditions in which connections between Pentecost and the covenant at Sinai are made, critical scholarship has begun to recognize this important aspect of the feast at the time of Christ. See, e.g., careful discussion of this in Josesph Fitzmeyer, *The Acts of the Apostles* (New Haven: Yale, 1998), and Luke Timothy Johnson, *The Acts of the Apostles*, Sacra Pagina (Collegeville, MN: Liturgical Press, 1992). Post-AD 70, Jubilees was known by and quoted by many early Christian authors. Given these data points, it is not unreasonable to assume that these connections were common in first-century Judaism, influenced the liturgies of the temple, and were assumed to be understood by the readers of Acts.

7. Tobit 1:3–9, the writings of Philo (*Spec. Laws* 2.162–63, 215–22), Josephus (*Antiquities* 3.250–53) and rabbinic literature (m. Bik. and Menah.) in general agree about the main symbols and rites. See J. Schwartz, "Sacrifice without the Rabbis," 139–41. See also Josephus, *Antiquities* 14.338; 17.254.

8. m. Bik. 1:3.

are provisions in the Mishnah that a woman could bring the firstfruits, but a man would have to recite the declaration for her.[9] He, or she, would put the firstfruits in a basket, decorate them, and then take them to Jerusalem. People often would make the pilgrimage up to Jerusalem in groups, celebrating along the way together, accompanied by the flute.[10] Pentecost marked the first day that Israelites could offer these individual firstfruits offerings. They could be offered later, until *Sukkot*, but not before.[11]

We find a lovely description of this firstfruits pilgrimage in the book of Tobit, which is part of the Apocrypha.[12] In this wisdom story, Tobit remembers regularly making this trek and offering these firstfruits as well as other tithes, even while living among the deported Jews near Nineveh in the eighth century BC. Probably written early in the second century BC, the story's action takes place centuries earlier. It starts with this description, highlighting Tobit's piety:

> But I alone went often to Jerusalem for the festivals, as it is prescribed for all Israel by an everlasting decree. I would hurry off to Jerusalem with the first fruits of the crops and the firstlings of the flock, the tithes of the cattle, and the first shearings of the sheep. I would give these to the priests, the sons of Aaron, at the altar; likewise the tenth of the grain, wine, olive oil, pomegranates, figs, and the rest of the fruits to the sons of Levi who ministered at Jerusalem. (Tobit 1:6–7)

After an Israelite arrived in Jerusalem with their offering, at the appointed time they would go to the Temple Mount and bring their offering to the priest at the altar.[13] With the basket on their shoulder they would say, "Today I declare to the LORD your God that I have come into the land that the LORD

9. m. Bik. 1:5. This is supposedly because they could not say "which the Lord your God has given me" (Deut. 26:10). This is based in part on Num. 26:54, where the land is apportioned according to the numbers of males in a tribe. But the spunk of the daughters of Zelophehad and the decree of the Lord (Num. 27:1–11) indicate that women could own land in certain circumstances and so would be the ones to properly bring the firstfruits.

10. m. Bik. 3:2, 8–10.

11. m. Bik. 1:3, 10.

12. A similar description is found in Philo, *Spec. Laws* 2:215–22.

13. Instructions in m. Bik. follow closely the directions given in Deut. 26:1–11.

swore to our ancestors to give us" (Deut. 26:3). The firstfruits were proof that the fruits of the covenant were being experienced. They were the culmination of that covenantal history. After this, they would take the basket and "wave" it before the Lord, moving it forward and backward and raising it up and down. They would set it down, and then the person would recite (following the promptings of the priest) Deuteronomy 26:5–10, beginning with the words, "A wandering Aramean was my ancestor; he went down into Egypt and lived there as an alien." The person would outline Israel's story from Abraham, to slavery to and deliverance from Egypt, to God's leading them to the promised land, and finally end with, "So now I bring the first of the fruit of the ground that you, O LORD, have given me" (Deut. 26:10). In this way they claimed this story as their own.

After this, they would prostrate themselves before God. In that bodily action, they showed their humility before God and their commitment to him. Then, they would get up and go celebrate! These individual offerings would be offered outside the times appointed for the corporate liturgies for the day.

On the day of Pentecost, the daily morning sacrifice of the nation would be made at dawn, and then later, the corporate festival sacrifices and liturgies were celebrated. For Pentecost, the main *olot* or burnt offerings that were part of the liturgies were "two young bulls, one ram, seven male lambs a year old," along with their accompanying *minhot* or grain offerings and drink offerings. These were all turned to smoke, symbolizing the total self-offering of Israel to God. Then a single male goat would be offered as a sin offering to "make atonement," and finally "two male lambs" would be sacrificed, part offered to God and part eaten later by the priests as a sacrificial celebration of shalom (Lev. 23:18–19; Num. 28:26–31).

The most significant offering that day, however, was the two loaves of specially made leavened bread, called simply "the two loaves."[14]

The grain for this bread was wheat. Remember that the *omer* given at Passover was barley. In some early sources, barley is considered to be grain poor people eat; other sources consider it grain fit for animals. Wheat is considered to be much better; it is better fit for humans.

The wheat for this offering was not prepared in the usual way that grain was typically handled. Instead, like the grain for the loaves of the bread of the

---

14. m. Menah. 5:1, 6:7.

Presence, it would be "rubbed" by hand to separate the grain from the fibers and chaff and then beat and made into flour. It was carefully sifted twelve times,[15] creating a very fine flour.

Leaven was then added. This was quite unusual. Pentecost was the only time that leaven was added to any corporate sacrifice at the temple. The Mishnah says, "All grain offerings must be offered unleavened, with the exception of the leavened cakes of the thanksgiving offering and the two loaves which are offered leavened."[16] This other sacrifice mentioned, the thanksgiving offering or *todah*, was a sacrifice brought by an individual. It consisted in part of ten leavened cakes and had similar meanings to the corporate Pentecost offering.

The leavened dough for the two loaves was then kneaded, and each loaf was baked separately in the temple using a special form, creating loaves that were "seven hand-breadths long, four hand-breadths wide and their sides were four finger-breadths tall."[17]

During the liturgy, a celebration filled with other sacrifices, prayers, and songs, these two loaves would be "waved" before God in the usual manner— forward and backward, up and down. They would then be eaten by the priests, along with the lamb, in a feast in the courts of the Lord in God's presence. Later traditions make clear that each priest would get at least a small portion of the sacrificial bread and lambs, but other food was added so that they all had their fill as they sat down together as at a regal feast.[18]

Central Meanings of the Rites

Given these central rites and symbols, how might one summarize the central meanings of this feast?

The firstfruits offering of the individual has a number of meanings associated with it. Most obviously it is a freewill thanksgiving sacrifice for the blessings of the promised land. The image is quite moving: thousands of Israelites joyfully streaming toward the temple with the fruits of the promised land in their hands, offering to God a symbol of the blessings they have received as

15. Versus thirteen times for the Passover *omer* and eleven times for the bread of the Presence according to m. Menah. 6:7.
16. m. Menah. 5:1.
17. m. Menah. 11:4.
18. Tosafot b. Yoma 25a; b. Zevah. 91a; b. Tem. 23a.

a result of their covenant relationship with God. Offering it to God, yes, and yet the firstfruits were then shared "with the Levites and the aliens who reside among you," while the tithes were then shared among "the Levites, the aliens, the orphans, and the widows" (Deut. 26:11–13). While much can be said about such a practice, at the least we see that in response to the blessings of their covenant relationship with God, the Israelites were commanded to enter into a cycle of generosity and blessing, initiated by the goodness of God. They were blessed to be a blessing.

The declaration they speak shows it is more than this, however. Their declaration is a form of covenant renewal. The Israelites publicly declare, on an annual basis, an interpretation of both their own identity and the blessings they have received. They are sons and daughters of "a wandering Aramean," children of Abraham. The land that they farm is "the land" and "the ground" promised to their ancestors. The fruits that they mark, harvest, and carry are seen and confessed to be blessings of this covenant relationship, blessings from God. It is a powerful moment of identity formation and covenant renewal for the people of Israel. While the covenant ceremony on Mount Sinai is not explicitly referenced in these words, the covenant relationship started with Abraham and sealed with the nation as a whole on Sinai is the background to it all.

It should be stressed that all this was to be done with great joy. "Rejoice before the LORD your God—you and your sons and your daughters, your male and female slaves, the Levites resident in your town, as well as the strangers, the orphans, and the widows who are among you" (Deut. 16:11). Israel is to enter into God's own joy and delight, the delight that God takes in prospering his people (Deut. 30:9), a joy that overflows in acts of generosity so that even the poorest and most vulnerable among the people will be able to celebrate.[19]

The loaves of leavened bread add depth to the meanings of the festival. The fact that this is the only leavened bread ever used in corporate sacrifices at the temple is highly significant. Just as care is taken at Passover to make sure that there is no leaven in the bread, here the fact that the loaves must be leavened is stressed.

The leavened loaves arguably have two central meanings. The first reflects the fact that it is *leavened* bread; the second that it is leavened *bread*. The mean-

---

19. See Christine Roy Yoder, "Sheaves, Shouts and *Shavuot*: Reflections on Joy," *Journal for Preachers* (Pentecost/Easter 2016), 16–19.

ing of leaven is likely carried over from the Passover—leaven is something small or unseen that has great consequences for the patterns of activity of a person or community. Just as Israel is to have left behind the "leaven" of Egypt, here they celebrate a new "leaven," new principles of action and life which should spread throughout their lives as a people. Later, Jesus compares the reign of God to this phenomenon of leavening: "It is like yeast that a woman took and mixed in with three measures of flour until all of it was leavened" (Luke 13:21; cf. Matt. 13:33).

What was that leaven? On Mount Sinai Israel was given the law, the *torah*, patterns of life that detail their relationships with God, with each other, and with the rest of creation. The law contained the patterns of the kingdom of God. It revealed what God desired and planned for them. This revelation was intended to shape and form them into a people suited for their covenant relationship with God. As we will see, in the Eucharist, the Holy Spirit is called upon, and like leaven, becomes a new principle of action within the people of God, forming us into the patterns of the New Covenant.

The second meaning is closely related. Unlike the unleavened bread or manna associated with Passover and the travels toward the promised land, here the bread is leavened and full. The leavened *bread* represents Israel and their life filled with the blessings of the promised land. The leavened bread is a symbol of the realized promises of God, the promises of fruitfulness and blessing.[20] In this way it is also like the other firstfruits offerings of the people, a symbol of the blessings of God. Both the inner principle of the people of Israel—the yeast of the law—and their outward life of prosperity and blessing—the fullness of the loaves—are symbolized in the two loaves.

Later Jewish traditions reflect similarly on these meanings of the leavened loaves. As one example, Lubavitcher Rebbe understands the *omer* of barley at Passover and the leavened loaves at Pentecost to represent two stages on Israel's journey with God. In the first stage, they were saved, led, and refined more according to their lower animal-like qualities—as the barley and unleavened bread represent. They followed God without a "taste" of what they were doing, he writes. But at Pentecost, as they are given the law, and they are able to follow

20. The significance of the *two* loaves is unclear. Several possibilities are found in the tradition: the two tablets of the law, two marriage partners (God and Israel, or perhaps Jews and Gentiles, especially since Ruth is often read at Pentecost), two witnesses, or thanksgiving for past and future (Philo, *Spec. Laws* 2.179, 187).

God more like adult humans, with their full understanding and intellect—as the wheat, a grain more fit for humans, and the leaven, which represents the gift of revelation and the law, represent.[21]

The final symbolic rite, the actions of the priests as they sit eating the feast in the courts of the Lord, a feast with bread, lamb, and wine, points in similar directions. Eating this bread, the bread symbolic of their covenant relationship to God, is an action that echoes all the many passages in the Old Testament that relate the *torah* and God's commandments to food, a food that nourishes, delights, and gives one health and life (e.g., Deut. 8:3; Ps. 119:102–3; Ezek. 2:8–3:3; Jer. 15:16). That meal represents and actually is a celebration of the blessings promised by God in the covenant, blessings that have already been realized in the lives of the people of Israel. Just as the leaders of Israel "ate and drank" with God on Sinai (Exod. 24:11) to seal the covenant, here the leaders remember and renew that covenant in a similar covenant feast. And, as we will see, Christians do something similar in the Eucharist.

So, putting all these symbols and symbolic acts together, Pentecost is a feast of celebration of the already realized blessings of Israel's covenant relationship with God. These fruits and blessings come as a result of Israel's relationship with God, a relationship described in part by the covenant given and committed to on Mount Sinai, and also described by the story they shared together. And it is a feast in which that covenant is renewed as individuals take on Israel's story as their own. The people of Israel prostrate themselves before God as a sign of God's lordship. They recommit themselves to that covenant relationship also by taking bread, the symbol of God's covenant relationship with them, lifting it up before the Lord, and eating it.

Understood in this full way, it is quite fitting that for the sectarian Jewish community at Qumran, *Shavuot* was their most central festival. As mentioned in an earlier chapter, this community, which flourished between 100 and 50 BC, could be considered a counter-temple movement, or better, a temple-renewal movement. They considered the leadership of the temple in Jerusalem hopelessly compromised and sought to live a pure life with pure worship in their separatist community. They saw themselves as a new spiritual temple

---

21. Lubavitcher Rebbe, *Likutei sichos* (Brooklyn, NY: Kehot Publication Society, 2002), vol. 32, pp. 134ff; vol. 22, p. 31.

that in some ways replaced the temple in Jerusalem.[22] For them, Pentecost was the high point in their year, a day on which every member would re-dedicate themselves in an elaborate ceremony to the covenant and to their covenant community.

Pentecost Connections: Pentecost and Eucharist in the New Testament and Early Church

Is there evidence that Pentecost, this feast of the Mosaic covenant, is picked up, extended, and in some way "fulfilled" in the life of the New Testament people of God, specifically in relationship to the Eucharist? And if so, how?

I will outline two methodological approaches to answering this question, one narrower and one broader. After outlining these approaches, I will back up and go deeper into each.

The narrower, and methodologically safer, approach is to look for specific places where the Eucharist is directly linked to the words "covenant" or "Pentecost" in New Testament or early church texts. Using this lens, we easily spot two primary references in the New Testament: the words of Christ about the "blood of the covenant" and the "new covenant" at the Last Supper, and the connections in Acts 2 between the Feast of Pentecost, the pouring out of the Spirit, and the following practice of the "breaking of bread" (Acts 2:42, 46).

The broader approach is typological. One examines the content of the Old Testament and the symbolic practices associated with *Shavuot* and compares them to the Eucharist. One should ask, are there eucharistic practices of the early church that "rhyme" with the Old Testament practices of Pentecost? In order to best answer that question, it is good to first state clearly what the people of God are being both *freed from* and *freed for* in each instance.

In the Old Testament, the good news of God's act to free his people from Egypt (and later freedom from Babylon) was followed by the giving of the law at Sinai. The law outlined the kind of blessed life under God that Israel was to live. That new life is what they were freed for. And so, the Feast of Passover was followed by the Feast of Pentecost, in which individuals celebrated and recommitted themselves to the law and the covenant relationship. In addition,

22. Perrin, *Jesus the Temple*, 29–37.

the fruits and blessings of that covenant relationship were celebrated, both in their joyful feasting and also in their practice of distributing those firstfruits so that the most vulnerable in the community were included, such as the poor, the widows and orphans, the slaves, and the resident aliens. The firstfruits ceremony and the leavened loaves were both symbols of the blessings of the land that was promised and Israel's full and good life as they were "leavened" by the law.

In the New Testament, the good news is first of all that the Messiah has come, the people of God are *freed from* their bondage to sin, the flesh, the world, and the devil, and their sins are forgiven. But what they are *freed for* is the new covenant relationship between God and God's people that centers on the way of Christ, the power of the Spirit, and love.

In the Old Testament, the law was revealed to Israel on tablets of stone, a law which outlined a way of life that brought Israel into proper relationship with God and brought fullness of life to the whole community. In the new covenant, the full ends of Israel's covenant relationship with God are revealed by Christ and the proper fulfillment of that covenant relationship is enabled by Christ. Christ fulfills the law by living as the true covenant partner God intended. He clearly teaches that new covenant life is a life of *agapē*, summed up as love of God and neighbor, even one's enemies.

But that fulfilled "law" does not remain outside of us. Instead of tablets of stone, it is written on our hearts as we become one with or united to Christ. As we are nourished by his body and blood, we take the shape or "law" of his life into ourselves. This is enabled through the pouring out of the Spirit, whose energy unites us to Christ's life. The body and blood of Christ, his humanity, together with the power of the Spirit are like "leaven." The Spirit acts as a hidden power that unites us with Christ and shapes us by writing the form or "law" of Christ onto our hearts.[23] This fulfills what was described by Jeremiah:

23. Aquinas, for one, writes clearly of such parallels between the Feast of Pentecost and the NT Pentecost: "Other solemnities of the Old Law have been succeeded by solemnities of the new law, because benefits conferred on that people were a sign of those granted us by Christ. Thus the feast of Passover was succeeded by that of Christ's passion and resurrection. The feast of Pentecost, when the Old Law was given, has been succeeded by the Pentecost in which was given the law of the Spirit of life." Aquinas, *Summa Theologiae*, trans. English Dominican Province, 5 vols. (London: Christian Classics, 1981), 1.2.103. Quoted in Fitzmyer, *Acts*, 237.

"I will put my law within them, and I will write it on their hearts; and I will be their God, and they shall be my people" (Jer. 31:33).

Given that understanding of the old and new covenants, what symbolic actions associated with the Eucharist represent the desire for, commitment to, and reception of the realities of the new covenant? The early church emphasized eating and drinking the body and blood of Christ, an eating that nourishes us and strengthens us for a new way of life, a calling on the Spirit to enable that to happen, and a saying of "Amen" to the story that one identifies with.

What symbolic actions represent the fruits and blessings of this new covenant life? We find the early church ritually performing actions in association with the Eucharist, such as washing one another's feet, sharing a meal together and referring to such meals as *agapē* feasts, sharing a kiss of peace, celebrating the Eucharist with great joy, praying for all, doing politically charged acts and behaviors that resist the world's classism and ways of dominating one another, and caring for the poor, the sick, the widow, and the stranger. These are the "firstfruits" of the new covenant, the signs that God's promised covenant life is being experienced.

So, while we do not find early church authors and liturgies that explicitly affirm a typological extension of the Feast of Pentecost, the fit is plain to see. Notice too how these figural performances of the Eucharist in the early church more naturally relate to Pentecost than to Passover. The feast of the Eucharist is not only a celebration of the deliverance brought about by the work of Christ. It is also a celebration of the new covenant relationship to God and the fruit-filled life of *agapē* given to us through Christ and the Spirit.

Textual Connections in the New Testament

Backing up, let us consider the details of these connections between *Shavuot* and the Eucharist more carefully, starting with the narrower methodological approach that emphasizes textual connections.

First, at the Last Supper Jesus speaks words that suggest what he is doing has a typological relationship to the giving and sealing of the covenant on Mount Sinai. Jesus says, "This is my blood of the covenant" (Mark 14:24; Matt. 26:28; cf. Luke 22:20; 1 Cor. 11:25). This phrase and its variants have three primary Old Testament backgrounds: the original Sinai covenant in Exodus, the promises of a renewed deliverance of Israel that is likened to a new exodus event in Isaiah, and the promises of a "new covenant" in Jeremiah ("new covenant" is found in Luke 22:20, 1 Cor. 11:25, and textual variants of Mark 14:24 and Matt. 26:28). None of these are directly connected to the Passover sacrifice, but rather to the covenant making and sacrifices on Mount Sinai, the events centrally celebrated in the Pentecost feast.

The phrase "blood of the covenant" strongly echoes Exodus 24:8: "Moses took the blood and dashed it on the people, and said, 'See the blood of the covenant that the LORD has made with you in accordance with all these words.'"[24]

In using that phrase, Jesus alerts his disciples that something similar is happening in the Last Supper, and by extension, in the Eucharist—both ritual celebrations of Christ's sacrificial life and death. Joel Green affirms this kind of typological connection: "By means of this allusion, a typological relationship is drawn between the covenant sacrifice of Exod. 24:8 and the death of Jesus, so that Jesus' death is said to atone for the sins of the people and thus to enable their participation in the renewed, eschatological covenant of God."[25]

The other echoes are in Isaiah, where God's servant is given as a "covenant" (Isa. 42:6; 49:8) and God promises not to remove his "covenant of peace" from Israel (54:10).[26] There, through the action of Israel as a servant, or through a Messianic figure, whose life was "poured out" and who "bore the sin of many" (53:12), God will bring about a new exodus (52:1–12), and renew his covenant relationship with Israel (54:10). These echoes also point back to the original exodus event and covenant as a type that will be renewed.

Finally, the phrase "new covenant" in Luke, 1 Corinthians 11, and some variants of Matthew 26 and Mark 14, has strong allusions back to Jer. 31:31–34.[27] There again, a new exodus is envisioned and we gain more information about

24. The only Old Testament instances of the phrase "the blood of the covenant" are Exod. 24:8 and Zech. 9:11. The writer of the book of Hebrews picks up this phrase in Heb. 9:20, 10:29, 12:24, and 13:20—clearly linking the work of Christ back to Exod. 24 and the covenant on Sinai. As for Zech. 9:11, it is interesting to note that Matt. 21:4–5 quotes Zech. 9:9, suggesting Christ's entrance into Jerusalem—followed by Christ's Last Supper and passion—is a fulfillment of Zechariah's larger vision of the ingathering of the dispersed Israelites. Perhaps there are intertextual echoes here as well.

25. Joel Green, *The Gospel of Luke*, New International Commentary on the New Testament (Grand Rapids: Eerdmans, 1997), 763. I wonder, however, in what sense the particular covenant-making sacrifice in Exod. 24:8 is atoning. Rather, the emphasis is on eschatological covenant-making.

26. See Donald Hagner, *Matthew*, Word Biblical Commentary (Dallas: Word, 1995), 773.

27. For example, Green, *Gospel of Luke*, 763: "The language of 'new covenant' is drawn from Jer 31:31–34."

what that new covenant entails: the writing of the law on the hearts of God's people (31:33), a more intimate knowledge of God (31:34), and forgiveness of the iniquity of the people (31:34).

Given these words of Christ at the Last Supper, the Eucharist as it grew in part out of the Last Supper should be seen at the very least as a remembrance of and thanksgiving for the sacrifice of Christ that sealed the new covenant.

But as we have seen, Pentecost at the temple was more than that. It was also a joyful feast where not only the giving of the covenant was remembered, but the fruits of that covenant were recognized and celebrated. In the New Testament, we get a greater sense of that in the Feast of Pentecost in Acts 2 and the "breaking of the bread" [Gr. in Acts 2:42 has an article not translated in the NRSV] that followed.

In Acts 2, Luke's narration of the coming of the Spirit has many details that allude to the events on Mount Sinai. While in the past such connections have not been emphasized in standard commentaries, some scholars now confidently say that "it has been convincingly argued elsewhere that Luke's depiction of the disciples' Spirit-filling and speaking in tongues in Acts 2:1–13 is modeled on the Sinai event, a decisive redemptive-historical moment in which God's glory descends so as to make Sinai itself a kind of temple."[28]

Luke Timothy Johnson lists the typological links as follows. First, the fire imagery at Pentecost draws up the "widespread use in Judaism of fire as a symbol for Torah." But the fire imagery combined with loud sounds, wind, and the descent of these signs from heaven points more specifically to Exod. 19:16–18. It is only in that passage that the "same cluster of symbols [are] all found together."[29]

Second, the way Philo (c. 25 BC–AD 50) describes the giving of the law at Sinai parallels the event at Pentecost, including intelligible speech:

Then from the midst of the fire that streamed from heaven there sounded forth to their utter amazement a voice, for the flame became articulate speech in the language familiar to the audience, and so clearly and distinctly were the words formed by it that they seemed to see rather than hear them.[30]

28. Perrin, *Jesus the Temple*, 63. He cites here Fitzmeyer, *Acts*, 234; Beale, *Temple and the Church's Mission*, 205.
29. Johnson, *Acts*, 46.
30. Philo, *On the Decalogue* 46.

Philo and/or the traditions he himself is drawing from seem to be in the background of Luke's description of this Pentecost event and the way he links it back to Mount Sinai. Perhaps even the striking image of "tongues, as of fire, appeared among them, and a tongue rested on each of them" (Acts 2:3) could be related to Philo's description of flame-like words that could be seen.

Third, Luke uses Moses and exodus imagery throughout his writings. We see this in the parallels between Stephen's description of the giving of the law by Moses and Peter's description of Christ's sending of the Holy Spirit. "Moses 'received living words to give to us' (Acts 7:38); Jesus 'received the Holy Spirit, and poured out this thing you see and hear' (Acts 2:33)."[31] But how is the Spirit like the law? The Spirit is a "power" (Acts 1:8) or "power from on high" (Luke 24:49) that shapes and empowers the church to shine with the ways of the "kingdom of God" (Acts 1:3, 6) and to be witnesses of the work of God to the ends of the earth. The same could be said of the *torah*. Both act like "leaven" within the people of God, shaping them into patterns of the kingdom of heaven and bringing them to fullness of life.

Part of the new covenant in which the kingdom of God furthers its entrance into the earth is the formation of a new temple or house of worship. Note the description of the "sound like the rush of a violent wind" coming down "from heaven" that "filled the entire house" (Acts 2:2). The phrase echoes the temple dedication when the presence of God "filled the house" (1 Kings 8:10), similar again to how the glory of the Lord "filled the tabernacle" which Moses constructed at Sinai (Exod. 40:34-35).[32]

Perhaps the house where the disciples were gathered was the temple itself. More likely, however, the house was the "upper room" where Jesus ate the Last Supper with his disciples (Luke 22:10-12) and where the disciples were "devoting themselves to prayer" (Acts 1:13-14) after Christ's death.[33] After the Spirit comes, the "house" becomes the center for, among other things, the "breaking of the bread" (Acts 2:42). The "breaking of the bread" was more than

31. Johnson, *Acts*, 46.

32. Note how Stephen's speech climaxes with the building of Solomon's temple—Stephen sees that a new kind of "house" is being built now, but that the people are resisting God's new work (Acts 7:47-50).

33. Luke links the upper room to both the Passover (Luke 22:7) and the exodus. In the transfiguration scene, Moses and Elijah "appeared in glory and were speaking of his departure [Gr. *exodus*], which he was about to accomplish at Jerusalem" (Luke 9:31).

an ordinary meal. It was an event in which the presence of Christ was "made known to them" (Luke 24:35; cf. Luke 24:41–42; Acts 1:4; 10:41). At Pentecost in Luke-Acts, a new house-temple is being created, centered on the practice of "breaking of the bread."

Summing up, the Pentecost event in Acts 2, occurring during this celebration of the older covenant, was the inauguration of a new covenant based on the type of the old. It was a new chapter in the history of the covenants between God and his people. A new temple, a new liturgy, a new law were being put into effect. While the temple in Jerusalem was not left behind—the disciples still went there to worship—the glory and presence of God was expanding beyond it to the "house" or "houses" where the followers of Christ were gathered and broke bread and which are filled with the glory and Spirit of God.

Solomon's final words at the dedication of the first temple were these: "Devote yourselves completely to the LORD our God, walking in his statutes and keeping his commandments" (1 Kings 8:61). Those words find resonance with a new covenant rendition of them: the disciples "devoted themselves to the apostles' teaching and fellowship, to the breaking of [the] bread and the prayers" (Acts 2:42). They did this in a way that showed honor both to the temple, "the house," and their "houses," which became new centers of worship: "Day by day, as they spent much time together in the temple, they broke bread from house to house and ate their food with glad and generous hearts, praising God and having the goodwill of all the people" (2:46–47). The temple is not destroyed, at least not yet, but rather expanded into new locations.

In their lives together centered on their worship, including the "breaking of the bread," the fruits of the new covenant were being experienced: "wonders and signs" were being performed (2:43; cf. Deut. 4:34; 6:22, etc.), all "were together and had all things in common" (2:44), and "there was not a needy person among them" (4:34). This last description seems to be a direct allusion to Deuteronomy 15:4: "there will, however, be no one in need among you, because the Lord is sure to bless you in the land. . . ." At this transformed Pentecost, the blessings and fruits of the covenant are being realized and celebrated by the people of God.

These connections between the Old Testament Feast of Pentecost and the giving of the law, and the New Testament events recorded in Luke-Acts, such as the gift of the Spirit, the creation of new spiritual "houses" centered in part on this rite of the breaking of the bread, and the fruits of the new covenant experienced by the early church, are quite suggestive. They imply that the breaking of the bread, an early description and form of eucharistic practice, was understood in Luke-Acts to be a new covenant celebration taking place in a new spiritual temple. In this celebration, the fruits of the new covenant were being experienced and celebrated. The presence of Christ, the gift of the Spirit, and the life of the kingdom were coming down from heaven to earth and expanding into the entire world.

Typological Connections to Early Church Practice

Broadening our vision beyond the words of institution and Acts 2, most of the earliest reflections on the Eucharist outside of the New Testament do not make explicit textual connections between the Feast of Pentecost and the Eucharist. But going beyond direct textual allusions to include typological themes and practices, we find deep resonances between the Feast of Pentecost and the Eucharist.

In early church eucharistic thought and practice, not only is thanksgiving given for the creation, not only is our redemption remembered, but also the new covenant relationship between God and God's people is renewed and the fruits of that relationship are celebrated. Specifically, the bread and wine are consecrated so that they might become the body and blood of Christ for the nourishment of the faithful, and the Holy Spirit is called upon to unite those gathered to Christ and to create a community that bears the fruits of this new covenant relationship in which the "law" of Christ is written on their hearts and expressed in their lives.

Let us consider a few examples.

In Justin Martyr's *Apology*, Justin speaks about the food of the Eucharist in this way:

> For not as common bread and common drink do we receive these; but in like manner as Jesus Christ our Savior, having been made flesh by the Word of God, had both flesh and blood for our salvation, so likewise have we been taught that the food which is blessed by the prayer of His word, and from which our blood and flesh by transmutation are nourished, is the flesh and blood of that Jesus who was made flesh.[34]

34. Justin, *Apology* 1.66.

Here Justin makes parallels between the way the Word of God became in-carnate in the flesh and blood of Jesus Christ, and the "transmutation" and "nourishment" of the congregation's flesh and blood through Jesus Christ's humanity, present to us in the bread and wine.

While Justin does not use the words "new covenant" explicitly, putting his words into such a context makes sense of the larger theology that forms the substructure of his thinking. Specifically, the body and blood of Christ are salvific and nourishing because Christ is the forerunner of a new, renewed humanity in proper covenant relationship to God. As the God-man, he is the new covenant relationship between God and God's people in a person. We enter into that relationship by partaking of the humanity of Christ, the true human covenant partner of God, and being formed or "transmuted" by par-taking of the "flesh and blood" of Christ. The Word of God, like leaven, enters into the congregation through the mediation of bread and wine, and nourishes, "transmutes," and shapes them in a way similar and yet deeper than that by which the law, the details of the covenant relationship revealed on Sinai, was to shape Israel.

Justin goes on to describe the Christian life that follows from this: "the wealthy among us help the needy," offerings are brought to and "deposited with the president, who succors the orphans and widows and those who, through sickness or any other cause, are in want, and those who are in bonds and the strangers sojourning among us, and in a word takes care of all who are in need."[35] This description echoes what was to happen at Pentecost at the temple through the bringing of the firstfruits and what did happen after the Pentecostal pouring out of the Spirit in Acts.

What Justin emphasizes—that through the consecration of the bread and wine Christ's humanity is made present to the gathered congregation who are united to it or transformed by it—is, of course, a standard part of Western eucharistic theology. My point here is that such a salvific process is the core content of the new covenant.

In the Clementine liturgy of the Apostolic Constitutions, however, the link to the new covenant is made explicit. As the president gets to the point in the long history of Israel and Christ when he speaks of the Last Supper, he says, "He took bread in his holy and undefiled hands, and looking up to Thee

35. Justin, *Apology* 1.67.

His God and Father, He brake it, and gave it to His disciples, saying, This is the mystery of the new covenant: this is my body."[36] In Christ's body and his offering of it we see the mystery of the new covenant—which we participate in by taking and eating the bread and drinking the wine.

Many early eucharistic liturgies also ask for the work of the Holy Spirit to bring about the same kind of new covenant salvific relationships and sanctifying processes. For example, the *Apostolic Tradition*, a text with parts dated from the late second century to the early fourth century and traditionally associated with Hippolytus of Rome, contains one of the earliest known eucharistic prayers. It ends with this *epiclesis* or calling upon the Holy Spirit: "And we ask that you would send your Holy Spirit in the oblation of [your] holy church, [that] gathering [them] into one you will give to all who partake of the holy things [to partake] in the fullness of the Holy Spirit, for the strengthening of faith in truth, that we may praise and glorify you through your Child Jesus Christ, through whom [be] glory and honor to you, Father and Son with the Holy Spirit, in your holy church, both now and to the ages of ages. Amen."[37]

Note that the focus of the work of the Holy Spirit is on the gathered congregation. The Spirit was called on to work "in" the eucharistic oblation, that is, in the church's rite of offering bread and wine, so that they might be united into one, strengthened in their faith, in order to bring glory and honor to God through Jesus Christ. Such is a common emphasis in the earliest known eucharistic prayers. John McKenna spells this out:

> In the earliest anaphoras, e.g., that of the *Apostolic Tradition* and that of Addai and Mari, the epiclesis seeks the sanctification of the assembled faithful. The transformation of the gifts goes unmentioned. Even later, when the epiclesis did come to appeal for a transformation of the bread and wine into Christ's body and blood, the epiclesis made it clear that the transformation was in view of the assembly's sanctification. Almost invariably we read of a trans-

---

36. Apostolic Constitutions 8.12.

37. Hippolytus, *Apostolic Tradition* 4.12–13, based on the Latin text. Paul F. Bradshaw, Maxwell E. Johnson, and L. Edward Phillips, *The Apostolic Tradition: A Commentary*, Hermeneia (Minneapolis: Augsburg Fortress, 2002), 40.

formation of the gifts *so that* the faithful might receive such benefits as unity, forgiveness, and life in the present and/or in the eschatological future.[38]

Again, while the "new covenant" itself is not mentioned, its core content is present: the Holy Spirit coming down on and into the faithful, joining them to Christ, and making them a holy people in which the kingdom of God is made manifest.

This lens of the new covenant helps make sense of the emphasis on both Christ and the Spirit in early prayers, and also the emphasis on the sanctification and unity of the congregation and other "ethical" aspects of the prayers.[39]

It also makes sense of previously mentioned practices that developed quite early in the church in connection with the Eucharist: the kiss of peace, the *agapē* meals, the sharing of goods, footwashing, and other "political" acts in which the reign of God was symbolized and experienced. I will briefly look at two of these practices.

First, there is the well-known but little understood phenomenon that in certain parts of the early church, eucharistic feasts were also known as *agapē* or love feasts. Older scholarly reconstructions of these practices identified one definable thing called the *agapē* feast that was either united with or eventually separated from another distinct ritual meal called the Eucharist. But Andrew McGowan has convincingly argued against this. There is no evidence of such a clear distinction. Instead, authors such as Ignatius of Antioch use the terms *eucharistia* and *agapē* to refer to the same event.[40] In Paul's first letter to the Corinthians, the practice Paul calls "the Lord's Supper" includes both what

---

38. John H. McKenna, C. M., "Eucharistic Epiclesis: Myopia or Microcosm?" *Theological Studies* 36 (1975): 265–84, here p. 266. See also McKenna, *The Eucharistic Epiclesis: A Detailed History from the Patristic to the Modern Era*, 2nd ed. (Chicago: Mundelein, 2009).

39. "Thus [Apostolic Constitutions] 7.26 asks God to 'free [the church] from every evil and make it perfect in your love and your truth and unite us, all of us, into your kingdom'; the Egyptian version of the Liturgy of St. Basil asks God to 'preserve us . . . in your faith and lead us into your kingdom'; and the Sacramentary of Sarapion prays 'for the destruction of evil and for the confirmation of the church,' and later asks God to give the departed 'a place of rest in your kingdom.'" Bradshaw, *Apostolic Tradition*, 45.

40. Ignatius, *To the Smyrneans* 7–8; *To the Romans* 7.3. Cited in Andrew McGowan, "Rethinking Agape and Eucharist in Early North African Christianity," *Studia Liturgica* 34 (2004): 166n4. See also McGowan, "Naming the Feast: The Agape and the Diversity of Early Christian Meals," *Studia Patristica* 30 (1997): 314–318.

interpreters have later called "the words of institution" and a larger communal meal—Paul makes no distinctions between them.[41] Instead, we find that the practices surrounding this central Christian rite and the names by which it was called varied from place to place and over time.

However, we do see over time a decline in the full meal character of these eucharistic practices and consequently a decline in calling them *agapē* feasts. McGowan, for example, traces such a development in North Africa between AD 200 and 250 and suggests reasons for the changes in eucharistic practice using the writings of Tertullian and Cyprian as data.

Without wandering too deeply into this murky territory of scholarship, let me simply suggest two uncontroversial things about such eucharistic celebrations. First, leaders of the church saw the importance of celebrating together as a communal body. In other words, the central ritual meanings of the celebration involved the relationships of the people to one another as well as their relationship to God. For example, in one of his letters, Cyprian, a bishop in North Africa, writes about problems concerning *agapē* feasts in his area. In his discussion, the importance of the communal aspect of their celebrations is apparent: "But when we dine, we cannot call the people together to our banquet, to celebrate the truth of the sacrament with all the brethren present."[42] Here, as McGowan argues, Cyprian sees the need for everyone to be gathered together in order for the full meaning of the rite to be celebrated, and so, it is a problem that they cannot avoid. As a solution, Cyprian suggests moving the rite to the morning rather than the evening, a time when they could all gather.[43]

Second, as the name *agapē* suggests, part of the meaning of the sacrament

---

41. Here I must note my genuine puzzlement. The best scholarly literature on the *agapē* feasts looks to the "Greco-Roman banquet tradition" as their background. For example, Dennis E. Smith, *From Symposium to Eucharist: The Banquet in the Early Christian World* (Minneapolis: Fortress, 2003). While this contextual information is important since Eucharistic practices developed in this environment, as far as origins, an even more important precedent to such combinations of meals and ritual practices is closer at hand and pre-dates the Greek and Roman empires: the pilgrim feasts of Israel. Especially given that the church understood itself as a new spiritual temple, the precedents of the pilgrim feasts should have occurred to scholars, given the references to them in early Christian literature. Certainly Greco-Roman traditions had their influence, but the thesis of Smith, that "the earliest Christian meals developed out of the model of the Greco-Roman banquet," misplaces the emphasis (Smith, 287).

42. Cyprian, *Epistle 63*.

43. McGowan, "Rethinking Agape and Eucharist," 172.

is a celebration of the church's love for one another. This emphasis on love and gathering together make sense against the backdrop of the new covenant. The understanding that Christ's work brings about a new community marked by love for one another is spoken of throughout the New Testament: "I give you a new commandment, that you love one another" (John 13:34); "Love the Lord your God," and "Love your neighbor as yourself" (Mark 12:30–31); "No one has ever seen God; if we love one another, God lives in us, and his love is perfected in us. By this we know that we abide in him and he in us, because he has given us of his Spirit" (1 John 4:12–13). The central feast of the Christian church is one in which the fruits of the new covenant are celebrated—and so aptly named at places and times in the early church an *agapē* feast.

Not only was the eucharistic assembly understood to be characterized by love, but also by peace and by the undercutting of common class-driven forms of honor and respect. Such ways of relating to one another were other key fruits of the new covenant. Practices commonly associated with the eucharistic rites in the early church were acts that were real symbols of these new covenant realities and relationships.

For example, in the *Didascalia Apostolorum*, a church order document from the churches in North Syria around AD 230, elements of their eucharistic worship focused on creating a "contrast society" that would show forth "light and peace" to all peoples.[44] One of these practices had to do with seating. The text says that if a guest arrives during their celebration and that person "has honour in the world," then a deacon must make sure they have a place. But if a "poor man or woman" should arrive, then the bishop was told to stop everything and "with all your heart appoint a place for them—and even if you have to sit upon the ground" so that the bishop would not "be as one who respects the persons of men," and so that his "ministry will be acceptable to God."[45]

Their eucharistic celebrations also contained moments of peacemaking within them, including the kiss of peace. In the *Didascalia apostolorum*, during the service, the deacon would stand up and say, "Is there perhaps a man that keeps some grudge against his fellow?" At that point right before or during the kiss of peace exchanged between members of the assembly,[46] members who

44. Drawing from Alan Kreider, "Peacemaking in Worship in the Syrian Church Orders," *Studia Liturgica* 34 (2004): 177–90.

45. *Didascalia apostolorum* 2.58 (Connolly).

46. Based on Apostolic Constitutions 2.57, a related document.

had a grudge would present themselves to the bishop who would "persuade them and make peace between them."[47]

The main rationales given for this practice were obedience to Christ's instructions in Matt. 5:23–24 and their related understanding of the central meanings of the Eucharist. The laity were instructed, "If then you keep any grudge against your brother, or he against you, your prayer is not heard, and your Eucharist is not accepted."[48] Included in this discussion of peacemaking is a reflection on the correspondence between the heavenly realms and that of the congregation: as the angels in heaven praise God in harmony and peace, so too should the congregation praise God in harmony and peace, as is prayed for in the Lord's Prayer, "Thy will be done on earth as in heaven."[49] The reasoning here is that the church's life, especially at worship, should be patterned on the commands of Jesus which reveal and mirror the patterns of God's heavenly kingdom. Given that the ways of heaven are ways of peace, relationships of peace among the congregation are part of what it means for the kingdom of heaven to come to earth.

More could be said about other practices associated with the Eucharist that were seen as reflecting the fruits of new covenant community life in communion with God. An example would be footwashing.[50] More could also be said

47. *Didascalia apostolorum* 2.54. See discussion in Kreider, "Peacemaking," 180–83. There were other longer processes set up for peacemaking within the congregation outside of their eucharistic celebration if that did not work.

48. *Didascalia apostolorum* 2.53.

49. *Didascalia apostolorum* 2.54.

50. In later Christian traditions, footwashing was and is practiced in conjunction with the Eucharist regularly or on special occasions, such as Maundy Thursday. In the Gospel of John, Christ's washing of the disciples' feet occupies the same narrative space as Christ's discussion of bread and wine in the Synoptic Gospels, and as such they are mutually illuminating. Sandra Schneiders writes this about the rite in the Gospel of John:

> The desire of the disciples (and others) to dominate one another and establish their superiority over others was frequently the object of Jesus' instruction and reproach in the synoptic Gospels (Matt 20:20–28 and par.; Matt 23:1–12; Mark 9:38–41 and par.; Mark 10:33–37 and par.; Luke 18:14; 22:24–27). There can be little doubt that this subject was a recurrent theme in the teaching of the historical Jesus. The foot washing is John's dramatic interpretation of this theme. In the Johannine perspective what definitively distinguishes the community which Jesus calls into existence from the power structures so universal in human society is the love of friendship expressing itself in joyful mutual service for which rank is irrelevant. By the foot washing Jesus has transcended and transformed the only ontologically based inequality among human beings, that between himself and us. Peter's refusal of Jesus' act of service was equivalent, then, to a rejection of the death of Jesus, un-

about assumed relationships between baptism and Eucharist and how the idea of a "new covenant" community forms the background for both.

The central point here is that, in the New Testament and early church, the Eucharist was not only a thanksgiving for God's creative work and a recommitment to humanity's proper place in the created order—similar to the daily, Sabbath, and monthly worship at the temple. Nor was it only a remembrance of how Christ's sacrificial life and death free us from sin and open up a new way of life—similar to the Passover feast at the temple. It was also a remembrance and celebration of the fact that God, through the work of Christ and pouring out of the Spirit, has created a new covenant relationship with God's people—similar to the Feast of Pentecost at the temple. In the celebration itself a fresh work of the Spirit was called for to unite those gathered to the body and blood of Christ and to one another. In the celebration itself fruits of those new covenant relationships with Christ and one another were experienced and symbolized.

In short, in the early church, a Christian might have rightly thought, "In the Eucharist, we give thanks for and recommit ourselves to the new covenant way of Christ; we pray for the Holy Spirit to unite us with Christ and one another, nourishing us and empowering us to live as Christ's body for the world."

Pentecost Pressure: Celebrating the New Covenant Today

These connections between the Old Testament celebration of the law, Pentecost, and the Eucharist should shape our understanding and practice of the Eucharist. But how? What would it mean for our eucharistic celebrations to recover and reflect more deeply, in New Testament–transposed fashion, the central meanings of *Shavuot*?

Most centrally, the Eucharist should be understood and celebrated in part as a rite in which God gathers and meets with the church to renew, deepen, and celebrate the new covenant between God and God's people. The Eucharist becomes in part a covenant renewal ceremony. The church not only remembers and celebrates their deliverance from the dominion of sin, flesh, the world,

---

derstood as the laying down of his life for those he loved, and implying a radically new order of human relationships.

(Sandra Schneiders, "The Foot Washing [John 13:1–20]: An Experiment in Hermeneutics," *Ex Auditu* [1985]: 135–46.)

and the devil, but also renews and deepens their new covenantal relationship with God. This involves a participation in the new humanity of Christ, his flesh and blood, through the power of the Holy Spirit. Christ pioneered a new way of being human, a renewed form of human desiring, thinking, and living in communion with God. His new humanity is the "new law" that gets carved onto the "tablets" of our hearts by the Spirit.

Along with this, the church should joyfully celebrate and symbolize in its feast the fruits of this new covenant way of life. Symbolic acts of love, peace, justice, unity, and purity should be on display. It also prays that this kingdom way of life will expand out from the temple of the church into the entire world. This is what these typological connections imply.

In our present day, however, such meanings are lacking in most of our eucharistic celebrations and theologies across traditions. As John Witvliet points out, "The image of covenant has been largely ignored by many recent contributions to sacramental theology."[51] For example, while *Baptism, Eucharist and Ministry* mentions it in passing, the new covenant is not given much importance and is not one of the central organizing images. And yet Witvliet and others, many not surprisingly from the Reformed tradition, have argued for the benefits of seeing the Eucharist in part through the image of covenant and covenant renewal.[52]

Witvliet and others point out that the earliest eucharistic prayers and historic liturgies took the shape of covenant ratification ceremonies inherited from the Old Testament. Old Testament covenant ceremonies began by narrating the saving deeds of God; this and other typical aspects of covenant renewal ceremonies find parallels in most early Eucharist prayers.[53]

Another argument is the fact that in the West, the Latin word *sacramentum*, "sacrament," became the term chosen for the class of church rites of which the Eucharist is part. In the time of the early church, this word referred to the rite in which a Roman soldier took an oath of loyalty to the Roman Empire. In AD 112, in the Roman governor Pliny's letter to Emperor Trajan, Pliny writes that Christians gathered "before dawn . . . to chant" and "to bind themselves by oath" (*se sacramento obstringere*).[54] While the meaning of the

51. John Witvliet, "Prospects for Covenant Theology in Ecumenical Discussions of the Eucharist," *Worship* 71 (1997): 99. Republished as chapter 3 of *Worship Seeking Understanding*.
52. John Reumann, *The Supper of the Lord: The New Testament, Ecumenical Dialogues, and Faith and Order on Eucharist* (Philadelphia: Fortress, 1985), 40.
53. Witvliet, "Prospects for Covenant Theology," 113.
54. Pliny, *Letters* 10.96. See Witvliet, "Prospects for Covenant Theology," 113.

term "sacrament" developed further, one can see that the early Christians, by taking on this term themselves, would have thought Pliny's description was a fair one. The Roman soldier's rite of oathtaking, the covenant ratification and renewal ceremonies of Israel, and the Eucharist all bear a strong family resemblance.

Of course a third complementary argument for recognizing and highlighting covenantal aspects is the present one, that the Eucharist is in part a typological extension of the Feast of Pentecost.

With the development of entire theological systems based on the idea of covenant from the sixteenth century forward in especially the Reformed tradition, and interpretations of the Eucharist within those theological systems up until the present day, a treasure-house of theological material and historic liturgies exists for filling out this facet of the Eucharist. John Calvin, Martin Luther, and John Wesley all featured the motif of covenant in their eucharistic theologies. This rich historical background makes it all the more striking that this motif is not more common in ecumenical discussions of the Eucharist.

Let me briefly suggest four implications of and possibilities for connecting our eucharistic theologies and practices back to covenant renewal ceremonies in general and more specifically the yearly pilgrim feast of covenant renewal and celebration, Pentecost.

The Communion Prayer: The Church Re-narrated into the Story of God and God's People

Connecting the Eucharist and the covenant renewal Feast of Pentecost highlights the importance of narrating the story of God's people in our eucharistic prayers. It also pressures us to tell this story in a certain way.

As mentioned above, by doing so we first of all continue in the long tradition of covenant ratifications and renewals begun by the ancient Hebrews. Let us examine this tradition more carefully.

Klaus Baltzer and others have analyzed the pattern or "formulary" of covenant texts and ceremonies in Israel (and neighboring regions) and discerned six typical elements in their overall structure. A written covenant or covenant ceremony would include: naming the parties involved, a retelling of the history of the relationship, a summary of the intended future relationship, specific stipulations of that relationship, invocation of the gods as witnesses, and pronouncements of blessings and curses for obedience to and breaking of the covenant.[55] Furthermore, covenant ceremonies between Israel and God often included a ritual meal that further sealed the covenant.[56]

One striking feature of this covenant formulary is its narrative pattern of past deeds, present stipulations, and anticipated future between the two parties at its core.[57] It envisions the covenant parties not simply as two parties of a contract in which certain stipulations are agreed to. Instead, the covenant partners are participants in an ongoing relationship with its own story. And in the case of the covenants between God and God's people, this story stretches from the beginning to the end of history.

At the Feast of Pentecost we see evidence of this pattern. During the presentation of their firstfruits, Israelites would reaffirm and reclaim their identity by reciting important parts of their history with God. In doing so, they identified themselves as children of Abraham, as part of a people in covenant relationship to God. As they reaffirmed that relationship, they gave voice to both who and whose they were.

This form of covenant ratification and renewal is reflected in the shape of later Jewish prayers and early Christian eucharistic prayers.[58] As one example among many, one of the earliest eucharistic liturgies we have a record of is the so-called Clementine liturgy found in the Apostolic Constitutions. It tells the story of God, Israel, Christ, Spirit, and church in great length and detail. The person presiding at the Eucharist retells, for example, that it was God who "didst deliver righteous Noah from that flood by an ark, with eight souls, the end of the foregoing generations, and the beginning of those that were to

---

55. Klaus Baltzer, *The Covenant Formulary in Old Testament, Jewish, and Early Christian Writings*, trans. David E. Green (Philadelphia: Fortress, 1971). One finds this pattern, including the retelling of the history of God's actions in relationship to Israel, also structured important covenant renewal ceremonies in the Old Testament (Exod. 34; Deut. 31:9–13; Josh. 24; 2 Kgs. 23:1–3; 2 Chron. 15:8–15; Neh. 9–10).

56. Witvliet, "Prospects for Covenant Theology," 108.

57. Another striking feature is that God, by entering into a covenant with God's people, is acting as a "person," as discussed above in chapter 5.

58. Baltzer analyzes the liturgies of the Qumran community as well as the Clementine liturgy found in Apostolic Constitutions 8, showing they follow the same form of the covenant formulary and thus can be thought of in part as covenant renewal ceremonies. Baltzer, *Covenant Formulary*, 167–72. He concludes that "in the formal structures the old and new covenant do not differ. The new element in the new covenant is its new historical foundation" (180). See also Witvliet, "Prospects for Covenant Theology," 105n25.

come; who didst kindle a fearful fire against the five cities of Sodom."[59] This level of detail is present throughout.

So, as contemporary Christians tell the larger story of God and God's people in the Eucharist, we also place ourselves in this larger history of covenant renewal.

The importance of this is not simply that we follow tradition. By entering into this covenant relationship, we not only agree to certain "stipulations" (which in the new covenant have to do with our willing openness to the work of Christ and Spirit in us in faith), but we enter into a grand story and an overarching interpretation of the world, a story in which our lives, our identities, and our actions gain their deepest meanings.[60]

Stories are the necessary background for understanding both actions and persons. As N. T. Wright puts it, "Stories are the most basic modes of human life."[61] The meaning and purposes of actions are only understood within a larger history, and similarly the character and identity of a person are only understood through their larger history. Both meaningful actions and personal identity are key aspects of what makes our lives "human." The philosopher Alasdair MacIntyre puts the point more technically: "Just as history is not a sequence of actions, but the concept of an action is that of a moment in an actual or possible history abstracted for some purpose from that history, so the characters in a history are not a collection of persons, but the concept of a person is that of a character abstracted from a history."[62] The stories that underlie both actions and persons are what make them understandable.

But what story or stories should we tell? We live in a world in which many alternative and conflicting stories are told. Our contemporary situation is one in which there is great doubt that any one particular overarching story or metanarrative can make sense of our lives, the meanings of our larger communities, and the world as a whole.[63] The loss of such an overarching story is one that causes great distress, anxiety, and a sense of meaninglessness to many people.

59. Apostolic Constitutions 8.
60. As John Witvliet affirms, "A covenant enacts a relationship and confers an identity" ("Prospects for Covenant Theology," 106).
61. N. T. Wright, *The New Testament and the People of God* (Minneapolis: Fortress, 1992), 38.
62. Alasdair MacIntyre, *After Virtue: A Study in Moral Theory*, 2nd ed. (Notre Dame: University of Notre Dame Press, 1985), 211.
63. Charles Taylor, *A Secular Age* (Cambridge: Harvard University Press, 2007).

At the Eucharist, the church tells such an overarching story. Part of the meaning of becoming the people of God in baptism and reaffirming that covenant relationship in the Eucharist is precisely entering into and affirming such an overarching history of the world, what Richard Bauckham calls the "non-modern metanarrative" that underlies the writings of the Bible.[64] Recognizing this, the narrative character of our eucharistic prayers should be emphasized.

But what portions of the story between God and God's people are important? Using the typological framework of the worship of the temple highlighted in this book as a guide, we should begin with God's creation of the world and ongoing providence, speak of God's acts of redemption, the gift of the covenant relationship between God and God's people, and in our telling we should look forward to the end of the story, the great feast to come.[65] Many ecumenical prayers exhibit this narrative progression. Seeing connections back to Pentecost and other acts of covenant renewal helps us to see why this is appropriate and good.

In sum, in the Eucharist, the church is re-narrated into this larger narrative of the world. As a person willingly and knowingly celebrates the Eucharist in part as a covenant renewal feast, they take on this larger narrative for themselves. As they join in and speak the "Amen" of the eucharistic prayer, and as they take, eat, and drink the bread and wine, they in their hearts, minds, and actions are saying, "This is who God is. This is who the church is. This is who I am. This story and all that it implies is what I am committed to."

A Central Dynamic of the New Covenant: Calling for the Work of the Holy Spirit

We find ourselves, our identities, and our mission within this larger story of God's covenant relationship with God's people. Pentecost also reminds us that the new covenant relationship is not only about Christ, but also about the work

---

64. Richard Bauckham, *Bible and Mission: Christian Witness in a Postmodern World* (Grand Rapids: Baker Academic, 2003), 90–94.

65. This is similar to what *BEM* suggests. It structures that prayer around thanksgiving for "the marvels of creation, redemption and sanctification" and the *anamnesis* or remembrance of "the great acts of redemption, passion, death, resurrection, ascension and Pentecost, which brought the Church into being." All are typical parts of full Eucharistic prayers and certainly part of early church liturgies. *BEM*, Eucharist 27.

of the Holy Spirit who unites us with the new humanity of Christ. The Spirit writes the "law" found in Christ on our hearts and lives.

So, Pentecost connections pressure us to emphasize the part of the prayer that is called the *epiclesis*, which in Greek means "calling upon." The *epiclesis* is the point in the eucharistic prayer when the people call upon God to send the Holy Spirit to act upon the elements of bread and wine as well as the congregation. The Holy Spirit acts so "that they may be for us the body and blood of Christ and that we may be his body for the world"—as one version goes.[66] The phrase above asks for the Holy Spirit to act upon both the elements and the congregation.

Three brief points about this moment in the eucharistic prayer.

Pentecost typology pressures us, first of all, to make sure that we include an epiclesis in our eucharistic prayers. "Come, Holy Spirit," or "We pray that you would send the Holy Spirit" should be part of every eucharistic prayer.

Secondly, Pentecost typology pressures us toward an equal emphasis on the elements of bread and wine and the congregation in our epiclesis. How we word this part of the prayer is deeply affected by our understanding of how God, Christ, and the Spirit are present in relationship to the eucharistic elements. But even given that, I do not see the need to take a stand on one particular detailed theory of real presence here. Instead, the larger new covenant reality pointed to in this moment as we take and eat bread and wine is that a fresh work of the Holy Spirit is happening that creates the possibility of a renewed and deeper union between those gathered and Christ. Given this, I am quite satisfied with what has become a typical phrasing in many contemporary eucharistic prayers: "Pour out your Holy Spirit upon us and upon these your gifts of bread and wine, that they may be for us the body and blood of Christ and that we may be his body for the world."[67]

Finally, Pentecostal pressure has something to say about what is called "the moment of consecration." There have been debates between the East and West about the moment when "the change" occurs in the elements, and this moment is called the moment of consecration. Typically Western traditions emphasize the "words of institution" while the Eastern Orthodox emphasize the *epiclesis*. In some traditions, bells are rung at the *epiclesis*, in others, at the words of insti-

66. *BCW*, 27.
67. *BCW*, 27.

tution, signaling the importance of these moments. The Trinitarian structure of these new covenant realities (i.e., that we are united to Christ through the work of the Spirit at the initiative of and for the glory of the Father) would seem to push for a "both-and" answer to this debate; both the "words of institution" and the epiclesis should be part of our prayers and seem essential for a full understanding and practice. So, perhaps we should think of the great "Amen" at the end of the eucharistic prayer as the moment of consecration of the elements of bread and wine, the point when all the congregation voices their yes and their openness to all that is spoken of in the prayer. But going further, an epiclesis with a double emphasis points us to the fact that "the change" is twofold—"the elements" include the congregation as well as the bread and wine. In Acts 2 at least, the change is when the Holy Spirit is poured out on the people (Acts 2:17). Perhaps then it is the moment of eating and drinking, the congregation's embodied yes to God's action, that is the ultimate moment of consecration.

Words During Distribution: Emphasizing Covenant Themes

Besides the words of the communion prayer, the words said as the elements of bread and wine are distributed are another opportunity for emphasizing covenant themes.

Congregations distribute the elements in many ways. Three of the most common ways I have seen are by servers who hold bread and wine at stations while people come forward in lines to receive them, by servers who serve bread and wine to individuals who are kneeling or standing at the altar rail, and by all the members of the congregation passing the bread and wine to one another as they either are sitting in pews or standing in a circle around the altar or table. In all of these cases the servers or the members of the congregation usually say a brief sentence to those who are receiving as they hand them the bread and wine. They say things such as "The body of Christ, broken for you," and "The blood of Christ, shed for you."

These brief statements are theologically packed. For many, they act as summary statements of the entire rite. And because they are not only said by the priest or pastor who is presiding at the Eucharist, but also memorized and said by other members of the congregation, they seem quite important to me.

When I hear or say the words just mentioned, I immediately imagine Christ's dying body on the cross. In this way the central meaning of my reception often centers on humble thanksgiving for the great sacrifice of Christ on my behalf. This of course is good and right, but other central meanings should be highlighted as well.

My suggestion is to vary these short phrases so that all the central meanings of the Eucharist might be brought out from time to time. This should be done quite deliberately and with some instruction in order to help people feel comfortable with different phrases, and so that people will know such phrases are approved or authorized (some people will care deeply about this; others will not care at all).

Using temple typology as a guide, one might want to develop four sets of typical phrases, one that corresponds to creation/providence themes, one that corresponds to Passover/redemption themes, one that corresponds to Pentecost/covenant themes, and one that corresponds to Booths/new creation themes. This seems a bit complicated to me, however, given the congregations I know.

Given my context, I would simply suggest two possibilities: "The body of Christ, the bread from heaven," and "The blood of Christ, the cup of the new covenant." The phrase "bread from heaven" picks up the biblical imagery of John 6 and alerts the receiver to unleavened bread and manna imagery; doing so will increase and vary the way Passover/redemption themes are received. "The cup of the new covenant" is taken directly from the words of institution, and in my estimation would greatly help people to attend to the covenant themes of the celebration.

In seminary classes, when I have the occasion to emphasize such covenant themes with students, I ask them to imagine raising or, if they are daring, to actually raise the communion cup just a bit as they receive, similar to what they would do with a glass of wine at a feast or dinner when they respond to a proposed toast. This small action is a way of saying, "I'll drink to that!" For that is what we are doing. As we take, eat, and drink the bread and the wine, we are symbolically resealing the covenant. We are saying in response to God's work, "Yes, Lord! I am in! I am part of that!" Or in more biblical language, "As for me and my house, we will serve the Lord!" (Josh. 24:15)

The eighteenth-century American theologian Jonathan Edwards emphasizes this covenantal aspect of the Eucharist: "The Lord's Supper is a mutual solemn profession of two parties transacting the covenant of grace."[68] A similar

68. Edwards, "Inquiry Concerning Qualifications for Communion," in *The Works*

emphasis is found in the eucharistic theology of Zwingli, who understood that "at the Lord's Supper the community of faith pledges their allegiance to Christ."[69] While I would argue Zwingli's understanding of God's presence is insufficient, I appreciate his attention to the covenantal aspects of the rite. Emphasizing such themes in both the words of institution as well as in these important phrases during the distribution could help congregations recover these themes in their practice, themes more common in the early church and Reformed tradition than they are today.

My other suggested alternative is this: "the body and blood of Christ, the firstfruits of the kingdom of God." In my own eucharistic practice, I am often in the position of serving the congregation one element, while another server distributes the other. When the entire congregation has been served bread and wine, the servers then offer each other both elements. In such a context, a phrase that refers to the bread and wine at the same time is appropriate. This alternative saying gives voice to the fact that Christ is the firstfruits of the new creation, and as we are joined to him through the Spirit, we begin to participate in the life of the coming kingdom of God. Such a theme highlights the Booths/new creation aspects of the Eucharist. It also emphasizes that we are experiencing some of the fruits of the new covenant even now.

Signs of the Kingdom among Us

A final improvement in eucharistic celebrations may come from attending to practices in which the firstfruits of the new covenant relationship between God and God's people are seen and symbolized. These practices are signs of the in-breaking of the kingdom among us.

As discussed above, the early church performed such ritual actions as part of their eucharistic celebrations, actions like washing one another's feet, sharing what could be called an *agapē* meal together, sharing a kiss of peace, celebrating the eucharistic feast with great joy, praying for all, politically charged acts that resist the world's classism and ways of dominating one another, and caring for the poor, the sick, the widow, and the stranger. We would do well

---

of Jonathan Edwards, vol. 1 (Edinburgh: Banner of Truth Trust, 1974), 458. Quoted in Moore-Keish, *Do This in Remembrance*, 19n12.

69. Moore-Keish, *Do This in Remembrance*, 19.

to include such actions in our celebrations. To spark the imagination in these directions, let me simply point out a few meaningful ways that such actions have been incorporated into eucharistic practices of communities I have been part of or know.

The kiss of peace of the early church has been recovered in many traditions as "the passing of the peace." In our seminary community, the leader says, "The peace of Christ be with you," and the congregation responds, "And also with you." Then the leader says, "Let us extend a sign of Christ's peace to one another." People then shake hands or hug one another while saying, "The peace of Christ be with you." This often is a powerful moment highlighting the importance of reconciled relationships within the community and joy in one another. If there are tensions or relationships that are in need of reconciliation, these are keenly felt at that moment—and hopefully such pangs become a spark to take quick action or to inwardly commit to follow up with people after the service.

The meanings of this exchange and its connection to the Eucharist should be clearly taught—perhaps mentioned occasionally in sermons or even in a moment of instruction before the passing of the peace.

In one church community I was part of when I lived in San Francisco, such moments of reconciliation and connection extended into the time of distribution. After the eucharistic prayer, communion music would be playing, and while some people were at the altar railing receiving, others would be up out of their seats and talking quietly with one another. These quiet conversations often involved exchanging apologies or having short discussions that led to reconciliation or to commitments to reconcile with one another. After such moments they would then go up to the altar rail together and receive. These communion services were intense and beautiful times, and people saw them as real symbols of the church's commitment to be a community of justice and love.

Another sign of the kingdom among us during the Eucharist is the way that racial, tribal, and class barriers are broken down during this feast. So often divisions within communities are symbolized and systematized through our meal practices. From lunch tables in school cafeterias to laws within countries and religions that exclude groups from eating with one another, the shared meal is a political event in which divisions are often reinforced. The Eucharist should be a place where such barriers between people groups are instead overcome.

Stories of places and times where this has not been the case are deep wounds in the church's history. From the class divisions within Paul's Corinthian congregation (1 Cor. 11:20–21) to the racial divisions within the churches of South Africa in which white South African Christians refused to commune with "coloured" (a historical term indicating mixed-race as opposed to black or white or Asian) South African Christians, refusals that were the seedbed out of which the demonic policies of Apartheid grew, our ability to understand that such practices are travesties proves the rule of what the Eucharist should be.

In the case of South Africa, the Uniting Reformed Church of South Africa, a union of the black Dutch Reformed Church in Africa and the mostly coloured Dutch Reformed Mission Church, did come together to show that the church must make its unity "visible" in part by "eat[ing] one bread and drink[ing] one cup" together.[70] Their eucharistic community was and is truly a sign of the kingdom breaking into a difficult place and time; and yet, the lack of full communion with the white Dutch Reformed Church shows the "not yet" situation of the universal church.

In our seminary, we try to intentionally manifest unity across typical dividing lines not only by opening our meal to any baptized believer who confesses Christ as Lord, but also by paying attention to who serves. Intentionally including people as eucharistic servers from all sides of class, gender, race, tribe, and even the so-called "abled"/"disabled" divisions within our community is an important symbol of equality within the family of God and our calling to be a unified and reconciled community.

Finally, other practices that can be included in our eucharistic celebrations are extending our celebration to those who are unable to attend due to age, sickness, or being in prison, and linking our eucharistic table to practices of feeding the poor and needy in our communities.

In some churches I have been part of, some of the eucharistic elements of bread and wine are presented to deacons, a short prayer is said, and those deacons then take those elements to elderly "shut-ins," people in the hospital, or those in prison. This practice shows love and care for them and extends the church's eucharistic community.

Related to this is the practice of linking the feast of the Eucharist to the feeding ministries of a congregation. Sara Miles, in her well-known and mov-

---

70. Confession of Belhar 2.3–4.

ing memoir, *Take This Bread*, tells her own story of the powerful way that she and her church connected the eucharistic table at which we are fed by God to another "table," a food distribution center, that her congregation prepared for the surrounding community. Their feeding ministry in one section of San Francisco was in fact centered on the eucharistic table—the food they distributed was physically placed around their altar, a wonderful sign of how the kingdom of God which breaks into the congregation's worship in the Eucharist then extends into the community in their congregation's mission.

In these and other ways, the *worship* of a church centered on the word and sacrament finds natural extensions into its *ethics* and *mission*—and those ethical and missional parts of the church's life find symbolic presence within the Eucharist itself. In these and other ways, the "firstfruits" of the new covenant are experienced in the Eucharist and extended into the world. As we draw bold lines of connection from Pentecost into the Eucharist, our practice is pushed in such directions.

10

THE FEAST OF BOOTHS

A Foretaste of the Feast to Come

Let the vineyards be fruitful, Lord, and fill to the brim our cup of
blessing. Gather a harvest from the seeds that were sown, that we
may be fed with the bread of life. Gather the hopes and dreams
of all; unite them with the prayers we offer. Grace our table with
your presence, and give us a foretaste of the feast to come.

—Song for Holy Communion,
Lutheran Book of Worship

In the seventh month of the year, Israel celebrated the greatest of the three
pilgrim feasts at the temple: *Sukkot*, the Feast of Booths. Its central themes
and images are all connected with God's final actions at the close of the year
and the close of the age. It leans into the future; it is an eschatological feast.

During the first convocation, the Feast of Trumpets, trumpets were blown
and sacrifices made, anticipating the coming of God to judge.[1] Nine days after
this announcement of judgment was the Day of Atonement or *Yom Kippur*. On
that day Israel experienced the mercy of God, as the sins of the people that were
uncovered in judgment were covered over during the elaborate ceremonies and
sacrifices at that important event. The final part of the festival sequence, called

---

1. In many biblical passages, trumpets are a symbol associated with the call to holy
battle and the coming of God to judge. The rabbinic tractate *Rosh Hashanah* shows that
later Jews understood this as a day devoted to penitence and judgment, when every
person had to give an account of their actions the past year.

the Feast of Booths, the Feast of Ingathering, or simply, the Feast, lasted a week. More sacrifices were made during this feast than all the other festivals put together. The details and meanings of this great feast and the "eighth day" which follows it are many, but more than in any other feast, the celebrants longed for the end of the age and celebrated a foretaste of the great feast to come.

Booths Foundations: The Great Feast at the Temple

Put all together, the three pilgrim festivals of *Pesach, Shavuot,* and *Sukkot* create a timeline stretching from past to future. Passover primarily looked backward to God's deliverance of Israel and their start as God's people. At Pentecost, the present covenant relationship between God and Israel was celebrated and recommitted to. Booths is a festival season that leans forward and anticipates the final ends of all of God's purposes for Israel, and indeed, for the entire creation.

In the chart below, you can see that the festival season of Booths encompasses four holy convocations that are part of three important celebrations: *Rosh Hashanah* or the Feast of Trumpets, *Yom Kippur* or the Day of Atonement, and *Sukkot* itself, the Feast of Booths. While these three celebrations are often treated separately in modern texts, they form a single festival cycle in this seventh month.[2] They are sometimes grouped together under the name "Booths," which (somewhat confusingly) can refer either to the entire festival cycle or more properly just to the final feast.[3] Their central meanings together form an overall narrative of what will happen at "the end": judgment, atonement, and grand celebration.

2. In ancient Jewish documents, they are treated together. For example, in the Temple Scroll 25–29 and in Josephus, *Antiquities* 3.10.1–4, these festivals and their sacrifices are treated together in order. In modern interpretations, however, this is not always the case. For example, in Edersheim's *The Temple,* the Feast of Booths is treated first (chapter 14), then *Rosh Hashanah* along with the regular monthly celebrations is examined (chapter 15), while the Day of Atonement gets the pride of place as the last Mosaic festival discussed (chapter 16). Edersheim, a convert to Christianity from Judaism, not surprisingly emphasizes forgiveness of sins as the most important meaning of the temple services and interprets the work of Christ similarly.

3. As an example, I take the mention in 1 Macc. 10:21 that Jonathan put on the high priestly "sacred vestments . . . at the festival of booths" to mean that he put them on during *Yom Kippur*—so here "the festival of booths" is used in the broad sense. See Deborah W. Rooke, "The Day of Atonement as a Ritual of Validation for the High Priest," in *Temple and Worship in Biblical Israel,* ed. John Day (London: T&T Clark, 2007), 360.

Date	Celebration	Key Symbols and Rituals
Tishri 1	Trumpets (*Rosh Hashanah*)	Trumpets and *shofar* blown (Convocation)
Tishri 10	Day of Atonement (*Yom Kippur*)	Repentance by people and preparations
		Convocation of the high priest
		Incense in the holy of holies
		Blood and fat of goats and bullock
		Sending the scapegoat
		Reading by high priest and his appearing in golden vestments
Tishri 15–21	Feast of Booths (*Sukkot*)	Joyous festivities (Convocation on 1st day)
		Water offerings
		Lighting lights in the Court of Women
		Numerous sacrifices
		Dwelling in "booths"
		Processions with *lulav* (palm frond) and *etrog* (fruit)
		Hoshanah Rabbah ("great hosannah")
Tishri 22	Eighth-day Feast (Convocation)	The Great Feast!

Let us take a closer look at these celebrations, their central symbols, and their central meanings in turn.

Trumpets

The first celebration is *Rosh Hashanah* or Trumpets. It was and still is a feast that marks the New Year. For the Jewish people, the close of a year was both a time of taking stock of the past and also looking forward to the future. It is similar to current New Year's practices in the United States: a person looks back on the past and, based on what he/she sees, makes resolutions for the future.

The fact that *Rosh Hashanah* is considered a New Year celebration might seem odd since it is on the first day of the seventh calendar month. The reason for this is that while Nisan 1 is the first day of the year for determining calendar months and the reign of Jewish kings, Tishri 1 is used for determining sabbatical years and Jubilee years as well as the years for non-Jewish kings.[4] Multiple year ends and beginnings are not foreign to us, even if it might seem odd at first glance. In the United States, we often distinguish between the calendar year, the academic year, and the fiscal year. We even celebrate the beginning of a new academic year in many institutions with a grand opening convocation. *Rosh Hashanah* similarly marks the end and beginning of one way of marking years.

As for how it was celebrated, the corporate liturgies at the temple involved offering several sacrifices to God.[5] However, the most distinctive symbolic rite was the blowing of trumpets and shofarot. As it is written in Leviticus: "In the seventh month, on the first day of the month, you shall observe a day of complete rest, a holy convocation commemorated with trumpet blasts [lit. a memorial of blowing]" (Lev. 23:24; cf. Num. 29:1 [a day of blowing]).

The English name of this feast, "trumpets," gets its name from the special metal trumpets [*hatzotzerot*] written about in Numbers 10:1–9. They blew these trumpets on *Rosh Hashanah* as well as in conjunction with many other sacrifices and ceremonies throughout the year. They blew not only trumpets but also shofarot—but they blew the shofarot only on *Rosh Hashanah* and the Day of Atonement. The shofar was made from the horn of an animal, preferably a ram.[6] Since the shofar was a special addition on those days, it had pride of place.[7]

In Jewish traditions dating back to before the destruction of the temple, three central meanings were associated with the day and the blowing of the trumpets and shofarot. These meanings were linked to three concepts listed in the Mishnah: kingship (*Malkuyot*), remembrance (*Zikronot*), and the blowing of the instrument of judgment and war (*Shofrot*).[8] Blessings and prayers that developed as part of the liturgy emphasized those ideas.

4. m. Rosh Hash. 1 identifies four New Years—four ways of accounting the year according to different purposes and harvests.
5. Descriptions of the sacrifices are listed in Num. 29:1–6.
6. m. Rosh Hash. 3.
7. m. Rosh Hash. 3. Num. 10:1–9 says that trumpets should be used at appointed festivals; Lev. 25:9 says that shofarot shall be used at Rosh Hashanah and the Day of Atonement. In practice both were used, as m. Rosh Hash. 3 notes.
8. m. Rosh Hash. 4:6. "In sum, the actual threefold concept of *Malkuyot, Zikronot,* and *Shofrot,* in its fundamental form, was already known in pre-destruction days. It was

The blowing of the trumpets and shofarot first calls to mind the coronation of a king. As one hears the trumpets sounding, one is reminded that God is king, not only of Israel, but over the whole earth. As the psalmist writes (Ps. 98:6):

> With trumpets and the sound of the horn [*shofar*]
> make a joyful noise before the King, the LORD.

The sounding of the shofar also helps Israel remember the covenant given on Mount Sinai. The blast of the shofar is first mentioned in Scripture in Exodus 19, when God met with Israel to give them the covenant: "On the morning of the third day there was thunder and lightning, as well as a thick cloud on the mountain, and a blast of a trumpet [*shofar*] so loud that all the people in the camp trembled.... As the blast of the trumpet [*shofar*] grew louder and louder, Moses would speak and God would answer him in thunder" (19:16, 19). Philo writes that one reason for this celebration is to cause Israel to remember that moment. It is "a commemoration of that most marvelous, wonderful, and miraculous event that took place when the holy oracles of the law were given."[9]

As the law is remembered, one is reminded of how one stands in relationship to it. And that is the third main meaning of this day—it is a day of judgment. It is a day when God the King comes and weighs humanity according to how they stand in relationship to the ways of God. As the Mishnah says, "On the New Year, all who have entered the earth pass before Him, one by one, like young sheep, as it says: 'He that fashioned the heart of them all, Who understands all their deeds' (*Psalms* 33:15)."[10]

The way the *shofar* is blown is related to this third meaning. Three sets of blasts were blown. A long sustained blast, called the *tekiah*, was followed by a quavering blast, the *teruah*, which was followed by another sustained blast. This set of three blasts was repeated three times.[11] The quavering blast, the *teruah*, was associated with war and the coming judgment of God. The quavering

---

only expressed differently in Judea and in the Diaspora. In the Temple it was voiced by the choice of Psalm 81 containing those aspects; in the Diaspora, specifically in the *proseuchē* of Alexandria, it was emphasized by such philosophic expressions as found in Philo's lesson of the 'trumpet day.'" Sidney B. Hoenig, "Origins of the Rosh Hashanah Liturgy," *The Jewish Quarterly Review* 57 (1967): 330–31.

9. Philo, *Special Laws* 2.188.

10. m. Rosh Hash. 1:2.

11. m. Rosh Hash. 4:9.

sound was an audible symbol of how a person might quaver or tremble with trepidation in the face of such realities.[12]

Putting these three meanings together, the trumpet blasts of that day were an announcement of the coming of the Great King to judge, a call for Israel to wake up, remember their covenant with God, repent, and prepare for the coming judgment. Maimonides, writing in the medieval era, explains: "It is a day of repentance, on which we are stirred up from our forgetfulness. For this reason the shofar is blown on this day. The day is . . . a preparation for and an introduction to the day of the Fast."[13] Psalm 81, the psalm appointed for that day, also features the blowing of the trumpet (vv. 3–5), a call for Israel to remember their deliverance and God's words to them (vv. 6–10), and a call to repentance (vv. 11–13).

This judgment of individuals at the end of the year is linked to the coming of the Lord to judge at the end of the age. In both Isaiah and Joel, the great "day of the Lord," the day when God comes both to bring judgment and to bring to fruition all of God's purposes, is announced with the shofar. "On that day a great trumpet [*shofar*] will be blown," prophesies Isaiah (Isa. 27:13). Similarly Joel proclaims, "Blow the trumpet [*shofar*] in Zion; sound the alarm on my holy mountain! Let all the inhabitants of the land tremble, for the day of the LORD is coming, it is near" (Joel 2:1).

But the judgments made on *Rosh Hashanah* are not final. Later Jewish traditions understood there was still time for repentance and for making amends during the days that led to the Day of Atonement. Those days came to be called "the Days of Awe." It was only on the Day of Atonement that the judgments of God were finally sealed. Mercifully, they were sealed after the rites of atonement.

The Day of Atonement

The Day of Atonement was a day filled with symbolic rites. Its main theme is implied by its name: atonement for sin.

But what does "atonement" mean? As discussed above, the meaning of the Hebrew word *kippur*, often translated as "atonement," most basically means "to

12. Hoenig, "Origins of the Rosh Hashanah Liturgy," 320–21.
13. Maimonides, *Guide for the Perplexed* 3.43.

cover."[14] While connected with the ideas of "wiping clean" or even "ransoming," "covering" is its most basic idea.[15] The ideas of covering and uncovering can be related to the ideas of revealing and hiding, but they also have several other metaphorical connotations in interpersonal and financial relationships even today in the English language, as in "I'll cover that" or "I've got you covered." Those meanings are also borne out in the larger narratives of Scripture— starting with the shameful self-covering of Adam and Eve in the aftermath of their sin against God's commandment and the merciful covering of them provided by God in the same story (Gen. 3:7, 21). Like the pitch that covered Noah's ark (Gen 6:14), the gifts of Jacob that covered (NRSV: "appeased") the face of Esau leading to their reconciliation (Gen 32:20), and the *kapporet* or mercy seat that covered the ark of the covenant, the actions taken on the day of atonement in some way cover over the sins of Israel. This covering is part of the process of forgiveness. "The priest shall make atonement [covering] for them, and they shall be forgiven" (Lev. 4:20).[16] They will also be considered "clean" again in God's eyes: "For on this day atonement [covering] shall be made for you, to cleanse you; from all your sins you shall be clean before the LORD" (Lev. 16:30).[17]

This atonement was vitally important in order that God could continue to dwell with his people in harmony. Otherwise, God would "set [God's] face against [Israel]" (Lev. 26:17) and Israel would be "vomited" out of the land (Lev. 18:24–30 and 26:14–39). But through atonement, what separated them could be put out of God's sight so they could be reconciled or "at one" with one another again.

The details of such atonement are better understood by examining and reflecting on the preparations for and details of the rites.[18]

14. See discussion in Stubbs, *Numbers*, 84–93.

15. For discussion of these different possibilities, see Richard Averbeck, "kipper," *NIDOTTE* 2.689–710. I disagree with the influential theory of Milgrom about the purification offering that has led many to privilege the idea of "wiping." See below for further discussion.

16. Marx, "Theology of the Sacrifice," 110. For "forgiveness" see also Lev. 4:26, 31, 35; Num. 15:25, 28.

17. On this dual result of atonement, see David Janzen, "Priestly Sacrifice in the Hebrew Bible: A Summary of Recent Scholarship and a Narrative Reading," *Religion Compass* 2 (2008): 44.

18. Such details are found especially in Lev. 16:1–34, 23:26–32, and Num. 29:7–11

The people prepared for these atoning rites during the days from *Rosh Hashanah* to *Yom Kippur*. They prepared by repenting from their sins and reconciling with each other. Then on *Yom Kippur* they participated in a strict fast: "You shall deny yourselves. . . . For anyone who does not practice self-denial [i.e., fasting] during that entire day shall be cut off from the people" (Lev. 23:27–29). This fast was the ritual culmination of their repentance and preparation. It included denying oneself "food and drink, bathing and anointing, fastening a sandal and sexual activity."[19] Such self-denial or turning away from these needs and pleasures symbolized turning away from sin while also cultivating the skills needed for doing so.

Besides turning away from sin, the people's repentance involved reconciling with others and obtaining pardon from them, if there were any unresolved transgressions between people. In the earliest strands of rabbinic traditions, it is written, "[If he says:] I will sin and the Day of Atonement atones—the Day of Atonement does not atone. Transgressions between a man and God—the Day of Atonement atones. Transgressions between a man and his fellow—the Day of Atonement does not atone, until he obtains pardon from his fellow."[20] In those statements we see also that repentance must be sincere. The offerings of the Day of Atonement are not "automatic" or "magical" but are instead symbols of or actions intertwined with changes of heart, actions, and relationships. Repentance and reconciliation were required in order for the rites of the Day of Atonement to have any effect on the relationships between God and the people.

There were also many preparations for the day that concerned the high priest. Many of the rites on the Day of Atonement, unlike other days, were required to be done by the high priest himself.[21] In preparation, the high priest

---

which form the basis for the more detailed ceremonies described in m. Yoma. These rites are also described in extra-biblical literature, such as in the Temple Scroll 25.14–16; Philo, *Special Laws* 1.72, 2.188–214; and Josephus, *Antiquities* 3.240–245.

19. m. Yoma 8.1. In Instone-Brewer, *Feasts and Sabbaths*, 311, this is considered pre-AD 70 material. In drawing from m. Yoma, I will only use what Instone-Brewer considers pre-AD 70 material unless otherwise noted.

20. Mish. Yoma 8.9. In Instone-Brewer, *Feasts and Sabbaths*, 322–23.

21. In fact, while not a central meaning of the whole event, an important meaning of the Day of Atonement was that, for the high priest, it "functions as a yearly ritual confirmation of his high priest-hood" (345) and in the centuries leading up to Christ was the day on which the high priest was installed. Rooke, "Day of Atonement," 342–64.

would leave his house and live in a chamber in the temple for the seven days before the feast. The high priest needed to be both fit enough to perform the rites and ritually pure; such seclusion helped keep him safe from injury and guarded him against any ritual impurity. An understudy was also appointed to make sure that any eventuality was covered. Some traditions describe this time as a period of training for or review of the duties of the high priest during the coming day.

On the day itself, the high priest would arise, put on his usual golden robes and vestments, and lead the morning sacrifice.

After the morning sacrifice, the high priest would unvest, bathe, and then put on special linen garments that he would wear only for the expiatory or purification rites of the day. There are a variety of opinions about the significance of the linen garments. A likely one is that by wearing linen, the high priest would be dressed like the angels in the heavenly realms, which would be appropriate for the high priest during this one time out of the entire year when he entered the holy of holies.

After changing into the linen garments, the high priest officiated over the central ritual events of the day. These rites centered on the *hattat*, or sin offering, of a bull on behalf of the high priest and his house, the sin offering of a goat on behalf of the people paired with another goat that was sent into the wilderness, an offering of incense, and the offering of two rams as *olot* or burnt offerings, one for himself and one for the people.

The high priest in his linen garments first stood beside the bull that was to be a sin offering for himself and his house. According to the Mishnah, he laid his two hands upon it while offering a prayer of confession. It was not yet killed.

Following this, he went to the two male goats that had been brought from the congregation in front of the temple. Two lots had been placed in an urn. Upon one was written "for the Lord" and on the other was written "for Azazel." The high priest put his hands into the urn, drew out the two lots and placed one on each goat. Each goat was thus designated for its sacrificial purpose. Later rabbinic tradition said that they tied a crimson cord around the horns of the one designated for Azazel, the "sent-away goat."[22]

The priest then went back to the bull, laid his hands on the bull and prayed

---

22. m. Yoma 4.2.

another prayer of confession. At this point the bull's throat was slit and its blood collected.

The high priest then prepared to offer incense in the holy of holies. He took a censer filled with live coals and a ladle of incense and carried them through the veil into the inner sanctum. He placed the coals on the ground and poured the incense over the coals in order to create a cloud of incense smoke. In the era of the First Temple when the ark of the covenant was still present, he would place the censer and incense between the poles of the ark so "the cloud of the incense may cover the mercy seat that is upon the covenant" (Lev. 16:13). In the era of the Second Temple, the ark was no longer there, so the priest placed the censer on the foundation stone in the empty holy of holies. The high priest would then say a prayer, keeping it short so as not to arouse the concern of the people waiting for him, and then emerged from the holy of holies.

At this point the goat that was designated "for the Lord" was slaughtered and its blood collected. Using the blood from the bull and the goat, the high priest re-entered the holy of holies and sprinkled blood there. Using his finger he would sprinkle the blood once upward and seven times downward. Exiting the holy of holies, he similarly sprinkled blood toward the veil from within the holy place. He then placed blood on each of the horns of the altar of incense, and sprinkled the altar as well. Finally, he poured out the rest of the blood of the bull and goat on the western side of the outer altar of sacrifice.

At that point, attention turned to the other goat designated "for Azazel." The priest would lay "both his hands on the head of the live goat, and confess over it all the iniquities of the people of Israel." He then turned it over to a person who would conduct it out "into the wilderness" where it would be "set free." That was the practice according to the biblical tradition (Lev. 16:21). But later traditions said he pushed the goat into "the ravine" where it would die because of the fall.[23]

After this goat was sent away, the high priest went to the carcasses of the first goat and the bull, removed the fat from them, and offered them on the altar (Lev. 16:25; m. Yoma 6:7). Their carcasses were taken "outside the camp" (Lev. 16:27) or outside "the Court wall" (m. Yoma 6:7) where they were burned.

The last acts the high priest performed in the linen garments would be reading selections from the Torah related to the Day of Atonement and then

23. m. Yoma 6:4, 6.

blessing the people with several benedictions. After that, the priest went in and took off the linen garments.

After washing and putting on the golden garments again, the high priest came back out. In his last official act of the feast, after all the atoning sacrifices were made, he offered two rams as burnt offerings, one for the priest and his house and one for the people, as well as other burnt offerings.

The account of Ben Sira, written c. 180 BC in Jerusalem, of these final acts when Simon the high priest was presiding is particularly striking:

> How glorious he was when the people gathered round him as he came out of the inner sanctuary! Like the morning star among clouds, like the moon when it is full; like the sun shining upon the temple of the Most High . . . he made the court of the sanctuary glorious. (Sirach 50:5–11, RSV)

Simon then made the burnt offerings, after which the account continues:

> Then the sons of Aaron shouted, they sounded the trumpets of hammered work, they made a great noise to be heard for remembrance before the Most High. Then all the people together made haste and fell to the ground to worship their Lord, the Almighty, God Most High. And the people besought the Lord Most High in prayer before him who is merciful, till the order of worship of the Lord was ended; so they completed his service.
>
> Then Simon came down, and lifted up his hands over the whole congregation of the sons of Israel, to pronounce the blessing of the Lord with his lips, and to glory in his name; and they bowed down in worship a second time, to receive the blessing from the Most High. (Sirach 50:16–21, RSV)

After the Day of Atonement rites were completed, the evening sacrificial rites were performed.

There are many, many details of these complex rites that could be commented on. However, three details especially convey the central meanings of the day: the sin offerings of the bull and goat, the sending away of the second goat that was designated "for Azazel," and the interplay between these sacrifices and the final burnt offerings.

What are the meanings of the bull and goat?

The priests physically handled sin offerings in a distinct way. As described above, the blood was sprinkled in the holy place, and on the Day of Atonement also in the holy of holies. The blood was then dabbed on the horns of the altar of incense, and the rest was poured out at the base of the altar. This differed from how the blood was handled in any other offering.

The way the rest of the animal was treated also has distinguishing marks. The fat was offered to God by being "turn[ed] . . . into smoke" (Lev. 4:10) just as in the *shelamim* offering, but unlike it the rest of the body is not eaten. Instead, the non-fat parts are disposed of by burning them outside the camp in a "clean place" (Lev. 4:12). This is different than both the *shelamim* and the *olah*.

The meaning of this offering—both its effect and its "mechanism"—has been disputed. As to the effects of the offering, there are two main camps of interpretation: either the offering addresses the disruption in the relationship between God and God's people because of sin and impurity, or it purifies the holy places that have become contaminated through the sin and impurity of the people.

The latter option—that the offering affects primarily places and things rather than people—is associated with the work of Jacob Milgrom.[24] Milgrom considers the *hattat* as the key for understanding the worldview of the priestly writers of the Pentateuch. For Milgrom the negative effects of sin do not so much defile the person or people who have sinned, but instead defile the temple or tabernacle. He calls attention to the fact that the blood of sacrifices is applied to the holy things of the sanctuary rather than to the people. He explains this through his idea that the priestly writers understood impurity to be like "a physical substance, an aerial miasma that possessed magnetic attraction for the realm of the sacred."[25] Due to the impurity and inadvertent sins of Israel and Israel's priests, this miasma is released and magnetically drawn to the temple. This impurity builds up and the sanctuary needs to be regularly cleansed or purified by the sacrifices. The blood—which as an agent of "life" counteracts the death-associated effects of impurity—acts like a "ritual detergent" cleansing the holy places so that God will continue to dwell in them.[26]

24. Jacob Milgrom, *Leviticus 1–16: A New Translation with Introduction and Commentary* (New York: Doubleday, 1991), 226–91. Milgrom, "Israel's Sanctuary: The Priestly 'Picture of Dorian Gray,'" *Revue biblique* 83 (1976): 390–99.

25. Milgrom, *Leviticus 1–16*, 257.

26. Milgrom, *Leviticus 1–16*, 253–60.

Thus the *hattat* sacrifices are better referred to as "purification" offerings rather than as "sin" offerings. Relatedly, for Milgrom the primary meaning of *kippur* is "to wipe" or to cleanse, rather than "to cover." As a result, Lev. 16:16 becomes a key verse for understanding the *hattat* sacrifices and the Day of Atonement as a whole: "Thus he shall make atonement for the sanctuary, because of the uncleannesses of the people of Israel, and because of their transgressions, all their sins; and so he shall do for the tent of meeting, which remains with them in the midst of their uncleannesses."

While this understanding of the effect of the *hattat* sacrifices has been quite influential, parts or all of it are often called into question by many scholars.[27] Here are a few of the reasons. As pointed out above, in the key texts that explain sin offerings other than Leviticus 16:16, the emphasized effect is "forgiveness" and not simply "purification": "The priest shall make atonement for them, and they shall be forgiven" (Lev. 4:20; also 4:26, 31, 35; 5:10, 13; Num. 15:25, 28).[28] Analyses of the word *kippur* also show that sacrifices purify "both physical impurities and moral sins" from those bringing the sacrifices.[29] In addition, sacrifices that do not involve blood, such as the *minhah*, are also said to bring about *kippur*, thus calling into question Milgrom's contention that its basic meaning is "to wipe" or purify and also raising the question why things other than blood can bring about atonement.[30] Other such counterarguments are made. In the end, I do not find Milgrom's overarching way of understanding the *hattat*, much less all of the sacrifices of Israel, convincing.

Instead, more traditional ways of understanding the primary effect of the sin offering—that through it both the sin or transgressions and impurity of

27. See Janzen, "Priestly Sacrifice in the Hebrew Bible," 43–46 for a good summary of "the challenges to Milgrom's theory."

28. Janzen, "Priestly Sacrifice in the Hebrew Bible," 43–44. John Dennis, "The Function of the *hattat* Sacrifice in the Priestly Literature: An Evaluation of the View of Jacob Milgrom," *Ephemerides Theologicae Lovanienses* 78 (2002), 117–18. N. Kiuchi, *The Purification Offering in the Priestly Literature: Its Meaning and Function* (Sheffield: Sheffield Academic, 1987), 98.

29. Janzen, "Priestly Sacrifice in the Hebrew Bible," 44. Roy Gane, *Cult and Character: Purification Offering, Day of Atonement, and Theodicy* (Winona Lake: Eisenbrauns, 2005), 106–30.

30. Janzen, "Priestly Sacrifice in the Hebrew Bible," 45. Rolf Rendtorff, *Leviticus 1, 1–10, 20,* 176–78.

the offerer are in some way dealt with, "atoned," covered over, or forgiven—fit the scriptural data more convincingly.

In his many works on sacrifice Alfred Marx offers clear analyses of the functions and meanings of the various offerings.[31] He makes a clear division between two different kinds of sacrifices, "the offerings of pleasant aroma and the sacrifices of atonement."[32] The first three sacrifices mentioned in Leviticus 1–7 are of the first kind. The *olah* along with the *minhah* and the *shelamim* were meant to establish communication and continue a positive relationship between the offerer and YHWH. All three were means for the worshipper, individual or corporate, to "draw near" to God. The second kind, the *hattat* and the *asham* or reparation offering, were only performed in light of certain transgressions of God's covenantal order. Marx writes, "They have as their object to obtain pardon for an offense against YHWH's prohibitions [for the *hattat*] or property [for the *asham*], to break thus with a faulty past, and restore the possibility for an untroubled relationship with YHWH."[33] While the animals, cereal, and other foodstuffs of the first type functioned as gifts of a meal,[34] the animals and other sacrifices of the second type functioned as "a sort of penalty imposed as a result of a transgression."[35]

Under this model, "Atonement is not the primary purpose of the sacrificial cult." Instead, the first three sacrifices convey that primary purpose, namely, expressing and strengthening those normal relations.[36] The sacrifices that bring about atonement were also critically important but served a subsidiary purpose, namely, to restore Israel back to proper relationship with God when God's covenantal order had been transgressed.

For the *hattat*, there were always two parts to the overall sacrifice. The blood functioned as the negative part, representing the penalty that was paid. The second part consisted of the burning of the fat of the animal, and this expressed a positive gift to God that was "a pleasing aroma to the LORD" (Lev. 4:31). So while the blood removed what hindered the relationship, the second

---

31. E.g., Marx, "Theology of the Sacrifice," 103–20; Marx, *Les systèmes sacrificiels*.
32. Marx, "Theology of the Sacrifice," 111.
33. Marx, "Theology of the Sacrifice," 111.
34. "These are brought to him not as raw materials, but ready to be prepared for a meal" (Marx, "Theology of the Sacrifice," 112).
35. Marx, "Theology of the Sacrifice," 115.
36. Marx, "Theology of the Sacrifice," 111.

part of the offering expressed the positive relationship with YHWH that had been broken but repaired.[37]

Perhaps that is all that can be said with assurance about the *hattat*: that it represents a kind of penalty paid that "covers" over a break in the relationship due to a transgression. The details of its "mechanism," how and why such a penalty repairs the relationship, are not clear as the Pentateuch offers no explicit "atonement theory" clarifying such details.

Still, three points can be made. First, blood is primarily a symbol of life.

When the symbol of blood is understood within the larger narrative context of the Pentateuch, we see that blood is not treated primarily as a detergent that cleans. It is a symbol of life, and more specifically a symbol that when offered to God expresses that God is the Lord of life. It also is a reminder that violations of God's covenantal order can be punishable by death.[38]

Such an understanding is found in Genesis 9:4-6, where humans are given permission to kill and eat animals, but not with their blood: "Only, you shall not eat flesh with its life, that is, its blood" (v. 4). This is followed by a severe warning against wanton violence and murder: "For your own lifeblood I will surely require a reckoning: from every animal I will require it and from human beings, each one for the blood of another. . . . Whoever sheds the blood of a human, by a human shall that person's blood be shed" (vv. 5-6).

Thus the blood of the sacrifices, especially in the *hattat*, functions as a symbol of rendering unto God what is due to God—life—and simultaneously as a warning against taking life into our own hands by transgressing God's order.

Second, while I do not subscribe to Milgrom's view of the blood primarily as a detergent, he rightly attends to the fact that the Day of Atonement rites not only make atonement for the people, but also for the "sanctuary" and the "tent of meeting" (Lev. 16:16). The "uncleannesses" of the people of Israel have effects that extend beyond themselves—they create an environmental disaster. Given the way the temple itself functions as a symbol not only for Israel, but

37. Marx, "Theology of the Sacrifice," 117.
38. See Janzen, "Priestly Sacrifice in the Hebrew Bible," 46-49, where he paints this larger narrative context. His conclusion: "The blood of sacrifice is ultimately not a detergent, but an indicator of something that belongs to God—an indication of God's authority to demand obedience and power to punish sin" (49).

also for the whole created order, one sees that the day could be considered a rite in which the entire creation is atoned for and renewed.[39]

Third, the rite as a whole can be understood as a fitting symbol of repentance. This was explicitly stated as the central meaning of the Day of Atonement sacrifices in the earliest strands of rabbinic literature, as discussed above.

The Christian tradition has reflected deeply on the process of repentance. The contemporary Catechism of the Catholic Church draws from these reflections as it points out three typical parts of this process of repentance: contrition, confession, and penance.[40] All three of these aspects of repentance can be read onto the *hattat.*

Contrition is explained as "sorrow of the soul and detestation for the sin committed, together with the resolution not to sin again."[41] In the confession of sin, the laying on of hands, and the slaughter, the *hattat* symbolizes "the death of one's sinful and worldly desires," an expression of one's sorrow and commitment to repent.[42] As it is written, "A broken and contrite heart, O God, you will not despise" (Ps. 51:17). The offering of the fat would then fittingly indicate a renewed resolution and commitment to God's lordship—as in the burnt offering.

Confession also occurred during the sin offering of the Day of Atonement according to the Mishnah. At least in the later strands of m. Yoma, the high priest lays both hands on the bull and verbally confesses, "I have disobeyed, transgressed and sinned before you—I and my household. Oh Lord, make atonement for disobediences, transgressions and sins" (m. Yoma 3.8). Such a practice of confession of transgressions and sins may have been a common practice for all the *hattat* sacrifices.

Penance too might be seen to be part of the rite. Penance is "doing something to make amends for the sin"—either undoing the damage or else undergoing some kind of hard treatment as a kind of penalty or punishment.[43] The offering of the animal itself might be considered a kind of penance.

---

39. Margaret Barker stresses this as a central meaning of the Day of Atonement in, for example, "Temple Roots," 1–19.

40. Catechism of the Catholic Church, §1448–1460.

41. Catechism of the Catholic Church, §1451.

42. This is Kiuchi's explanation of the *olah*—such an explanation seems to fit more with the sin offering in my opinion. Kiuchi, *Leviticus,* 61.

43. Catechism of the Catholic Church, §1459.

Giving an animal from one's own livelihood and property would be a personal hardship. Alternatively, the "cost" of the animal to the offerer might be considered a kind of "ransom" paid that frees one from the punishment, perhaps death, that one should properly undergo.[44] Or perhaps through the laying on of hands, the animal might be considered a substitute, taking on the punishment, specifically death, that the person rightly would have suffered. On this latter account perhaps it is imagined that God's wrath is pacified by the death of the animal—someone has to die, one might say—but possibly God is propitiated instead by the act of repentance and contrition that this public representation of one's rightful penalty would entail. All are possible explanations of how the sacrifice might be considered as penance and all have been suggested by interpreters. All of these interpretations are possibilities given the evidence in the Old Testament.

While the Pentateuch sources are ambiguous at this level of detail, the main point is clear: the rite is a fitting act of true repentance.

As for the rite of the goat that is sent away, scholars again disagree as to the details of the mechanism of this rite. The word "Azazel" itself is ambiguous, having at least three common interpretations.[45] (1) First, some consider it the proper name given to the goat as it is designated. The name may derive from the combination of the verb *azal*, "to go away," with the word *ez*, meaning "she-goat." Thus the name may mean "the go-away goat." This is an ancient explanation and is the understanding of the Septuagint and Vulgate translations. It is also behind the Tyndale English translation of "scapegoat," which for Tyndale meant the goat that escaped—a meaning quite different from contemporary understandings of the term. A related yet different alternative is the one proposed by the influential *A Hebrew and English Lexicon of the Old Testament*, in which the Arabic word *azala* is the root, meaning to "entirely remove."[46] The goat, by escaping, entirely removes the sin it carries. (2) A second possibility is that Azazel is a name suggestive of the place where

---

44. Gordon Wenham's explanation of the *olah* falls into a similar pattern. Wenham, *Leviticus*, 245.

45. Mary Douglas, "The Go-Away Goat," in *The Book of Leviticus: Composition and Reception*, ed. Rolf Rendtorff (Leiden: Brill, 2003), 121–41. Levine, *Leviticus*, 102–257. Milgrom, *Leviticus 1–16*, 1020–21.

46. Francis Brown, S. R. Driver, and Charles A. Briggs, eds., *A Hebrew and English Lexicon of the Old Testament* (Oxford: Clarendon, 1951), s.v. "לַעֲזָאזֵל."

the goat was sent, a rugged place or precipice in the wilderness, derived from *azaz*, "rough ground," and *el*, "of God." Rabbinic interpreters often followed this explanation. (3) A third possibility is that it is a variation on the name of the demon *Azel* mentioned first in 1 Enoch, a book written long after the final redaction of Leviticus.

The third explanation, while considered the "most plausible" by Milgrom, needs some explanation, given both the timing of the writings and because offering sacrifices to demons is explicitly forbidden in the following chapter (Lev. 17:7). Milgrom explains that the goat is neither an offering to a demon, nor even a sacrifice, but rather the goat is the means of banishing Israel's sins back to where they could do no harm or to where they came from.[47]

As for the meaning of this rite, the anthropologist Mary Douglas offers a quite compelling reading in her article, "The Go-Away Goat."[48] Noting the change from Leviticus 16:22 where it is "set free in the wilderness" to later rabbinic literature where it is apparently pushed over a cliff and killed, she thinks that the meaning of the rite may have changed over time. In creating her interpretation, Douglas works with biblical ceremonies and narratives that feature pairs of animals or people, such as the ceremony of the offering of two birds for the cured leper and narratives about pairs of brothers in Genesis. In the Genesis narratives, Isaac and Jacob are like the goat chosen "for YHWH," while Ishmael and Esau are like the goat which is sent away and set free in the wilderness. Ishmael and Esau are not killed. Instead, God ensures a good future; the nations that surround Israel descend from them. Similarly Joseph is sent away; he becomes associated with Egypt. Douglas suggests the ceremony of sending one goat into the wilderness stems in part from these stories. Given these narrative echoes, her proposal is that in the rite the sins of Israel, sins associated with the people chosen "for YHWH," are confessed onto the goat. It is then sent into the wilderness as an emissary bearing Israel's confession to the nations. Such a symbolic act becomes a national confession with the hope that atonement and reconciliation between Israel and her estranged neighbors might occur. Like the gifts that Jacob sends to "cover" the face of Esau, the "go-away goat" is sent from Israel outward to the descendants of Esau. In the

---

47. Milgrom, *Leviticus 1–16*, 1044–45
48. Mary Douglas, "The Go-Away Goat," in *The Book of Leviticus: Composition and Reception*, ed. Rendtorff (Leiden: Brill, 2003), 121–41.

Day of Atonement, this act is paired with the goat for God. With the goat "for YHWH," Israel performs an act of contrition, confession, and penance that brings atonement between Israel and the Lord. Through this rite with the "go-away" goat—so different from most other sacrifices—Israel seeks atonement with the surrounding nations.

Given our twenty-first-century political climate, I find Douglas's reading of the rite incredibly appealing. Oh, that we as a church and a nation would regularly act that way! But even if it was originally the case, when the goat was killed in later times as part of the ceremony, that meaning of the rite had been lost. Instead, the "go-away goat" functioned as a second sin offering to God. One can interpret it as a visual representation of the bearing away and entire removal of sins that occurs through the more regular rite of the sin offering of its twin. While the sin offering "covers" iniquities, the "sent-away goat" dispatches them into the wilderness.[49] In this case, the death of the goat who bears away the sins of the people is not the primary point. Whether it is let go as in Leviticus or pushed over a ravine as in later rabbinical writings, the point is that sin is transported away and removed.

In the centuries immediately before Christ, when the Temple Scroll of the Qumran community was written, this seems to be the understanding of at least that community:

> He shall wash his hands and feet of the blood of the sin-offering and shall come to the living goat and shall confess over its head the iniquities of the children of Israel together with all their guilt, all their sins. He shall put them on the head of the goat and dispatch it to Azazel in the desert by the hand of the man who is waiting ready. The goat shall bear all the iniquities of (the children of Israel) . . . [and he shall expiate] for all the children of Israel and it shall be forgiven to them.[50]

The result is that, as in the text of Isaiah, "though your sins be as scarlet, they shall be as white as snow" (1:18 KJV). In later rabbinic traditions, it was reported that a portion of the scarlet thread that marked the sent-away goat was

---

49. Milgrom, *Leviticus 1–16*, 1044, in his explanation of a possible origin of the rite.
50. Temple Scroll 26–27.

kept, and that miraculously, when the sending away or killing of the goat was accomplished, the scarlet thread at the temple turned white.[51]

Another way of interpreting the rite is that the death of the goat is precisely the point—it bears sin in another way. It becomes a substitute for the sinner; it is killed in a kind of substitute punishment. This understanding is closest to modern "scapegoating." However, it is hard to reconcile this interpretation with the Levitical text in which the goat is to be let go. And, as Mary Douglas at least claims, such an act, which is finally like the more contemporary notions of "scapegoating," is "banal, foreign-inspired," and "full of contradictions."[52] On this, Milgrom and Douglas are agreed: "Killing the goat was not essential."[53] While bearing some resemblance to some Christian penal-substitution atonement theories, if "exile" is understood as the punishment given, this interpretation does not have the support of Old Testament interpreters such as Douglas.

One final aspect of the Day of Atonement that should be noted is the relationship of these expiatory rites to the final whole burnt offerings. After the expiatory rites, the high priest changed out of his linen vestments into his golden vestments. This signaled the change from sin offering rites to whole burnt offering rites, or using Marx's categories, from rites of "atonement" to "offerings of pleasing aroma." When the priest changed vestments and emerged back from the holy of holies alive and well, this signaled to the people gathered that the expiatory rites were successful and the relationship between Israel and God was repaired. This explains the great fanfare that greeted the high priest when he emerged. After expiation, the primary or normal relationship of homage, self-giving, and nearness signaled by whole burnt offerings at the end of the day was restarted.

Summing up our findings of this rather detailed discussion, the central meanings of the Day of Atonement were that Israel repented, her sins were covered, and she was forgiven by God. In the Feast of Trumpets the coming of God to judge was announced. Here in the Day of Atonement, we see that God is ready to forgive Israel's sins, transgressions, and guilt. The result of this holy day was that Israel, the temple, and perhaps even the entire creation were atoned for and their relationships with God set right.

51. It was also reported that in the forty years before the destruction of the temple, that miracle ceased to regularly happen. b. Yoma 39a-b.

52. Douglas, "Go-Away Goat," 141.

53. Milgrom, *Leviticus 1–16*, 1045.

The Feast

The Day of Atonement is followed by the eight-day celebration of the Feast of Booths. In Scripture, besides being called the Feast of Booths (*Hag Hasukkot*), it is also referred to as the Festival of Ingathering (Exod. 23:16; 34:22; "feast" in RSV) or even simply "the Festival" (1 Kgs. 8:2; 12:32; "feast" in RSV). It was by far the greatest and largest feast of the year. The number of sacrifices was greater than all the other festivals put together. Just taking the number of bulls listed in the book of Numbers (29:12–38), we see that thirteen are to be sacrificed on the first day, twelve on the second day, proceeding likewise down to 7 on the seventh day and 1 on the eighth day, for a total of 70 bulls sacrificed for the festival as a whole. These were sacrificed and then eaten as *shelamim* or shalom celebration offerings. The whole week was like a grand celebratory meal eaten by Israel and also offered to God.

The feast is linked to the ingathering of all the final produce from the fields, especially the grape harvest. Like all the pilgrim feasts, the concrete and more agricultural meanings of the feast took on symbolic freight as the feast was tied to the history of God with Israel. The feast looked backward to the wilderness period of Israel, the forty years that Israel lived in the wilderness after they received the law at Pentecost but before they entered the promised land: "You shall live in booths for seven days . . . so that your generations may know that I made the people of Israel live in booths when I brought them out of the land of Egypt" (Lev. 23:42–43). And just as the people of Israel during that wilderness time looked forward to the realization of God's promises when they finally reached the promised land, so too the feast itself became associated with eschatological and messianic hopes and expectations. As Israel celebrated the feast, they looked forward to the realization of God's promises as a result of an anticipated new exodus-like experience. They anticipated the great feast and eschatological banquet envisioned by the prophets.

While it is debated when these eschatological expectations became major themes of the feast, it is clear that at least some Jews, such as the author of Zechariah 14, early on understood the Feast of *Sukkot* in precisely that way.[54]

---

54. It has been common to understand the Feast of *Sukkot* as the eschatological feast *par excellence*. But some scholars, such as Jeffrey Rubenstein, call into question those associations and interpret it almost entirely as a yearly harvest festival that is thoroughly this-worldly. Rubenstein lists nine typical arguments that scholars make for such escha-

Certainly the early Christians did. Jean Daniélou speaks for many interpreters of the festival when he claims that *Sukkot* "more than any other festival took on eschatological significance."[55]

Besides the sacrifices, another major symbolic practice was the making of the booths, from which the feast got its name. The actual building of these booths first became standard practice at the time of Ezra. Before that time, "From the days of Jeshua son of Nun to that day the people of Israel had not done so" (Neh. 8:17). During the festival, the people built and lived in these temporary abodes.[56] The temporary and fragile nature of them became symbols and reminders of the temporariness and fragility of our lives.

The meanings of these booths and the feast as a whole had a multifaceted "now and not yet" quality. Both Philo and Maimonides understand the booths as in part a reminder to Israel of the hard times of the past so that they would live with humility and thankfulness during times of plenty.[57] The feast was accordingly in part a celebration of the goodness of the present and the fruits of the promised land as Israel looked back on the hard journey it took to get there. But the booths also reminded Israel of the fragility of one's present life as they anticipated God's good future. So the feast was also filled with expectation and longing for the final "day of the Lord" when the full fruits of God's promises would fully come to pass.

One might think that a reminder of the temporariness and fragility of our lives would be a somber occasion, but this was not at all the case. Instead, the entire week was the grandest and most joyful feast of the year. All the different

---

tological associations and calls them all into question. He grants that "on the other hand, a few marginal and eschatologically oriented groups, perhaps cut off or alienated from the contemporary Jerusalem temple, dreamed of a restored and purified temple" and modeled their visions on the *Sukkot* rites. But given the double meanings of both Passover and Pentecost that also have links to Israel's salvation history, given the quickness with which such eschatological resonances found their way into rabbinic and Christian literature, given the eschatological orientation of many Jews during the first century (evident in the Dead Sea Scrolls), and given arguments that could be mounted against Rubenstein's own interpretations of the evidence, I find Rubenstein's arguments overly cautious. Jeffrey L. Rubenstein, "Sukkot, Eschatology and Zechariah 14," *Revue Biblique* 103 (1996):761–95.

55. Jean Daniélou, *Primitive Christian Symbols* (London: Burns & Oates, 1961), 2–3. Quoted in Rubenstein, "Sukkot," 162.

56. m. Suk. 1.1.

57. Philo, *Spec. Laws* 2.204–209; Maimonides, *Guide for the Perplexed* 3.43.

rites and festivities pointed toward one central meaning: *Sukkot* was a feast of great thanksgiving for the present blessings given by God, while simultaneously a foretaste of the great feast to come at the end of the age or the end of one's life, when all the promises of God would come to pass and the people of God would feast with God. After the Feast of Trumpets, announcing the coming of God to judge, and the Day of Atonement, when their sins were covered, Israel rejoiced with all their might that they had been forgiven, that they were experiencing many blessings now, and that in the future there would be an even greater feast when God's kingdom would fully come.

In addition to building and living in booths, each day people would participate in various worship services at the temple. They would carry with them an arrangement made out of four species of trees and fruits: a palm branch (*lulav*), the branch of a myrtle tree (*hadas*), the branch of a willow tree (*aravah*), and the fruit of a citron tree (*etrog*). These in part represented the fruits of the promised land. During the daily rites, worshippers would recite or sing the Hallel Psalms, Psalms 113–118, and during certain phrases, "Give thanks to the LORD, for he is good" (Ps. 118:1) and "Save us, we beseech you, O LORD" (Ps. 118:25), they would wave them.[58] That phrase in Psalm 118:25, "save, Oh Lord, I pray" (my translation) is in Hebrew, "*Yahweh hoshi'ah anna*," or, shortened in Greek, "*hosanna*." Large palm branches or possibly willow branches would also be marched around the altar once every day. The people would say, "Save us, we beseech you, O LORD," and then lean the branches against the altar.[59] On the seventh day of the feast, they would march around the altar with palm branches seven times. Here again, thanksgiving for all that God has done is joined together with a longing for an even greater salvation.

An important rite came at the end of the first day of the festival. Four giant "candlesticks," poles with golden bowls on top of them, were positioned in the Court of Women. They were so high that four youths would climb ladders in order to pour into them large jars of the oil that fueled these lights. On that day they were lit amidst great fanfare. This practice provides the background to Jesus's claim, "I am the light of the world" (John 8:12; 9:5), a claim he made

58. m. Suk. 3.9.

59. m. Suk. 4.6 mentions both possibilities, willow or palm. In Jub. 16:31, Abraham foreshadows the feast, celebrating with palm branches. 2 Macc. 10:6–8 also mentions palm branches. Plutarch (*Quaestiones convivialium* 4.6.2) also mentions palm branches. The use of palm branches in the Gospels with the cry of "Hosanna!" seems to echo this use.

during the Feast of Booths in John's Gospel. Jesus is the incarnation of the type that the lights pointed to. These lights most likely had similar meanings to the lights of the menorah in the temple. They represented the light and wisdom that God gave to Israel and that Israel would herself shine with as a result of God's blessing.

Another daily rite during the festival centered on the symbol of water. A golden flagon of water was filled in the pool of Shiloah by a priest and then brought into the temple to the sounds of flutes and trumpets. It was then poured into bowls at the corners of the altar from which it would flow outward. This rite was another point of great celebration: "He who has not seen the rejoicing at the place of the water-drawing has never seen rejoicing in his life," say the rabbis.[60] This rite was an enacted prayer for God's blessing of water in the coming year.[61] But it was also connected with expectations of God's blessings in the coming age. This water in rabbinic literature is connected with Isaiah 12:3,

> With joy you will draw water from the wells of salvation. And you
>   will say in that day:
> Give thanks to the LORD,
>   call on his name;
> make known his deeds among the nations;
>   proclaim that his name is exalted.[62]

"That day" is the great day of the Lord, when the Messiah, the "shoot" that will come out of the "stump of Jesse" (Isa. 11:1), will come and restore the fortunes of Israel and Israel will again see the salvation of God (Isa. 9–12). In the Gospel of John, Jesus connects this water with himself: "Let anyone who is thirsty come to me" (John 7:37). This rite shared in the meanings of all the water symbolism of the temple—like the garden of Eden, the temple was a source of life-giving water. Given this practice and the water systems of the temple, water actually did flow out of the temple, just as it does quite dramatically in Ezekiel's vision (Ezek. 47:1–12).

60. m. Suk. 5.1.
61. Rubenstein, "Sukkot," 182–84.
62. m. Suk. 4.9.

A final important symbolic practice tied to the central meanings of the feast was the celebration of the eighth day. Philo calls the eighth day the "seal" or "crown" of all the feasts of the year.[63] For Israel, the seventh day hearkens back to the seventh day of God's creation when all was completed. So, the eighth day suggests a new beginning, here a new beginning after judgment and final atonement. The association of the number eight and the eighth day with new beginnings finds its way into Christian eucharistic practices as we will see. There is a strong connection to the day of Christ's resurrection, which took place on the day after the sabbath or seventh day, so, on the eighth day. It is also the reason why many ancient Christian baptistries and baptismal fonts had eight sides.[64]

Such a new beginning is seen in the vision of the prophet Zechariah. In his vision, "a day is coming" when there will be a great judgment of the nations (14:1–5), but after the judgment, there will be "light" and "continuous day" (14:7), when "waters [will] flow out from Jerusalem" (14:8). And "all who survive of the nations . . . shall go up year after year to worship the King . . . and to keep the festival of booths" (14:16).

In sum, this great festival season of *Sukkot* was the crown of the Jewish liturgical year. Booths completes the cycle begun with Passover and Pentecost by looking forward to the consummation of all God's promises for Israel. It not only celebrates the foretaste of blessings already given by God, but strains forward in joyful expectation toward "the day of the Lord," when God will judge the nations, sins and transgressions will be fully and finally atoned for, and the people of God will be called to the great feast where they will celebrate God's shalom with each other and with their Lord.

New Testament and Early Church Connections

For early Christians, the Eucharist had an eschatological aspect to it that was similar to the Feast of *Sukkot*. Christ's real presence was celebrated in the feast, but Christ's presence was also understood as a foretaste of or a "projection" of

---

63. Philo, *Spec. Laws* 2.211.
64. Everett Ferguson, *Catechesis, Baptism, Eschatology, and Martyrdom*, vol. 2 of *The Early Church at Work and Worship* (Cambridge: James Clarke, 2014), 252–53.

Christ's second coming.[65] Christ's coming in the Eucharist was both "now and not yet." The early church understood and expressed those "comings" of Christ and the Spirit using the same themes and symbols that *Sukkot* did, and by using types shared with the *Sukkot* celebrations—as if *Sukkot* was transposed into a new key given Christ and the Spirit's work.

The eschatological aspects of the Eucharist, while often forgotten in some Christian traditions, have been recovered and argued for in the past half-century. Two authors in particular stand out. From the Protestant tradition, Geoffrey Wainwright's *Eucharist and Eschatology* highlights the eschatological aspects of the early church's eucharistic worship. From the Orthodox tradition, Alexander Schmemann's writings, such as *For the Life of the World* and *The Eucharist: Sacrament of the Kingdom*, also highlight eschatological aspects implicit in traditional eucharistic liturgies. While these and other works have helpfully injected eschatological themes back into eucharistic theology, bold lines of connection back to the same eschatological themes and symbols central to *Sukkot*, the great eschatological feast of the Old Testament, have, unfortunately, not been emphasized in these important works.

So much could be written here—as evidenced by Wainwright's and Schmemann's book-length treatments of these themes. A few examples of how early liturgies, scriptures, and other patristic writings about the Eucharist can be seen in typological relation to the themes and symbols of the Feast of Trumpets, the Day of Atonement, and the Great Feast will need to suffice.

Maranatha, Hosanna, and the Benedictus

One of the earliest records of directions and words used in the Christian meal assemblies which came to be called the Eucharist is found in the Didache. At the end of the Didache (10:6), we find several significant phrases used in the prayers associated with the meal. The first is the Aramaic word "Maranatha," which was not translated into Greek. It could mean either "Our Lord, come!" or "Our Lord has come." It is part of the end of the section that outlines the

---

65. For "projection," see Wainwright, *Eucharist and Eschatology*, 92–93. Projection in two senses: Christ's coming is a projection in a "temporal" sense, "a 'throwing forward' of Christ's final advent into the present." It is also a projection in a "map-maker's sense of projection." "It is a representation of a large reality by means of a set of comprehensible symbols" (92). In both senses the symbols are real symbols in that they participate in that which they symbolize.

thanksgiving or "eucharist" spoken over the meal of the Christian assembly. That section might have formed a dialogue between the president of the assembly and the people, as suggested by Wainwright:

> *President:* Let grace come and this world pass away.
> *People:* Hosanna to the Son of David.
> *President:* If anyone is holy, let him come. If any is not, let him repent. Maranatha.
> *People:* Amen.[66]

"Maranatha" also occurs at the end of 1 Corinthians in a list of phrases (arguably liturgical) that are strikingly similar to the ending of the Didache: "Greet one another with a holy kiss"; "Let anyone be accursed who has no love for the Lord"; "Maranatha"; "The grace of the Lord Jesus Christ be with you" (16:20, 22–23)

These instances of "Maranatha" resonate with the phrase "Come, Lord Jesus!" at the end of Revelation (22:20; this time in Greek, so the imperative form is certain there). This cry anticipates the great day when "a new heaven and a new earth" are revealed, the first earth has "passed away" (Rev. 21:1), and the great "marriage supper of the Lamb" (Rev. 19:9) is to be celebrated. It looks forward to the *parousia*—the second coming of Christ. The context of the entire letter might also indicate that such a coming is anticipated in the worship of the church in their eucharistic celebration on "the Lord's Day" (Rev. 1:10).[67]

Taken together, these texts suggest that the word "Maranatha" was a regular part of the eucharistic liturgy. It was a call for Christ's presence in the Eucharist, an invocation or *epiclesis*. And yet it was more. It was also "at least a partial anticipation of the *parousia*," the second coming of Christ.[68]

This call for Christ's coming is related to the phrase "Hosanna to the Son of David." Hosanna, another word preserved in its original language in Christian

66. Wainwright, *Eucharist and Eschatology*, 68, drawing from H. Lietzmann, *Messe und Herrenmahl* (Berlin: de Gruyter, 1955), 230–38.

67. As suggested by, e.g., Wilfrid J. Harrington, O. P., *Revelation*, Sacra Pagina (Collegeville, MN: Liturgical Press, 1993), 224–27. Craig R. Koester, *Revelation: A New Translation with Introduction and Commentary* (New Haven: Yale University Press, 2014), 845–46, disagrees, but he also holds there are no "clear allusions to the Lord's Supper" (846) anywhere in the book.

68. Wainwright, *Eucharist and Eschatology*, 70.

liturgies, means "save us." This phrase alludes back to Matthew 21 and Jesus's triumphal entry into Jerusalem and the temple. The crowds "cut branches from the trees and spread them on the road" (21:8), followed him, and shouted, "Hosanna to the Son of David!" and "Blessed is the one who comes in the name of the Lord!" (21:9; cf. Mark 11:9–10; Luke 19:38).

Applied to the Eucharist, this phrase suggests the triumphal entry of Christ into the Christian temple. It also suggests the Eucharist is in part a calling for Christ's second coming, a coming anticipated in the eucharistic assembly itself. Thus the phrase has polysemic connotations similar to "Maranatha!"

As we have seen above, the Old Testament precedent for such cries and actions is the Feast of *Sukkot*. The Gospels and the eucharistic liturgies are themselves quoting or alluding to Psalm 118:25–26:

> Save us, we beseech you, O LORD!
> O LORD, we beseech you, give us success!
> Blessed is the one who comes in the name of the LORD.

Those phrases are part of the Hallel Psalms (113–118) used in the *Sukkot* liturgies. They were in fact the climax of the recitation of the Hallel Psalms. And, as noted above, according to the Mishnah, as those very phrases were recited by the people, while marching around the altar—once each day and seven times on the day called the Great Hosanna—all the people were supposed to wave their festal branches.[69] The people waved their *lulavim*, calling on God to come and bring to culmination his final victory and fulfill his purposes for them. In this way the patterns and central meanings of *Sukkot* were extended into the earliest Christian eucharistic celebrations.

The phrase "Blessed is the one who comes in the name of the Lord!" eventually came to play a role in typical eucharistic liturgies. In Wainwright's analysis, that phrase, called in Latin the *Benedictus qui venit*, seems to have replaced the "Maranatha!" of the earliest liturgies.[70] Many readers will be familiar with its place in traditional eucharistic liturgies right after the opening lines of the *Sanctus* that begin with "Holy, Holy, Holy." This combination of the *Sanctus*

69. m. Suk. 3.9. Apparently, Rabbi Gamaliel and Rabbi Yehoshua waved their *lulavim* only at "Hosanna, we beseech you, O Lord." Others waved theirs also at the beginning and end of Ps. 118, three places in total, Ps. 118:1, 25, and 29.
70. Wainwright, *Eucharist and Eschatology*, 70–72.

and *Benedictus* in the eucharistic liturgy is first attested in the sixth century, and since has become common in both Western and Eastern liturgies.[71] But earlier, the place of the *Benedictus* seems to have been right before communion, as in the Testament of Our Lord (fifth century), or in response to the elevation of the elements right before communion, as in the Apostolic Constitutions 8 (fourth century).[72] Both placements suggest the phrase anticipated the coming again of Christ not only in the future, but especially during the eating or elevating of the bread and wine. In early Syrian liturgies, the phrase appears as "Blessed is he that came and cometh," making clear the multiple comings of Christ. The literary context of that prayer makes clear that "cometh" refers to the second coming of Christ.[73]

"Hosanna!," the Benedictus, and by association "Maranatha!" all arguably have their ultimate ritual roots in Psalm 118 and its climactic use in the Feast of *Sukkot*. As Israel celebrated with joy the already experienced signs of shalom and God's realized reign in the Great Feast of *Sukkot*, they also cried "Hosanna!" They called for God to come and save them even more fully in the future. Those practices became types, which the Eucharist then employed. Christians gave these expressions new meanings as they called for and celebrated the coming of Christ's presence into their midst, while understanding Christ's presence now in the eucharistic feast was but a foretaste of his coming at the end of the age.

Judgment and Atonement

As Christ comes into the presence of his people in the Eucharist, he brings both judgment and atonement before ushering in the Great Feast. Early eucharistic services exhibit a pattern similar to the narrative movement of the larger season of *Sukkot*, in which the Day of Trumpets announces judgment and then the Day of Atonement announces the possibility of forgiveness and reconciliation. [74]

71. Wainwright, *Eucharist and Eschatology*, 70, 179n223.
72. Wainwright, *Eucharist and Eschatology*, 71.
73. Wainwright, *Eucharist and Eschatology*, 71. The prayer of Severus of Antioch is used as one example (63–64).
74. See discussion of the Eucharist and judgment in Wainwright, *Eucharist and Eschatology*, 80–91.

As far as judgment, Christians typically affirm a great day of judgment when "all . . . must appear before the judgment seat of Christ" (2 Cor. 5:10). Christians also recognize that whenever people encounter Christ—in the incarnation, in preaching, through Scripture—a projection of that final judgment takes place according to their reaction to him. "Those who believe in him are not condemned; but those who do not believe are condemned already, because they have not believed in the name of the only Son of God," Jesus tells Nicodemus (John 3:18).[75] At the end of his ministry to the people in John's Gospel, Jesus reiterates that his purpose is to save rather than to condemn; yet, if people reject him and his word they bring judgment on themselves, a judgment that will be sealed on the final day of judgment: "I do not judge anyone who hears my words and does not keep them, for I came not to judge the world, but to save the world. The one who rejects me and does not receive my word has a judge; on the last day the word that I have spoken will serve as judge" (John 12:47–48).

Early Christians recognized a similar scenario in the Eucharist as people encountered the presence of Christ there. In this way the central themes of *Rosh Hashanah*, the Day of Trumpets, are taken up and transformed in the Christian Eucharist.

An important scriptural passage that reflects such an understanding is 1 Corinthians 11:27–34 where Paul chastises the Corinthian church for their poor eucharistic behavior. In the passage, two things are clear: one, the eucharistic celebration itself can become an occasion for judgment, and two, the reason for a negative judgment in the case of the Corinthian church was that they were celebrating the Eucharist wrongly.

Paul writes, "For all who eat and drink without discerning the body, eat and drink judgment against themselves" (1 Cor. 11:29). The image of eating and drinking judgment needs unpacking.[76] It suggests that in their eucharistic

---

75. The theme of judgment throughout John's Gospel makes this clear. See also 5:30–47, 12:44–50, and the ironic trial scene of Christ before Pilate and the Jewish leaders.

76. There was an Old Testament rite called the *Sotah* (Num. 5:11–31), a rite used in the case of a jealous husband. In that ordeal certain words were written on paper, scraped into a cup for the woman to drink. The reaction the woman had to the drink proved either her innocence or her guilt. There are similarities in imagery here, and Paul's mentioning of both "cup" and "jealousy" in 1 Cor. 10 raises the question whether such a rite formed part of Paul's imagination here. Raymond Collins notes the possible connection, *1 Corinthians*, 439.

eating and drinking, the Corinthian people have a close encounter with the risen Christ, and that the encounter is an anticipation of or projection of the encounter they will have with the risen Christ in the day of judgment. That second coming of Christ is mentioned in v. 26: "For as often as you eat this bread and drink the cup, you proclaim the Lord's death until he comes." The second coming of Christ is the springboard for Paul's "therefore" in v. 27 and this whole section (vv. 27–34) on judgment.

What are they being judged for? For not "discerning the body" and "eating and drinking in an unworthy manner" (vv. 27, 29). These phrases have been interpreted in quite different ways throughout Christian history. I am persuaded by the interpretation that the core of the issue here has to do with their "divisions" (v. 18) and their humiliating treatment of one another across class lines (v. 22).[77] I understand, along with many recent interpreters, that what Paul means by "discerning [*diakrinōn*] the body" concerns primarily the *ecclesial body*, discerning that they are all parts of the church and thus connected to and gifts to one another. But since this discerning is tied to their eucharistic feast, this *ecclesial body* (the church) of Christ relates to both the *incarnate* (Jesus incarnate) and *sacramental* bodies of Christ (in the Eucharist). In the incarnation, Christ inaugurates a new righteous humanity in proper relationship to God. But in the Eucharist, the risen and living Christ is present to us sacramentally. As one participates in the Eucharist, one should also discern, accept, and commit to what this means for oneself as part of Christ's ecclesial body.[78]

This meaning of "discerning the body" clarifies why their eucharistic meal behavior in which they humiliate one another by not sharing with, waiting for, or receiving one another and by having visible divisions is "not really" eating "the Lord's supper" (v. 20). They in their practice are rejecting Christ and his way, thereby bringing judgment on themselves. Nevertheless, that judgment results only in "discipline" (v. 32) so that they will not suffer condemnation in the final judgment along with those who totally reject Christ and his way, here called "the world" (v. 32).

77. For example, Gordon Fee, *1 Corinthians*, 558–67; Richard Hays, *1 Corinthians*, 200–206.

78. I understand such a complex activity of discerning and committing to the implications of what one discerns to be similar to what John means by receiving and believing in Christ in his Gospel (John 1:12).

Many early liturgies also understand the Eucharist as anticipating the final judgment.[79] This recognition of judgment is paired with the equal recognition that Christ came not to condemn, but rather to offer himself as a sacrifice for sins. Those who believe and receive him partake in the fruits of that sacrifice, the forgiveness of sins. This mirrors the Jewish *Sukkot* cycle, where the judgment announced in the Feast of Trumpets is paired with the forgiveness announced in the Day of Atonement.

Jesus's words about the cup at the Last Supper point to this meaning of the Eucharist. Christ said, "For this is my blood of the covenant, which is poured out for many for the forgiveness of sins" (Matt. 26:28).

Many liturgies treat "the forgiveness of sins" as a present effect of the communion rite, and also as an anticipation of God's forgiveness at the final judgment. Here is one example, from the liturgy of St. James, one of the oldest liturgies that is still in use in Orthodox churches today:

> And to us, O Lord, who have eaten thy holy body and drunk thy propitiatory blood, let it not be for judgment, for vengeance nor for condemnation nor for accusation to me and to thy faithful people but for the pardon of offenses and for the remission of sins and for a blessed resurrection from the house of the dead and for boldness before thy fearful judgment seat, O our Lord and our God for ever.[80]

Early Christians explicitly connect the sacrifice of Christ for the forgiveness of sins celebrated in the Eucharist to the Day of Atonement. For example, Origen, commenting on Leviticus 9, writes, "Christ [is] the true high priest who made atonement for you. . . . Hear him saying to you: 'This is my blood which is poured out for you for the forgiveness of sins.'"[81] Scripture itself makes similar claims, as in Romans 3:25 and above all in Hebrews. The latter understands the significance of Christ's saving death explicitly and at length in terms of Old Testament rites at the tabernacle, above all the rites of the Day of Atone-

---

79. See many examples in Wainwright, *Eucharist and Eschatology*, 83–89.

80. Quoted in Wainwright, *Eucharist and Eschatology*, 87. "The Divine Liturgy of James the Holy Apostle and Brother of the Lord," *The Ante-Nicene Fathers*, vol. 7.

81. Quoted in Barker, "Temple Roots," 17–18. Origen, *Homilies on Leviticus 1–16*, The Fathers of the Church 83 (Washington, DC: Catholic University of America Press, 1990), 9.10.

ment.[82] It provides detailed comparisons between Christ's priesthood and sacrifice and "the high priest" (9:7) at the tabernacle and "the blood of goats and bulls" (9:13) sacrificed on that day. Prevailing contemporary interpretations of Hebrews suggest that the author did not have the Eucharist explicitly in mind as a celebration in which the priestly and sacrificial work of Christ is remembered and experienced anew. However, Hebrews' interpretation of the work of Christ in light of the Day of Atonement rites had tremendous influence on later sacramental theologies.

What does this tell us? Both New Testament and early church texts consider participation in the Eucharist as a participation in the death of Christ, a death which was seen as an atoning sacrifice. Christ's death was like the Old Testament sin offerings presented in God's presence on the Day of Atonement, only it was the perfection and fulfillment of those offerings. Thus in the Eucharist, the congregation comes into the presence of God, into the presence of the one who will be our judge at the end of the age. Through our repentance and our relationship to Christ, however, we benefit from the priestly and sacrificial work of Christ. Like the high priest at the Day of Atonement, Christ has offered a sin offering—himself—which brings about "the forgiveness of sins." We experience this forgiveness now in each celebration of the Eucharist. This present forgiveness also anticipates the final application of the atoning work of Christ at the end of the age.

A Foretaste of the Feast to Come

But, just as in the Feast of *Sukkot*, that is not all.

Throughout Jesus's ministry, he often portrayed the end or goal of God's plans for his people as a great feast. Jesus, in a statement about the expansiveness of God's work, says, "I tell you, many will come from east and west and will eat with Abraham and Isaac and Jacob in the kingdom of heaven" (Matt. 8:11; cf. Luke 13:29). In the beatitudes, Jesus speaks of those who hunger and

---

82. For the relationship of Hebrews to sacramental theology, see, for example, L. T. Johnson, "Sacramentality and Sacraments in Hebrews," in *Oxford Handbook of Sacramental Theology*, ed. John Webster, Kathryn Tanner, and Iain Torrance (Oxford: Oxford University Press, 2015), 109–22. For an interpretation of Hebrews in the same volume more open to seeing the "altar" in Heb. 13:10 as the Eucharistic table, see Nicolas Perrin, "Sacraments and Sacramentality in the New Testament," 52–67.

thirst now, but will then be "filled" (Matt. 5:6; cf. Luke 6:21). And in his parables about and visions of the end, Jesus sometimes likens the kingdom to a "wedding banquet" (Matt 25:1–13; cf. Luke 12:35–38). Such a banquet will occur after a time of judgment (Matt. 25:31–46), a time announced by the sound of the trumpet (Matt. 24:31).

But such a feast was not simply a future reality. Central to Jesus's ministry were his many symbolic acts concerning meals and miraculous feedings of thousands. He often ate with "tax collectors and sinners" (Mark 2:15–17; cf. Matt. 9:9–13, Luke 5:27–32). His miraculous feedings of the five thousand and four thousand (Mark 6:30–44; 8:1–10; Matt. 14:13–21; 15:32–39; Luke 9:11–17; John 6:3–15) resonate with Isaiah's vision of the great feast: "On this mountain the Lord of hosts will make for all peoples a feast of rich food, a feast of well-aged wines, of rich food filled with marrow, of well-aged wines strained clear" (Isa. 25:6). By these acts Jesus was providing a foretaste of the feast to come.

The same may be said of the early church's Eucharist celebrations. In the Eucharist, they experienced a foretaste, an appetizer, of that great feast to come. Their meal was a projection into the present of the heavenly or kingdom feast that would take place after the second coming of Christ. This kingdom meal is directly mentioned in Christ's words at the Last Supper: "I tell you, I will never again drink of this fruit of the vine until that day when I drink it new with you in my Father's kingdom" (Matt. 26:29; cf. Luke 22:18).

Geoffrey Wainwright's *Eucharist and Eschatology* dedicates a chapter to this theme: "The Antepast [i.e., Appetizer] of Heaven."[83] As Wainwright unpacks this theme, he highlights the fact that early Christians saw the Eucharist as a meal. And at this meal, they considered Jesus to be present not only in the elements of bread and wine but also as a host and a participant in the meal—just as he was in the Last Supper. Furthermore, they understood their eucharistic meal to be an anticipation of the great banquet of the future age, itself a symbol of resurrection life.

Such themes are reflected in many writings of the early Christians concerning the Eucharist. For example, Balai, a fifth-century Syrian leader of the church, composed these words as part of a hymn for the dedication of a church:

83. Pp. 21–74 in Wainwright, *Eucharist and Eschatology*.

His altar is ready, and he takes his meal with us;
his glory is offered to men, and they take their place at table;
we eat with him at our table; one day he will eat with us at his.[84]

Celebrating the Eucharist on Sunday, or the "eighth" day, is also tied to this theme. What happens on our "eighth day" is a sacrament or foretaste of what will take place in the new creation. Basil the Great, for example, writes that the church celebrates the Eucharist on the eighth day because "this day foreshadows the state which is to follow the present age: a day without sunset, nightfall, or successor, an age which does not grow old or come to an end."[85]

So, in this way as well, the early Christians saw that the Eucharist was in part a transformation of the themes that characterized *Sukkot*, the festival celebrating and prefiguring the end of all. In the Eucharist they expected that God in Christ would come and be present at their celebration, that in their midst Christ's judgment and atonement would be anticipated, and that they would gain a foretaste of the great feast to come.

Pressure: Celebrating the End in the Now

How might drawing these lines of connection between the Feast of Booths and the Eucharist affect our eucharistic theology and practice today? Two possibilities stand out.

Passover and Day of Atonement Sacrifices and Christian Atonement Theories

Early Christians often viewed the cross through the framework of Jewish temple sacrifice. The writers of the New Testament made sense of Christ's saving work on the cross by relating it to one or more of the main sacrifices of the temple. However, over time Christian reflections have prioritized other theories of atonement.

84. From the German translation by P. S. Langersdorfer in *Ausgewählte Schriften der syrischen Dichter*, vol. 6 of *Bibliothek der Kirchenväter* (Kempten: Jos. Kösel, 1913), 13. Quoted in Wainwright, *Eucharist and Eschatology*, 57.
85. Basil, *On the Holy Spirit* (Yonkers, NY: St. Vladimir's Seminary Press, 2011), 27.66.

Let me offer two major examples. Anselm's reflections in *Cur Deus homo?* find their home and basic logic in the relationship between a feudal lord and his subject. Neither the temple nor sacrifice is mentioned in the entire treatise. Instead the logic of human redemption by Christ is worked through, and argued to be "necessary" by Anselm, using the categories of justice, obedience, debt, honor, and payment of satisfaction. Notably, Anselm uses the two basic categories of a positive gift of justice and obedience as well as a "payment" for disobedience. And, I applaud Anselm for contextualizing biblical notions into the categories of his day. But what is he contextualizing? Would it not have been better to link those categories back to Passover and Day of Atonement sacrifices—in this way basing his "logic" on or at least relating it to more central biblical notions? My question of Anselm, which is often the critique of Anselm by his detractors, has to do with the necessity of his conception of justice. While Anselm, who is so cautious and lovely about this in his opening chapters, wants to move beyond the "fittingness" of the "pictures" of Scripture to "the rational soundness of the truth," I wonder whether he is simply moving from one set of pictures to another.[86]

Relatedly, Karl Barth's discussion in *Church Dogmatics* IV/1 of Christ's "priestly" work finds its logical ground not in the images of the temple, but rather the courtroom: the "judge judged in our place" is a key phrase of his.[87] Barth gives two main reasons for moving from temple to courtroom, for selecting what he calls the "forensic" over the "cultic" framework in his explanations of the logic of Christ's work. He claims that the temple is "now rather remote from us" and that forensic concepts are more "distinct" and "comprehensive."[88] However, he raises this question: "May it not be that the most primitive Christianity, because of its great nearness to the Old Testament, partly in agreement with it and partly in opposition to it, did in fact think and speak far more in the

---

86. Anselm, *Cur Deus homo?*, 1.3–4.

87. Barth, *Church Dogmatics* IV/1 (London: T&T Clark, 1956), 211–83.

88. Barth, *CD* IV/1, 275. Given advancements in scholarship about the temple in the last half century discussed in the opening chapter, plus the fact that courtroom "justice" is not quite as distinct as Barth suggests—as the growing discussion about "restorative justice" versus "punitive justice" in our culture makes clear—I do not find those reasons compelling for *preferring* forensic over cultic. That being said, I agree with Barth that forensic metaphors and language also find their home in Scripture and that, as Barth's exposition shows, they provide quite a rich alternative angle on the work of Christ as well.

images and categories of this group [i.e., the cultic framework] than we can detect from the New Testament?"[89] Yes, the temple framework provided a sometimes hidden, sometimes plain to see substructure for early Christian thought. However, the temple framework is not actually very difficult to "detect" in the New Testament. Like Anselm, Barth develops two aspects of Christ's work, the positive gift of his life of obedience, indeed the creation of a new humanity (especially in IV/2), as well as Christ's gift of taking on punishment due for sin (especially in IV/1). These two facets of Christ's work parallel Passover and the Day of Atonement. I would also point out that his brief exposition of those cultic metaphors and the way he relates priesthood and sacrifice to Christ's work are quite amenable to the major points I am making here.[90] I am not arguing that Anselm and Barth were "wrong," but simply that the temple imagery of Scripture is a strong or stronger place to both ground and check our understandings of the work of Christ than feudal understandings of satisfaction or even the courtroom.

Temple imagery forms the thinking of the New Testament writers; it is arguably their first language for speaking about the work of Christ, as Barth suggests. If we wish to ground our theology in the apostolic tradition, we would do well to pay attention to those images, categories, and understandings. And, as pointed out in the first chapter, we are in a much better place to do so in our culture than Barth and the church of his day or Anselm in his culture.

How then might the typological connections to the Day of Atonement and Passover shape our eucharistic reflections on Christ's sacrifice?

First, they invite a multifaceted approach. Many people reading this book will be familiar with the "facets of a diamond" analogy: Christ's life, death, and resurrection are multifaceted, and Scripture employs many metaphors to understand them. They are all valid facets of the precious diamond of Christ's saving work. There is not simply one biblical "atonement" theory that comprehends it all. Linking Christ's sacrifice to both Passover and the Day of Atonement allows for a fuller appreciation of its various facets. Thus, our eucharistic celebrations and theologies should recognize and use the imagery of more than one "atonement theory" or way of approaching the central meanings of the cross.

89. Barth, CD IV/1, 274.
90. Barth, CD IV/1, 274–83.

Secondly, I find it important that there are precisely two main typological relationships or links back to Jewish sacrifice. In connection to the Passover sacrifice, Christ is seen as a new and model human being who functions as the true "firstborn." His offering and sacrifice is one of obedience, and his obedience is that of fulfilling the proper priestly role that ultimately all human beings should also perform—one of true worship of God. That worship is total self-offering of oneself and one's life, a kind of *olah* or burnt offering that is pleasing to God. It is in this way that Christ overcomes and is victorious over sin, the world, the devil, and ultimately death. Rather than hard-heartedly and tight-fistedly closing oneself to God, as Pharaoh did, Christ as the true human priest and sacrifice opened himself to God and was obedient to the way of life that God intended for all of humanity. He fulfilled and began anew who and what humanity was intended by God to be. And as one participates in this new humanity, one is "redeemed" from slavery and a way is opened into God's kingdom, God's intended way for all human living.

This typological understanding of Christ's sacrifice connects to the *Christus Victor* theory, as well as to what is often called the recapitulation theory, and also to aspects of what is called deification or "theosis." Christ is the vicarious substitute or representative of all humanity in a positive way—he fully expresses God's intentions for human life in all its relationships and roles.

But, given the fact that humanity has not followed this positive way, humanity also requires an act or sacrifice that brings about a "covering" for sin. And that is precisely the role of the Day of Atonement sacrifices and the rite of the sent-away goat.

Here, the primary sacrificial type is that of the "sin offering." As argued above, this offering is an enacted prayer for forgiveness, representing perhaps the punishment due to the person being transferred onto the animal, or perhaps contrition and penance as the offerer's sin is symbolically transferred onto the animal before killing it. Either way, both the offerer and the offering undergo a hard thing, and this paves the way for forgiveness and a restored relationship to God. And in the mystery of the divine economy, Christ has operated in a similar way for us as both priest and sin offering, thereby taking on the difficult work needed to bring about reconciliation.

Thus the sacrificial economy of the temple highlights two basic aspects of Christ's work. The Passover sacrifice represents the primary or positive form of justice which is due to God, a symbolic representation of what righteous human life is intended to be. Jesus's total self-giving is the antitype of this sacrifice. The Day of Atonement sacrifice symbolically represents the "rectifying" or "corrective" form of justice that is required to bring forgiveness and restore the relationship between God and humanity when things have gone wrong. God in Christ offers this sin offering on behalf of all humanity.[91]

As pointed out above, the structure of Barth's theology of reconciliation also reflects these two primary ways of understanding the significance of Christ's work. The two main parts of his Christology revolve around recognition of Christ's fulfillment of true humanity ("The Royal Man" in IV/2), and God in Christ bearing the hard treatment necessary for reconciliation ("The Judge Judged in Our Place" in IV/1). In the unity of the two, treated in IV/3, Christ becomes "The True Witness." Much of this is a reworking of the venerable Reformed dyad of "justification" and "sanctification," both of which are christologically grounded.

Barth's work clarifies that two primary aspects of Christ's work are commonly recognized. Christ, joined to humanity through the incarnation of the Word by the power of the Spirit, fulfills God's ultimate intentions for human life, thus fulfilling primary justice. At the same time Christ makes proper contrition or penance in response to sin, paying the penalty that brings about the possibility for a restored relationship to God once things have gone awry. Temple typology allows for easy reference to both of these aspects in our communion prayers and eucharistic celebrations.

Third, the relationship between the temple sacrifices is also worthy of consideration. The Passover sacrifice holds a certain priority—it shows us what should be the "normal" way of humanity with God. The Day of Atonement sacrifice, while absolutely necessary given our situation as sinful but loved creatures, has a secondary or ancillary character to it. The prayer in the next chapter attempts to signal this priority.

In summary, connections between Christ's sacrifice and the Day of Atonement enable appreciation for the multifaceted nature of his sacrifice, provide a helpful structure for reflecting on both its positive and negative facets, and prioritize the positive facets of his sacrifice as more basic.

91. These two aspects of Christ's sacrifice map onto Wolterstorff's discussions regarding primary and corrective justice (see above, chap. 8) and Marx's analysis of the Hebrew sacrificial system as a whole (see above, chap. 7)

This priority calls into question the appropriateness of both the gloomy tone and the sole focus on Christ's sacrifice as a sin offering in many eucharistic prayers and practices—a subject to which we now turn.

The Tone and Focus of Eucharistic Celebrations: Moving Toward the Great Feast

Sukkot ends the festival season with the Great Feast—the most central biblical image of the life to come when Christ returns, the dead are raised, and God and the new creation are enjoyed. This eighth-day celebration foreshadows the Eucharist, a meal celebrated with Christ in anticipation of the life to come.

In the previous chapter, we discussed various practices such as passing the peace that are symbolic of and in themselves actually firstfruits of the kingdom of God. These firstfruits relate to the themes of *Sukkot* as well.

But the overarching tone of *Sukkot* is not most centrally a tone of commitment and striving for justice, or even love. Those seem most appropriate to Pentecost, in which the ways of the new covenant are front and center. The final end of *Sukkot,* the eighth-day celebration, is about enjoyment and delight—in God, in each other, and in all the spiritual and physical blessings that flow from the hand of God. Our Eucharists should also have the same final end.

In the West, the church has had a difficult time finding the proper relationship between the world-affirming and world-denying aspects of the Christian life. Often, it has tended to overemphasize the world-denying aspects of the Christian life. For example, take the typical monastic vows of poverty, chastity, and obedience. These are understandable and laudable as prophetic rejections of the worldly temptations of money, sex, and power. In a context where Christianity became entangled with imperial ambitions and papal leaders often looked indistinguishable from other monarchs, these vows can be seen in part as a creative and prophetic response. But such vows of denial on their own cannot carry the full weight of a positive vision of the kingdom of God, of what it means for God's people to be a "priestly kingdom and a holy nation" (Exod. 19:6; cf. 1 Peter 2:9). For that, one needs a more positive vision of God's designs—visions of an abundant and fruitful creation, joyful feasting at the coming of God's kingdom, human love and sexuality, and our creative royal calling to not only be "servants" but also "friends" of God (John 15:15).

Themes of "the cross"—which include the rejection of the distorted aspects of our selves and the world and the suffering that often accompanies this rejection—must find their place within the larger narrative that includes the goodness of creation and the joyful end of resurrection life. The cross is not the end or goal of the Christian life; it is the means by which one arrives at the resurrection. The meals of Jesus throughout his ministry and the image of the Last Supper itself as a meal provide the context within which the cross itself is best understood. As the writer of Hebrews put it, "for the sake of the joy that was set before him [Christ] endured the cross, disregarding its shame" (Heb. 12:2). He understood that the end was *joy*—even if his way involved suffering and the submission of his will to the Father—and that strengthened him for the difficult journey.

Themes of cross and resurrection are also tied together in a deeper way. There is no true joy without entering into the world's suffering. Nor is there a proper Christian self-denial and suffering for the sake of righteousness without an embrace of the goodness of the world and humanity. How these themes best go together in life and practice is not always obvious; it is a matter of practical wisdom and an "aesthetic" sense developed as part of Christian maturity.

This kind of wisdom can be found in the patterns of the feast of *Sukkot* in its journey from judgment, through atonement, to the Great Feast. And *Sukkot* itself is part of the overall rhythm of the worship calendar given to Israel by God in which, I would claim, a wise relationship between such themes is exhibited and cultivated.

Similarly, the Eucharist can and should be a full symbol and summary of the Christian life—as well as a full summary of the Christian story of the cosmos. For example, follow the symbolism of bread and wine through the four central meanings of the temple practices that organize this book. Bread and wine are fitting symbols of creation—both the good gifts that God gives us and the proper human response of wisely and creatively using the gifts of creation. As symbols of the Passover sacrifice, they represent the multifaceted sacrifice that God in Christ made for our reconciliation and sanctification. Like the two loaves at Pentecost, they symbolize our new covenant commitment and life that follow after God's freeing us from bondage, a life that includes "the way of the cross" as we are united to Christ and his way. As elements of the Great Feast at *Sukkot*, they are also fitting symbols of the joyful feast that awaits when God is all in all. Creation, past deliverance, present new covenant life, and future feasting are all "summed up" in this celebration.

And so, it is a shame if the fullness of our gospel story is not proclaimed in our eucharistic celebrations. If we start and end with simply the remembrance of Christ's sacrifice on the cross then we have not told the full story.

Practically, we can signal this full story in our eucharistic prayer. To be a full prayer, it should include elements of creation, redemption, new covenant, and the coming great feast. Of course, there are times and places for shorter prayers and times and seasons when one aspect or another is emphasized. But over a full year, all those aspects should be brought out. Furthermore, I would suggest—for the sake of the comprehension of the congregation—that the eucharistic prayer follows the order of that sweeping story. This means that the "words of institution" most naturally will be in the middle of the prayer, when Christ's redeeming work is emphasized. This also means that the end of the prayer is a joyful looking forward to the great feast.

As far as the physical elements of bread and wine, wafers and grape juice are acceptable—but are they the most fitting? If we want to emphasize the goodness of creation, the fullness of the new covenant life, or the great feast to come, it would be more fitting to use full, tasty, leavened bread—bread that you would be pleased to serve guests you invited to your house for dinner. "Taste and see that the LORD is good" (Ps. 34:8), a phrase often incorporated into communion hymns, should not be the occasion of ironic smirks when a tasteless wafer or stale piece of bread is passed around during communion. Dry communion wafers seem to be symbols best suited for the remembrance of Christ's suffering and the unleavened bread that Israel used as they fled from Egypt. So, they are not inappropriate—but I would use them only in Lent or other times when especially the congregation or church is specifically focusing on the hard road of the cross that Jesus trod. The cross is a crucial element of the story that the Eucharist celebrates—but it is not the only one.

I—and others—reflect similarly on the element of wine. My own rule of thumb is to buy and serve wine that I would be pleased to serve guests at my home. I do not serve grape juice at a joyful feast in my home (although I do also serve attractive non-alcoholic beverages for those who prefer them)—nor did Christ when he acted as host at the wedding feast at Cana, his first sign (John 2:1–11). Of course, out of respect for those who abstain for any reason, a non-alcoholic option should also be available and clearly indicated at our Eucharists. This is the rule at least in the PC(USA), my home denomination.[92]

92. "The session will determine whether wine is used; a non-alcoholic option shall

As far as music, I also prefer to have a full range of emotions and themes present during the eucharistic feast. Some music directors consciously choose communion hymns and songs that begin on the more somber and reflective side—quite appropriate for remembrance of Christ's sacrifice and the awe of coming into God's presence where our sin so quickly becomes clear to us. A hymn such as "Let All Mortal Flesh Keep Silence," originally based on the Liturgy of St. James from the fifth century, accomplishes this—in fact the first verse of it brings to mind some of the central meanings of the Feast of Trumpets, even the trembling blast of the *shofar*:

> Let all mortal flesh keep silence,
> And with fear and trembling stand;
> Ponder nothing earthly-minded,
> For with blessing in His hand,
> Christ our God to earth descendeth,
> Our full homage to demand.[93]

But we do not end there. Such moments of awe and confession should be part of every eucharistic feast, but the typical eucharistic service should not stay in this mode. Rather, it should move toward the joy of the Great Feast, even in the midst of what can be a difficult life.

Chris Tomlin's song "The Table" expresses these complex emotions well in both its music and its lyrics. The bridge of this song explicitly names the hope and joy anticipated in our Eucharists, drawing from the temple image of the saints gathering around the *kapporet* or mercy seat of God, an image straight out of Revelation 4:

> I know he has a place for me;
> Oh, what joy will fill my heart
> with the saints around the mercy seat of God.

The final verse repeats the main theme of the song:

---

be provided and clearly identified." "Directory for Worship," *Book of Order 2017–2019: The Constitution of the Presbyterian Church (USA) Part II* (Louisville: Office of the General Assembly), W-3.0414.

93. Adapted by Gerard Moultrie (1864). Trinity Psalter Hymnal #292.

I'm invited to the table of the Lord,
I'm invited to the table of the Lord;
He says come just as you are to His table.[94]

It is a wonderful contemporary composition that recognizes the temple background of the eucharistic feast.

Drawing bold lines of connection from all the main celebrations of the temple into our eucharistic celebrations leads us to move toward "the end" in the end. Our celebrations should follow the movements of the great biblical story summed up in the worship life of the temple, a story transposed into a new key given the full work of Christ and Spirit. That story does not end with freedom and forgiveness; nor does it end with the call to the justice and love of new covenant life; it ends with the joy of the great feast eaten together with the Lord and one another. Our Eucharists—our prayers, our elements, our music, and our thoughts and emotions—should move in that way as well. They should move toward the joyful feast to come.

94. Chris Tomlin, Ed Cash, Wayne Jolley, "The Table," CCLI#: 7028956.

PART FOUR

Cultivating a Table-Temple Imagination
among Protestants

11

On Music, Intentions, Space, and Prayers

Cultivating a Temple-Table Imagination

One thing have I desired of the LORD, that will I seek after;
that I may dwell in the house of the LORD all the days of my life,
to behold the beauty of the LORD, and to inquire in his temple.

—Psalm 27:4 (KJV)

Drawing bold lines of connection from the Lord's Supper back to the temple and its worship sparks our imaginations and guides our understandings of the Eucharist. That is the main claim of this book. Bridging the gap between temple and table transforms our conceptual understandings of the Eucharist. But another imposing gap must be bridged, the gap between intellectually agreeing with an argument and applying its conclusions within a worshipping community.

So, what would it take for Protestants to imagine as they gather together for worship on the Lord's Day that they are coming to and creating a new spiritual temple? That as they gather together for worship they are doing something similar to what the Israelites did as they ascended to the "hill of the Lord" (Ps. 24:3) for their regular daily, weekly, and monthly worship rites and the pilgrim feasts?

As I have reflected on this question over the years, I have felt pulled in different directions. On the one hand, biblical literacy is decreasing in general, and as the title of Brent Strawn's book suggests, the Old Testament in particular can be likened to a dying language.[1]

---

1. Brent Strawn, *The Old Testament Is Dying: A Diagnosis and Recommended Treatment* (Grand Rapids: Baker Academic, 2017).

And yet, in many congregations and communities, that gap is not as large as it might at first seem. Images of the congregation worshipping as a spiritual temple are common especially in the church's hymnody, both traditional and contemporary. Since the beginning of what is called "contemporary Christian music," images of the worshipping congregation as a kind of spiritual temple have been relatively common. Brent Chamber's well-known 1979 song "Let Our Praise to You Be as Incense" has been translated into many languages, and is found in many compilations of music and hymnbooks; it clearly pictures the worshipping congregation as if they were before the throne of God offering worship. Petra's 1997 worship song displays the same impulse and imagery:

> Let our voices rise like incense.
> Let them be as sweet perfume.
> Let our praises fill the temple.
> Hallelujah's ringing ever new.[2]

Present-day examples are too numerous to cite here: many contemporary new songs and hymns mention or are centrally organized around temple imagery. A quick search for the word "temple" on www.hymnary.org will generate thousands of hits.

The temple is and has been a common image in the church's psalms, hymns, and spiritual songs throughout its history. This is in part because much of the book of Psalms was written for worship in the temple—a book still used in Christian worship today. This is as it should be, since, as argued throughout this book, the temple and its worship form the ritual center of the Old Testament people of God, and this image or "type" is extended into and helps structure the worship of the New Testament people of God in New Testament Scripture, in the early church, and in the great traditions of Christianity.

But for the many reasons spoken of in the opening chapter, it has not been a central organizing image for the overall worship life of Protestants in their theology or practice. Oftentimes temple imagery is limited to the musical component of worship. Some extend it to prayer as well; these activities are considered the places and times when heaven and earth meet. This is a good start. I see it as a subversive way biblical imagery is pushing back against mod-

2. "Let Our Voices Rise Like Incense," *Petra Praise, Vol. 2: We Need Jesus* (1997).

ern Protestant allergies to all things ritual, Catholic and Jewish. My hope is simply to extend the imagery to include the entire worship service, both the "sacrament" of scriptural reading and preaching, when the Spirit opens our hearts and illumines our minds to receive the Word of the Father, and then also the sacrament of the Eucharist, when God—Father, Word, and Spirit—is also specially present to God's people. In this rite the Word is tasted and received, and the kingdom of God breaks into the lives of the gathered people of God in a powerful way.

In this final chapter, I will reflect on three practical ways other than lyrics that these connections between the temple and our eucharistic practice might be made bolder: our teaching about and "intentions" we hold as we participate in the Eucharist, our design, renovation, and arrangement of worship spaces, and the eucharistic prayer itself.

Intentions: The Five Central Meanings of the Eucharist

The temple rhythms of worship gifted to Israel at Sinai and which structured the worship of Israel in Jerusalem can be summed up according to the central meanings of the temple building itself, the daily/weekly/monthly worship services, and the three yearly pilgrim feasts, Passover (*Pesach*), Pentecost (*Shavuot*), and Booths (*Sukkot*). Throughout its history, the church has at times applied one or another aspect of these five types to the Eucharist. But a more methodical approach in which they are put together as a set and grounded in the temple can broaden overly narrow understandings of the Eucharist, organize confused understandings, help major themes remain major and minor themes remain minor, and enrich our imaginations and practice.

These meanings should not remain in written theological texts, however. These five meanings can become five conscious "intentions" or main thoughts held by those who celebrate the Eucharist.

The term "eucharistic intention" has been used in Roman Catholic theology to refer especially to the intentions of the priest as they celebrate. Here, I am extending the term to *all* Christians as they celebrate—these are things they can "intend" to do as they participate in the eucharistic service.

Temple typology suggests the following thoughts to Christians as they approach the table:

- "God is really and personally present; the Kingdom of God is breaking in."
- "We give thanks for God's creation and providence; we commit ourselves to wisely and creatively participate in God's creational order."
- "We remember God's deliverance of us through Christ's sacrificial life and death; in faith, we reject the old way of life and follow in the steps of Christ."
- "We give thanks for and recommit ourselves to the new covenant way of Christ; we call on the Holy Spirit to unite us with Christ and one another, empowering us to live as Christ's body for the world."
- "We celebrate with hope the feast to come in God's Kingdom; we will be judged, yet forgiven, and so we rejoice that we can experience a foretaste of that feast even now."

Or, even shorter: "God and God's kingdom are here." "We give thanks for God's creation and providence." "We remember Christ's sacrificial life and death." "We recommit ourselves to the new covenant." "We celebrate with hope the feast to come."

Even though I am highlighting what *we* are doing, it should be recognized that our actions and intentions are responses. God is the primary actor. God gathers and gives gifts. And yet, in God's grace, God enables and equips us as a community to respond to those gifts with genuine intention and action. Recognizing this, a stress on intention need not run afoul of the salutary stress of Reformed theology on the priority of God's action. Nor need it exclude those among us who are less able to fully intend such things, such as young children and those with limited cognitive abilities. They too fully participate as their activity is embraced by the arms of God and the "we" of the community.

As a way of bringing together the main results of the above chapters while also thinking about them through the lens of eucharistic intentions, let me comment briefly on each of these in turn.

1. "God is really and personally present; the kingdom of God is breaking in."

Like an Israelite approaching the temple in Jerusalem, Christians approaching the eucharistic service should anticipate coming into God's real and personal presence. God is everywhere—and yet, as at the temple, God has covenanted to be with us in a real and personal way in our eucharistic worship. Given the incarnation of the Word in Jesus Christ, and the pouring out of the Spirit, and given that the church is a new spiritual temple, we would expect this presence to take a full trinitarian shape. Still, we would expect—as the New Testament writers and early church did—continuities between the old and new. Additionally, as at the temple, Christians should also recognize that in some way, the kingdom of God is breaking in—the heavenly ways of God's kingdom are intersecting with, seen in, and shape the earthly "elements" of our rite.

I have purposely avoided typical debates about how God is present in the bread and wine. While not unimportant, such debates needlessly divide orthodox Christians from one another. But temple typology does push our understandings about God's presence in certain ways, as detailed above. First, one should expect the *real* presence of God in the midst of God's people during these rites. Second, it pushes us to consider that God is *personally* present—present to act with intention with those gathered in order to form mutual relationships. God is not merely present as an "element," as a kind of divine substance (here meaning a kind of "sub-animal" thing); instead, God is really and personally present.

Furthermore, as at the temple, the congregation not only encounters God, but they also encounter and are formed into the ways of the kingdom of God. The Eucharist is, or should be, an ethically charged event. In this rite the congregation's ethical imagination is formed, and, through certain practices such as the passing of the peace, the congregation's interactions with God and each other are parables of God's designs for human life with God and with each other. These ways of acting are detailed in the specifics of the following meanings.

2. *"We give thanks for God's creation and providence; we commit ourselves to wisely and creatively participate in God's creational order."*

Like the Israelites as they celebrated the daily, weekly, and monthly rites at the temple, Christians approaching the eucharistic table should give thanks for the many creational (creaturely, worldly) blessings God has provided them, both in general and specifically in their own life. Similar to what the Israelites did, Christians bring offerings to God, the "firstfruits" of their work. These are tokens that all that we have as creatures—our being, life, energy, skill for work, and any possessions—are gifts from God. Both monetary gifts of the offering and the gifts of bread and wine are appropriately raised up at the table or altar—similar to the wave offerings of the Israelites—as words of thanksgiving are spoken.

These offerings to God further the cycle of gift-giving we find ourselves in as creatures. They are also symbols of commitment to wise and creative participation in God's creational order. We not only recognize that the *things* we have are from God, but we also recognize that the *healthy systems* and *purposes* of things and creatures are not solely or principally determined by us. We commit ourselves anew to attempt to discern and fit into the orders and purposes that God sustains for all creatures. These orders and purposes bring health and life. As we offer our offerings we commit ourselves to act as wise stewards and priests of all creation, both *things* and *systems*.

Incorporating these meanings of the Eucharist back into our practice will help reconnect us to the thinking of the early church, guard us against gnostic tendencies in our theologies, and also better connect this central act of worship to our lives of work and our place as human, embodied creatures within the created order.

3. *"We remember God's deliverance of us through Christ's sacrificial life and death; in faith, we reject the old way of life and follow in the steps of Christ."*

Like the Israelites as they celebrated the Passover at the temple, Christians approaching the eucharistic table should give thanks for the way God has delivered his people from evil and sin. Similar to the way Israel remembered God's deliverance of them from Egypt and slavery, Christians remember and give thanks for God's work in and through Christ to bring about the forgiveness of sins and to deliver us from the grip of sin, death, and the devil.

As the Israelites cleaned out leaven from their households during the Feast of Passover and Unleavened Bread, Christians similarly repent, confess their sins, and reject the ways of the world which are against the ways of God. We remember the bitterness of all that God has delivered us from, and instead commit ourselves anew to follow in the ways of Christ.

In this joyful feast, we remember that Christ is our Passover lamb; he has been sacrificed, given for us. He in his life fulfilled the calling of God's people to act as God's "firstborn," to offer themselves fully and obediently to God. This substitutionary gift of Christ's righteous and obedient life "covers" us and provides a way for us to leave behind our old ways of life. We also remember that Christ's sacrifice is like a sin offering—but that is more appropriately related to the Day of Atonement sacrifices, as mentioned below. Freed from the slavery of sin, those gathered around the table remember this great gift of deliverance which is simultaneously also a gift of reconciliation with God. In receiving it in faith, we recommit ourselves to follow God as disciples of Christ.

4. *"We give thanks for and recommit ourselves to the new covenant way of Christ; we call on the Holy Spirit to unite us with Christ and one another, empowering us to live as Christ's body for the world."*

Like the Israelites as they celebrated Pentecost at the temple, Christians approaching the eucharistic table should give thanks for the gift of the new covenant. This New Testament law was not written on stone, but first on the flesh of Jesus Christ through the power of the Spirit. Just as the Israelites were not only freed from Egypt, but also freed for the new life of the promised land, a way of life sketched in the laws given on Mount Sinai, so too Christians are not only forgiven and *freed from* sin and the ways of the fallen world. They are also *freed for* the way of the new covenant.

The heart of the new covenant is the mystery that Christ not only teaches us the ways of God, but also is the way. The law of the new covenant is seen in Jesus—both in his teachings and in the patterns of his own life. He in his person is the way, the life, the patterns of living that God intends for all humanity.

But the new covenant relationship between God and his people involves more than Christ's fulfillment of and teaching about the law. As Christians, in a relationship of faith, we participate in his life. Through the work of the Spirit, the patterns of the divine life and its power seen in the earthly body of Christ are written on and linked to the human flesh of his disciples. This is symbolized and realized in and through the Eucharist. Christ tells us, "This is my body," and as we eat the bread and wine in faith, his life and way enter more fully into us. We as individuals and as a church take and eat his body and blood in order to be more fully his body, to be Christians.

This covenant relationship with God obviously has an ethical aspect. This covenant way of life is another way of talking about the patterns and ways of life of the kingdom of God. In the eucharistic rite as a whole, the ways that the congregation interacts with each other also embody the patterns of the kingdom of God in summary fashion. For example, in the passing of the peace, the peaceful ways of the kingdom of God are imaged and symbolized. As we eat together at the same table, divisions of race, class, and gender are symbolically and to some extent really overcome. As we pray together, we take an appropriate human posture of receptivity toward God and of love toward our neighbors, and we pray that the church in all its life might witness to and extend these kingdom ways into the world.

5. *"We celebrate with hope the feast to come in God's kingdom; we will be judged, yet forgiven, and so we rejoice that we can experience a foretaste of that feast even now."*

Like the Israelites as they celebrated the Feast of Booths at the temple, Christians approaching the eucharistic table should anticipate with hope the coming feast of the kingdom of God.

And, similar to the celebration of Booths, as we look forward we realize that there is a coming judgment. Yet we are assured by the atoning sacrifice offered by Christ that for those who cling to Christ by faith, mercy accompanies judgment. Like the sin offerings at the temple on the Day of Atonement that follow on the heels of the Day of Trumpets, Christ's once-for-all sacrifice covers our sins. He is our once-for-all-time sin offering. In remembering his death, his blood shed for us and for many, we can look forward to Christ's second coming with assurance.

But mercy is not the final word. Feasting is a common image and symbol given throughout Scripture of what awaits us after our death, after Christ returns again. Our eucharistic feast is a sign and anticipation of that good future. As such it should ring with sounds and actions that are themselves a foretaste of the joy of that coming feast.

Taking all these meanings together, the Eucharist becomes a summary of our Christian faith. It is a preaching of the gospel—the good news of God with us, the good news of what God has done, is doing, and will do from creation to new creation. And the Eucharist is not simply a preaching of the gospel. It is also an altar call. "Come to the table" is a call to come and receive, to open ourselves to God, to recommit ourselves to God's work in our lives and in the church, and to recommit ourselves to the vocation of being the body of Christ for the world.

Seen in this way, the Eucharist is a celebration that comprehends the main aspects of God's creating, reconciling, and redeeming work—just as the year-long Israelite calendar at the temple was comprehensive.

My hope is that this way of thinking will help Christians see the expansiveness of our central rite, and through it the wonder of God's work in the world. A table-temple imagination—seeing the Eucharist in light of the central meanings and practices of the temple—is expansive and comprehensive.

Spaces: The Clothing of the New Temple

In what ways would taking seriously the relationships between the temple, the church, and the Eucharist put pressure on the design, construction, arrangement, or renovation of worship spaces? Here I have in mind everything from the design of new multimillion dollar construction projects to the arrangement of movable chairs, podiums, tables, and basins of water.

Let us tackle this question first with a broad brush, by thinking through what the implications of this table-temple typological relationship are for worship spaces in general. I will do so in light of two influential proposals about worship space by Louis Bouyer and Mark Torgerson. Then I will get more practical and detail what taking seriously such a relationship might mean for a single concrete space, using the chapel renovation of my own place of work and worship, Western Theological Seminary, as a case in point.

To begin, let us assume that a person or community sees such a typological relationship between the temple in Jerusalem and the church at worship. How then might this affect how one envisions or renovates a worship building? A first obvious answer might be direct imitation of design: build churches on the plan of the temple or tabernacle as given in Scripture. This is not a bad idea. In fact, as Louis Bouyer points out in *Liturgy and Architecture*, some of the earliest known Christian churches in Syria imitated many features of Jewish synagogues, which in turn were based on features of the temple.[3]

But even the synagogues were not direct imitations. They did retain similar features, such as the menorah, the veil, and an "ark" in which Torah scrolls were kept. In fact, during the service, scrolls were taken out of the ark and then read from a bema, a raised space much like a pulpit. This important action con-

---

3. Bouyer, *Liturgy and Architecture*, 24–39.

nected the scrolls to the ark of the covenant of the temple, showing a certain understanding of how God was present and speaking to the community. But in many other ways the buildings differed. Synagogues had no altar of sacrifice, and building materials, scale, and a host of other aspects were changed. This raises the question: by what criteria did they make decisions about which features should be imitated and which left behind in the transposition from temple to synagogue?

The same question may be asked of the church. The transformation of God's covenant relationship to God's people brought about by the New Testament work of Christ and the Spirit—what impact should this have on worship space design and practices? It is crucially important to note that the early church imitated numerous aspects of the temple in their worship spaces. But it is important to have some criteria that help explain both the similarities as well as differences. What should these be?[4]

A final group of questions emerges given the fact that simple imitation of design does not account for the way that changes in the place, time, and culture surrounding a symbol change the meanings of those symbols. For example, a woman professor wearing a black bowler hat in a twenty-first-century American classroom means something different than a male banker wearing it on a promenade through the park in nineteenth-century England. Similarly, building designs and even building materials take on different connotations in different contexts. This again suggests the need to ask deeper questions and not settle for surface imitations.

So, if one considers the church at worship to be "a new temple," what precisely should one aim for when designing, renovating, or arranging a worship space in the twenty-first century? What criteria might we use to think about what in our contemporary spaces might be similar to or different than the temple in Jerusalem?

Perhaps a good place to start is by considering building materials. In the Old Testament, the temple was a building and system of worship commanded by God according to exact specifications and built primarily with stone. In the New Testament, this building is understood to be replaced not by a new stone

4. As I have presented on this project, amid excited reactions, some have asked with concern if I wanted to reinstitute animal sacrifices and hereditary priestly hierarchies. I do not, but such questions raise the need for criteria for discernment.

building, but instead constructed out of "living stones" (1 Pet. 2:4–5), people who together in their worship fulfill the main impulses of the old temple, but in a new key.

This shift might at first seem to undercut the need to attend to architecture at all. Buildings and things don't matter, just the people. There is some truth to this.

However, the oft-quoted words of bishop John Robinson, "The building will always win," caution us against taking this too far. Here is the fuller quote:

> But we are now being reminded that the church people go to has an immensely powerful psychological effect on their vision of the Church they are meant to be. The church building is a prime aid, or a prime hindrance, to the building up of the Body of Christ. And what the building says so often shouts something entirely contrary to all that we are seeking to express through the liturgy. And the building will always win—unless and until we can make it say something else.[5]

Robinson is claiming that the church building affects how the Church envisions both itself and what it is doing in its worship. Furthermore, what might at first seem to be a strong difference between Mosaic and new covenants—that the older covenant stresses a building, while the new puts stress on people—may not be all that great, and may not be the best avenue into understanding the differences between these two covenants. After all, the meanings of the temple building that we have been focusing on pertain to who God is, who Israel is to be, and what is happening at the temple in this encounter between God and God's people. The Old Testament itself emphasizes that the realities of the temple are to find expression in the people of God—they are to be shaped into a priestly people and a holy nation. In the Old Testament, even the word "house" is played with. God promises to build "the house" of David, a people, in response to David's desire to build God "a house," the temple (2 Sam. 7:11, 27). In both houses God's name will dwell. Perhaps this transition from stones to people is not as much a distinction between the two covenants as one might at first think.

---

5. John A. T. Robinson, "Preface" in *Making the Building Serve the Liturgy: Studies in the Re-ordering of Churches,* ed. Gilbert Cope (London: Mowbray, 1962), 5.

So, what should the building or worship space "say," as Robinson puts it?

A common emphasis in church architectural literature is that the building says, or should say, something about God. In particular, church buildings might emphasize either that God is transcendent or immanent. For example, Mark Torgerson, in his recent and important study *An Architecture of Immanence: Architecture for Worship and Ministry Today*, structures his analysis of church buildings in precisely this way.[6]

While Torgerson sets up his book around this contrast—which is a helpful way to show the effects of modern liberal theology and modern architectural theory on church design—he notes the need to maintain both in complex relation. He appreciates the reactions against an overly transcendent architectural style, but questions the way modern liberal theology emphasized immanence of God in the people of God in a one-sided fashion: "The solutions that were intended to express a theological affirmation of the people of God did achieve their effect in the built environment, but sometimes this was achieved at the cost of affirming the significance of God's holiness."[7] Instead, Torgerson prefers the way the ecumenical and liturgical movements emphasized what he calls the "paradox" of the two together, which he knowingly relates to the "two natures—divine and human—of Christ."[8]

Such a complex relationship between transcendence and immanence also characterized the temple. In fact, a central meaning of the temple building itself—that God, while transcendent, is really and personally present, and that the kingdom of God is breaking in—seems to be quite similar to Torgerson's desires for the paradox of God's transcendence and immanence in church architecture. The Gospels also connect the incarnation to the temple. "Destroy this temple, and in three days I will raise it up again," says Jesus (John 2:19). This connection of incarnation with temple supports building churches in a way that communicates both transcendence and immanence.

6. Mark Torgerson, *An Architecture of Immanence: Architecture for Worship and Ministry Today* (Grand Rapids: Eerdmans, 2007). Torgerson goes on to trace and analyze the immense changes in church architecture that took place from the nineteenth century to the present day. He sees these shifts as a result of primarily four main forces: the rise of modern liberal theology, the ecumenical movement, the liturgical renewal movement, and emphases of modern architecture. As a result of these movements, there has been a great shift in church design, from a stress on God's transcendence to God's immanence.

7. Torgerson, *Architecture of Immanence*, 182.

8. Torgerson, *Architecture of Immanence*, 4.

How does a building speak such things? Torgerson writes: "A number of factors in church design can work toward reminding us of the transcendence and immanence of God. Scale (relative size in relation to the human person) and volume, the control of light, the elaboration or simplification of the décor, and the organization of the space have all been used through various designs to help remind the worshipper of the nature of God."[9] And it is certainly not only the physical building which speaks, but the traditions of interpretation and use of buildings play important roles in understanding what buildings are "saying." A "prayer chapel" could become "the coffee hour space" without substantially altering the physical space. As he writes, "Meanings are also assigned to objects and can be learned over time."[10] Without going further into specifics, let us say simply that such a question should be important to us: "How can we signal in our space that the transcendent God is also really present here?" Just as the temple spoke of the transcendence and yet real and personal presence of God, so too should our churches.

A different, and to some extent complementary, approach to how worship spaces speak and what they should say is found in Louis Bouyer's *Liturgy and Architecture.*

Bouyer writes: "Where is the spirit of men more apparent than in the homes that they build to house their lives? In the same manner, it is the way in which we shall build our churches which will be a manifestation par excellence of the kind of Church life, of common life in the Body of Christ, that will be ours."[11] Here we see that Bouyer is interested in more than what these houses say about God. He emphasizes what they say about the "life" and "spirit" of the Christian community in its relationship to God.[12]

And *how* is this life made apparent? Bouyer writes:

When we look at the churches which were arranged or built on purpose to house the Christian liturgy at the height of its freshness and creative power, we see that it is not a series of fixed details, all taken in isolation or together, which is important. It is rather a dynamic relation between some different

9. Torgerson, *Architecture of Immanence*, 4.
10. Torgerson, *Architecture of Immanence*, 3.
11. Bouyer, *Liturgy and Architecture*, 6.
12. It should be noted that this is part of what Torgerson means by an architecture of immanence.

focuses of the celebration, embodied in various elements and their coherent disposition. This may give, and has given, rise to an almost unlimited variety of patterns. But all of these patterns become dead as soon as they are copied materially, without the right understanding of what gave them their sense.[13]

Bouyer emphasizes that it is not the individual details of the building that speak loudest. Rather, it is the overall "dynamic relation" between foci of the liturgy. These foci include things like the congregation, font, table, and pulpit. What speaks are the "patterns" between them, namely, their relative placement and the patterned ways the congregation and its leaders interact with the places where God's presence is mediated. That is what does the talking in a space. Bouyer is quick to point out that these patterns can only be fully understood when they are seen in terms of the part they play in the actual worship life or liturgy of Christian churches. It is this actual lived worship practice which gives these architectural features and the dynamic relations between them "their sense."

But *what* is "their sense" for Bouyer? Bouyer finds his greatest inspiration in the early Syrian churches mentioned above. Their worship spaces were based on synagogues, which were in turn based in part on temple themes and patterns. Several aspects of their liturgy and architecture resonate quite deeply with the temple themes we have been discussing. Their physical orientation, toward the East now rather than toward the holy of holies in the temple in Jerusalem, calls to mind the New Jerusalem, the future where the "Son of Righteousness" will rise like the sun.[14] And on every Lord's Day, this coming is localized first at the "ark" (similar to the place in synagogues where torah scrolls were kept) and bema (a raised platform similar to the place in synagogues where scriptural teaching was done) where Christ meets us in Scripture and preaching. After this,

the Christians in their churches, hearing the word, are led by it from the Ark to the altar. And beyond the altar itself, they look toward no other earthly place but only toward the rising sun as toward the symbol of the *Sol justitiae*

13. Bouyer, *Liturgy and Architecture*, 7–8.
14. Bouyer, *Liturgy and Architecture*, 29–30.

they are expecting. The holy table, for them, is the only possible equivalent on earth of what was for the Jews their Holy of holies.[15]

In Syrian churches, there were two veils—before the ark and before the table—which allude back to the entrances to the holy place and holy of holies at the temple.[16] And before the ark, where the Scriptures were kept, was a copy of the menorah—a symbol of the light which God gives to God's people.

Thus for Bouyer, the architectural features of the worship spaces in these early churches knowingly alluded back to the temple. In the interplay between their primary furniture and the liturgy, the overall "senses" of these Old and New Testament spaces were quite analogous. Syrian architecture and liturgy communicated that the congregation was on a journey toward the New Jerusalem, toward the temple in heaven, toward their eschatological future, and that each Lord's Day provided a foretaste of this future reality.

How this sense is given expression, how the space speaks, is through the dynamic relations between bema, table, veils, menorah, and physical orientation to the East. Bouyer helpfully guides our primary attention to the central symbols and spaces involved in sacramental movements and moments in the liturgy—in the reading of Scripture, in baptism, in the Eucharist. Thus the dynamic relations between the primary sacramental elements should shape the building's design and ornamentation.

The end result of our reflections on Torgerson and Bouyer is that we should think from the liturgy outward. Put differently, the building that clothes the people of God at worship should fit the central activities of the people of God in their encounter with God and each other. Form should follow function. The central senses or meanings of the sacramental encounters between God and God's people in font, pulpit, and table should guide our building designs, renovations, and worship space arrangements. Thus, the typological relationships between the Old Testament temple worship and the worship of the New Testament "temple" people should determine what we bring forward, change, or leave behind from Israel's temple architecture.

More specific to the Eucharist and its central meanings, our spaces should "fit" the senses that (a) the transcendent God is really and personally present

---

15. Bouyer, *Liturgy and Architecture*, 31.
16. Bouyer, *Liturgy and Architecture*, 31.

and the kingdom of God is breaking in, (b) the people of God are giving thanks for the created order and rededicating themselves to be wise creatures within it, (c) the people of God are remembering and giving thanks for deliverance, (d) the people of God are recommitting themselves to the new covenant relationship between God and God's people and among God's people, and (e) the people of God are experiencing a foretaste of the feast to come.

A church building or worship space should provide an appropriate context in which these meanings can be expressed. And, the building itself to some extent should "say" these things. At the very least, the building should not be saying something different.

But is this practical? Yes it is. These meanings have very practical implications, and there are many worship spaces that have been modeled on or renovated according to similar themes, and can serve as examples of what such temple pressure might look like. Of these, some have been inspired by Louis Bouyer's book directly, others by aspects of the liturgical renewal movement inspired by the liturgical sense of the early church. Three spaces I am personally familiar with are the Church of the Servant in Grand Rapids, Michigan, St. Gregory of Nyssa Episcopal Church in San Francisco, California, and the renovation of the chapel at Western Theological Seminary in Holland, Michigan.[17] These sacred spaces have been intentionally planned and show the possibilities and promise of how such emphases can shape worship spaces.

Let me describe the thinking and the results of the renovation of the John R. Mulder chapel at Western Theological Seminary in Holland, Michigan.[18] In

17. Nicholas Wolterstorff wrote a booklet, "Worship at Church of the Servant," that is available at that church that explains much of the vision of the new construction of their building as well as their liturgy. More information is available on their website: https://www.churchoftheservantcrc.org/worship/worship-at-cos-frequently-asked-questions/. Many articles have been written about worship at St. Gregory of Nyssa Episcopal Church in San Francisco. In one, the fourth-century style of worship is also seen as quite "seeker" friendly: Trudy Bush, "Back to the Future: Fourth Century Style Reaches Bay Area Seekers," *Christian Century*, November 20, 2002, 18–22. Donald Schell, one of the founders of St. Gregory of Nyssa Episcopal Church, writes about church design in "Rending the Temple Veil: Holy Space in Holy Community," in *Searching for Sacred Space*, ed. John Runkle (New York: Church, 2002), 149–81.

18. Western Theological Seminary, "The Transformation of the John R. Mulder Memorial Chapel 2011–2012," ed. Carla Plumert (Grand Rapids: Western Theological Seminary, 2012). http://www.westernsem.edu/wp-content/uploads/2016/06/Chapel-piece-final-lowres.pdf.

2011, an extensive renovation of Mulder Chapel was undertaken. It had been constructed in 1954 and had a typical Reformed design: raised chancel and central pulpit, with wooden pews facing forward. Such a design emphasized the centrality of God speaking through the written Scriptures and preached Word. God "showed up" in and through Scripture, the chapel said. The chapel was a typical Reformed space and somewhat attractive. However, during my time at the seminary, students and faculty were given the opportunity to choose which worship space to use as they planned our daily chapel services. Nine out of ten times in the years preceding the renovation, students and faculty chose to have our community worship in another hall, Semmelink Hall, in which moveable chairs could be used to create what most considered a better space given the central meanings of our worship together. It is interesting to note that our faculty in general consider ourselves "sacramental Calvinists," in that in our thinking and teaching, we often emphasize the sacramental aspects of Calvin's theology and consider his "sacramental" worldview important, namely, that the world is the "theatre of God's glory."[19]

The renovation of Mulder Chapel created a space that better matched our community's sensibilities. The renovation allowed pulpit, table, and font to be in the center of the worshipping congregation, and also created a central open space in the middle of the ceiling of the chapel. The walls were slightly curved, like an oval, creating a kind of embrace of the congregation. Colorful art glass was added, with symbols and colors creating links to the world the congregation comes from and is sent back into.

The central values of the committee which helped guide the renovation are expressed well in the following statement:

19. Several faculty publications evidence this: Leanne Van Dyk (our then academic dean), ed., *A More Profound Alleluia: Theology and Worship in Harmony* (Grand Rapids: Eerdmans, 2004); Carol Bechtel (professor of Old Testament), ed., *Touching the Altar: The Old Testament for Christian Worship* (Grand Rapids: Eerdmans, 2008); James Brownson (professor of New Testament), *The Promise of Baptism* (Grand Rapids: Eerdmans, 2006); J. Todd Billings (professor of theology), *Remembrance, Communion, and Hope: Rediscovering the Gospel at the Lord's Table* (Grand Rapids: Eerdmans, 2018); and the many contributions by two of our professors that were trained as liturgical theologians, Ron Rienstra and Sue Rozeboom, including Rozeboom's "Doctrine of the Lord's Supper," in *Calvin's Theology and Its Reception*, ed. J. Todd Billings and I. John Hesselink (Louisville: Westminster John Knox, 2012), and Debra Rienstra and Ron Rienstra's *Worship Words* (Grand Rapids: Baker Academic, 2009).

Much theological thought and planning went into the renovation. Perhaps the most dramatic change is the removal of the pews, giving seating flexibility, but there is much more going on than that. The new chapel helps to shape our theophanic expectation in particular ways. It encourages us to look for God to "show up" primarily in the central things, located in the center: Pulpit, Table, and Font. Secondarily, we expect to meet God in the very people gathered around these central things, surrounded by God's good gifts in music and in creation (communicated in part by the art glass).

The most significant element is the alignment of the horizontal and vertical axes of the building. The former space functioned on a horizontal plane, focusing attention on the raised chancel. By curving the walls, dropping the ceiling four feet, and adding a carved oculus emanating warm light, attention is focused on a central circle, where most often the pulpit, table, and font are placed. The horizontal and vertical axes of the building converge on the center, and the community is simultaneously focused on Word and Sacrament, where we meet God and neighbor.[20]

Notice that the space was designed so that "theophanic expectations"—where we expect God to appear—were centered on pulpit, table, and font. More precisely, God is expected to show up in, under, and through the ritual activities that are centered on these entities.

But not only there. As one of our students, Samantha Kadzban, emphasized in her words during the dedication, God is present to shape and form the people who are present into the body of Christ:

This sanctuary speaks an ancient and abiding truth: Immanuel, God is with us. All who enter are invited to experience both the presence of God and the reality of community. The vertical axis speaks of God who is not far away but near to us; the horizontal axis speaks of community—we are not autonomous but together form the church, the body of Christ. In this sanctuary, these two axes come beautifully and seamlessly together. Immanuel, God is with us.[21]

20. Plumert, "The Transformation," 10 (drafted by Ron Rienstra).
21. Plumert, "The Transformation," 9 (drafted by Ron Rienstra).

I would add that the vertical axis speaks simultaneously of the transcendence of God and God's immanence. It is precisely the great transcendence of God that makes God's intimate immanence possible. The peculiar transcendence of our God who is beyond all creation allows God to be immanent in the entire creation but especially in font, table, and pulpit—and in God's people. As opposed to the older space, the renovation clearly says that God is expected to show up in more than simply through the reading and preaching of Scripture.

And finally, a value in the design of especially the windows and art glass—materials that both separate the space from and communicate with the outside world—was our sense that our worship comes from, represents, and speaks on behalf of all the creation surrounding us.[22] Rather than the typical white of many Reformed worship spaces which emphasizes God's transcendence and possibly suggests the exit of the community from the world or the antithesis between the community and the world, the art glass for us represents God's love for the world and God's power to renew it and make it beautiful—common meanings behind the tradition of stained glass. It also suggests that in worship, God is present to transform and equip the people of God for their mission in and to the world. We as a community speak of how God is with us not simply to forgive or to rescue us from the world, but also to transform us and the world in a proleptic way into the patterns of the kingdom of God.

The results of the renovation exceeded our expectations. The space has become like a dearly loved member of our community, teaching, forming, and speaking the central meanings of our worship together. It is difficult to exaggerate the great impact that the renewed space has had on our community.

While a temple imagination was not explicitly part of the design discussion, the renovation project fits precisely with the central values and expectations of what I am proposing. And that is not unexpected, since the thinking of our community has been shaped in part by much of the literature of the liturgical renewal movement, combined with a missional understanding of the church—namely, that the church is being equipped not only to preach the gospel, but also to exhibit the patterns of the kingdom of God to the wider world.

22. See this meaning in yet another publication by one of our faculty members that has relevance for worship: Suzanne McDonald, *Re-imaging Election: Divine Election as Representing God to Others and Others to God* (Grand Rapids: Eerdmans, 2010).

Both of those movements draw upon aspects of the early church's worship and life, which themselves drew upon the types and images of Israel's worship and life centered at the temple.[23]

The Liturgy of Word and Table: A Renewed Eucharistic Prayer

Probably the most important way that a temple imagination can be fostered among Protestants is through renewing the communion prayer itself. It is in this prayer, more than anywhere else, that the eucharistic theology of the celebrating congregation comes into ritual focus and verbal expression. Below I offer a possible eucharistic prayer in which I seek to highlight its central meanings—making the connections between table and temple transparent without being overbearing or pedantic. I offer this prayer and these reflections humbly and yet hopefully, realizing that the communion prayer in many traditions is a jealously guarded treasure. In my own tradition, those who lead at the Eucharist are given a choice in the *Book of Common Worship* between several eucharistic prayers. The final prayer is in fact a guide for those who wish to pray the prayer "in a free style."[24] I offer this prayer in that spirit of structured freedom. I hope it will be used in traditions that allow alternative prayers, and I hope that it may inspire committees as they write prayers that will be approved for use in other traditions.

Four principal facets stand out.

First, it has a fourfold structure. Our first theme concerning the temple itself—that God is present and the kingdom of God is breaking in—is assumed throughout the prayer. The remaining themes structure the prayer: creation, deliverance, new covenant, and future feast. I make this structure clear by having the congregation join in with the minister and recite well-known phrases that are part of many eucharistic prayers. Each of these congregational affirmations sums up the main theme of the preceding section. It is striking to me how well these biblical statements or phrases developed within the tradition fit so well with this temple typology structure.

Second, I have included both the words of institution and a double *epiclesis*

23. See Presa, *Liturgical-Missional*.
24. *BCW*, 156.

(calling on the Spirit to transform both the elements of bread and wine and the congregation) within the prayer. Roman Catholics consider the words of institution to be the moment of consecration, Eastern Orthodox consider the *epiclesis* to be the moment of consecration, while Protestants have a variety of opinions (as usual!). To honor these traditions, and because I believe both are critical, I include both.

I placed the *epiclesis* in the third section, the section that highlights God's work in the new covenant. While the Spirit is involved in every work of God, it seems to me that the most appropriate place to call on the Holy Spirit would be in the Pentecost section—the section that highlights the gift of the Spirit that unites us to Christ and writes the law or way of Christ onto our hearts and lives.

I placed the words of institution in the final section, the section that, like Booths, looks forward to the great feast to come. They certainly could have been placed in the second section corresponding to Passover, or the third section corresponding to Pentecost, or, as is often done, after the communion prayer. There are several reasons for placing it here. Reciting the words outside of the prayer—with more ceremony and importance than the prayer itself— makes the prayer seem almost superfluous, a kind of preamble to the words of institution. I find that problematic in that it downplays many themes of the prayer, tends to reduce the entire Eucharist to a memorial of Christ's death, and can make the words of institution seem like a magical incantation more than a prayerful remembrance.[25] Its placement below highlights the coming feast, the eschatological aspect of the Eucharist, alongside the remembrance of the past. Certainly I do not want to downplay Christ's sacrifice, but I think it is best remembered in combination with the aims of that sacrifice: "who for the sake of the joy that was set before him endured the cross" (Heb. 12:2). Kingdom joy is the culmination of the eucharistic "journey," as Bouyer would say.

Third, in regards to style, the words I have used are drawn from many sources, especially the PC(USA) Prayer E, which itself is an adaption of an ecumenical prayer written by the International Commission of English in the Liturgy. As such, the language is traditional, semi-formal, and somewhat po-

---

25. Many readers may not be aware that the common magical phrase, "hocus pocus," is probably a corruption of the Latin phrase *hoc est corpus*, from the larger phrase we translate "this is my body." Speculations about this connection began as early as 1694 by John Tillotson, *Sermons Preach'd Upon Several Occasions* (1694), xxvi.II.237.

etic. My goal is not to be original, but rather to draw from the traditions of the church as much as possible, especially its earliest strands, and to do so in a way that highlights the relationship between table and temple. Because most of the language is biblical and traditional, it may not seem as contemporary or modern as many would like. While I am deeply concerned with making Christianity relevant to our present contexts, I myself am attracted to many contextually aware movements in the present day that do so precisely by recovering the premodern past as we move into a post-modern future. I simply offer this as one possibility among many. There are certainly other stylistic ways to make these themes transparent in a eucharistic prayer.

Finally, while I offer a communion prayer, typological connections push us to include other aspects of the liturgy within our larger eucharistic celebration—particularly the confession and the offering. In some traditions, the phrase "the eucharistic liturgy" incorporates these rites, but not in others.

For example, temple liturgies always started with ritual acts of cleansing— an embodied confession that indeed our lives need cleansing. Accordingly, our eucharistic services might similarly include acts of confession at some point before we approach the Lord's table.[26] Another central part of temple liturgies was the offering of tithes and gifts. Such acts are easily included within a larger eucharistic rite as well.[27] Additionally, the passing of the peace or a "holy kiss" was integrated into the eucharistic rites of the early church as a symbol of new covenant life; it is often integrated into contemporary eucharistic celebrations. All this to say that while a carefully structured eucharistic prayer is a central aspect of our eucharistic celebration, I recognize that it is part of a larger liturgy that altogether is beneficially seen as typologically related to Old Testament temple worship.

Parenthetically, I should say that I understand that the eucharistic service should be paired with a "service of the Word" as well. I do not want to downplay the importance of reading Scripture or preaching—a key emphasis of the Reformation. It is simply that this project is focused on the Eucharist. A Lord's Day service in which preaching and Eucharist are equally emphasized should be the rule. In so doing, God is encountered in several ways in the spiritual

26. In the PC(USA) standard Lord's day service, "Confession and Pardon" are standard parts of the gathering movement of the service. *BCW*, 35.

27. Again, as it is in the PC(USA) service. *BCW*, 41.

temple of the church. We are illumined by the Spirit to hear the Word of God through the Spirit-inspired words of Scripture and biblical preaching, and then the entire gospel is heard in the eucharistic prayer and encountered through the rite and the elements of the table. In the entire service, God is present and the kingdom of God is breaking in.

But at the center of the Eucharist is the Great Prayer of Thanksgiving. It can be shaped to highlight these table-temple themes, as in the following example. May such a prayer be acceptable to God, and may the imagination of the church in praying such a prayer be formed to see how, as "living stones," they are "being built into a spiritual house, to offer spiritual sacrifices acceptable to God through Jesus Christ" (1 Pet. 2:5).

Great Prayer of Thanksgiving

Leader: The Lord be with you!
People: And also with you.
Leader: Open your hearts.[28]
People: We open them to the Lord.
Leader: Let us give thanks to the Lord our God.
People: It is right to give our thanks and praise.
Leader: Blessed are you, strong and faithful God.
             All your works, the height and the depth,
             echo the silent music of your praise.
             In the beginning your Word summoned light,
             night withdrew, creation dawned.
             As ages passed unseen,
             waters gathered on the face of the earth and life appeared.
             When the times at last had ripened
             and the earth grown full in abundance,
             you created in your image man and woman,

---

28. Here I follow the suggestion of Paul Santmire for a slight change to the *Sursum Corda*. See chapter 7 above for discussion. In our context, I think making this change is preferable to the more traditional "lift up your hearts" in order to emphasize that in the Eucharist heaven and earth are meeting and God is coming into our hearts, guarding against the interpretation that we are escaping from the earth to heaven in the Eucharist as we "lift up" our hearts.

> the stewards of all creation.
> You gave us breath and speech,
> that all the living might find a voice to sing your praise,
> and to celebrate the creation you call good.
> So now, with all the powers of heaven and earth,
> we sing this ageless hymn:[29]

People: Holy, holy, holy, God of power and might,
> Heaven and earth are full of your glory.
> Hosanna in the highest.

Leader: All holy God, how wonderful is the work of your hands!
> When sin had scarred the world, you entered into covenant
> to renew the whole creation.
> You chose a people as your own: Abraham, Sarah, and their
> children.
> When they had fallen into slavery,
> you heard their cries and delivered them from oppression.
> You gave them your presence and showed them how to live.
> You filled them with hunger for yourself,
> for a peace that would last,
> and for a justice that would never fail.
> From them, you raised up Jesus, your Son, the living bread,
> in whom ancient hungers are satisfied.
> His perfect life, with neither fault nor sin, is the true unleav-
> ened bread.
> Through the bitterness of his own suffering and death,
> he accomplished a new exodus for us.
> He defeated sin, the forces of evil, and death itself
> through his obedient life, death, and resurrection.
> He frees us and opens a way to abundant and eternal life.
> He is our Passover lamb.
> In this meal, we remember his sacrifice,
> once, upon the cross,
> for the redemption of the whole world.

29. This section on the creation, slightly altered here, was prepared by the ICEL and is the first part of "Great Thanksgiving: E," in *BCW.* I appreciate especially the poetic imagery regarding humanity as the "priests of all creation"—a theme of the daily, weekly, and monthly worship at the temple.

People:	Christ our Passover Lamb is sacrificed for us; therefore let us celebrate the feast.
Leader:	Gracious God, you not only delivered us from the shadow of death,
	but in Jesus you showed us the paths of life.
	He healed the sick, he preached good news to the poor,
	he offered his life to sinners,
	and he showed us true love of you and love of neighbor.
	Truly he is the way; he is the bread of life.
	Holy Father, you not only gave us
	a new commandment of love through your Son.
	You also sent your Holy Spirit
	so we might hunger for your ways
	and have power to live as your children.
	As we eat this bread and drink this wine,
	we open ourselves to Christ's life in us.
	We recommit ourselves to follow in the way of Christ,
	the way of the new covenant.
	Eternal God, let your Holy Spirit move in power over us
	and over these earthly gifts of bread and wine,
	that they may be for us the body and blood of Christ,
	and that we may be his body for the world.
People:	Come, Holy Spirit. Make us one in Christ.
	Renew us and make us the body of Christ for the world.

[Here take each element at the word "took" and raise them at "gave thanks"]

People:	On the night before he met with death,
	Jesus came to the table with those he loved.
	He took bread, and gave thanks to you, God of all creation.
	He broke the bread among his disciples and said:
	"Take this, all of you, and eat it.
	This is my body, which is given for you."
	When the supper was ended, he took a cup of wine
	and gave thanks to you, God of all creation.
	He passed the wine among his disciples and said:
	"Take this, all of you, and drink from it.
	This is my blood of the new covenant, poured out for many.

Truly I tell you, I will never again drink of the
fruit of the vine until that day when I drink it new
in the kingdom of God."
Almighty Father,
we remember and give thanks for Christ,
our Passover lamb.
We recommit ourselves to the new covenant
and open ourselves to the work of your Spirit.
We anticipate with hope and joy that great banquet
when we will eat and drink with Christ and one another
in your kingdom.
May his coming in glory find us watchful in prayer,
strong in truth and love,
and faithful in the breaking of the bread.
Then, at last, all peoples will be free, all divisions healed,
and with your whole creation
we will sing your praise, through your Son, Jesus Christ.

People: Christ has died; Christ is risen; Christ will come again.
Come, Lord Jesus. Amen.

Leader: Come to the feast! All things are ready.

Bibliography

Anderson, Gary. "Sacrifice and Sacrificial Offerings." In *Anchor Bible Dictionary* vol. 5, 870–86. New York: Doubleday, 1992.

The Ante-Nicene Fathers. Edited by Alexander Roberts and James Donaldson. 1885–1887. 10 vols. Repr., Peabody, MA: Hendrickson, 1994.

Aquinas, Thomas. *Summa Theologica*. Translated by English Dominican Province. 5 vols. London: Christian Classics, 1981.

Aulén, Gustaf. *Christus Victor: An Historical Study of the Three Main Types of the Idea of Atonement*. New York: Macmillan, 1960.

Awad, Nageed G. "Personhood as Particularity: John Zizioulas, Colin Gunton and the Trinitarian Theology of Personhood." *Journal of Reformed Theology* 4 (2010): 1–22.

Bahat, Dan. "The Second Temple in Jerusalem." Pages 59–74 in *Jesus and Temple: Textual and Archaeological Explorations*, edited by James H. Charlesworth. Minneapolis: Fortress Press, 2014.

Balentine, Samuel E. *The Torah's Vision of Worship*. Minneapolis: Fortress, 1999.

Baltzer, Klaus. *The Covenant Formulary in Old Testament, Jewish, and Early Christian Writings*. Translated by David E. Green. Philadelphia: Fortress, 1971.

Barker, Margaret. *The Great High Priest: Temple Roots of Christian Liturgy*. London: T&T Clark, 2003.

———. *On Earth As It Is in Heaven: Temple Symbolism in the New Testament*. Edinburgh: T&T Clark, 1995.

———. "The Temple Roots of the Liturgy." Unpublished paper, 2000.

———. *Temple Themes in Christian Worship*. London: T&T Clark, 2007.

———. *Temple Theology: An Introduction*. London: SPCK, 2004.

Barth, Karl. *Church Dogmatics*. Vol. IV/1. London: T&T Clark, 1956.

St. Basil the Great. *On the Holy Spirit*. New York: St. Vladimir's Seminary Press, 1980.

Bauckham, Richard. *Bible and Ecology: Rediscovering the Community of Creation*. Waco, TX: Baylor University Press, 2010.

———. *Bible and Mission: Christian Witness in a Postmodern World*. Grand Rapids: Baker Academic, 2003.

Beale, Gregory K. *The Temple and the Church's Mission: A Biblical Theology of the Dwelling Place of God.* Downers Grove, IL: InterVarsity Press, 2004.

Beale, Gregory, and Mitchell Kim. *God Dwells Among Us: Expanding Eden to the Ends of the Earth.* Downers Grove, IL: InterVarsity Press, 2014.

Bechtel, Carol, ed. *Touching the Altar: The Old Testament for Christian Worship.* Grand Rapids: Eerdmans, 2008.

Bell, Catherine. *Ritual Theory, Ritual Practice.* Oxford: Oxford University Press, 1992.

Berry, Wendell. *Home Economics.* New York: Farrar, Straus & Giroux, 1987.

Bieringer, Reimund, Emmanuel Nathan, Didier Pollefeyt, and Peter L. Tomson, eds. *Second Corinthians in the Perspective of Late Second Temple Judaism.* CRINT 14. Leiden: Brill, 2014.

Billings, J. Todd. *Remembrance, Communion, and Hope: Rediscovering the Gospel at the Lord's Table.* Grand Rapids: Eerdmans, 2018.

Boersma, Hans. *Heavenly Participation: The Weaving of a Sacramental Tapestry.* Grand Rapids: Eerdmans, 2011.

———. "The Sacramental Reading of Nicene Theology: Athanasius and Gregory of Nyssa on Proverbs 8." *Journal of Theological Interpretation* 10 (2016): 1–30.

Boulton, Matthew. "Supersession or Subsession? Exodus Typology, the Christian Eucharist and the Jewish Passover Meal." *Scottish Journal of Theology* 66 (2013): 18–29.

Bouma-Prediger, Steve. *For the Beauty of the Earth: A Christian Vision for Creation Care.* 2nd ed. Grand Rapids: Baker Academic, 2010.

Bouyer, Louis. *Liturgy and Architecture.* Notre Dame: University of Notre Dame Press, 1967.

Bradshaw, Paul F. *Eucharistic Origins.* London: SPCK, 2004.

———. *Reconstructing Early Christian Worship.* London: SPCK, 2009.

———. *The Search for the Origins of Christian Worship.* 2nd ed. Oxford: Oxford University Press, 2002.

Bradshaw, Paul, and Maxwell Johnson. *The Origins of Feasts, Fasts and Seasons in Early Christianity.* Collegeville, MN: Liturgical Press, 2011.

Bradshaw, Paul F., Maxwell E. Johnson, and L. Edward Phillips. *The Apostolic Tradition: A Commentary.* Hermeneia. Minneapolis: Augsburg Fortress, 2002.

Brightman, F. E., ed. *Liturgies Eastern and Western.* Oxford: Clarendon, 1896.

Brown, Raymond. *The Gospel According to John I-XII.* Anchor Bible 29. New Haven: Yale Univ. Press, 1966.

———. *The Gospel According to John XIII-XXI.* Anchor Bible 29A. New Haven: Yale Univ. Press, 1970.

Brown, Sally A., and Patrick D. Miller, eds. *Lament.* Louisville: Westminster John Knox Press, 2005.

Brownson, James. *The Promise of Baptism.* Grand Rapids: Eerdmans, 2006.

Brueggemann, Walter. *Theology of the Old Testament: Testimony, Dispute, Advocacy.* Minneapolis: Fortress, 2012.

———. *Worship in Ancient Israel: An Essential Guide.* Nashville: Abingdon, 2005.

Calvin, John. *Institutes of the Christian Religion,* ed. John T. McNeill. The Library of Christian Classics. Louisville: Westminster John Knox, 1960.

Campolo, Tony. *How to Rescue the Earth without Worshipping Nature.* Nashville: Nelson, 1992.

Canlis, Julie. *Calvin's Ladder: A Spiritual Theology of Ascent and Ascension.* Grand Rapids: Eerdmans, 2010.

Carroll, Anthony J., S. J. "Disenchantment, Rationality and the Modernity of Max Weber." *Forum Philosophicum* (2011): 117–37.

Cavalletti, Sofia. "Memorial and Typology in Jewish and Christian Liturgy." *Letter & Spirit* 1 (2005): 69–86.

Cavanaugh, William. "Eucharistic Sacrifice in the Social Imagination in Early Modern Europe." *Journal of Medieval and Early Modern Studies* 31 (2001): 585–605.

Charlesworth, James H, ed. *Jesus and Temple: Textual and Archaeological Explorations.* Minneapolis: Fortress, 2014.

Chilton, Bruce. *The Temple of Jesus: His Sacrificial Program within a Cultural History of Sacrifice.* Philadelphia: Pennsylvania State University Press, 1992.

Chryssavgis, John, ed. *Cosmic Grace, Humble Prayer: The Ecological Vision of the Green Patriarch Bartholomew I.* Grand Rapids: Eerdmans, 2003.

Chryssavgis, John, and Bruce V. Foltz, eds. *Toward an Ecology of Transfiguration: Orthodox Perspectives on Environment, Nature, and Creation.* New York: Fordham University Press, 2013.

Clavier, Mark. *Stewards of God's Delight: Becoming Priests of the New Creation.* Eugene, OR: Wipf & Stock, 2009.

Cochran, Daniel C. "Projecting Power in Sixth-Century Rome: The Church of Santi Cosma e Damiano in the Late Antique Forum Romanum." *Journal of History and Cultures* 3 (2013): 1–32.

Collins, Raymond. *First Corinthians.* Sacra Pagina. Collegeville, MN: Liturgical Press, 1999.

Coloe, Mary. *God Dwells with Us: Temple Symbolism in the Fourth Gospel.* Collegeville, MN: Liturgical Press, 2001.

Connolly, R. Hugh. *Didascalia Apostolorum.* Oxford: Clarendon, 1929.

Crouch, Andy. *Culture Making: Recovering Our Creative Calling.* Downers Grove, IL: InterVarsity Press, 2008.

Dalferth, Ingolf. "The Stuff of Revelation: Austin Farrer's Doctrine of Inspired Images." Pages 149–66 in *Scripture, Metaphysics, and Poetry: Austin Farrer's "The Glass of Vision" with Critical Commentary,* edited by Robert MacSwain. Surrey, England: Ashgate Publishing Limited, 2013.

Daniélou, Jean. *The Bible and the Liturgy.* Notre Dame: University of Notre Dame Press, 1956.

———. *Primitive Christian Symbols.* London: Burns & Oates, 1961.

———. *The Theology of Jewish Christianity.* London: Darton, Longman & Todd, 1964.

Dawson, John David. *Christian Figural Reading and the Fashioning of Identity.* Berkeley: Univ. of California Press, 2001.

de Jong, Huib Looren. "Levels of Explanation in Biological Psychology." *Philosophical Psychology* 15 (2002): 441–62.

DeWitt, Calvin. *Caring for Creation: Responsible Stewardship of God's Handiwork.* Grand Rapids: Baker, 1998.

Dennis, John. "The Function of the *hattat* Sacrifice in the Priestly Literature: An Evaluation of the View of Jacob Milgrom." *Ephemerides theologicae Lovanienses* 78 (2002): 108–29.

Dimant, Devorah. *History, Ideology and Bible Interpretation in the Dead Sea Scrolls.* Forshungen zum Alt Testament 90. Tübingen: Mohr Siebeck, 2014.

Dix, Dom Gregory. *The Shape of the Liturgy.* New York: Seabury, 1982.

Douglas, Mary. "The Go-Away Goat." Pages 121–41 in *The Book of Leviticus: Composition and Reception.* Edited by Rolf Rendtorff and Robert A. Kugler. Leiden: Brill, 2003.

———. *In the Wilderness: The Doctrine of Defilement in the Book of Numbers.* Sheffield: Sheffield Academic, 1993.

Edersheim, Alfred. *The Temple: Its Ministry and Services.* 1874. Repr., Peabody, MA: Hendrickson, 1995.

Elior, Rachel. *The Three Temples: On the Emergence of Jewish Mysticism.* Translated by David Louvish. Oxford: The Littman Library of Jewish Civilization, 2004.

St. Ephrem the Syrian. *Hymns on Paradise.* Translated by S. P. Brock. Crestwood, NY: St. Vladimir's Seminary Press, 1990.

Fee, Gordon D. *The First Epistle to the Corinthians.* The New International Commentary on the New Testament. Grand Rapids: Eerdmans, 1987.

Ferguson, Everett. *Catechesis, Baptism, Eschatology, and Martyrdom.* Vol. 2 in *The Early Church at Work and Worship.* Cambridge: James Clarke & Co., 2014.

Fitzmyer, Joseph. *The Acts of the Apostles.* The Anchor Bible. New Haven: Yale, 1998.

Flannery, Austin, O. P., ed. *Vatican Council II: Constitutions, Decrees, Declarations: A Completely Revised Translation in Inclusive Language.* Northport, NY: Costello, 1996.

Forrester, Duncan, and Doug Gay, eds. *Worship and Liturgy in Context: Studies and Case Studies in Theology and Practice.* London: SCM, 2009.

Friedländer, M., ed. *The Guide of the Perplexed of Maimonides.* London: Trübner, 1885.

Gane, Roy. *Cult and Character: Purification Offering, Day of Atonement, and Theodicy.* Winona Lake: Eisenbrauns, 2005.

Gardner, Philip. "'A House for Sorrow and a School for Compassion': Recovering Lament in Contemporary Worship." *Touchstone* 20.1 (2007): 16–28.

Garland, David. *1 Corinthians.* Baker Exegetical Commentary on the New Testament. Grand Rapids: Baker Academic, 2003.

Gelston, A. *The Eucharistic Prayer of Addai and Mari.* Oxford: Clarendon, 1992.

Goppelt, Leonhard. *Typos: The Typological Interpretation of the Old Testament in the New.* Translated by Donald H. Madvig. Grand Rapids: Eerdmans, 1982.

Green, Joel. *The Gospel of Luke.* The New International Commentary on the New Testament. Grand Rapids: Eerdmans, 1997.

Grenz, Stanley, and John Franke. *Beyond Foundationalism: Shaping Theology in a Postmodern Context.* Louisville: Westminster John Knox, 2001.

Grypeon, Emmanouela, and Helen Spurling. *The Book of Genesis in Late Antiquity: Encounters Between Jewish and Christian Exegesis.* Leiden: Brill, 2013.

Hachlili, R. "The Niche and the Ark in Ancient Synagogues." *Bulletin of the American Schools of Oriental Research* 223 (1976): 43–53.

Hagner, Donald. *Matthew.* Word Biblical Commentary. Dallas: Word, 1995.

Harrington, Wilfrid J., O. P. *Revelation*. Sacra Pagina. Collegeville, MN: Liturgical Press, 1993.

Harris, Forrest E., Sr. "The Children Have Come to Birth: A Theological Response for Survival and Quality of Life." Pages 26–41 in *Walk Together Children: Black and Womanist Theologies, Church and Theological Education*. Eugene, OR: Cascade, 2010.

Harrison, Carol. *Beauty and Revelation in the Thought of Saint Augustine*. Oxford: Clarendon Press, 1992.

Hauerwas, Stanley, and Samuel Wells, eds. *The Blackwell Companion to Christian Ethics*. Malden, MA: Blackwell, 2004.

Hawn, C. Michael. "The Wild Goose Sings: Themes in the Worship and Music of the Iona Community." *Worship* (2000): 504–21.

Hays, Richard B. *The Conversion of the Imagination: Paul as Interpreter of Israel's Scripture*. Grand Rapids: Eerdmans, 2005.

———. *Echoes of Scripture in the Letters of Paul*. New Haven: Yale University Press, 1989.

———. *First Corinthians*. Interpretation. Louisville: John Knox Press, 1997.

———. *Reading Backwards: Figural Christology and the Fourfold Gospel Witness*. Waco, TX: Baylor University Press, 2014.

Hays, Richard B., and Ellen Davis, eds., *The Art of Reading Scripture*. Grand Rapids: Eerdmans, 2003.

Hayward, C. T. R. *The Jewish Temple: A Non-Biblical Sourcebook*. New York: Routledge, 1996.

Heinemann, Joseph. *Prayer in the Talmud: Forms and Patterns*. Studia Judaica 9. New York: De Gruyter, 1977.

Heron, Alasdair. *Table and Tradition: Toward an Ecumenical Understanding of the Eucharist*. Philadelphia: Westminster, 1983.

Heschel, Abraham Joshua. *God in Search of Man: A Philosophy of Judaism*. New York: Farrer, Straus & Giroux, 1983.

Hill, Andrew. *Malachi*. The Anchor Bible. New York: Doubleday, 1998.

Hirsch, Samson R. "The Menorah: Components and Workmanship." Pages 209–35 in vol. 1 of *Collected Writings*. New York: Philipp Feldheim, 1996.

Hoenig, Sidney B. "Origins of the Rosh Hashanah Liturgy." *The Jewish Quarterly Review* 57 (1967): 312–31.

Holmes, Michael W. *The Apostolic Fathers*. Grand Rapids: Baker Academic, 1999.

Hoskins, Paul. "Freedom from Slavery to Sin and the Devil: John 8:31–47 and the Passover Theme of the Gospel of John." *Trinity Journal* 31 (2010): 47–63.

———. *Jesus as the Fulfillment of the Temple in the Gospel of John*. Bletchley, UK: Paternoster, 2006.

Houtman, Cornelis. *Exodus*. Historical Commentary on the Old Testament. 4 vols. Kampen: Kok Publishing House, 1996.

Hutton, Rodney. *Charisma and Authority in Israelite Society*. Minneapolis: Fortress, 1994.

Instone-Brewer, David. "The Eighteen Benedictions and the Minim Before 70 CE." *Journal of Theological Studies* 54 (2003): 25–44.

———. *Feasts and Sabbaths: Passover and Atonement*. Vol. 2a of *Traditions of the Rabbis from the Era of the New Testament*. Grand Rapids: Eerdmans, 2011.

Janzen, David. "Priestly Sacrifice in the Hebrew Bible: A Summary of Recent Scholarship and a Narrative Reading." *Religion Compass* 2 (2007): 38–52.

Jasper, R. C. D., and G. J. Cuming. *Prayers of the Eucharist: Early and Reformed.* 3rd ed. New York: Pueblo, 1980.

Jennings, William. *The Christian Imagination: Theology and the Origins of Race.* New Haven: Yale University Press, 2010.

Jensen, Robin M. "Recovering Ancient Ecclesiology: The Place of the Altar and the Orientation of Prayer in the Early Latin Church." *Worship* 89 (2015): 99–124.

Jeremias, Joachim. *The Eucharistic Words of Jesus.* Translated by Norman Perrin. London: SCM, 1966.

Johnson, Luke Timothy. *The Acts of the Apostles.* Sacra Pagina. Collegeville, MN: Liturgical Press, 1992.

———. "Sacramentality and Sacraments in Hebrews." Pages 109–22 in *Oxford Handbook of Sacramental Theology.* Edited by John Webster, Kathryn Tanner, and Iain Torrance Oxford: Oxford University Press, 2015.

Jones, Serene. *Feminist Theory and Christian Theology: Cartographies of Grace.* Minneapolis: Fortress, 2000.

Josephus. *The Works of Josephus: Complete and Unabridged.* Translated by William Whiston. Peabody, MA: Hendrickson, 1987.

Just, Arthur, Jr. "Entering Holiness: Christology and Eucharist in Hebrews." *Concordia Theological Quarterly* 69 (2005): 75–95.

Keener, Craig. *The Gospel of John: A Commentary.* Peabody, MA: Hendrickson, 2003.

Kelsey, David. *Eccentric Existence: A Theological Anthropology.* 2 vols. Louisville: Westminster John Knox, 2009.

Kerr, Alan. *The Temple of Jesus' Body: The Temple Theme in the Gospel of John.* Sheffield, UK: Sheffield Academic, 2002.

Kimball, Dan. *The Emerging Church: Vintage Christianity for New Generations.* Grand Rapids: Zondervan, 2003.

Kiuchi, Nobuyoshi. *Leviticus.* Apollos Old Testament Commentary. Downers Grove, IL: InterVarsity, 2007.

———. *The Purification Offering in the Priestly Literature: Its Meaning and Function.* Sheffield: Sheffield Academic, 1987.

Klawans, Jonathan. *Impurity and Sin in Ancient Judaism.* New York: Oxford University Press, 2000.

Kline, Meredith. *Kingdom Prologue: Genesis Foundations for a Covenantal Worldview.* Eugene, OR: Wipf & Stock, 2006.

Koehler, Ludwig. *Old Testament Theology.* London: Lutterworth Press, 1957.

Koester, Craig. *The Dwelling of God: The Tabernacle in the Old Testament, Intertestamental Jewish Literature, and the New Testament.* Washington, DC: Catholic Biblical Association of America, 1989.

———. *Revelation: A New Translation with Introduction and Commentary.* New Haven: Yale University Press, 2014.

Kraft, R. A. "In Search of 'Jewish Christianity' and Its 'Theology.'" Pages 1–13 in *Early Christianity and Judaism,* ed. Everett Ferguson. New York: Garland, 1993.

Kraus, Hans-Joachim. *Worship in Israel: A Cultic History of the Old Testament.* Richmond: John Knox Press, 1966.

Krautheimer, Richard. *Early Christian and Byzantine Architecture.* 4th ed. New Haven: Yale University Press, 1984.

Kreider, Alan. "Peacemaking in Worship in the Syrian Church Orders." *Studia Liturgica* 34 (2004): 177–90.

Kugel, James. *A Walk through Jubilees.* Leiden: Brill, 2012.

Kulp, Joshua. "The Origins of the Seder and Haggadah." *Currents in Biblical Research* 4 (2005): 109–34.

Kuyper, Abraham. *Common Grace: God's Gifts for a Fallen World.* Vol. 1. Bellingham, WA: Lexham, 2015.

Lakatos, Imre. *The Methodology of Scientific Research Programmes: Philosophical Papers, Vol. 1.* Cambridge: Cambridge University Press, 1978.

Lang, Uwe Michael. "Louis Bouyer and Church Architecture: Resourcing Benedict XVI's The Spirit of the Liturgy." *Journal of the Institute for Sacred Architecture* 19 (2011): 14–17.

Leithart, Peter. "Conjugating the Rites: Old and New in Augustine's Theory of Signs." *Calvin Theological Journal* 34 (1999): 136–47.

———. "Embracing Ritual: Sacraments as Rites." *Calvin Theological Journal* 40 (2005): 6–20.

———. *1 and 2 Kings.* Brazos Theological Commentary on the Bible. Grand Rapids: Brazos, 2006.

———. *A House for My Name: A Survey of the Old Testament.* Moscow, ID: Canon Press, 2000.

———. "Marburg and Modernity." *First Things* (Jan. 1992): 8–9.

———. "Old Covenant and New in Sacramental Theology Old and New." *Pro Ecclesia* 14 (2005): 174–90.

———. "What's Wrong with Transubstantiation: Evaluating Theological Models." *Westminster Theological Journal* 53 (1991): 295–324.

Levenson, Jon D. *The Death and Resurrection of the Beloved Son: The Transformation of Child Sacrifice in Judaism and Christianity.* New Haven: Yale University Press, 1993.

———. *Inheriting Abraham: The Patriarch in Judaism, Christianity and Islam.* Princeton: Princeton University Press, 2012.

———. *Sinai and Zion: An Entry into the Jewish Bible.* San Francisco: HarperSanFrancisco, 1985.

Levering, Matthew. *Christ's Fulfillment of Torah and Temple.* Notre Dame: University of Notre Dame Press, 2002.

———. *Sacrifice and Community: Jewish Offering and Christian Eucharist.* Malden, MA: Blackwell, 2005.

Levine, Baruch. *Leviticus.* JPS Torah Commentary. Philadelphia: Jewish Publication Society, 1989.

Lewis, C. S. *Is Theology Poetry?* London: Geoffrey Bles, 1962.

Lossky, Vladimir, and Léonide Ouspensky. *The Meaning of Icons.* Crestwood, NY: St. Vladimir's Seminary Press, 1982.

Lovejoy, Arthur. *The Great Chain of Being: A Study of the History of an Idea*. Cambridge: Harvard University Press, 1971.

Lubac, Henri de, S. J. "Lumen Gentium and the Fathers." In *Vatican II: An Interfaith Appraisal*. Notre Dame: University of Notre Dame Press, 1966.

MacIntyre, Alasdair. *After Virtue: A Study in Moral Theory*. 2nd ed. Notre Dame: University of Notre Dame Press, 1985.

————. *Dependent Rational Animals: Why Human Beings Need the Virtues*. London: Duckworth, 1999.

————. *First Principles, Final Ends and Contemporary Philosophical Issues*. Milwaukee: Marquette University Press, 1990.

————. *Whose Justice? Which Rationality?* Notre Dame: University of Notre Dame Press, 1988.

Macmurray, John. *Persons in Relation*. Atlantic Highlands: Humanities Press, 1996.

————. *The Self as Agent*. New York: Harper and Brothers, 1957.

MacSwain, Robert, ed. *Scripture, Metaphysics, and Poetry: Austin Farrer's* The Glass of Vision *With Critical Commentary*. Surrey, UK: Ashgate, 2013.

Marx, Alfred. *Les systèmes sacrificiels de l'Ancien Testament: Formes et fonctions du culte sacrificiel à Yhwh*. Leiden: Brill, 2005.

————. "The Theology of the Sacrifice According to Leviticus 1–7." Pages 103–20 in *The Book of Leviticus: Composition and Reception*, ed. Rolf Rendtorff and Robert A. Kugler. Leiden: Brill, 2003.

Mauser, Ulrich. *The Gospel of Peace: A Scriptural Message for Today's World*. Louisville: Westminster John Knox, 1992.

McBride, S. Dean, Jr. "Divine Protocol: Genesis 1:1–2:3 as Prologue to the Pentateuch." Pages 3–41 in *God Who Creates: Essays in Honor of W. Sibley Towner*. Edited by William Brown and S. Dean McBride, Jr. Grand Rapids: Eerdmans, 2000.

McConville, J. G. *Deuteronomy*. Apollos Old Testament Commentary. Downers Grove, IL: InterVarsity, 2002.

McDonald, Suzanne. *Re-imaging Election: Divine Election as Representing God to Others and Others to God*. Grand Rapids: Eerdmans, 2010.

McGowan, Andrew. *Ancient Christian Worship: Early Church Practices in Social, Historical, and Theological Perspective*. Grand Rapids: Baker Academic, 2014.

————. "Naming the Feast: The Agape and the Diversity of Early Christian Meals." *Studia Patristica* 30 (1997): 314–18.

————. "Rethinking Agape and Eucharist in Early North African Christianity." *Studia Liturgica* 34 (2004): 165–76.

McGrath, Alister. *Christian Theology: An Introduction*. 3rd ed. Malden, MA: Blackwell, 2001.

McKenna, John H., C. M. *The Eucharistic Epiclesis: A Detailed History from the Patristic to the Modern Era*. 2nd ed. Chicago: Mundelein, 2009.

————. "Eucharistic Epiclesis: Myopia or Microcosm?" *Theological Studies* 36 (1975): 265–84.

Melito of Sardis. *On Pascha and Fragments*. Edited by Stuart Hall. Oxford: Clarendon, 1979.

Mettinger, Tryggve N. D. *In Search of God: The Meaning and Message of the Everlasting Names*. Philadelphia: Fortress, 1988.

Meyer, Ben F. *The Aims of Jesus*. London: SCM, 1979.

———. *Christus Faber: The Master-Builder and the House of God*. Princeton Theological Monograph Series. Allison Park, PA: Pickwick, 1992.

Meyers, Carol, and Eric Meyers. *Zechariah 9–14*. The Anchor Bible. Garden City, NY: Doubleday, 1993.

Milgrom, Jacob. "Encroaching on the Sacred: Purity and Polity in Num. 1–10." *Interpretation* 51 (1997): 241–53.

———. "Israel's Sanctuary: The Priestly 'Picture of Dorian Gray.'" *Revue biblique* 83 (1976): 390–99.

———. *Leviticus 1–16: A New Translation with Introduction and Commentary*. New York: Doubleday, 1991.

———. *Leviticus: A Book of Ritual and Ethics*. Minneapolis: Fortress, 2004.

Miller, Patrick. "Property and Possession in Light of the Ten Commandments." Pages 17–50 in *Having: Property and Possession in Religious and Social Life*. Edited by William Schweiker and Charles Mathewes. Grand Rapids: Eerdmans, 2004.

Moore-Keish, Martha. *Do This in Remembrance of Me: A Ritual Approach to Reformed Eucharistic Theology*. Grand Rapids: Eerdmans, 2008.

Morray-Jones, Christopher R. A. "The Ascent into Paradise (2 Cor 12:1–12): Paul's Merkava Vision and Apostolic Call." Pages 245–85 in *Second Corinthians in the Perspective of Late Second Temple Judaism*. Edited by Reimund Bieringer, Emmanuel Nathan, Didier Pollefeyt, and Peter L. Tomson. Leiden: Brill, 2014.

Morris, Leon. *The Gospel According to John*. Rev. ed. New International Commentary on the New Testament. Grand Rapids: Eerdmans, 1995.

Nelson, Richard D. *Raising Up a Faithful Priest: Community and Priesthood in Biblical Theology*. Louisville: Westminster John Knox, 1993.

Neusner, Jacob. *The Mishnah: A New Translation*. New Haven: Yale University Press, 1991.

Niederwimmer, Kurt. *The Didache: A Commentary*. Minneapolis: Fortress, 1998.

Nolloth, C. F. *The Fourth Evangelist*. London: John Murray, 1925.

Nowak, Martin A. *Evolutionary Dynamics*. Cambridge: Belknap, 2006.

———. "Evolving Cooperation." *Journal of Theoretical Biology* 299 (2012): 1–8.

———. "Five Rules for the Evolution of Cooperation." *Science* 314 (2006): 1560–63.

Ochs, Peter. *Another Reformation: Postliberal Christianity and the Jews*. Grand Rapids: Baker Academic, 2011.

Orr, William F., and James Arthur Walther. *1 Corinthians: A New Translation*. The Anchor Bible. Garden City, NY: Doubleday, 1976.

Paesler, Kurt. *Das Tempelwort Jesu: Die Traditionen von Tempelzerstörung und Tempelerneuerung im Neuen Testament*. Göttingen: Vandenhoeck und Ruprecht Verlag, 1999.

Partee, Charles. *The Theology of John Calvin*. Louisville: Westminster John Knox, 2010.

Origen. *Homilies on Leviticus 1–16*. Catholic University of America Press, 1990.

Patrologia Graeca. Edited by J.-P. Migne. 162 vols. Paris, 1857–1886.

Patrologia Latina. Edited by J.-P. Migne. 217 vols. Paris, 1844–1864.

Perrin, Nicholas. *Jesus the Temple*. Grand Rapids: Baker Academic, 2010.

————. "Sacraments and Sacramentality in the New Testament." Pages 52–67 in *The Oxford Handbook of Sacramental Theology*. Edited by Hans Boersma and Matthew Levering. Oxford: Oxford University Press, 2015.

Pitre, Brant. *Jesus and the Jewish Roots of the Eucharist*. New York: Doubleday, 2011.

————. *Jesus and the Last Supper*. Grand Rapids: Eerdmans, 2015.

Presa, Neal, ed. *Liturgical-Missional: Perspectives on a Reformed Ecclesiology*. Eugene, OR: Wipf & Stock, 2016.

Presbyterian Church (USA), General Assembly Mission Council. *Christians and Jews: People of God*. Louisville: Presbyterian Church (USA), 2010.

Presbyterian Church (USA), Office of Research Services. "How Frequently Do PCUSA Congregations Celebrate the Lord's Supper?" Louisville: Presbyterian Church (USA), 2007.

————. "The Presbyterian Panel: The Sacraments: The February 2009 Survey." Louisville: Presbyterian Church (USA), 2009.

Presbyterian Church (USA), Office of Theology and Worship. *Invitation to Christ: A Guide to Sacramental Practices*. Louisville: Presbyterian Church (USA), 2006.

Presbyterian Church (USA), Theology and Worship Ministry Unit. *Book of Common Worship*. Louisville: Westminster John Knox, 2018.

Rahner, Karl. *Hearers of the Word*. Translated by M. Richards. New York: Herder & Herder, 1969.

Ramshaw, Gail. "The Place of Lament Within Praise: Theses for Discussion." *Worship* 61 (1987): 317.

Ratzinger, Joseph Cardinal. *The Spirit of the Liturgy*. San Francisco: Ignatius Press, 2000.

Rendtorff, Rolf. *Leviticus 1, 1–10, 20*. Neukirchen-Vluyn: Neukirchener Verlag, 2004.

Reumann, John. *The Supper of the Lord: The New Testament, Ecumenical Dialogues, and Faith and Order on Eucharist*. Philadelphia: Fortress, 1985.

Rienstra, Debra, and Ron Rienstra. *Worship Words*. Grand Rapids: Baker Academic, 2009.

Ritmeyer, Leen. "Imagining the Temple Known to Jesus and to Early Jews." Pages 19–57 in *Jesus and Temple: Textual and Archaeological Explorations*. Edited by James H. Charlesworth. Minneapolis: Fortress Press, 2014.

Robinson, John A. T. "Preface." In *Making the Building Serve the Liturgy: Studies in the Re-Ordering of Churches*. Edited by Gilbert Cope. London: Mowbray, 1962.

Rooke, Deborah W. "The Day of Atonement as a Ritual of Validation for the High Priest." Pages 342–64 in *Temple and Worship in Biblical Israel*. Edited by John Day. London: T&T Clark, 2007.

Rowe, C. Kavin. "Biblical Pressure and Trinitarian Hermeneutics." *Pro Ecclesia* 11 (2002): 295–312.

Rowley, H. H. *Worship in Ancient Israel: Its Forms and Meanings*. London: SPCK, 1976.

Rozeboom, Sue. "Doctrine of the Lord's Supper." Pages 143–65 in *Calvin's Theology and Its Reception*. Edited by Todd Billings and I. John Hesselink. Louisville: Westminster John Knox, 2012.

Rubenstein, Jeffrey L. "Sukkot, Eschatology and Zechariah 14." *Revue Biblique* 103 (1996): 161–95.

Sanders, E. P. *Jesus and Judaism*. London: SCM, 1985.

———. *Paul and Palestinian Judaism*. Philadelphia: Fortress, 1977.

Santmire, Paul. *Ritualizing Nature: Renewing Christian Liturgy in a Time of Crisis*. Minneapolis: Fortress, 2008.

———. *The Travail of Nature: The Ambiguous Ecological Promise of Christian Theology*. Minneapolis: Fortress, 1985.

Schauss, Hayyim. *The Jewish Festivals: A Guide to Their History and Observance*. Translated by S. Jaffe. New York: Schocken, 1962.

Schell, Donald. "Rending the Temple Veil: Holy Space in Holy Community." Pages 149–81 in *Searching for Sacred Space*. New York: Church, 2002.

Schiffman, L. H. *Reclaiming the Dead Sea Scrolls: The History of Judaism, the Background of Christianity, the Lost Library of Qumran*. Philadelphia: Jewish Publication Society, 1994.

Schindler, David. "'In the Beginning Was the Word': Mercy as a 'Reality Illuminated by Reason.'" *Communio* 41 (2014): 759–62.

Schmemann, Alexander. *The Eucharist: Sacrament of the Kingdom*. Crestwood, NY: St. Vladimir's Seminary Press, 2003.

———. *For the Life of the World: Sacraments and Orthodoxy*. Crestwood, NY: St. Vladimir's Seminary Press, 2000.

Schneiders, Sandra. "The Foot Washing (John 13:1–20): An Experiment in Hermeneutics." *Ex Auditu* (1985): 135–46.

Schreiner, Susan E. *The Theater of His Glory: Nature and the Natural Order in the Thought of John Calvin*. Grand Rapids: Baker Academic, 1991.

Schwartz, Baruch. *The Jewish Study Bible*. New York: Oxford University Press, 2014.

Schwartz, Joshua. "Sacrifice without the Rabbis." Pages 123–49 in *The Actuality of Sacrifice: Past and Present*. Leiden: Brill, 2014.

Segal, J. B. *The Hebrew Passover: From the Earliest Times to A.D. 70*. London: Oxford University Press, 1963.

Seitz, Christopher. *Figured Out: Typology and Providence in Christian Scripture*. Louisville: Westminster John Knox, 2001.

Skarsaune, Oskar. *In the Shadow of the Temple: Jewish Influences on Early Christianity*. Downers Grove, IL: InterVarsity Press, 2002.

Smith, Dennis E. *From Symposium to Eucharist: The Banquet in the Early Christian World*. Minneapolis: Fortress, 2003.

Smith, Ralph. *Micah-Malachi*. Word Biblical Commentary. Waco, TX: Word, 1984.

Snyder, Graydon F. *Ante Pacem: Archeological Evidence of Church Life before Constantine*. Macon: Mercer University Press, 2003.

Sokolowski, Robert. *The God of Faith and Reason*. Notre Dame: University of Notre Dame Press, 1982.

Spinks, Bryan. *Do This in Remembrance of Me: The Eucharist from the Early Church to the Present Day*. London: SCM, 2013.

———. *The Sanctus in the Eucharistic Prayer*. Cambridge University Press, 1991.

Stendahl, Krister. "The Apostle Paul and Introspective Conscience of the West." *Harvard Theological Review* 56 (1963): 199–215.

Strawn, Brent. *The Old Testament Is Dying: A Diagnosis and Recommended Treatment*. Grand Rapids: Baker Academic, 2017.

Stubbs, David. "Ending of Worship—Ethics." Pages 133–55 in *A More Profound Alleluia*. Edited by Leanne Van Dyk. Grand Rapids: Eerdmans, 2005.

———. "Kuyper's Common Grace and Kelsey: Polishing a Reformed Gem." *Journal of Reformed Theology* 10 (2016): 314–39.

———. "Locating the Liturgical-Missional Church in the Bible's Story." Pages 15–32 in *Liturgical-Missional: Perspectives on a Reformed Ecclesiology*. Edited by Neal Presa. Eugene, OR: Wipf & Stock, 2016.

———. *Numbers*. Brazos Theological Commentary on the Bible. Grand Rapids: Brazos Press, 2009.

Tanner, Kathryn. *Jesus, Humanity and the Trinity*. Minneapolis: Fortress, 2001.

Taylor, Charles. *Human Agency and Language*. Cambridge: Cambridge University Press, 1985.

———. *The Language Animal: The Full Shape of the Human Linguistic Capacity*. Cambridge: Belknap, 2016.

———. *A Secular Age*. Cambridge: Harvard University Press, 2007.

Terrien, Samuel. *The Elusive Presence: Toward a New Biblical Theology*. San Francisco: Harper & Row, 1978.

Theissen, Gerd. "Soziale Integration und sakramentales Handeln: Eine Analyse von 1 Cor 11:17–34." *Novum Testamentum* 16 (1974): 179–206.

Thurian, Max. "Toward a Renewal of the Doctrine of Transubstantiation." In *Christianity Divided*. Edited by D. J. Callahan. New York: Sheed & Ward, 1961.

Tickle, Phyllis. *The Great Emergence: How Christianity Is Changing and Why*. Grand Rapids: Baker, 2008.

Tigay, Jeffrey H. "The Torah Scroll and God's Presence." Pages 323–40 in *Built by Wisdom, Established by Understanding: Essays on Biblical and Near Eastern Literature in Honor of Adele Berlin*. Edited by Maxine L. Grossman. Bethesda: University Press of Maryland, 2013.

Torgerson, Mark. *An Architecture of Immanence: Architecture for Worship and Ministry Today*. Grand Rapids: Eerdmans, 2007.

Torrance, James. *Worship, Community and the Triune God of Grace*. Downers Grove, IL: InterVarsity Press, 1996.

Torrance, T. F. *The Doctrine of Grace in the Apostolic Fathers*. Edinburgh: Oliver & Boyd, 1948.

United States Conference of Catholic Bishops. *Sacramental Catechesis: An Online Resource for Dioceses and Eparchies*. Washington, DC: US Conference of Catholic Bishops, 2012.

VanderKam, James C. "Covenant and Pentecost." *Calvin Theological Journal* 37 (2002): 239–54.

Van Dyk, Leanne, ed. *A More Profound Alleluia: Theology and Worship in Harmony*. Grand Rapids: Eerdmans, 2004.

VanGemeren, Willem A., ed. *New International Dictionary of Old Testament Theology and Exegesis*. 5 vols. Grand Rapids: Zondervan, 1997.

Vanhoozer, Kevin J. *Dictionary for Theological Interpretation of the Bible*. Grand Rapids: Baker Academic, 2005.

Vermes, Geza. *The Complete Dead Sea Scrolls in English, Revised Edition.* London: Penguin, 2004.

Wainwright, Geoffrey. *Eucharist and Eschatology.* Akron: OSL, 2002.

Walsh, Bryan, and Sylvia Keesmaat. *Colossians Remixed: Subverting the Empire.* Downers Grove, IL: InterVarsity Press, 2004.

Walton, J. H. *Genesis.* NIV Application Commentary. Grand Rapids: Zondervan, 2001.

Webber, Robert. *Ancient-Future Evangelism.* Grand Rapids: Baker, 2003.

———. *Ancient-Future Worship: Proclaiming and Enacting God's Narrative.* Grand Rapids: Baker, 2008.

Webber, Robert, ed. *Twenty Centuries of Christian Worship.* Peabody, MA: Hendrickson, 1994.

Weinfeld, Moshe. "Pentecost as Festival of the Giving of the Law." *Immanuel* 8 (1978): 7–18.

Welker, Michael. *What Happens in Holy Communion?* Grand Rapids: Eerdmans, 2000.

Wells, Samuel, and Ben Quash. *Introducing Christian Ethics.* Malden, MA: Wiley-Blackwell, 2010.

Wenham, Gordon. *The Book of Leviticus.* New International Commentary on the Old Testament. Grand Rapids: Eerdmans, 1979.

———. "Sanctuary Symbolism in the Garden of Eden Story." Pages 399–404 in *"I Studied Inscriptions from Before the Flood": Ancient Near Eastern, Literary and Linguistic Approaches to Genesis 1–11.* Edited by Richard Hess and David Tsumura. Winona Lake, IN: Eisenbrauns, 1994.

White, James F. *Protestant Worship: Traditions in Transition.* Louisville: Westminster John Knox, 1989.

White, L. Michael. *Building God's House in the Roman World: Architectural Adaption among Pagans, Jews, and Christians.* Johns Hopkins University Press, 1990.

Williams, Rowan. *On Augustine.* London: Bloomsbury, 2016.

Wilson, Marvin. *Our Father Abraham: Jewish Roots of the Christian Faith.* Grand Rapids: Eerdmans, 1989.

Witvliet, John. "Prospects for Covenant Theology in Ecumenical Discussions of the Eucharist." *Worship* 71 (1997): 98–123.

———. *Worship Seeking Understanding.* Grand Rapids: Baker Academic, 2003.

Wolterstorff, Nicholas. *Hearing the Call.* Grand Rapids: Eerdmans, 2011.

———. *Justice in Love.* Grand Rapids: Eerdmans, 2011.

———. *Justice: Rights and Wrongs.* Princeton: Princeton University Press, 2008.

———. *Until Justice and Peace Embrace: The Kuyper Lectures for 1981 Delivered at the Free University of Amsterdam.* Grand Rapids: Eerdmans, 1983.

World Council of Churches. *Baptism, Eucharist and Ministry: Faith and Order Paper No. 111.* Geneva: World Council of Churches, 1982.

Wright, G. E. *God Who Acts: Biblical Theology as Recital.* London: SCM, 1952.

Wright, N. T. *The Climax of the Covenant.* Minneapolis: Fortress, 1991.

———. "Jesus and the Identity of God." *Ex Auditu* (1998): 14–56.

———. *Jesus and the Victory of God.* Minneapolis: Fortress, 1996.

———. *Justification: God's Plan and Paul's Vision.* Downers Grove, IL: IVP Academic, 2009.

————. *The New Testament and the People of God*. Minneapolis: Fortress, 1992.

————. *Paul and the Faithfulness of God*. Minneapolis: Fortress, 2013.

————. *Pauline Perspectives: Essays on Paul, 1978–2013*. London: SPCK, 2013.

————. "Worship and Spirit in the New Testament." Pages 3–25 in *The Spirit in Worship— Worship in the Spirit*. Edited by Teresa Berger and Bryan Spinks. Collegeville, MN: Liturgical Press, 2009.

Yoder, Christine Roy. "Sheaves, Shouts and *Shavuot*: Reflections on Joy." *Journal for Preachers* (Pentecost/Easter 2016): 16–19.

Zuijdwegt, Geertjan. "'Utrum Caritas Sit Aliquid Creatum in Anima': Aquinas on the Lombard's Identification of Charity with the Holy Spirit." *Recherches de Théologie et Philosophie Médiévales* 79 (2012): 39–74.

Modern Authors Index

Subject Index

Aaron, 72, 76, 183
Aaronic blessing, 61, 164, 171, 180
Abraham, 262, 282; and *Aqedah*, binding of Isaac, 219–20, 221–23, 228, 239
Adam, 63, 71, 81–82n6; and Eve, 69, 76, 298
Addai and Mari, prayer of, 96, 274
African churches, 104, 276, 290
agapē, love meals, 95, 176n44, 267, 275–77, 288
allegorical reading, 40n30, 41, 42
altars, 101, 103–5, 136–37, 352–53
altruism, 247–48
angels, 63, 65, 66, 96, 200, 300
Anselm, 327, 328
Apostolic Constitutions, 97, 320; Clementine liturgy, 273–74, 282–83
Apostolic Tradition, 274
apostolic tradition, 6
Aqedah, binding of Isaac, 219–20, 221–23, 228, 239
Aquinas, Thomas, 124–25, 128n46, 266n23
archaeology, 23, 53
architecture, 99; church buildings, 99–102, 103–5, 346–47; early church, 99–102, 103–5; synagogue, 102–4, 347–48, 352–53; temple, 54, 62, 67–68, 70, 350–51, 352–53
Aristotle, Aristotelianism, 125
ark of the covenant, 62, 67–68, 102, 181, 347–48

art, church, 106–7, 355, 356, 357
Asa (king), 257
asceticism, 194–95
atonement, 223, 230n41, 245–46, 297–98, 304–5
Atonement, Day of. *See* Day of Atonement, *Yom Kippur*
atonement theories, 246; Day of Atonement sacrifice, 327–28, 329, 330–31; evolutionary theory, 247–49; Passover sacrifice, 223, 240–45, 247–48, 327–30; penal substitution, 240–44, 245–46, 248–49, 311
Augustine of Hippo, 121–23, 139n77, 246
Azazel, goat for, 300, 308–11, 329

Bacon, Francis, 198
Balai, 325–26
baptism, 5, 24–25; Eucharist and, 252–53; exodus and, 41–42; Passover and, 252–53
Baptism, Eucharist and Ministry (BEM), 132–33, 137n74, 180, 280, 284n65
baptistries, 101, 103n52, 316
barley, 260, 263; *omer* of, firstfruits, 12–13, 216, 224, 233, 255–56, 260–61, 263
Basil of Caesarea, the Great, 24–25, 275n39, 326
bema, 102–3, 104–5, 352–53
benedictus qui venit, 319–20
berith olam, 174

383

Scripture and Ancient Sources Index